KU-012-149

Strategy Safari

FT Prentice Hall
FINANCIAL TIMES

In an increasingly competitive world, we believe it's quality
of thinking that gives you the edge – an idea that opens new
doors, a technique that solves a problem, or an insight that
simply makes sense of it all. The more you know, the
smarter and faster you can go.

That's why we work with the best minds in business and
finance to bring cutting-edge thinking and best learning
practice to a global market.

Under a range of leading imprints, including *Financial Times
Prentice Hall*, we create world-class print publications and
electronic products bringing our readers knowledge, skills
and understanding, which can be applied whether
studying or at work.

To find out more about Pearson Education publications, or
tell us about the books you'd like to find, you can visit us at
www.pearsoned.co.uk

PEARSON
Education

Strategy Safari

The complete guide through the wilds of
strategic management

Henry Mintzberg

Bruce Ahlstrand

Joseph Lampel

Second Edition

LEARNING
RESOURCES
CENTRE

FT Prentice Hall
FINANCIAL TIMES

An imprint of **Pearson Education**
Harlow, England • London • New York • Boston • San Francisco • Toronto • Sydney • Singapore • Hong Kong
Tokyo • Seoul • Taipei • New Delhi • Cape Town • Madrid • Mexico City • Amsterdam • Munich • Paris • Milan

658.4012   AG   202151
138243

PEARSON EDUCATION LIMITED

Edinburgh Gate
Harlow CM20 2JE
United Kingdom
Tel: +44 (0)1279 623623
Fax: +44 (0)1279 431059
Website: www.pearsoned.co.uk

First edition published in the United States of America
by The Free Press, a Division of Simon & Schuster, Inc
First edition published in Great Britain in 1998
Second edition published in Great Britain in 2009

© Henry Mintzberg, Bruce Ahlstrand and Joseph Lampel 1998, 2009

The rights of Henry Mintzberg, Bruce Ahlstrand and Joseph Lampel to be identified as
authors of this work has been asserted by them in accordance with the Copyright, Designs
and Patents Act 1988.

All rights reserved; no part of this publication may be reproduced, stored in a retrieval
system, or transmitted in any form or by any means, electronic, mechanical, photocopying,
recording, or otherwise without either the prior written permission of the Publishers or a
licence permitting restricted copying in the United Kingdom issued by the Copyright
Licensing Agency Ltd, Saffron House, 6–10 Kirby Street, London EC1N 8TS. This book
may not be lent, resold, hired out or otherwise disposed of by way of trade in any form
of binding or cover other than that in which it is published, without the prior consent of
the Publishers.

ISBN: 978-0-273-71958-8

British Library Cataloguing in Publication Data
A CIP catalogue record for this book can be obtained from the British Library

Library of Congress Cataloging in Publication Data
Mintzberg, Henry.
    Strategy safari : the complete guide through the wilds of strategic management /
Henry Mintzberg, Bruce Ahlstrand, Joseph Lampel. -- 2nd ed.
        p. cm.
    Includes bibliographical references and index.
    ISBN 978-0-273-71958-8 (pbk.)
    1.   Strategic planning.   2.   Business planning.   I.   Ahlstrand, Bruce W.   II.   Lampel,
Joseph.   III.   Title.
    HD30.28.M564 2009
    658.4'012--dc22

                                                                    2008034094

10 9 8 7 6 5
12 11 10

Set by 30
Printed and bound in Great Britain by Ashford Colour Press Ltd, Gosport, Hants

The Publisher's policy is to use paper manufactured from sustainable forests.

Dedication

There are some people who begin the Zoo at the beginning, called WAYIN, and walk as quickly as they can past every cage until they come to the one called WAYOUT, but the nicest people go straight to the animal they love the most, and stay there.

—A.A. Milne, in the Introduction to *Winnie-The-Pooh*

We dedicate this book to such people who are more interested in open fields than closed cages.

Contents

Publisher's acknowledgements

We are grateful to the following for permission to reproduce copyright material:

Table 2.1 and 2.2 from *Strategic Management Skills*, Addison-Wesley, (Power, D., M. Gannon, M. McGinnis and D. Schweiger. 1986). Reprinted with permission of Daniel Power; Figure 3.1 reprinted with the permission of The Free Press, a Division of Simon & Schuster Adult Publishing Group, from *TOP MANAGEMENT PLANNING* by George A. Steiner. Copyright © 1969 by the Trustees of Columbia University in the City of New York. All rights reserved; Figure 3.2 from *A Framework for Business Planning*, Stanford Research Institute, (Stewart, R. F. 1963). Figure courtesy of SRI International; Figure 3.3 from "Annual Planning Cycle at General Electric" in "How to Ensure the Continued Growth of Strategic Planning", *Journal of Business Strategy*, (Rothschild, William E. 1980). Bill Rothschild, CEO Rothschild Strategies Unlimited LLC and author of 'global best seller' *The Secret to GE's Success* and blog on www.strategyleader.com. © Emerald Group Publishing Limited. Originally published in *Journal of Business Strategy* Volume 1 Issue 1; Figure 3.4 adapted with the permission of The Free Press, a Division of Simon & Schuster Adult Publishing Group, from *The RISE AND FALL OF STRATEGIC PLANNING: Reconceiving Roles of Planning, Plans, Planners* by Henry Mintzberg. Copyright © 1994 by Henry Mintzberg. All rights reserved; Figure 4.1, Figure 4.2 and Figure 7.3 used by permission of The Boston Consulting Group, Inc; Figure 4.3 reprinted with the permission of The Free Press, a Division of Simon & Schuster Adult Publishing Group, from *COMPETITIVE STRATEGY: Techniques for Analyzing Industries and Competitors* by Michael E. Porter. Copyright © 1980, 1998 by The Free Press. All rights reserved; Figure 4.4 and Figure 4.5 reprinted with the permission of The Free Press, a Division of Simon & Schuster Adult Publishing Group, from *COMPETITIVE ADVANTAGE: Creating and Sustaining Superior Performance* by Michael E. Porter. Copyright © 1985, 1998 by Michael E. Porter. All rights reserved; Figure 6.1 reprinted by permission, Patricia Doyle Corner, Angelo J. Kinicki, Barbara W. Keats, Integrating organizational and individual information processing perspectives on choice, *Organization Science*, volume 5, number 3, August 1994. Copyright 1994, the Institute for Operations Research and the Management Sciences (INFORMS), 7240 Parkway Drive, Suite 310, Hanover, MD 21076 USA. INFORMS is not responsible for errors introduced in the English translation of the original figure; Table 6.1 reprinted with the permission of The Free Press, a Division of Simon & Schuster Adult Publishing Group, from *FORECASTING, PLANNING, AND STRATEGY FOR THE 21st CENTURY* by Spyros G. Makridakis. Copyright © 1990 by Spyros G. Makridakis. All rights reserved; Figure 7.1 reprinted from "A Process Model of Internal Corporate Venturing in the Diversified Major Firm" by Mr Robert Burgelman published in *Administrative Science Quarterly* Vol. 28, No. 2 (June 1983) by permission of Vol. 28, No. 2. © Johnson Graduate School of Management, Cornell University; Figure 7.4 from *The Knowledge-Creating Company* by Nonaka I & Takeuchi H (OUP, 1995) reprinted by permission of Oxford University Press Inc; Table 7.5 from *ACADEMY OF MANAGEMENT REVIEW* by Mary Crossan, Henry Lane, and Roderick White. Copyright 1999 by Academy of Management (NY). Reproduced with permission of Academy of Management (NY) in the format Tradebook via Copyright Clearance Center; Table 8.1 was published in *Long Range Planning*, Vol. 27, Pekar and Allio, "Types of strategic alliances" in "Making Alliances Work: Guidelines for Success" by Pekar and Allio, pp. 12-24, Copyright Elsevier (1994); Figure 11.2 from *Crisis & Renewal: Meeting the Challenge of Organizational Change* by D. K. Hurst, Harvard Business School Press Copyright © 1995; all rights reserved; Figure 11.4 from *CONTROL YOUR DESTINY OR SOMEONE ELSE WILL* by Noel M. Tichy, Stratford Sherman, copyright © 1993 by Noel M. Tichy and Stratford Sherman. Used by permission of Doubleday, a division of Random House, Inc; Figure 11.5 was published in *Organizational Dynamics*, Vol. 20, Richard W. Beatty and David O. Ulrich, "Re-energizing the mature organization", 1 page only, Copyright Elsevier (1991)

We are grateful to the following for permission to reproduce the following texts:

Box 1.1 from *ACADEMY OF MANAGEMENT REVIEW* by E. E. Chaffee. Copyright 1985 by Academy of Management (NY). Reproduced with permission of Academy of Management (NY) in the format Tradebook via Copyright Clearance Center; Box 1.2 from "The Seeking of Strategy Where It Is Not: Toward a Theory of Strategy Absence" in *Strategic Management Journal*, Vo. 16, Inkpen, A, and Choudhury, N. 1995. © John Wiley & Sons Limited. Reproduced with permission; Box 3.2 was published in *Long Range Planner*, Vol. 27, Wilson, "The Seven Deadly Sins Of Strategic Planning" in "Strategic Planning Isn't Dead-It Changed", pp. 12-24, Copyright Elsevier (1994); Box 4.1 from Harry G. Summers, Jr., *On Strategy: The Vietnam War in Context*, originally published by Carlisle, PA: Strategic Studies Institute, U.S. Army War College, 1981; reprinted by Washington, DC: U.S. Government Printing Office, 1981, pp. 59-97; Box 4.4 used with permission from Richard Rumelt; Box 5.1 from *Arenas of Strategic Thinking*, Foundations for Economic Education, (Nasi, J., 1991); Box 5.3 from "How Entrepreneurs Craft Strategies That Work" by Amar V. Bhide, *Harvard Business Review*, March 1994; all rights reserved; Box 5.5 and Box 6.3 from *ACADEMY OF MANAGEMENT REVIEW* by Dane and Pratt. Copyright 2007 by Academy of Management (NY). Reproduced with permission of Academy of Management (NY) in the format Tradebook via Copyright Clearance Center; Box 6.1 reprinted by permission of Inderscience Enterprises Limited, www.inderscience.com, who retain copyright; Box 6.4 from *ACADEMY OF MANAGEMENT REVIEW* by Smircich and Stubbart. Copyright 1985 by Academy of Management (NY). Reproduced with permission of Academy of Management (NY) in the format Tradebook via Copyright Clearance Center; Box 7.2 was published in *Omega*, Vol. 10, J.B Quinn, "Prescriptions For Logical Incrementalism" in "Managing Strategies Incrementally", pp. 613-627, Copyright Elsevier (1982); Box 7.6 from Robert H. Miles, *Coffin Nails and Corporate Strategies* (Englewood Cliffs, New Jersey: Prentice-Hall/Pearson), 1982. Reprinted in abbreviated form by permission; Box 7.7 "How does strategy emerge" in "Strategy Innovation and the Quest for Value" from *MIT Sloan Management Review*, (Hamel, G. 1998). Copyright 1998 by Massachusetts Institute of Technology. All rights reserved. Distributed by Tribune Media Services; Box 7.9 from "The Seeking of Strategy Where It Is Not: Toward a Theory of Strategy Absence" in *Strategic Management Journal*, Vo.16, Inkpen, A, and Choudhury, N. 1995. © John Wiley & Sons Limited. Reproduced with permission; Box 8.2 from *The 48 Laws of Power*, Profile Books, (Greene,

R. 1998). With the permission of Profile Books Ltd; Box 8.2 from *THE 48 LAWS OF POWER* by Robert Greene and Joost Elffers, copyright © 1998 by Robert Greene and Joost Elffers. Use by permission Viking Penguin, a division of Penguin Group (USA) Inc; Box 8.3 was published in *Advances in Strategic Management: A Research Annual*, Vol. 3, I.C. Macmillan and W.D. Guth, "Strategy Implementation and Middle Management Coalitions", pp. 233-254, Copyright Elsevier (1985); Box 8.4 reprinted with the permission of The Free Press, a Division of Simon & Schuster Adult Publishing Group, from *COMPETITIVE STRATEGY: Techniques for Analyzing Industries and Competitors* by Michael E. Porter. Copyright © 1980, 1998 by The Free Press. All rights reserved; Box 8.5 from "Collaborate with Your Competitors - and Win" by Gary Hamel, Yves L. Doz, and C. K. Prahalad, *Harvard Business Review*, January 1989; all rights reserved; Box 9.1 from "What holds the modern company together?" by Goffee R. E., in Kerr S. ed., *Ultimate rewards*, Harvard Business School Press, Copyright © 1997; all rights reserved.; Box 11.2 was published in *Beyond Strategy: Configuration as a Pillar of Competitive Advantage*, Danny Miller and John O. Whitney, "What are Configurations?", Copyright Elsevier (1999); Box 11.3 from *Pathways to Performance,* Clemmer Group, (Clemmer, J. 1995). Jim Clemmer's practical leadership books, keynote presentations, workshops, and team retreats have helped hundreds of thousands of people worldwide improve personal, team, and organizational leadership. Visit his web site, http://jimclemmer.com/, for a huge selection of free practical resources including nearly 300 articles, dozens of video clips, team assessments, leadership newsletter, Improvement Points service, and popular leadership blog. Jim's five international bestselling books include The VIP Strategy, Firing on All Cylinders, Pathways to Performance, Growing the Distance, and The Leader's Digest. His latest book is Moose on the Table: A Novel Approach to Communications @ Work; Box 11.5 from "Why Change Programs Don't Produce Change" by M. Beer, R. A. Eisenstat, B. Spector, *Harvard Business Review*, Copyright © 1990; all rights reserved.; Box 11.6 from "Leading Change: Why Transformation Efforts Fail" by J. P. Kotter, *Harvard Business Review*, Copyright © 1995; all rights reserved.; "To be perfectly frank..." © The New Yorker Collection 1983 W.B. Park from cartoonbank.com. All Rights

Reserved; "Gentlemen, let us pool..." © The New Yorker Collection 1975 Stan Hunt from cartoonbank.com. All Rights Reserved; "What I especially like..." ScienceCartoonPlus.com; "Send in two eggs..." © P.C Vey; "Before we talk about direction..." Cartoon by permission of Mark Litzler; "Miss Denby, bring in my rose-colored glasses." © 2008 Robert Mankoff from cartoonbank.com. All Rights Reserved; "I didn't think it would be so..." ScienceCartoonPlus.com; "They can't find their hidden agenda" © 2008 by Nick Downes; "No wonder he never forgets." ScienceCartoonPlus.com; "Because I've already said..." © The New Yorker Collection 1995 Mort Gerberg from cartoonbank.com. All Rights Reserved; "Is that it?" ScienceCartoonPlus.com

In some instances we have been unable to trace the owners of copyright material, and we would appreciate any information that would enable us to do so.

Embarkation

This trip began with a paper by Henry called "Strategy Formation: Schools of Thought" published by Jim Fredrickson in a collection entitled *Perspectives on Strategic Management*. Bruce used the paper in a course at Trent University and found that it worked well. "Why don't you do a book on it?" he suggested. "Why don't we do it together?" Henry replied. They both thought that Joe would make an excellent member of the team. So the safari got underway.

We did not, however, write this as a textbook or some sort of academic treatise. From the outset, we believed that the book should have as much relevance for managers and consultants in practice as students and professors in the classroom. So we set out to write an easily accessible explanation of the fascinating field of strategic management. Sure, some parts are tougher than others; this is in the nature of the beast. We have not set out to domesticate it, but to make it friendly. We want readers from everywhere to join our safari, but at the same time we want to challenge them. As we argue throughout, the field of strategic management needs to be opened up, not closed down; it needs reconciliation among its many different tendencies, not the isolation of each.

To enrich the experience of this safari, we have also published *Strategy Bites Back*, a companion book with a similar structure and more playful content. We have also prepared an Instructor's Manual to facilitate the use of the rather unconventional nature of *Strategy Safari* in the classroom.

We owe many thank-yous. For the first edition, Bob Wallace of The Free Press must be especially singled out. Abby Luthin gave welcome support there as well. Kate Maguire provided great help. (Kate labeled the manuscript "The Beast" long before it received its current title.) She was supported admirably by Elana Trager, especially in tracking down some tricky bits of information. Coralie Clement dealt with all the references and permissions, plus lots more, working across countries, authors, and problems with remarkable skill. At one point, she wrote in an e-mail, "I think it's pretty awesome that I am communicating with a Franco-Anglo-Canadian in India about a book being published in the U.S. and Europe. . . . Ahhh, modern life."

Particularly wise and helpful in the first edition were comments on the manuscript provided by Joëlle Méric. Thanks also go to the doctoral students of Henry's colloquium in Montreal, who made a number of helpful suggestions.

The second edition is a re-embarkation: We went back and looked again at what we wrote, clarifying some parts, and adding where new ideas have emerged. Many people had a hand in making this re-embarkation possible. We would like to thank all the readers who over the years kept sending us comments and ideas: the students who forced us to rethink this or that part of the book; and the instructors who elected to use the book, often in surprising and innovative fashion. Our particular thanks go to Liz Gooster, Richard Stagg, Ajay Bhalla, Shiva Nadavulakere, Melissa Nadler and Santa Balanca-Rodrigues, with special appreciation to Pushkar Jha for his help.

The new edition contains numerous minor changes and some major additions. We added new sections on topics as varied as dynamic capabilities, the relationship between cognition and competition, real options theory, the impact of top and middle-management on strategic decision making, and the "strategy-as-practice" movement.

Bon Voyage!

'And over here, ladies and gentlemen: the strategic management beast'

"To be perfectly frank, I'm not nearly as smart as you seem to think I am."

© The New Yorker Collection 1983 W.B. Park from cartoonbank.com. All Rights Reserved.

A fable to begin, often referred to, seldom known:

THE BLIND MEN AND THE ELEPHANT
by John Godfrey Saxe (1816–87)

It was six men of Indostan
To learning much inclined,
Who went to see the Elephant
(Though all of them were blind)
That each by observation
Might satisfy his mind.

The First approached the Elephant,
And happening to fall
Against his broad and sturdy side,
At once began to brawl:
"God bless me but the Elephant
Is very like a wall."

The Second, feeling of the tusk,
Cried, "Ho! What have we here
So very round and smooth and sharp?
To me 'tis mighty clear
This wonder of an Elephant
Is very like a spear!"

The Third approached the animal,
And happening to take
The squirming trunk within his hands,
Thus boldly up and spake:
"I see," quoth he, "The Elephant
Is very like a snake!"

The Fourth reached out an eager hand,
And felt around the knee,
"What most this wondrous beast is like
Is mighty plain," quoth he;
" 'Tis clear enough the Elephant
Is very like a tree!"

The Fifth, who chanced to touch the ear,
Said: "E'en the blindest man
Can tell what this resembles most;
Deny the fact who can,
This marvel of an Elephant
Is very like a fan!"

The Sixth no sooner had begun
About the beast to grope,
Than, seizing on the swinging tail
That fell within his scope,
"I see," quoth he, "the Elephant
is very like a rope!"

And so these men of Indostan
Disputed loud and long,
Each of his own opinion
Exceeding stiff and strong,
Though each was partly in the right,
And all were in the wrong!

Moral

So oft in theologic wars,
The disputants, I ween,
Rail on in utter ignorance
Of what each other mean,
And prate about an Elephant
Not one of them has seen!

We are the blind people and strategy formation is our elephant. Since no one has had the vision to see the entire beast, everyone has grabbed hold of some part or other and 'railed on in utter ignorance' about the rest. We certainly do not get an elephant by adding up its parts. An elephant is more than that. Yet to comprehend the whole we also need to understand the parts.

> we are the blind people and strategy formation is our elephant

The next ten chapters describe ten parts of our strategy-formation beast. Each represents one 'school of thought.' These ten chapters are framed by this first chapter, which introduces the schools as well as some ideas about strategy itself, and a last chapter which returns to the whole beast.

Why ten?

In a colourful article entitled 'The magical number seven, plus or minus two: some limits on our capacity for processing information,' psychologist George Miller (1956) asked why we tend to favour a quantity of about seven for categorizing things—for example seven wonders of the world, seven deadly sins and seven days of the week. This reflects our cognitive makeup, he concluded: seven is about the number of 'chunks' of information that we can comfortably retain in our short-term memories.[1] Three wonders of the world would fall a little flat, so to speak, while eighteen would be daunting. But those of us interested in strategy are, of course, no ordinary mortals—at least in terms of our cognitive capacities—and so should be able to comprehend, say, one more than the magic number seven plus two. Accordingly, this book proposes ten schools of thought on strategy formation.

Cognition aside, in reviewing a large body of literature, ten distinct points of view did emerge, most of which are reflected in management practice. Each has a unique perspective that focuses, like each of the blind men, on one major aspect of the strategy-formation process. Every one, in a sense, is narrow and overstated. Yet in another sense, each is also interesting and insightful. An elephant may not *be* a trunk, but it certainly *has* a trunk, and it would be difficult to comprehend elephants without reference to trunks. The handicap of blindness does have an unexpected advantage, sharpening the other senses to the subtleties that can escape those who see clearly.

The schools

Accordingly, in each of the ten subsequent chapters, we present one of the schools from its own limited perspective. Then we critique it,

---

1 Actually, Miller argues for a limit of this order to the number of 'bits' we can handle in what he refers to as 'absolute judgment' and the number of 'chunks'—combinations of these bits—in 'intermediate memory.'

to extract both its limitations and its contributions. These schools, together with the single adjective that seems best to capture its view of the strategy process, are listed below:

The Design School:	strategy formation as a process of *conception*
The Planning School:	strategy formation as a *formal* process
The Positioning School:	strategy formation as an *analytical* process
The Entrepreneurial School:	strategy formation as a *visionary* process
The Cognitive School:	strategy formation as a *mental* process
The Learning School:	strategy formation as an *emergent* process
The Power School:	strategy formation as a process of *negotiation*
The Cultural School:	strategy formation as a *collective* process
The Environmental School:	strategy formation as a *reactive* process
The Configuration School:	strategy formation as a process of *transformation*[2]

The first three schools are *prescriptive* in nature—more concerned with how strategies *should* be formulated than with how they necessarily *do* form. The first of these, which in the 1960s presented the basic framework on which the other two were built, focuses on strategy formation as a process of informal *design*, essentially one of conception. The second school, which developed in parallel in the 1960s and peaked in a flurry of publications and practice in the 1970s, formalized that perspective, seeing strategy making as a more detached and systematic process of formal *planning*. That school was somewhat displaced in the 1980s by the third prescriptive school, less concerned with the process of strategy formation than with the actual content of strategies. It is referred to as the *positioning* school

---

2 In an interesting alternative mapping Martinet (1996) divided the field into *teleologic, sociologic, ideologic,* and *ecologic*. (Lauriol, 1996, has mapped our ten schools onto these four.) See also Bowman (1995) for another interesting cut of the field.

because it focuses on the selection of strategic positions in the economic marketplace.

The six schools that follow consider specific aspects of the process of strategy formation. They have been concerned less with prescribing ideal strategic behavior than with *describing* how strategies do, in fact, get made.

Some prominent writers have long associated strategy with *entrepreneurship*, and have described the process in terms of the creation of vision by the great leader. But if strategy can be personalized vision, then strategy formation has also to be understood as the process of concept attainment in a person's head. Accordingly, a small but important *cognitive* school has also developed that seeks to use the messages of cognitive psychology to enter the strategist's mind.

Each of the four schools that follows has tried to open up the process of strategy formation beyond the individual, to other forces and other actors. For the *learning* school, the world is too complex to allow strategies to be developed all at once as clear plans or visions. Hence strategies must emerge in small steps, as an organization adapts, or 'learns.' Similar to this, but with a different twist, is the *power* school, which treats strategy formation as a process of negotiation, whether by conflicting groups within an organization or by organizations themselves as they confront their external environments. In contrast to this is another school of thought that considers strategy formation to be rooted in the *culture* of the organization. Hence the process is viewed as fundamentally collective and cooperative. And then there are the proponents of an *environmental* school, organization theorists who believe strategy formation is a reactive process in which the initiative lies not inside the organization, but with its external context. Accordingly, these people seek to understand the pressures imposed on organizations.

Finally is one school which it could be argued really combines the others. We call it *configuration*. People in this school, in seeking to be integrative, cluster the various elements of our beast—the strategy-making process, the content of strategies, the structure of the organization and its context—into distinct stages or episodes, for example, of entrepreneurial growth or stable maturity. Sometimes these are sequenced over time to describe the life cycles of organizations. But if they settle into stable states, then their strategy making processes have to describe the leap from one state to another. And so, another side of this school describes the process as one of transformation, which incorporates much of the huge literature and practice on how to achieve 'strategic change.'

It will become evident, as we go along, that some of there schools tilt toward the art, the craft, or the science (meaning analysis) of managing. For example, the entrepreneurial school is most definitely oriented to the art, the learning and perhaps political schools to the craft, and the planning and positioning schools to the science.

These schools have appeared at different stages in the development of strategic management. A few have already peaked and declined, others are now developing, and some remain as thin but nonetheless significant trickles of publication and practice. We shall describe each school in turn, with our own interpretation of its development and its difficulties, before concluding with our final integrative comments in the closing chapter.

Note that all of these schools can be found in the literature, often in clearly delineated pockets: particular academic journals, special practitioner magazines, certain types of books. But most are, or have been, equally evident in practice, both within organizations and from the consulting firms that serve them. Practitioners read and are influenced by the literature just as the literature is influenced by the practice. So this is a book of the school of thought on strategy formation both in publication and in practice.

A field review

The literature of strategic management is vast—the number of items we reviewed over the years for the first edition alone numbered close to 2,000—and it continues to grow larger every day. Of course, not all of this comes from the field of management. All kinds of other fields make important contributions to our understanding of the strategy process.

William Starbuck has written that to discuss 'all aspects of organization which are relevant to adaptation . . . means . . . that one could legitimately discuss everything that has been written about organizations' (1965: 468). This is, in fact, an understatement, because the last word in the quotation should read 'collective systems of all kinds.'

What biologists write about the adaptation of species (for example 'punctuated equilibrium') can have relevance for our understanding of strategy as position ('niche'). What historians conclude about periods in the development of societies (such as 'revolution') can help explain different stages in the development of strategies in organizations (for example, 'turnaround' as a form of 'cultural revolution'). Physicists' descriptions of quantum mechanics and mathematicians' theories of chaos can provide insights into how organizations change. And so on. Add to this all the other literatures that are more commonly recognized as relevant to the study of organizations—psychology on human cognition as well as on leader charisma, anthropology on cultures in society, economics on industrial organization, urban planning on formal planning processes, political science on public policy making, military history on strat- egies of conflict, and on—and the result is an enormous, dispersed body of literature capable of rendering all sorts of insights. At the limit, strategy formation is not just about values and vision, competences and capabilities, but also about the military and Machiavelli, crisis and commitment, organizational learning and punctuated equilibrium, industrial organization and social revolution.

“ strategy formation is not just about values and vision, competences and capabilities ”

We consider this literature in its own terms. We do not, however, seek to *review* it comprehensively. (We had no more wish to write several thousand pages than most people have to read it.) This, in other words, is a *field* review, not a literature review. We seek to *cover* the literature and the practice—to set out its different angles, orientations, tendencies. In so doing, we cite published work either because it has been key to a school or else because it well illustrates a body of work. We apologize to the many insightful writers and consultants whose work is not mentioned; we hope that we have left out no significant bodies of work.

We must add one point, however. There is a terrible bias in today's management literature toward the current, the latest, the 'hottest.' This does a disservice, not only to all those wonderful old writers, but especially to the readers who are all too frequently offered the trivial new instead of the significant old. We express no such bias in this book. Ours is a review of the evolution as well as the current state of this field. Later in this book we argue that ignorance of an organization's past can undermine the development of strategies for its future. The same is true for the field of strategic management. We ignore past work at our own peril. Indeed, we believe that time works on the literature and practice of strategic management much like it works on wine in barrels: it reveals what is excellent. We therefore apologize to no one for reminding the reader of so many wonderful old publications.

Five Ps for strategy

The word *strategy* has been around for a long time. Managers now use it both freely and fondly. It is also considered to be the high point of managerial activity. For their part, academics have studied strategy extensively for about four decades, while business schools usually have as their final required capstone a course in strategic management. The word *strategy* is so influential. But what does it really mean?

It is part of human nature to look for *the* definition of every concept. Most of the standard textbooks on strategy offer that definition, usually presented in the introductory chapter, more or less as follows: 'top management's plans to attain outcomes consistent with the organization's missions and goals' (Wright *et al.*, 1992: 3). No doubt such definitions have been dutifully memorized by generations of students, who have later used them in thousands of corporate reports. We offer no such easy definition here. Instead, we argue that strategy (not to mention ten different schools about it) requires a number of definitions, five in particular (based on Mintzberg, 1987).

Strategies as plans and patterns

Ask someone to define strategy and you will likely be told that *strategy is a plan*, or something equivalent—a direction, a guide or course of action into the future, a path to get from here to there. Then ask that person to describe the strategy that his or her own organization *actually* pursued over the past five years—not what they intended to do but what they really did. You will find that most people are perfectly happy to answer that question, oblivious to the fact that doing so violates their very own definition of the term.

It turns out that strategy is one of those words that we inevitably define in one way yet often also use in another. *Strategy is a pattern*, that is, consistency in behaviour over time. A company that perpetually markets the most expensive products in its industry pursues what is commonly called a high-end strategy, just as a person who always accepts the most challenging of jobs may be described as pursuing a high-risk strategy. Figure 1.1 contrasts strategy as plan—looking ahead—with strategy as pattern—looking at past behaviour.

Now, both definitions appear to be valid: organizations develop plans for their future and they also evolve patterns out of their past. We can call one *intended* strategy and the other *realized* strategy. The important question thus becomes: must realized strategies always have been intended? (That intended strategies are not always realized is all too evident in practice.)

There is a simple way to find out. Just ask those people who happily described their (realized) strategies over the past five years what their intended strategies were five years earlier. Were they the same? Did the organization achieve what it intended? A few may claim that their intentions were realized perfectly. Suspect their honesty. A few others may answer that what they realized as strategies had nothing to do with what they intended. Suspect their behavior. In our experience, the vast majority of people give an answer that falls between these two extremes—a bit of this and a bit of that, they say. They did not stray completely from their intentions, but neither did they achieve them perfectly. For, after all, perfect realization implies brilliant foresight, not to mention an unwillingness to adapt to unexpected events, while no realization at all suggests a certain mindlessness. The real world inevitably involves some thinking ahead as well as some adaptation en route.

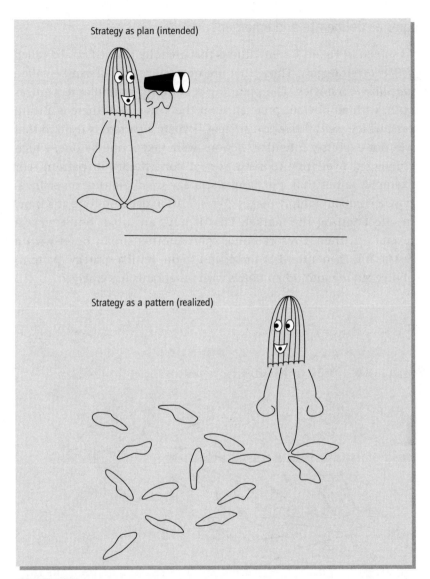

Strategy as plan (intended)

Strategy as a pattern (realized)

figure 1.1 Strategies ahead and behind

Strategies as deliberate and emergent

As shown in Figure 1.2, intentions that are fully realized can be called *deliberate* strategies. Those that are not realized at all can be called *unrealized* strategies. The planning school, for example, recognizes both, with an obvious preference for the former. But there is a third case, which we call *emergent* strategy—where a pattern is realized that was not expressly intended. Actions were taken, one by one, which converged over time to some sort of consistency, or pattern. For example, rather than pursuing a strategy (read plan) of diversification, a company simply makes diversification decisions one at a time, in effect testing the market. First it buys an urban hotel, next a restaurant, then a resort hotel, then another urban hotel with a restaurant, then a third of these, and so on, until a strategy (pattern) of diversifying into urban hotels with restaurants has emerged.

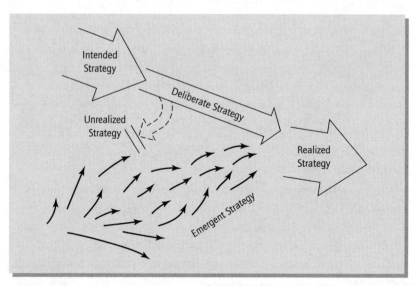

figure 1.2 Strategies deliberate and emergent

As implied earlier, few, if any, strategies are purely deliberate, just as few are purely emergent. One means no learning, the other means no control. All real-world strategies need to mix these in some way: to exercise control while fostering learning. Strategies, in other words, have to *form* as well as be *formulated*. An *umbrella* strategy, for example, means that the broad outlines are deliberate (such as to move upmarket), while the details are allowed to emerge en route (when, where and how). Thus, emergent strategies are not necessarily bad and deliberate strategies good; effective strategists mix these in ways that reflect the conditions at hand, notably the ability to predict as well as the need to react to unexpected events.

❝❝emergent strategies are not necessarily bad and deliberate strategies good❞❞

Strategies as positions and perspective

Alongside plan and pattern, we can add two more 'p' words. Some years ago, McDonald's introduced a new product called Egg McMuffin—the American breakfast in a bun. This was to encourage the use of their restaurant facilities in the morning. If you ask people whether Egg McMuffin was a strategic change for McDonald's—stop here and ask yourself the question—you will inevitably hear two answers: 'Yes, of course: it brought them into the breakfast market,' and 'Aw, come on, it's the same old stuff—the McDonald's way—just in a different package.' In our view, the real difference between these people is in how they implicitly define the content of strategy.

To some people, *strategy is a position*, namely the locating of particular products in particular markets—Egg McMuffin, for the breakfast market. To others, *strategy is a perspective*, namely an organization's fundamental way of doing things—for example, the McDonald's way. In Peter Drucker's memorable phrase, this is its 'theory of the business' (1970: 5; 1994). As shown in Figure 1.3, as position, strategy looks *down*—to the 'x' that marks the spot where the product meets the customer, as well as *out*—to the external marketplace. As perspective, in contrast, strategy looks *in*—inside the organization, indeed, inside the heads of the strategists, but it also looks *up*—to the grand vision of the enterprise.

Again, we need both definitions. McDonald's introduced Egg McMuffin successfully because the new position was consistent with the existing perspective. The executives of McDonald's seemed to understand well (although not necessarily in these terms) that one does not casually ignore perspective. (Anyone for McDuckling à

figure 1.3 Strategies above and below

l'Orange?) But while changing position within perspective may be easy, changing perspective, even while trying to maintain position, is not. (Just ask the big airlines about having to compete with their new discount rivals.) Figure 1.4 illustrates examples of this.

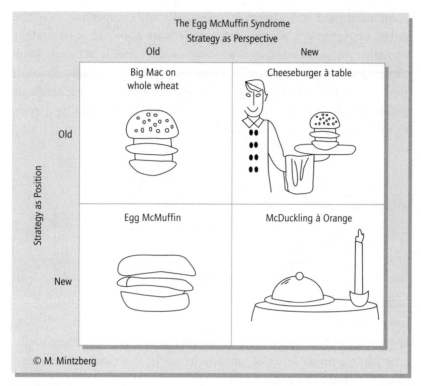

figure 1.4 Changing position and perspective

All the Ps

Thus, we have four different definitions of strategy. A fifth is in common usage too: *strategy is a ploy*, that is, a specific 'manoeuvre' intended to outwit an opponent or competitor. A kid may hop over a fence to draw a bully into his yard, where his Doberman Pinscher waits for intruders. Likewise, a corporation may buy land to give the impression it plans to expand its capacity, in order to discourage a competitor from building a new plant. Here the real strategy (as plan, that is, the real intention) is the threat, not the expansion itself, and as such is a ploy.

Five definitions and ten schools. As we shall see, the relationships between them are varied, although some of the schools have their preferences—for example, plan in the planning school, position in the positioning school, perspective in the entrepreneurial school, pattern in the learning school, ploy in the power school.

Combining plan and pattern with position and perspective, as in the matrix of Figure 1.5, we can derive four basic approaches to strategy formation, which correspond to some of the schools: strategic *planning* (planning, design and positioning schools), strategic *visioning* (entrepreneurial, design, cultural and cognitive schools); strategic *venturing* (learning, power and cognitive schools); and strategic *learning* (learning and entrepreneurial schools).

		Strategic Process to:	
		Deliberate Plans	Emergent Patterns
Strategy Content as:	Tangible Positions	Strategic Planning	Strategic Venturing
	Broad Perspective	Strategic Visioning	Strategic Learning

figure 1.5 Four basic approaches to strategy formation

There may not be one simple definition of strategy, but there are by now some general areas of agreement about the nature of strategy. Box 1.1 summarizes these.

Strategies for better and for worse

Any discussion of strategy inevitably ends on a knife-edge. For every advantage associated with strategy, there is an associated drawback or disadvantage:

1   **'Strategy sets direction.'**

Advantage: The main role of strategy is to chart the course of an organization in order for it to sail cohesively through its environment.

Disadvantage: Strategic direction can also serve as a set of blinders to hide potential dangers. Setting out on a predetermined course in unknown waters is the perfect way to sail into an iceberg. It is also important to look sideways.

---

box 1.1

The strategy beast: areas of agreement

(adapted from Chaffee, 1985: 89–90)

■ **Strategy concerns both organization and environment**. 'A basic premise of thinking about strategy concerns the inseparability of organization and environment. . . . The organization uses strategy to deal with changing environments.'

■ **The substance of strategy is complex**. 'Because change brings novel combinations of circumstances to the organization, the substance of strategy remains unstructured, unprogrammed, nonroutine, and non-repetitive. . . .'

■ **Strategy affects overall welfare of the organization**. '. . . Strategic decisions . . . are considered important enough to affect the overall welfare of the organization. . . .'

■ **Strategy involves issues of both content and process**. '. . . The study of strategy includes both the actions taken, or the content of strategy, and the processes by which actions are decided and implemented.'

■ **Strategies are not purely deliberate**. 'Theorists . . . agree that intended, emergent, and realized strategies may differ from one another.'

■ **Strategies exist on different levels**. '. . . Firms have . . . corporate strategy (What businesses shall we be in?) and business strategy (How shall we compete in each business?)'

■ **Strategy involves various thought processes**. '. . . Strategy involves conceptual as well as analytical exercises. Some authors stress the analytical dimension more than others, but most affirm that the heart of strategy making is the conceptual work done by leaders of the organization.'

---

2 **'Strategy focuses effort.'**

Advantage: Strategy promotes coordination of activity. Without strategy to focus effort, chaos can ensue as people pull in a variety of different directions.

Disadvantage: 'Groupthink' arises when effort is too carefully focused. There may be no peripheral vision, to open other possibilities.

3 **'Strategy defines the organization.'**

Advantage: Strategy provides people with a shorthand way to understand their organization and to distinguish it from others.

Disadvantage: To define an organization too sharply may also mean to define it too simply, sometimes to the point of stereotyping, so that the rich complexity of the system is lost.

4 **'Strategy provides consistency.'**

Advantage: Strategy is needed to reduce ambiguity and provide order. In this sense, a strategy is like a theory: a cognitive structure to simplify and explain the world, and thereby facilitate action.

Disadvantage: Ralph Waldo Emerson said that 'A foolish consistency is the hobgoblin of little minds. . . .' Creativity thrives on inconsistency—by finding new combinations of hitherto separate phenomena. It has to be realized that every strategy, like every theory, is a simplification that necessarily distorts reality. Strategies and theories are not reality themselves, only representations (or abstractions) of reality in the minds of people. No one has ever touched or seen a strategy. This means that every strategy can have a misrepresenting or distorting effect. That is the price of having a strategy.

> a foolish consistency is the hobgoblin of little minds

We function best when we can take some things for granted, at least for a time. And that is a major role of strategy in organizations: it resolves the big issues so that people can get on with the little details—like serving customers instead of debating which markets are best. Even chief executives, most of the time, must get on with managing their organizations in a given context; they cannot constantly put that context into question.

There is a tendency to picture the chief executive as a strategist, up there conceiving the big ideas while everyone else gets on with the little details. But the job is not like that at all. A great deal of it has to do with its own little details—reinforcing the existing perspective (and 'culture') through all kinds of figurehead duties, developing contacts to find important information, negotiating agreements to reinforce existing positions, and so on.

The problem with this, of course, is that eventually situations change—environments destabilize, niches disappear, opportunities open up. Then all that is constructive and effective about an established strategy becomes a liability. That is why, even though the concept of strategy is rooted in stability, so much of the study of strategy focuses on change. But while prescription for strategic change may come easily, the management of that change, especially when it involves shifting perspective, comes hard. The very encouragement of strategy to get on with it—its very role in protecting people in the organization from distraction—impedes their capacity to respond to changes in the environment. In other words, retooling is expensive, especially when it is human minds, and not just machines, that have to be retooled. Strategy, as mental set, can blind the organization to its own outdatedness. Thus we conclude that strategies are to organizations what blinders are to horses: they keep them going in a straight line but hardly encourage peripheral vision.

All this leads to the conclusion that strategies (and the strategic management process) can be vital to organizations by their *absence* as well as their presence. (See Box 1.2.)

Strategic management in the classroom

Also for better and for worse, strategic management has become an academic discipline in its own right, like marketing and finance. The field has its own academic journals, its own 'clubs', its own conferences. Its literature is vast and, since 1980, has been growing at an astonishing rate.

For the most part, the teaching of strategic management has highlighted the rational and prescriptive side of the process, namely our first three schools (design, planning and positioning). Strategic management has commonly been portrayed as revolving around the discrete phases of formulation, implementation, and control, carried out in almost cascading steps. This bias is heavily reflected in practice, particularly in the work of corporate and governmental planning departments as well as of many consulting firms.

This book departs from this traditional view in its attempt to provide a more balanced survey of the field, with all of its contradictions and controversies. Significant space is given to the nonrational/nonprescriptive schools, which point to other ways of looking at strategic management. Some of these schools have a less optimistic view about the possibility for formal strategic intervention. Where we become unbalanced somewhat is in our critiques of the different schools. The three prescriptive schools have so dominated the literature

---

box 1.2

Strategy absence as virtue

(from Inkpen and Choudhury, 1995: 313–23)

■ ... Strategy absence need not be associated with organizational failure.... Deliberate building in of strategy absence may promote flexibility in an organization.... Organizations with tight controls, high reliance on formalized procedures, and a passion for consistency may lose the ability to experiment and innovate.

■ Management may use the absence of strategy to send unequivocal signals to both internal and external stakeholders of its preference not to engage in resource-consuming ceremony.... For [one company] an absence of many of the supposed elements of strategy is symbolic of the no-frills, non-bureaucratic organization [it] has worked hard to become.

■ An absence of a rigid pattern of strategic decision making may ensure that 'noise' is retained in organizational systems, without which strategy may become a specialized recipe that decreases flexibility and blocks learning and adaptation....

---

and practice that we find it appropriate to include rather extensive discussions that bring much of this conventional wisdom into question. Of course, we critique all ten schools, since each has its own weaknesses. But when people are seated on one side of a see-saw, it makes no sense to try to get them into balance by pulling from the center. Put differently, to maintain balance among our critiques of the ten schools would only help to perpetuate the unbalance that we believe currently exists in the literature and practice.

Pervasive strategic failure in many large corporations may well be attributed to the army of business school graduates who have been sent out with an incomplete tool kit. This book seeks to open up the range of perspectives by providing a more varied set of ideas for such students as well as practising managers. As Hart has noted, 'High performing firms appear capable of blending competing frames of reference in strategy making. They are simultaneously planful and incremental, directive and participative, controlling and empowering, visionary and detailed' (1991:121). Or, as F. Scott Fitzgerald put

❝ high performing firms appear capable of blending competing frames of reference ❞

it, more bluntly: 'The test of a first-rate intelligence is the ability to hold two opposed ideas in the mind at the same time and still retain the ability to function.' To function as a strategist, of course, means not just to hold such opposing views, but as Spender (1992) has pointed out, to be able to synthesize them. We ask you, the reader, to hold ten such views!

The field of strategic management may itself be moving toward such synthesis. As we shall see, some of the newer work cuts across our schools, and there are increasing efforts to combine them. We applaud such work, and cite it where we can. It suggests a certain coming of age of the field.

But synthesis cannot happen in general. It must ultimately take place in the specific mind of the beholder, namely you the reader. We shall provide help where we can, but the task is up to those of you who deal with strategy in your jobs. We all know what a whole elephant is, yet we often have to describe it by its parts. That is in the nature of verbal description: words in linear order, chapters in a book.

So hang on—here we go!

The design school:
strategy formation as a
process of conception

"Gentlemen, let us pool our expertise."

© The New Yorker Collection 1975 Stan Hunt from cartoonbank.com. All Rights Reserved.

"The damn guy just sits there waiting for a case study."

—Manager, about a Harvard MBA

The design school represents, without question, the most influential view of the strategy-formation process. Its key concepts continue to form the base of undergraduate and MBA strategy courses as well as a great deal of the practice of strategic management. Professors, consultants, and planners worldwide have filled untold numbers of blackboards and PowerPoints with its famous notion of SWOT—the assessment of Strengths and Weaknesses of an organization in light of the Opportunities and Threats in its environment.

At its simplest, the design school proposes a model of strategy making that seeks to attain a match, or *fit*, between internal capabilities and external possibilities. In the words of this school's best-known proponents, 'Economic strategy will be seen as the match between qualifications and opportunity that positions a firm in its environment' (Christensen *et al.*, in the Harvard policy textbook, 1982: 164). 'Establish fit' is the motto of the design school (see Miles and Snow, 1994).

This chapter discusses and then critiques this school, which contains some of the most deeply seated assumptions about strategic management. Unexamined assumptions that appear perfectly plausible can sometimes prove to be rather misleading. We wish to raise doubts about these assumptions, not to dismiss the important contribution of the design school, but to understand better where it fits, alongside the very different views of some of the other schools. We must appreciate where the early ideas of strategic management came from, why they became so influential, and what role they should and should not play today.

Origins of the design school

The origins of the design school can be traced back to two influential books written at the University of California (Berkeley) and at MIT: Philip Selznick's *Leadership in Administration* of 1957, and Alfred D. Chandler's *Strategy and Structure* of 1962. Selznick, in particular, introduced the notion of 'distinctive competence' (1957: 42–56), discussed the need to bring together the organization's 'internal state' with its 'external expectations' (67–74), and argued for building 'policy into the organization's social structure' (1957: 91–107), which later came to be called 'implementation.' Chandler, in turn, established this school's notion of business strategy and its relationship to structure.

But the real impetus for the design school came from the General Management group at the Harvard Business School, beginning especially with the publication of its basic textbook, *Business Policy: Text and Cases* (cited above), which first appeared in 1965 (by Learned *et al.*). This quickly became the most popular classroom book in the field, as well as the dominant voice for this school of thought. Certainly its text portion, attributed in the various editions to co-author Kenneth Andrews (see also Andrews, 1987), stands as the most outspoken and one of the clearest statements of this school. But by the 1980s, this textbook was one of the few left that represented the ideas of the design school in their pure form, most others having come to favour the more elaborated renditions of them in the planning and positioning schools.

Accordingly, we use the Andrews text (in Christensen *et al.*, 1982) as a primary source of our discussion, and shall cite pages there in the following discussion (unless otherwise noted). As we shall see, in a sense the Harvard group pursued its own strategy, for there is a clear fit between the view of strategy formation that it has promoted for several decades and its own favored pedagogy of case study teaching.

The basic design school model

Our depiction of the basic design school model (similar to Andrews's own [187], but with other elements added) is shown in Figure 2.1. Consistent with the attention accorded in the Andrews text, the model places primary emphasis on the appraisals of the external and internal situations, the former uncovering threats and opportunities in the environment, the latter revealing strengths and weaknesses of the organization. Andrews's text on each of these is not extensive (nor, for that matter, is the whole text portion of the book, which numbers just 114 pages in the 1982 edition; the other 724 pages are devoted to cases).

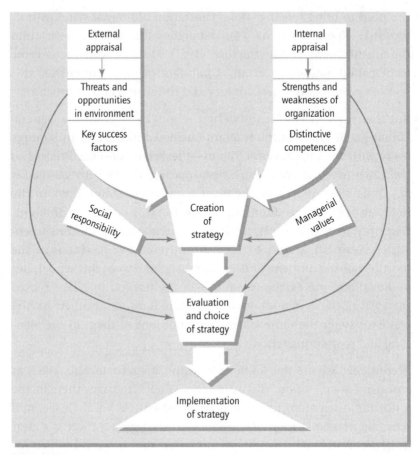

figure 2.1 Basic design school model

On external appraisal, aside from 12 pages inserted in this edition from Michael Porter's (1980) book (whose work, as we shall see, clearly falls into the positioning school), there are eight pages on the technological, economic, social, and political aspects of a company's environment, and brief consideration of the issues of forecasting and scanning. Andrews concluded his discussion with questions such as 'What is the underlying structure of the industry in which the firm participates?' and 'How might foreseeable change in the social, political, and macro-economic context impact the industry or the firm?' (179–80).

On internal appraisal, Andrews touched on a variety of points, such as the difficulty 'for organizations as well as for individuals to know themselves' (183) and the idea that 'individual and unsupported flashes of strength are not as dependable as the gradually accumulated product-and-market-related fruits of experience' (185). This ties back to an important theme in Selznick's book, that 'commitments to ways of acting and responding are built into the organization,' indeed are intrinsic to its very 'character' (1957: 67).

Figure 2.1 shows two other factors believed important in strategy making. One is managerial values—the beliefs and preferences of those who formally lead the organization, and the other is social responsibilities, specifically the ethics of the society in which the organization functions, at least as these are perceived by its managers. With the notable exception of Selznick (1957), however, most authors associated with this school do not accord a great deal of attention to values and ethics. Andrews, for example, offered his two brief chapters well after he developed the framework dealing with external and internal appraisals.

On the actual generation of strategies, little has been written in this school besides an emphasis on this being a 'creative act,' to quote Andrews (186). A recent extension of the design school by Hambrick and Fredrickson (2005), for instance, note that strategy development is not a linear process, but adds little beyond urging managers to consider the iterative nature of strategy formation.

Once alternative strategies have been determined, the next step in the model is to evaluate them and choose the best one. The assumption, in other words, is that several alternative strategies have been designed and are to be evaluated so that one can be selected (105, 109). Richard Rumelt (1997), a DBA from the Harvard General Management group, has perhaps provided the best framework for making this evaluation, in terms of a series of tests:

Consistency: The strategy must not present mutually inconsistent goals and policies.

Consonance: The strategy must represent an adaptive response to the external environment and to the critical changes occurring within it.

Advantage: The strategy must provide for the creation and/or maintenance of a competitive advantage in the selected area of activity.

Feasibility: The strategy must neither overtax available resources nor create unsolvable subproblems.

Finally, virtually all of the writings of this school make clear that once a strategy has been agreed upon, it is then implemented. We show implementation in the diagram as flaring out from formulation, to suggest that after the appraisals have been completed to narrow down to a convergent choice, the process diverges again to ensure implementation across the entire organization. Interestingly, here is one place where Andrews became rather specific: he listed twelve steps in the implementation process (backed up by a fair amount of text), encompassing many aspects of the strategy process not considered in formulation.

While, as we shall see, the strategic management field has developed and grown in many different directions, most standard textbooks continue to use the SWOT model as their centerpiece. Tables 2.1 and 2.2 show typical guidelines on internal and external approaches from one such book. Likewise, despite the rate at which they introduce new techniques, many strategy consultants continue to rely on the SWOT model and other design school notions.

❝ keep strategies clear, simple, and specific ❞

As the planning school faltered in the 1980s, as discussed in the next chapter, attention turned back to the language of the design school. Consulting firm Kepner-Tregoe's 'law of parsimony,' for example, was an almost direct quote from Andrews's early work: '. . . keep strategies clear, simple, and specific' (Tregoe and Tobia, 1990: 16–17). Jeannie Liedtka of the University of Virginia, Darden School, sees Coco Chanel's 'little black dress' as the perfect example of a simple but enduring design (see Box 2.1).

In our opinion, this school has not developed so much as provide the basis for developments in other schools. In other words, people took some of these ideas and elaborated them in terms of other assumptions about the strategy process (often, as we shall see, in contradiction to Andrews's own stated beliefs): for example, by adding the formality of the planning school or the analyses of the positioning school, or, in the work of Hamel and Prahalad, the adaptability of the learning school.

---

box 2.1

Strategy as a 'Little Black Dress'

(excerpted from Liedtka, 2005)

Coco Chanel is credited with the 'invention' of one of the great designs of the twentieth century – the 'little black dress' (or LBD), whose lessons for strategy makers are profound. Taking its inspiration from the uniforms of domestic help in Paris in the 1920s, it quickly established itself as a design of astonishing endurance in the notoriously fickle world of women's fashion. Anyone seeking to understand business strategy would do well to begin by understanding the enduring allure of Chanel's design.

What would business strategies designed with the LBD model look like? Of course, they would be simple in an elegant way – neither incomprehensibly obtuse to all save their creators, nor mind-numbingly banal and self-evident as in wallet sized statements of vision. They would eschew the faddish, and focus instead on basic elements of an enduring nature, incorporating a versatility and openness that invited their 'wearers' to add the adornments that saw fit to the occasion at hand. Perhaps most importantly, they would make us feel better about ourselves when we worked with them. And not in an insincere, preachy kind of 'call-to-greatness' way, but in a quiet way that emphasized our positives while acknowledging our flaws, all in the service of offering us hope for a better/thinner tomorrow.

In doing so, the stories that these strategies tell would echo the familiar, while translating these themes into something fresh and exciting. Perhaps even making us all feel a trifle frisky as a result – confident, open to new adventures, ready to find something special around the corner. If a little black dress can do all that, why can't a business strategy?

Premises of the design school

A number of basic premises underlie the design school, some fully evident, others only implicitly recognized. Seven are listed on pages 30 through 33 (together with supporting references to Andrews's writings in the 1982 Christensen *et al.* Harvard text):

table 2.1   Environmental variables checklist

1 **Societal changes**

   Changing customer preferences—Impacting product demand or design

   Population trends—Impacting distribution, product demand or design

2 **Governmental changes**

   New legislation—Impacting product costs

   New enforcement priorities—Impacting investments, products, demand

3 **Economic changes**

   Interest rates—Impacting expansion, debt costs

   Exchange rates—Impacting domestic and overseas demand, profits

   Real personal income changes—Impacting demand

4 **Competitive changes**

   Adoption of new technologies—Impacting cost position, product quality

   New competitors—Impacting prices, market share, contribution margin

   Price changes—Impacting market share, contribution margin

   New products—Impacting demand, advertising expenditures

5 **Supplier changes**

   Changes in input costs—Impacting prices, demand, contribution margin

   Supply changes—Impacting production processes, investment requirements

   Changes in number of suppliers—Impacting costs, availability

6 **Market changes**

   New uses of products—Impacting demand, capacity utilization

   New markets—Impacting distribution channels, demand, capacity utilization

   Product obsolescence—Impacting prices, demand, capacity utilization

Source: From Power *et al*. (1986: 38).

1 **Strategy formation should be a deliberate process of conscious thought** (94, 543). Action must flow from reason: effective strategies derive from a tightly controlled process of human thinking. Andrews suggested in another publication, for example, that managers 'know what they are really doing' only if they make strategy as 'deliberate' as possible (1981a: 24). Strategy making in this sense is an acquired, not a natural, skill (185), nor an intuitive one—it must be learned formally (6).

> **action must flow from reason**

table 2.2 Strengths and weaknesses checklist

1 **Marketing**
   Product quality
   Number of product lines
   Product differentiation
   Market share
   Pricing policies
   Distribution channels
   Promotional programs
   Customer service
   Marketing research
   Advertising
   Sales force
2 **Research and Development**
   Product R&D capabilities
   Process R&D capabilities
   Pilot plant capabilities
3 **Management information system**
   Speed and responsiveness
   Quality of current information
   Expandability
   User-oriented system
4 **Management team**
   Skills
   Value congruence

   Team spirit
   Experience
   Coordination of effort
5 **Operations**
   Control of raw materials
   Production capacity
   Production cost structure
   Facilities and equipment
   Inventory control
   Quality control
   Energy efficiency
6 **Finance**
   Financial leverage
   Operating leverage
   Balance sheet ratios
   Stockholder relations
   Tax situation
7 **Human resources**
   Employee capabilities
   Personnel systems
   Employee turnover
   Employee morale
   Employee development

Source: From Power, et al. (1986: 37).

2   **Responsibility for that control and consciousness must rest with the chief executive officer: that person is the strategist** (3, 19, 545). To the design school, ultimately, there is only one strategist, and that is the manager who sits at the apex of the organizational pyramid. Thus Andrews associated the whole process with the 'point of view' of the 'chief executive or general manager' (3), and he titled one section of his book 'the president as architect of organizational purpose.' Michael Porter sums up this view of the CEO's role in the box below. Robert Hayes, on the other hand, is not as sanguine as Porter about the implications:

'this "command-and-control" mentality allocates all major decisions to top management, which imposes them on the organization and monitors them through elaborate planning, budgeting, and control systems' (1985: 117). It might be noted that this premise not only relegates other members of the organization to subordinate roles in strategy formation, but also precludes external actors from the process altogether (except for members of the board of directors, who Andrews believed must review strategy (1980, 1981a, b)). This, in fact, is just one aspect of a larger issue associated with the design school—the relegation of the environment to a minor role, to be accounted for and then navigated through but not so much interacted with.

3 **The model of strategy formation must be kept simple and informal**. The preface to the Harvard textbook contains a quotation by Andrews that 'the idea of corporate strategy constitutes a simple practitioner's theory, a kind of Everyman's conceptual scheme' (14). Fundamental to this view is the belief that elaboration and formalization will sap the model of its essence. This premise, in fact, goes with the last: one way to ensure that strategy is controlled in one mind is to keep the process simple (182). However, this point, together with the first, forced Andrews to tread a fine line throughout his text between nonconscious intuition on one side and formal analysis on the other. In between was 'an act of judgment' (108). This distinguishes the design school from the entrepreneurial school on one side and the planning and especially positioning schools on the other.

4 **Strategies should be one of a kind: the best ones result from a process of individualized design** (187). As suggested above, it is the specific situation that matters, not any system of general variables. It follows therefore that strategies have to be tailored to the individual case. As a result, the design school says little about the content of strategies themselves, but instead concentrates on the process by which they should be developed. And that process above all should be a 'creative act' (186), to build on *distinctive* competence.

5 **The design process is complete when strategy appears fully formulated, as perspective.** This school offers little room for incrementalist views or emergent strategies, which allow 'formulation' to continue during and after 'implementation.' The big picture must appear—the grand strategy, an overall concept of the business. Here, in other words, we find not a Darwinian view of strategy formation, but the Biblical version, with strategy as the grand conception, the ultimate choice. That strategy appears as perspective, at some point in time, fully formulated, ready to be implemented.

6 **These strategies should be explicit, so they have to be kept simple** (105–6). Andrews, in common with virtually all the writers of this school, believed that strategies should be explicit for those who make them, and, if at all possible, articulated so that others in the organization can understand them. It follows, therefore, that they have to be kept rather simple. 'Simplicity is the essence of good art,' Andrews wrote, 'a conception of strategy brings simplicity to complex organizations' (554).

7 **Finally, only after these unique, full-blown, explicit, and simple strategies are fully formulated can they then be implemented.** We have already noted the sharp distinction made in this school between the formulation of strategies on one hand and their implementation on the other. Consistent with classical notions of rationality—diagnosis followed by prescription and then action—the design school clearly separates thinking from acting. Central to this distinction is the associated premise that structure must follow strategy. It appears to be assumed that each time a new strategy is formulated, the state of structure and everything else in the organization must be considered anew. According to Andrews, 'Until we know the strategy we cannot begin to specify the appropriate structure' (551).

If we need one image to capture the sense of this school, it is that famous picture of Thomas J. Watson Sr. sitting, looking very proper, under a sign that says THINK. Thousands of copies of this picture were distributed in the late 1940s to his employees at IBM.

---

box 2.2

Michael Porter on the CEO as strategist

(2005: 44–5)

The chief strategist of an organization has to be the leader—the CEO. A lot of business thinking has stressed the notion of empowerment, of pushing down and getting a lot of people involved. That's very important, but empowerment and involvement don't apply to the ultimate act of choice. To be successful, an organization must have a very strong leader who's willing to make choices and define the trade-offs. I've found that there's a striking relationship between really good strategies and really strong leaders.

That doesn't mean that leaders have to invent strategy. At some point in every organization, there has to be a fundamental act of creativity where someone divines the new activity that no one else is doing. Some leaders are really good at that, but that ability is not universal. The more critical job for a leader is to provide the discipline and the glue that keeps such a unique position sustained over time.

Another way to look at it is that the leader has to be the guardian of trade-offs. In any organization, thousands of ideas pour in every day—from employees with suggestions, from customers asking for things, from suppliers trying to sell things. There's all this input, and 99 percent of it is inconsistent with the organization's strategy.

Great leaders are able to enforce the trade-offs: 'Yes, it would be great if we could offer meals on Southwest Airlines, but if we did that, it wouldn't fit our low-cost strategy. Plus, it would make us look like United, and United is just as good as we are at serving meals.' At the same time, great leaders understand that there's nothing rigid or passive about strategy—it's something that a company is continually getting better at—so they can create a sense of urgency and progress while adhering to a clear and very sustained direction.

A leader also has to make sure that every one understands the strategy. Strategy used to be thought of as some mystical vision that only the people at the top understood. But that violated the most fundamental purpose of a strategy, which is to inform each of the many thousands of things that get done in an organization every day, and to make sure that those things are all aligned in the same basic direction.

If people in the organization don't understand how a company is supposed to be different—how it creates value compared to its rivals—then how can they possibly make all of the myriad choices they have to make? Every salesman has to know the strategy, otherwise, he won't know who to call on. Every engineer has to understand it, or she won't know what to build.

> The best CEOs I know are teachers, and at the core of what they teach is strategy. They go out to employees, to suppliers, and to customers, and they repeat, 'This is what we stand for, this is what we stand for.' So everyone understands it. This is what leaders do. In great companies, strategy becomes a cause. That's because a strategy is about being different. So if you have a really great strategy, people are fired up: 'We're not just another airline. We're bringing something new to the world.'

Critique of the design school

A strategy that locates an organization in a niche can narrow its own perspective. This seems to have happened to the design school itself (not to mention all the other schools) with regard to strategy formation. We have already suggested that the premises of the model deny certain important aspects of strategy formation, including incremental development and emergent strategy, the influence of existing structure on strategy, and the full participation of actors other than the chief executive. We wish to elaborate on these shortcomings in this critique, to indicate how they narrow the perspectives of the design school to particular contexts.

One point should be made first. Proponents of this school may well argue that we are interpreting their writings too literally, that it is unfair to take apart a *model*—a specified sequence of prescriptive steps—when all that was intended was a simple *framework*. In our view, however, both rest on the same set of assumptions, a critique of which forms the basis of our argument. These assumptions concern the central role of conscious thought in strategy formation, that such thought must necessarily precede action, and, correspondingly, that the organization must separate the work of thinkers from that of doers. We develop our critique at some length because of the influence the design school has had—and continues to have, all too often without being realized—on the teaching and practice of strategic management as well as on the planning and positioning schools in particular (which renders much of this critique applicable to them as well, as we shall see).

Assessment of strengths and weaknesses: bypassing learning

Our comments here revolve around one central theme: this school's promotion of thought independent of action, strategy formation above all as a process of *conception* rather than as one of *learning*. We can see this most clearly in a fundamental step in the formulation process, the assessment of strengths and weaknesses.

How does an organization *know* its strengths and weaknesses? On this, the design school has been quite clear—by consideration, assessment, judgment supported by analysis; in other words, by conscious thought expressed verbally and on paper. One gets the image of executives sitting around a table (as in the cartoon at the beginning of this chapter), discussing the strengths, weaknesses, and distinctive competences of an organization, much as do students in a case study class. Having decided what these are, they are then ready to design strategies.

But are competences distinct even to an organization? Might they not also be distinct to context, to time, even to application? In other words, can any organization really be sure of its strengths before it tests them?

Every strategic change involves some new experience, a step into the unknown, the taking of some kind of risk. Therefore no organization can ever be sure in advance whether an established competence will prove to be a strength or a weakness. In its retail diversification efforts, a supermarket chain was surprised to learn that discount stores, which seemed so compatible with its food store operations, did not work out well, while fast-food restaurants, ostensibly so different, did. The similarities of the discount store business—how products are displayed, moved about by customers, and checked out—were apparently overwhelmed by subtle differences of merchandising: styling, obsolescence, and the like. On the other hand, the restaurants may have looked very different, but they moved simple, perishable products through an efficient chain of distribution—much as did the supermarket (Mintzberg and Waters, 1982).

The point we wish to emphasize is: how could the firm have known this ahead of time? The discovery of 'what business are we in' could

LEARNING
RESOURCES
CENTRE

not be undertaken merely on paper; it had to benefit from the results of testing and experience. And the conclusion suggested from such experiences is that strengths often turn out to be far narrower than expected, and weaknesses far broader.

Nowhere does this come through more clearly in practice than in all those attempts at related diversification by acquisition. Obviously, no organization can undertake such an effort without a prior assessment of its strengths and weaknesses. Yet so many experiences reported in the popular press and the published research suggest that related diversification is above all a process of learning in which the acquiring firm has to make a number of mistakes until it gradually figures out, if it ever does, what works for it (see, for example, Miles, 1982; also Quinn, 1980a: 28).

Structure follows strategy . . . as the left foot follows the right

The design school promotes the dictum, first articulated by Chandler (1962), that structure should follow strategy and be determined by it. Yet what ongoing organization can ever wipe the slate clean when it changes its strategy? The past counts, just as does the environment, and organization structure is a significant part of that past. Claiming that strategy must take precedence over structure amounts to claiming that strategy must take precedence over the established capabilities of the organization, which are embedded in its structure. (Indeed, in this school's own model, as in Figure 2.1, these capabilities are inevitably shown as inputs to strategy formulation, part of the organization's strengths.) Structure may be somewhat malleable, but it cannot be altered at will just because a leader has conceived a new strategy. Many organizations have come to grief over just such a belief. Sitting and concocting strategies in an office rather than digging down in the pit with real products and real customers can be a dangerous business!

❝ strategists need to dig down in the pit with real products and real customers ❞

We conclude, therefore, that structure follows strategy the way the left foot follows the right foot in walking. In effect, the development of strategy and the design of structure both support the organization, as well as each other. Each always precedes the other, and follows it, except when the two move together, as the organization jumps to a new position. Strategy formation is an integrated system, not an arbitrary sequence.

Making strategy explicit: promoting inflexibility

Once strategies have been created, then the model calls for their articulation. 'Can you summarize your company's strategy in 35 words or less?' ask Collis and Rukstad (2008). Failure to do so is considered evidence of fuzzy thinking, or else of political motive. But there are other, often more important reasons, not to articulate strategy, which strike at the basic assumptions of the design school.

To so articulate strategy, a strategist must know for sure where he or she wishes to go, with few serious doubts. But organizations have to cope with conditions of uncertainty too. How can a company come 'to grips with a changing environment' when its 'strategy is [already] known' (Andrews, 1981a: 24)?

Our point is that organizations must function, not only *with* strategy, but also *during* periods of the formation of strategy, which can endure for long periods. As James Brian Quinn has noted, 'It is virtually impossible for a manager to orchestrate all internal decisions, external environmental events, behavioral and power relationships, technical and informational needs, and actions of intelligent opponents so that they come together at a precise moment' (1978: 17). During periods of uncertainty, the danger is not the lack of explicit strategy but the opposite—'premature closure.'

Moreover, even when uncertainty is low, the dangers of articulating strategies must still be recognized. Explicit strategies are blinders designed to focus direction and so to block out peripheral vision. They can thus impede strategic change when it does become necessary. Put differently, while strategists may be sure for now, they can never be sure forever. The more clearly articulated the strategy, the more deeply imbedded it becomes in the habits of the organization as well as in the mind of its strategists. There is, in fact, evidence from the laboratories of cognitive psychology that the articulation of a strategy—just having someone talk about what he or she is going to do anyway—locks it in, breeding a resistance to later change (Kiesler, 1971).

To summarize, certainly strategies must often be made explicit, for purposes of investigation, coordination, and support. The questions are: when? and how? and when not? These are questions assumed away in the design school.

Separation of formulation from implementation: detaching thinking from acting

The formulation-implementation dichotomy is central to the design school—whether taken as a tight model or a loose framework. This separation is convenient for the case study classroom, where students can formulate but cannot implement. In an hour or so, based on twenty pages read the night before, the class can assess the external environment, identify distinctive competences, generate alternative strategies, and discuss which one should be selected. Through 'disciplined classroom drill with the concept of strategy,' drill 'in the formal and analytic' that 'focuses attention on . . . selecting and ordering data,' claimed one of Harvard's most famous case study teachers and senior author of the textbook, students can be taught to ask 'the critical questions appropriate to a situation' (Christensen, in Christensen *et al.*, 1982: ix–x).

But how can a student who has read a short résumé of a company but has never seen the products, never met the customers, never visited the factories, possibly know these things? Is this the kind of data necessary to ask the 'critical questions'?

The case study method may be a powerful device to bring a wide variety of experience into the classroom for descriptive purposes. But it can become dangerous when used for prescription: to teach a process by which strategies *should* be made. If case study teaching has left managers with the impression that, to make strategy, they can remain in their offices surrounded by documents and think—*formulate* so that others can *implement*—then it may well have done them and their organizations a great disservice sometimes encouraging strategies that violate the very distinctive competences of their organizations.

Here is how Robert McNamara, one of Harvard's most famous MBAs, spelled out his approach to military strategy as Secretary of Defense: 'We must first determine what our foreign policy is to be, formulate a military strategy to carry out that policy, then build the military forces to successfully conduct this strategy' (quoted in Smalter and Ruggles, 1966: 70). He did just this in Vietnam, obsessed with the 'formal and the analytic' as his means of 'selecting and ordering data,' and the results were devastating. It was in the rice paddies of Vietnam that the failures of such an approach became all too apparent.

“ immerse yourself in the details and try things; get all sorts of people involved ””

Likewise in consulting, the design school model has often proved to be an all too convenient tool. Outsiders could descend on a corporation, much as did students in their case study classes, and do a SWOT analysis—in more ways than one. To quote from a popular book by two consultants: 'Four or five working days over a two-month period are required to set strategy. Two or three working days are required for the review and one-year update of strategy' (Tregoe and Zimmerman, 1980: 120). There is not a lot of money to be made by saying, 'It's too complicated for us. Go back and do your own homework: learn about your distinctive competences by immersing yourself in the details and trying things; get all sorts of people involved; eventually you may be able to come up with an effective strategy. We can't do it for you.'

The reality—if you are to believe a 1997 survey by Hill and Westbrook—is rather different. They surveyed fifty companies, and found that 'over 20 [of them] used a SWOT involving 14 consulting companies.' Yet 'no one subsequently used the outputs within the later stages of the strategy process' (1997: 46). Hence the title for their article: 'SWOT Analysis: It's Time for a Product Recall!'

Is 'think then do' really the best way, especially when the thinkers sit on top of some imagined 'hierarchy,' or worse, out in some consulting firm, while the doers are supposed to beaver away on implementation down below? How much does this 'mover and shaker' view of the organization—the powerful leader, educated in the right school, working it all out in some office—correspond to real need? The accompanying box presents an all too common example of how disconnected thinking can get in the way of real world acting.

If the design school model has encouraged leaders to oversimplify strategy, if it has given them the impression that 'you give me a synopsis and I'll give you a strategy,' if it has denied strategy formation as a long, subtle, and difficult process of learning, if it has encouraged managers to detach thinking from acting, remaining in their headquarters instead of getting into factories and meeting customers where the real information may have to be dug out, then it may be a root cause of some of the serious problems faced by so many of today's organizations. As Stirling Livingston, a Harvard professor critical of the case study method, put it years ago in an article entitled 'The Myth of the Well-Educated Manager,' management education based on 'secondhandedness' produces managers 'poorly prepared to learn and grow as they gain experience' (1971: 83, 89).

---

box 2.3

'Marketing myopia' myopia

(adapted from Mintzberg, 1994: 279–81)

In 1960, Theodore Levitt, a marketing professor at the Harvard Business School, published a celebrated article entitled 'Marketing myopia.' It is difficult to find a manager or planner who does not know the theme, even if he or she has never read the article.

The basic point was that firms should define themselves in terms of broad industry orientation—'underlying generic need' in the words of Kotler and Singh (1981:39)—rather than narrow product or technology terms. To take Levitt's favourite examples, railroad companies were to see themselves in the transportation business, oil refiners in the energy business.

Companies had a field day with the idea, rushing to redefine themselves in all kinds of fancy ways—for example, the articulated mission of one ball bearing company became 'reducing friction.' It was even better for the business schools. What better way to stimulate the students than to get them dreaming about how the chicken factory could be in the business of providing human energy or garbage collection could become beautification? Unfortunately, it was all too easy, a cerebral exercise that, while opening vistas, could also detach people from the mundane world of plucking and compacting.

Often the problem came down to some awfully ambitious assumptions about the strategic capabilities of an organization—namely that these are almost limitless, or at least very adaptable. Thus we have the example from George Steiner, presented in apparent seriousness, that 'buggy whip manufacturers might still be around if they had said their business was not making buggy whips but self-starters for carriages' (1979: 156). But what in the world would have made them capable of doing that? These products shared nothing in common—no material supply, no technology, no production process, no distribution channel—save a thought in somebody's head about making vehicles move. Why should starters have been any more of a logical product diversification for them than, say, fan belts, or the pumping of gas? As Heller suggested, 'instead of being in transportation accessories or guidance systems,' why could they not have defined their business as 'flagellation'? (quoted in Normann, 1977: 34).

Why should a few clever words on a piece of paper enable a railroad company to fly airplanes, or for that matter, run taxicabs? Levitt wrote that 'once it genuinely *thinks* of its business as taking care of people's transportation needs, nothing can stop it from creating its own extravagantly profitable growth' (1960: 53, italics added). Nothing except the limitations of its own distinctive competences. Words on paper do not transform a company.

Levitt's intention was to broaden the vision of managers. At that he may have succeeded—all too well. As Kotler and Singh, also from marketing, argued: 'very little in the world . . . is not potentially the energy business' (1981: 34). Ironically, by in effect redefining strategy from position to perspective, Levitt really *reduced* its breadth. Internal capability got lost; only the market opportunity mattered. Products did not count (railroad executives defined their industry 'wrong' because 'they were product-oriented instead of consumer-oriented' [45]), nor did production ('the particular form of manufacturing, processing, or what-have-you cannot be considered as a vital aspect of the industry' [55]). But what makes market intrinsically more important than product or production, or, for that matter, a smart researcher in the laboratory? Organizations have to build on whatever strengths they can make use of.

Critics of Levitt's article have had their own field day with the terminology, pointing out the dangers of 'marketing hyperopia,' where 'vision is better for distant than for near objects' (Kotler and Singh, 1981: 39), or of 'marketing macropia,' which escalates previously narrow market segments 'beyond experience or prudence' (Baughman, 1974: 65). We prefer to conclude simply that Levitt's notion of marketing myopia itself proved myopic.

In an article on the dysfunctions of traditional military organization, Feld (1959) has noted the sharp distinction that is made between the officers in the rear, who have the power to formulate plans and direct their execution, and the troops on the fronts, who, despite their first-hand experience, can only implement the plans given them. This 'is based on the assumption that [the officers'] position serves to keep them informed about what is happening to the army as a whole . . . [which] is supported by the hierarchical structure of military organization' (22).

This assumption is, in fact, fundamental to the separation between formulation and implementation: that data can be aggregated and transmitted up the hierarchy without significant loss or distortion. It is an assumption that often fails, destroying carefully formulated strategies in the process.

The external environment is not some kind of pear to be plucked from the tree of external appraisal. It is, instead, a major and sometimes unpredictable force to be reckoned with. Sometimes conditions change unexpectedly so that intended strategies become useless. Other times environments are so unstable that no intended strategy can be useful. In still other cases, it is the 'implementors' that resist. They may, of course, be narrow-minded bureaucrats, too wedded to their traditional ways to know a good new strategy when they see one. But they can also be right-minded people who simply wish to serve the organization despite its leadership. For example, they may be the first ones to realize that an intended strategy is unfeasible—that the organization will not be capable of implementing it or, once implemented, that it is failing because it does not suit the external conditions.

Behind the very distinction between formulation and implementation lies a set of very ambitious assumptions: that environments can always be understood, currently and for a period well into the future, either by the senior management or in ways that can be transmitted to that management; and that the environment itself is sufficiently stable, or at least predictable, to ensure that the formulated strategies today will remain viable after implementation. Under some conditions at least.

In an unstable or complex environment, this distinction has to be collapsed, in one of two ways. Either the 'formulator' has to be the 'implementor,' or else the 'implementors' have to 'formulate.' In other words, thinking and action have to proceed in tandem, closely associated. In one case, the thinker exercises close control over the consequent actions. This is characteristic of the highly personalized entrepreneurial approach to strategy making (discussed in Chapter 5), which, as noted earlier, tends to be dismissed in the design school. In the other case, when there is too much to know in one brain, as in high-technology firms or hospitals, then strategies have to be worked out on some kind of collective basis. As the implementors formulate, the organization *learns*.

Out of this discussion comes a whole range of possible relationships between thought and action. There are times when thought should precede action, and guide it, so that the dichotomy between formulation and implementation holds up, more or less, as in the design school. Other times, however, especially during or immediately after major unexpected shifts in the environment, thought must be so bound up with action that 'learning' becomes a better notion than 'designing' for what has to happen. But perhaps most common are a whole range of possibilities in between, where thought and action respond to each other. Intended strategies exist, but realized strategies also emerge. Here words like 'formulation' and 'implementation' should be used with caution, as should the design school model of strategy formation.

To conclude this critique, this seemingly innocent model—this mere 'informing idea'—in fact contains some ambitious assumptions about the capabilities of organizations and their leaders, assumptions that break down in whole or in good part under many common conditions. The problem may be seen in the very concept of design, which is a noun as well as a verb in the English language. There is a process of *designing* that leads to outputs called *designs*. What we are here calling the design school has focused on the process, not the product. But it has assumed that the two are intrinsically linked: that strategy is a grand design that requires a grand designer.

> ❝ strategy is a grand design that requires a grand designer ❞

There is, however, no one best route to truth in strategy, indeed no route there at all. As we progress through the chapters of this book, we shall find increasing reason to question the limiting premises of the design school—and those of the other schools as well!

The design school: contexts and contributions

Our critique has been intended to dismiss, not the design school, but its assumption of universality, that it somehow represents the 'one best way' to make strategy. In particular, use of the model is questionable when strategy formation has to emphasize learning, especially on a collective basis, under conditions of uncertainty and complexity. We also reject the model when it tends to be applied with superficial understanding of the operations in question.

We see a set of four conditions in particular that should encourage an organization to tilt toward the design school model:

1 **One brain can, in principle, handle all of the information relevant for strategy formation**. There are times when organizations do need grand designs: a chief executive who is highly capable of synthesis can take full charge of a process of designing strategy. Here the situation must be relatively simple, involving a base of knowledge that can be comprehended in one brain.

2 **That brain is able to have full, detailed, intimate knowledge of the situation in question**. This potential for centralizing knowledge must be backed up by sufficient access to, and experience of, the organization and its situation, so that one strategist can understand *in* a *deep sense* what is going on. We might add that he or she can only *know* the organization by truly being *in* the organization. In addition to IBM's Watson's THINK, therefore, there is the need for another image—perhaps someone picking flowers in a field—that says 'FEEL!'

   We must add here that the case study classroom trains people in exactly the opposite way: it encourages quick responses to situations barely known. This, unfortunately, is all too often paralleled in practice by the remote chief executive with a pithy report, the roving consultant with a 'quick fix,' the quarterly ritual at the directors' meeting. In fact, the design school model requires a strategist who has developed a rich, intimate knowledge base over a substantial period of time.

3 **The relevant knowledge must be established before a new intended strategy has to be implemented—in other words, the situation has to remain relatively stable or at least predictable.** Not only must the strategist have access to the relevant knowledge base, but there must also be some sense of closure on that base. Individual learning has to come to an end before organizational action can begin. In other words, at some point the strategist must know what needs to be known to conceive an intended strategic perspective that will have relevance well beyond the period of implementation. Put most simply, the world must hold still, or—what amounts to a much more demanding assumption—the strategist must have the capability to predict the changes that will come about. Of course, who can ever know? The world has no need to cooperate with a particular view of strategy making. So we can conclude, rather, that when the world so cooperates, the design school model may work.

4 **The organization in question must be prepared to cope with a centrally articulated strategy.** Other people in the organization must be willing to defer to a central strategist. They must also have the time, the energy, and the resources to implement a centrally determined strategy. And, of course, there has to be the will to do that implementation.

These conditions suggest some clear contexts in which the design school model would seem to apply best—its own particular niche, so to speak. Above all is the organization that needs a major reorientation, a period of *reconception* of its strategy, at least under two conditions. First, there has to have been a major change in the situation, so that the existing strategy has been seriously undermined. And second, there has to have developed the beginnings of a new stability, one that will support a new conception of strategy. In other words, *the design school model would seem to apply best at the junction of a major shift for an organization, coming out of a period of changing circumstances and into one of operating stability*. Of course, a clever new management might also wish to impose a better strategy on an organization whose circumstances have not changed. But lots of *clever* managements have gone astray; needed here is *wise* management.

There is another context where the design school model might apply, and that is the new organization, since it must have a clear sense of direction in order to compete with its more established rivals (or else position itself in a niche free of their direct influence). This period of *initial conception* of strategy is, of course, often the consequence of an entrepreneur with a vision, the person who created the organization in the first place. And that really brings us closer to the entrepreneurial school (which, as we shall see in Chapter 5, favours a less formal, more 'intuitive' process). During this period when entrepreneurs focus on initial conception, Hambrick and Fredrickson's (2005) insistence that mission and objectives must stand apart from the strategy process may indeed make sense–but not we would argue with the practice of strategy in complex and more diversified organizations.

To conclude, in critiquing the design *model*, perhaps we should be careful to preserve the design *school*. For while the model may be restricted in its application and often overly simplified, this school's contribution as an 'informing idea' has been profound. The design school has developed important vocabulary by which to discuss grand strategy, and it has provided the central notion that underlies so much of the prescription in the field of strategic management, namely that strategy represents a fundamental fit between external opportunity and internal capability (Venkatraman and Camillus, 1984). The original concept of fit, as articulated by Andrews and his Harvard colleagues, continues to be developed by researchers – in particular those who wish to transform fit into a dynamic process of adjustment (see Zajac *et al.*, 2000). Thus, this school exercises, and will continue to exercise, influence on those who see strategy as an activity principally directed towards establishing an alignment between organization and environment (Venkatraman and Prescott, 1990). The important contributions of this school therefore stand, no matter how many of the model's specific premises fall away.

3

The planning school: strategy formation as a formal process

"What I especially like about being a philosopher-scientist is that I don't have to get my hands dirty."

"I was in a warm bed, and suddenly I'm part of a plan."

Woody Allen in *Shadows and Fog*

The 1970s saw the publication of literally thousands of articles, in both the academic journals and the popular business press, that extolled the virtues of formal 'strategic planning.' In one sense, this was hugely successful, for it implanted in managers' minds everywhere a kind of imperative about the process: that it was something modern and progressive for which managers could only wish they had more time.

The central messages of the planning school fitted in neatly with the whole trend in management education and big business as well as big government practice: formal procedure, formal training, formal analysis, lots of numbers. Strategy was to be guided by a cadre of highly educated planners, part of a specialized strategic planning department with direct access to the chief executive. The appearance of 'strategic management' as an official field for courses and conferences capped all this activity.

In fact, the planning school originated at the same time as the design school; its most influential book, *Corporate Strategy*, by H. Igor Ansoff, was, like that of the Harvard group, published in 1965. But the fortunes of this school followed a rather different course. While it grew to have an enormous impact on the practice of strategic management in the 1970s, major setbacks seriously undermined it. Today, while hardly absent, it casts barely a pale shadow of its former influence.

The problem was that, quantitatively, this strategic planning literature grew dramatically, but qualitatively, it grew hardly at all. One basic set of ideas, rooted in the basic model of the design school, was repeated in this literature in endless variety. When not propagating these ideas, planning enthusiasts preached about organizations engaging in planning as some kind of imperative, or else about the 'pitfalls' that impeded them from doing so—above all that senior managers were not giving strategic planning the attention it deserved. Never was the possibility entertained that these managers might have been giving it far more attention than it deserved.

To many of these writers, planning became not just an approach to strategy formation but a virtual religion to be promulgated with the fervour of missionaries. Concurrently, hardly any research was undertaken to find out how planning really worked in practice. Peter Lorange, who attempted 'to survey the empirically based research on long range formal planning processes for corporate strategy' (1979: 226), cited less than thirty empirical studies, many of them questionnaire surveys from a distance which set out to prove that planning pays. The few in-depth studies of strategic planning were rarely conducted by people associated with this school.

This chapter begins with a discussion of the basic strategic planning model and then outlines the key premises of the planning school. After discussing some of its more recent developments, we present our critique of it, followed by an assessment of the context and contribution of this school.

The basic strategic planning model

There are hundreds of different strategic planning models. Every textbook on the subject as well as every self-respecting consulting 'strategy boutique' has one. But most reduce to the same basic ideas: take the SWOT model, divide it into neatly delineated steps, articulate each of these with lots of checklists and techniques, and giving special attention to the setting of objectives on the front end and the elaboration of budgets and operating plans on the back end. Of course, there is at least one and often several diagrams to show the overall flow. For example, Figure 3.1 shows the summary diagram from George Steiner's book, *Top Management Planning* (1969). Let us review the main steps, one at a time.

The objectives-setting stage

In place of thinking about values in the design school, proponents of the planning school developed extensive procedures for explicating and, wherever possible, quantifying the goals of the organization (generally referred to in numerical form as *objectives*). Unfortunately, there has been considerable confusion here. In their well-known book,

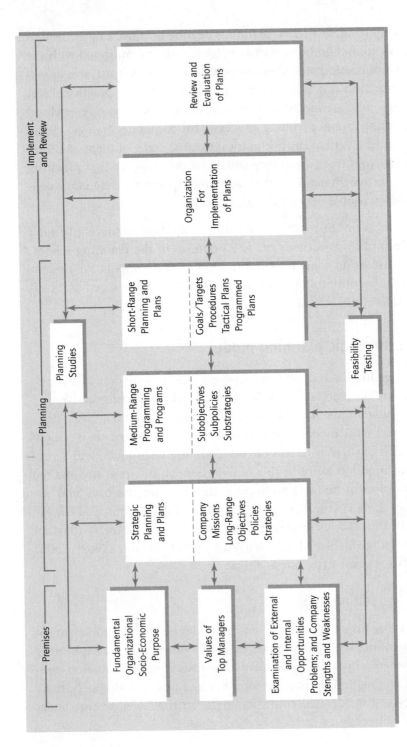

figure 3.1 **The Steiner model of strategic planning.**

Source: Reprinted with permission of The Free Press, a Division of Simon & Schuster Adult Publishing Group, from TOP MANAGEMENT PLANNING by George A. Steiner. Copyright © 1969 by the Trustees of Columbia University in the City of New York. All rights reserved.

Strategic Management, Schendel and Hofer made an issue of the distinction between 'those [models] that separate the goal and strategy
formulation tasks . . . and those that combine them' (1979: 16). As it
happens, it has almost inevitably been the planning people who have
tried to distinguish goals from strategies, while subscribers to the design
school rarely did so. But one is not very encouraged when such a
prominent planning writer as Ansoff (1965) included 'expansion of
product lines' and 'merger' under his list of objectives, and Peter
Lorange (1980), almost equally prominent in this school, used the word
objectives to mean strategies.[1] Values, or goals, as anyone in the design
school is happy to tell you, are very difficult to formalize. Perhaps that
is why so much of so-called strategic planning has been reduced to not
much more than the quantification of goals as a means of control.

The external audit stage

Once the objectives have been set, the next two stages, as in the
design school model, are to assess the external and the internal conditions of the organization. In the spirit of the more formalized
approach of planning, we shall refer to these as audits.

A major element of the audit of the organization's external environment is the set of forecasts made about future conditions. Planners
have long been preoccupied with such forecasting because, short of
being able to control the environment, an inability to predict means
an inability to plan. Thus 'predict and prepare' (Ackoff, 1983: 59)
became the motto of this school of thought. Extensive checklists
were proposed, to cover every conceivable external factor, and a
myriad of techniques were developed, ranging from the simple (such
as moving averages) to the immensely complex. Particularly popular
in more recent years has been scenario building, which seeks to pos-
tulate alternative states of an organization's upcoming situation. In
the 1980s, attention turned to *industry* or *competitor analysis*, stimulated in particular by Michael Porter's 1980 book, *Competitive Strategy*
(which is discussed in the next chapter).

---

1 'The first stage, objectives setting, serves primarily to identify relevant
strategic alternatives, where or in what strategic direction the firm as a whole
as well as its organizational subunits should go' (1980: 31).

The internal audit stage

Consistent with the planning approach, the study of strengths and weaknesses was also subjected to extensive decomposition. But here, perhaps because the assessment of *distinctive* competences is necessarily judgmental, the use of formalized technique generally gave way to simpler checklists and tables of various kinds—what Jelinek and Amar have referred to as 'corporate strategy by laundry lists' (1983: 1).

The strategy evaluation stage

In this next stage, the evaluation of strategies, the planning literature made up for what it lost in the last one. Because the process of evaluation lends itself to elaboration and qualification, techniques abound, ranging from the simple, early ones of return-on-investment calculation to a rash of later techniques such as 'competitive strategy valuation,' 'risk analysis,' 'the value curve,' and the various methods associated with calculating 'shareholder value.' As is evident in their labels, most are oriented to financial analysis. 'Value creation' has become a particularly popular term in the planning community, concerned with such things as the market-to-book value of the firm and the cost of equity capital. The underlying assumption here appears to be that firms make money by managing money. A further assumption about the whole notion of an evaluation stage must also be borne in mind here (as in the design school): that strategies are not evaluated or developed so much as *delineated*, at a particular point in time. And not one but several are delineated, so that these can be evaluated and one selected.

The strategy operationalization stage

Here is where most of the models become very detailed, almost as if the planning process has suddenly passed through the restricted strategy-formulation neck of a wind tunnel to accelerate into the seemingly open spaces of implementation. The reality of the process may, in fact, be exactly the opposite: that formulation has to be the open-ended, divergent process (in which imagination can flourish), while implementation should be more closed-ended and convergent (to subject the new strategies to the constraints of operationalization).

But because of planning's preference for formalization, it is formulation that becomes more tightly constrained, while implementation provides the freedom to decompose, elaborate, and rationalize, down an ever-widening hierarchy. Hence the inevitable association of planning with control.

Decomposition is clearly the order of the day in this stage. As Steiner has stated: 'All strategies must be broken down into substrategies for successful implementation' (1979: 177). The operationalization of strategies thus gives rise to a whole set of hierarchies, believed to exist on different levels and with different time perspectives. Long-term (usually five years) comprehensive, 'strategic' plans sit on top, followed by medium-term plans, which in turn give rise to short-term operating plans for the next year. Paralleling this is a hierarchy of objectives, a hierarchy of budgets, and a hierarchy of substrategies (corporate, business, and functional—in this school usually seen as positions rather than perspectives), and a hierarchy of action programmes.

❝ there is an inevitable association between planning and control ❞

Finally, the whole works—objectives, budgets, strategies, programmes—is brought together into a system of operating plans, sometimes referred to as the 'master plan.' Needless to say, this could become awfully elaborate, as suggested in Figure 3.2, which shows the Stanford Research Institute's widely publicized 'System of Plans.'

The label for all this effort at operationalization is *planning*, but, as suggested above, the intention has often really been *control*. Each budget, subobjective, operating plan, and action programme is overlaid on some kind of distinct entity of the organization—division, department, branch, or individual—to be carried out as specified.

Scheduling the whole process

Not only the steps in the process, but also the timetable by which they are carried out, has to be programmed. In his 1979 book, Steiner added to the front of his whole model an initial step, called the 'plan to plan.' Figure 3.3 depicts the process (according to the head of planning) used at General Electric in 1980, then the most famous of

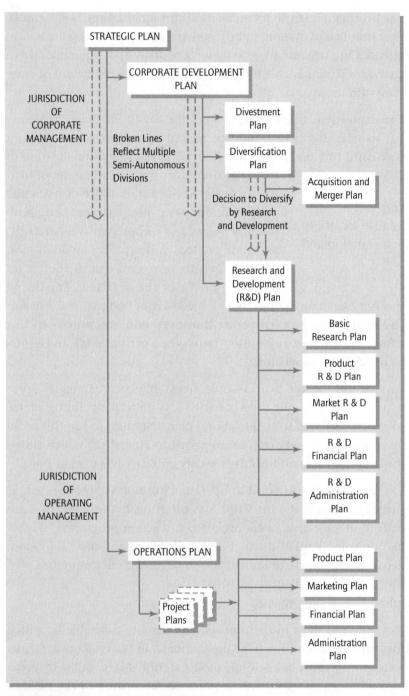

figure 3.2 Stanford Research Institute's proposed 'system of plans'

Source: Figure Courtesy of SRI International

the strategic planning companies. Each year, it began on 3 January and ended on 6 December. 'By the middle of June,' wrote Lorange and Vancil of planning in another large diversified multinational, 'top management has prepared an explicit statement of corporate strategy and goals' (1977: 31). One gets the picture of executives sitting around a table at 11:00 p.m. on 14 June working desperately to complete their strategy.

Sorting out the hierarchies

Put this all together, and you end up with a comprehensive model of strategic planning. But did that model ever get beyond its own decomposition? Figure 3.4 shows its main component parts, the four hierarchies—one for objectives, one for budgets, one for strategies, and one for programmes. A big line is drawn down the middle, because that seems to be the 'great divide' of planning.

On one side are strategies and programmes under the label *action planning*. These are concerned with making decisions before the fact in order to drive behaviour. On the other side are objectives and budgets labelled *performance control*, since these are designed to assess the results of behaviour after the fact.

In the fully developed model, objectives drive the formulation of strategies which in turn evoke programmes, the results of which influence budgets for purposes of control. Back and forth across the great divide. The question is whether these connections were ever really made. Or else, did 'strategic planning' simply reduce to routine 'number crunching' on the performance side and capital budgeting as ad hoc decision making on the action side?

Premises of the planning school

The planning school accepted most of the premises of the design school, save one and a half. But these made a considerable difference. First, as we have seen, the model was the same, but its execution was prescribed to be highly formal—at the limit almost mechanically programmed. The simple, informal model of the design school thus became an elaborated sequence of steps.

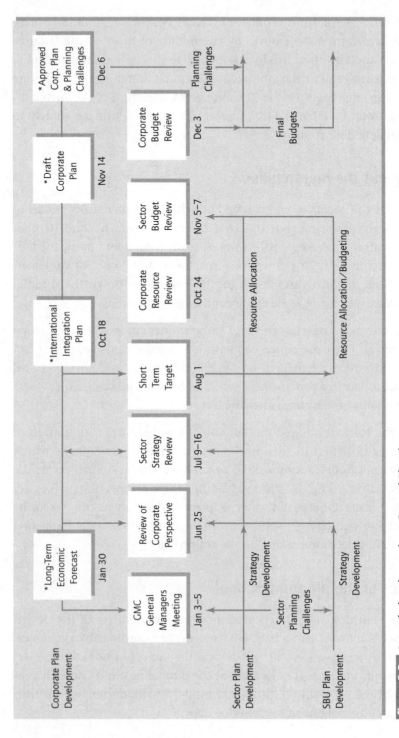

figure 3.3 Annual planning cycle at General Electric

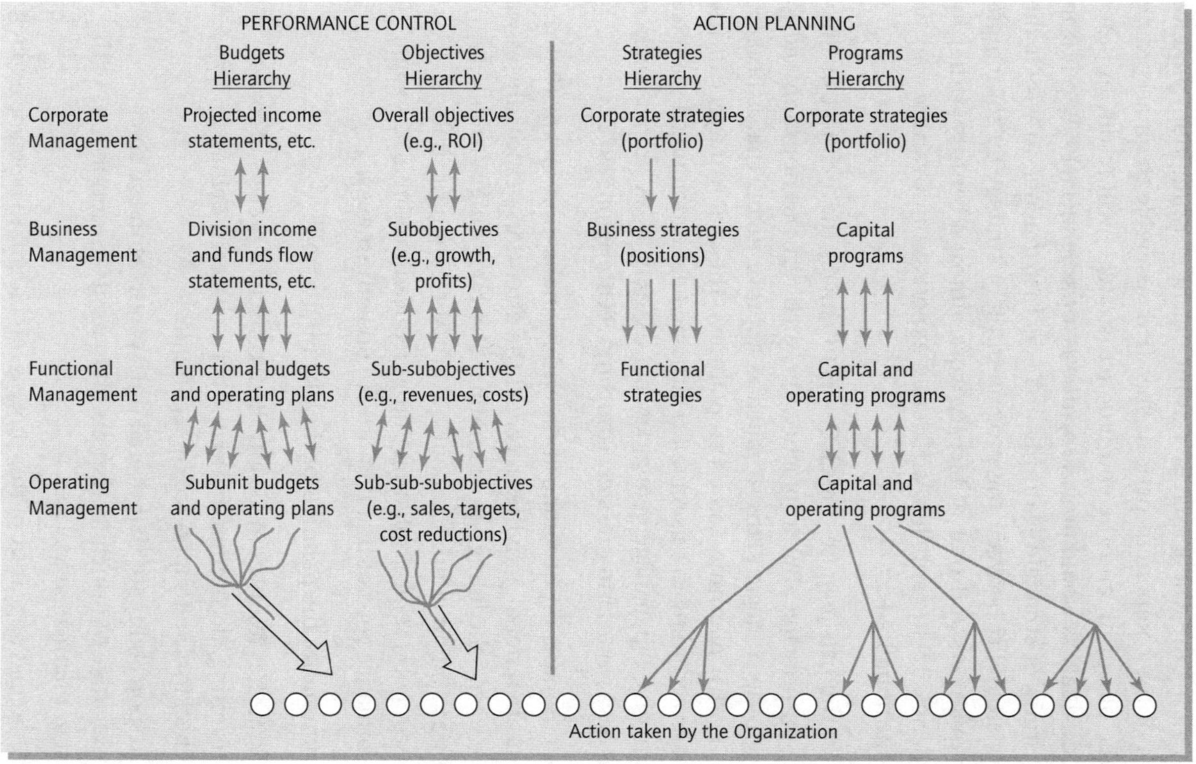

figure 3.4 Four planning hierarchies

Source: Adapted with the permission of The Free Press, a Division of Simon & Schuster Adult Publishing Group, from *The RISE AND FALL OF STRATEGIC PLANNING: Reconceiving Roles of Planning, Plans, Planners* by Henry Mintzberg. Copyright © 1994 by Henry Mintzberg. All rights reserved.

Underlying the whole exercise was the machine assumption: produce each of the component parts as specified, assemble them according to the blueprint, and the end product (strategy) will result. In other words, analysis would provide synthesis, or as Jelinek (1979) put it in her study of strategic planning at Texas Instruments, in which she drew a parallel between the programming of strategy by contemporary planners and that of factory work almost a century earlier by Frederick Taylor and his 'efficiency experts': 'innovation' can be 'institutionalized.'

As for the half premise, the CEO was to remain the architect of strategy—in principle. But in practice, this architect was not supposed to design the strategic plans so much as approve them. That is because along with planning came the planners, the major players in the process according to this school. Thus, one publication urged planners to 'involve top management at key points, only at key points,' such as four days per year in one steel company! (Pennington, 1972: 3)

The emphasis on decomposition and formalization meant that the most operational activities received the attention—especially, as we have seen, scheduling, programming, and budgeting. Virtually nothing was said, in contrast, about the actual creation of strategies. As a consequence, *strategic* planning often reduced to a 'numbers game' of performance control that had little to do with strategy.

To summarize the premises of the planning school:

1 Strategies result from a controlled, conscious process of formal planning, decomposed into distinct steps, each delineated by checklists and supported by techniques.

2 Responsibility for that overall process rests with the chief executive in principle; responsibility for its execution rests with staff planners in practice.

3 Strategies appear from this process full blown, to be made explicit so that they can then be implemented through detailed attention to objectives, budgets, programmes, and operating plans of various kinds.

Some more recent developments

While much of this literature has revolved around the models presented above, there have been other developments—in the spirit of these premises but more focused in application. We discuss briefly here three in particular—scenario planning, real options, and strategic control—as well as some summary comments by one of the authors of this book about the role of planners. (Other developments, concerning stakeholder planning and culture planning, will be discussed in the power and cultural schools respectively.)

Scenario planning

The *scenario*, a 'tool' in the 'strategist's arsenal,' to quote Porter (1985: 481), is predicated on the assumption that if you cannot predict *the* future, then by speculating upon a variety of them, you might open up your mind and even, perhaps, hit upon the right one.

There has been a good deal of interest in this since an article by Pierre Wack (1985) described a scenario-building exercise at Royal Dutch Shell that anticipated the nature (if not the timing) of the 1973 dramatic increase in the world petroleum prices. Wack described the complexity and subtlety of the exercise, which depended on judgment beyond simply the formal analysis—in his words, 'less on figures and more on insight' (84).

Planners' time is not limitless; they need enough scenarios to cover the important possible contingencies, yet few enough to be manageable (quite literally). Then the question arises of what to do with them: bet on the most probable or the most beneficial, hedge, remain flexible, make one happen (Porter, 1985). There also arises the need to convince management to do what seems best with a given scenario, a problem to which Wack devotes considerable attention. Changing the managerial worldview proved to be a 'much more demanding task' than actually building the scenario (84). But it was worth the effort:

" in scenario building, managers need to share some common view **"**   When the world changes, managers need to share some common view of the new world. Otherwise, decentralized strategic decisions will result in management anarchy. Scenarios express and communicate this common view, a shared understanding of the new realities to all parts of the organization. (89)

They also open up perspectives, so that the whole exercise can also be seen as one of stimulating creative activity, even if no one scenario applies perfectly. In these respects, scenario building might be described as *planners* at their best, rather than planning per se, because the intention is not to formalize strategy making so much as improve however managers do it. In Box 3.1, Laurence Wilkinson, elaborates further on scenario planning.

---

box 1.1

How to build scenarios

Planning for 'long fuse, big bang' problems in an era of uncertainty

(Excerpted from Wilkinson, 1995)

Anything that can help make a decision in the midst of uncertainty [is] valuable. One such tool is scenario planning. A growing number of corporate executives are using scenario planning to make big, hard decisions more effectively. And it's not just for bigwigs: scenario planning can help us at a personal level as well.

Scenario planning derives from the observation that, given the impossibility of knowing precisely how the future will play out, a good decision or strategy to adopt is one that plays out well across several possible futures. To find that 'robust' strategy, scenarios are created in plural, such that each scenario diverges markedly from the others. These sets of scenarios are, essentially, specially constructed stories about the future, each one modeling a distinct, plausible world in which we might someday have to live and work.

Yet, the purpose of scenario planning is not to pinpoint future events but to highlight large-scale forces that push the future in different directions. It's about making these forces visible—so that if they do happen, the planner will at least recognize them. It's about helping make better decisions today.

This all sounds rather esoteric, but as my partner Peter Schwartz . . . is fond of saying, 'scenario making isn't rocket science.' He should know. Not only did he help develop the technique back in the 1970s, but he's also a rocket scientist.

> Scenario planning begins by identifying the focal issue or decision. There are an infinite number of stories that we could tell about the future; our purpose is to tell those that matter, that lead to better decisions. So we begin the process by agreeing on the issue that we want to address. Sometimes the question is rather broad (What's the future of the former Soviet Union?); sometimes, it's pretty specific (Should we introduce a new operating system?). Either way, the point is to agree on the issue(s) that will be used as a test of relevance as we go through the rest of the scenario-making process. . . .
>
> Since scenarios are a way of understanding the dynamics shaping the future, we next attempt to identify the primary 'driving forces' at work in the present. These fall roughly into four categories:
>
> 1 **Social dynamics**—quantitative, demographic issues (How influential will youth be in 10 years?); softer issues of values, lifestyle, demand, or political energy (Will people get bored with online chatting?).
> 2 **Economic issues**—macroeconomic trends and forces shaping the economy as a whole (How will international trade flow and exchange rates affect the price of chips?); microeconomic dynamics (What might my competitors do? How might the very structure of the industry change?); and forces at work, on or within the company itself (Will we be able to find the skilled employees we need?).
> 3 **Political issues**—electoral (Who'll be the next president or premier?); legislative (Will tax policies be changed?); regulatory (Will the FCC loosen its grip on radio spectrum?); and litigative (Will the courts break up Microsoft?).
> 4 **Technological issues**—direct (How will high bandwidth wireless affect land-line telephony?); enabling (Will X-ray lithography bring in the next chip revolution?); and indirect (Will biotech allow easy 'body hacking' and thus compete with more traditional forms of entertainment?)

Real options

Scenario planning is useful for exploring the future, but it is ambiguous when it comes to addressing the question of which scenarios the organization should take seriously (Cornelius *et al.*, 2005). The simplest approach to moving forward would be to use a SWOT analysis to evaluate each scenario. However, as the case of Shell prior to the 1973 oil crisis suggests, this approach is essentially defensive: organizations explore threats and take steps to reduce their vulnerabilities, and prepare for opportunities should they arise. For many planning specialists, this approach is reactive, and it also lacks rigour. Managers would rather take action than wait for events to unfold. Thus, not surprisingly, when informed about scenarios they often ask for precise impact—in terms of costs and benefits.

To address these limitations, planning specialists are increasingly reaching out to the theory of 'real options.' Real options are the managerial equivalent of options theory in finance (Trigeorgis, 1993). In financial markets, options are contracts that specify a price at which the holder of the option can buy or sell an asset such as shares at a particular time in the future. The holders of the option do not have to buy or sell the asset; they simply have the right to do so in some future date. The catch is that they have to pay to obtain this right in proportion to the benefits that this right confers. In the financial markets, the value of this right to the holder can be calculated using tested and well-established formulas; in the managerial world so far this has not been possible.

Real options translate this logic to the world of managerial action. The option here is not on shares, but on investments (Dixit and Pindyck, 1995; Trigeorgis, 1990). When examining a scenario, managers usually want to know what investments would be needed to address or take advantage of a scenario (McGrath and MacMillan, 2000). Once the size of the total investment is calculated, the next step is to decide whether to go ahead with the investment. Traditionally, managers had to commit fully to a course of action, or abandon it altogether. Real options present a third alternative. Managers can buy what amounts to an option on a course of action, without fully committing themselves (Amram and Kulatilaka, 1999). For example, an energy company that wants to build wind turbines may pay landowners for the right to build wind turbines on their land, with a promise of further payments should it choose to do so. Another interesting example comes from the movie industry. Producers often pay screen writers a fee for a guarantee to have a 'first look' at their script once it is completed. Buying this option allows producers to get a jump on the competition, should the script turn out to be promising.

Real options theory fits well within the planning school: it is analytical, it is forward looking, and it builds on methodologies that provide specific answers to common managerial problems. The theory, however, is having difficulties being implemented in practice. To begin with, many managerial decisions are not susceptible to an options approach. For example, it is often difficult to take an option on launching a radical innovation: one takes the full risk and launches the innovation, or one does not (Garud *et al.*, 1998). At a more technical level, the valuing of real options does not have the same well-established methods that are available for their counterparts in finance. Without a reliable system, the valuing of options is ultimately a matter of human judgment (van Putten and MacMillan, 2004). Judgment of options is often reliable when it comes to well defined investment propositions, or to incremental technological change, but it runs into problems that are familiar to forecasters when the options deal with uncertain or rapidly evolving situations.

Strategic control

A subject of growing interest is that of strategic control. Most obvious here is control of strategy itself—keeping organizations on their intended strategic tracks, what Simons has referred to as the 'cybernetic view' (1988: 2). Indeed, we shall argue in our critique that a great deal of what has been called strategic planning really amounts to this kind of strategic control (see Ketokivi and Castañer, 2004). Beyond this is the view of strategic control as a means to review and accept proposed strategies.

In their book *Strategies and Styles: The Role of the Center in Managing Diversified Corporations*, Goold and Campbell (1987) treat strategic control in this way, as one of three strategy-making styles available to the headquarters of a multibusiness, diversified company:

1 **Strategic planning**: Here headquarters is involved in many of the key strategic decisions of the individual businesses (for the sake of the corporation as a whole). This style is most consistent with the planning school, whereby the centre acts as an organizing office to determine through careful analysis how resources are to be coordinated and redistributed among businesses.

2 **Financial control**: This style is defined by minimal involvement of the centre or corporate office in strategy formation.

Responsibility is devolved to the individual businesses within the corporation. The centre maintains control principally through short-term budgeting.

3 **Strategic control**: This is a hybrid style, which involves both business unit autonomy and promotion of corporate interests. Responsibility for strategy rests with the division, but strategies must ultimately be approved by headquarters. The centre uses 'planning reviews to test logic, to pinpoint weak arguments, and to encourage businesses to raise the quality of their strategic thinking' (1987: 74). Once headquarters approves a plan and budget (with financial targets set in a separate budgeting process), it monitors business performance against strategic milestones, such as market share and budgets (75).

Goold *et al.*, (1994) more recently developed their work on multibusiness strategy through a 'parenting' metaphor: there are different roles within the family, for the parent (headquarters) and the children (businesses). Of course, metaphors are not always neutral: this one certainly conveys some messages about control of divisions by corporate headquarters.

The parent needs to balance advice and encouragement with control and discipline. It also needs to recognize that the businesses (children) change and mature over time, and that a relationship that may have worked well in their early years will probably need to change as they grow. Businesses (children) like to know where they stand with their parents, including what will be regarded as good and bad behavior. . . . The parent has an important role in creating a family environment in which friendly relationships between the businesses (children) are fostered, and mutual antagonism is diffused. (1994: 47)

> ❝ the parent needs to balance advice and encouragement with control and discipline ❞

In another article, published in 1990, Goold and Quinn found evidence that 'in practice . . . few companies . . . identify formal and explicit strategic control measures [to monitor strategic progress and ensure the implementation of strategic plans] and build them into their control systems' (43). They call for a 'broader conception of strategic control, such that differences between actual and planned outcomes lead not just to modification in the actions of individuals, but also to questioning of the assumptions of the plan itself' (46). Their own survey of the 200 largest companies in Great Britain 'revealed that only a small number of companies (11 percent) would claim to employ a strategic control system of the type' they describe as 'fully fledged' (47).

But does this go far enough? There is certainly the need to assess success in the implementation of realized strategies, and then to see whether the resulting deliberate strategies actually worked out in the world. But what about the assessment of realized strategies that were not necessarily intended (namely the emergent ones)?

Put differently, strategic control has to broaden its scope beyond strategic planning. Strategies need not be deliberate to be effective. As suggested in the matrix of Figure 3.5, emergent strategies can be effective too, while many deliberate strategies, successfully implemented, have proved to be disasters. It is the performance of the organization that matters, not the performance of its planning.

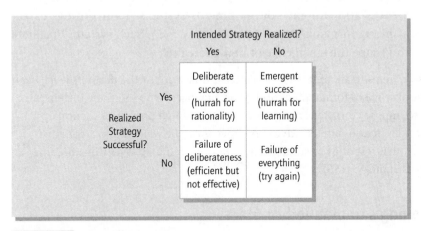

figure 3.5 **Broadening strategic control**   Source: From Mintzberg (1994: 360).

One book on strategic control consistent with this approach is *Levers of Control: How Managers Use Innovative Control Systems to Drive Strategic Renewal*, by Robert Simons (1995). Defining management control systems as 'the formal, information-based routines and procedures managers use to maintain or alter patterns in organizational activities' (5), Simons introduces four levers of control: *belief* systems (to 'provide values, purpose, direction for the organization' [34]), *boundary* systems (which establish limits to action), *diagnostic* control systems (more conventional feedback systems, 'to ensure predictable goal achievement' [59], 'the tools of strategy implementation' [90]), and *interactive* control systems.

Despite the ubiquity of the diagnostic control systems, Simons argues that managers pay little attention to them, focusing more on the interactive control systems. These, in contrast, 'stimulate research and learning, allowing new strategies to emerge as participants throughout the organization respond to perceived opportunities and threats' (91). Senior managers tend to select one of these for special attention, and use it to 'involve themselves regularly and personally in the decision activities of subordinates' (95).

In his study of thirty businesses in American health-care products, Simons identified five such systems: project management systems, profit planning systems, brand revenue budgets, intelligence systems (to gather and disseminate information about the external environment), and human development systems (concerning career planning or management by objectives, etc.). Such systems 'facilitate and shape the emergence of new strategies':

These systems relate to strategy as patterns of action. At the business level, even in the absence of formal plans and goals, managers who use these systems are able to impose consistency and guide creative search processes. Tactical day-to-day actions and creative experiments can be welded into a cohesive pattern that responds to strategic uncertainties and may, over time, become realized strategy. (155)

Planning's unplanned troubles

Strategic planning ran into trouble in the early 1980s when the activity was cut back in many companies. Most dramatic was its emasculation at General Electric, the company that 'literally wrote the book on the subject' (Potts, 1984).

Business Week documented the troubles in a cover story of 17 September 1984. 'After more than a decade of near-dictatorial sway over the future of US corporations, the reign of the strategic planner may be at an end,' the magazine exclaimed '. . . few of the supposedly brilliant strategies concocted by planners were successfully implemented.' To *Business Week*, the upheaval was 'nothing less' than a 'bloody battle between planners and managers' (1984: 62). The General Electric story dominated the article, as it had the lore of strategic planning almost from the very beginning.

> ❝ few of the supposedly brilliant strategies concocted by planners were successfully implemented ❞

As *Business Week* told this story, in the early 1980s, soon after he became Chairman and CEO, Jack Welch dismantled the strategic planning system. The vice-president of the Major Appliances Business Group was quoted about finally '"gaining ownership of the business, grabbing hold of it" from "an isolated bureaucracy" of planners' (62). *No* planners were left in that division by 1984.

The signs of troubles in the planning camp had hardly been absent earlier. Indeed the most enthusiastic proponent of strategic planning, Igor Ansoff, wrote in 1977, twelve years after the publication of his key book *Corporate Strategy*, that 'in spite of almost twenty years of existence of the strategic planning technology, a majority of firms today engage in the far less threatening and perturbing extrapolative long-range planning' (1977: 20). And the problems hardly abated after 1984. In *The Rise and Fall of Strategic Planning*, from which this chapter draws, Mintzberg (1994) documented the evidence that piled up against the process, including stories in the popular press and empirical findings from the research, which contained a long string of studies that set out to prove that strategic planning pays but never did.[2] Wilson's 'seven deadly sins of strategic planning,' reproduced in the accompanying box, summarize some of the problems that had undermined the process.

Planners' response to this evidence ranged from pure faith ('Plans are sometimes useless but the planning process is always indispensable' (Steiner and Kunin, 1983: 15)) to various forms of elaboration (calls

---

2 See the reviews by Bresser and Bishop (1983); Shrader *et al.*, (1984); Lorange (1979: 230); and Boyd (1991). For more on the General Electric story, see Hamermesh (1986) and Wilson (1994).

for more sophisticated forecasting, stakeholder analysis, etc.), each an effort to plug the holes while upping the ante. But the most popular response was to fall back on a set of 'pitfalls' of planning, notably the lack of managerial support for planning and the absence of an organizational climate congenial to the process.

Yet surely no technique had ever had more managerial attention than strategic planning. Moreover, might it not be equally fair to ask whether a climate hostile to planning may be right for certain other kinds of strategy making? And what about climates congenial to planning? Are they necessarily effective for strategy making?

As we have seen above, planning can undermine commitment to strategy making, not only of the middle managers subjected to its centralized controls, but even of top managers who may be largely bypassed in the process. Has anyone ever met a manager who, after filling out all the forms of the annual planning ritual, said: 'Boy that was fun. I can't wait to do it again next year!'?

Plans by their very nature are designed to promote *inflexibility*—they are meant to establish clear direction, to impose stability on an organization. Even the planning process itself may favour incremental change and a short-term orientation. Recall that planning is built around the categories that *already* exist in the organization, such as established corporate, business, and functional strategies, as well as existing structural units (around which the whole process is organized). That hardly makes it easy to change the categories, which is what true strategic change is all about. Of course, organizations manage around the categories—for example, by creating cross-unit task forces. But as the categories break down, so too does the notion of strategy formation as a formal (namely planned) process. Thus we have the conclusion of Harvard operations management professor Robert Hayes that 'line managers complained not about the *mis*functioning of strategic planning but about the harmful aspects of its *proper* functioning' (1985: 111).

box 3.2

The seven deadly sins of strategic planning

(from Wilson, 1994:13)

1 **The staff took over the process**. This situation arose partly because CEOs created new staff components to deal with a new function, partly because the staff moved in to fill a vacuum created by middle management's indifference to a new responsibility, and partly because of arrogance and empire building. As a result, planning staffs all too often cut executives out of the strategy development process, turning them into little more than rubber stamps. . . .

2 **The process dominated the staff**. The process's methodologies became increasingly elaborate. Staff placed too much emphasis on analysis, too little on true strategic insights. . . . Strategic thinking became equated with strategic planning. . . . Jack Welch, the chairman and CEO of GE, described the outcome graphically: 'The books got thicker, the printing got more sophisticated, the covers got harder, and the drawings got better.' . . .

3 **Planning systems were virtually designed to produce no results**. . . . The main design failure lay in denying, or diminishing, the planning role of the very executives whose mandate was to execute the strategy. . . .The attitude of many was typified by the angry retort of one executive. 'The matrix picked the strategy—let the matrix implement it!' The other design fault was the failure to integrate the strategic planning system with the operations system, resulting in a strategy that did not drive action.

4 **Planning focused on the more exciting game of mergers, acquisitions, and divestitures at the expense of core business development**. This problem stemmed in part from the temper of the times. But it also resulted from the inappropriate use of planning tools. . . .

5 **Planning processes failed to develop true strategic choices**. . . . Planners and executives rushed to adopt the first strategy that 'satisfied' (i.e. met certain basic conditions in an acceptable manner). They made no real effort to search for, or analyze, an array of strategy alternatives before making a decision. As a result, companies all too often adopted strategies by default rather than by choice.

6 **Planning neglected the organizational and cultural requirements of strategy**. . . . The process focused, rightly, on the external environment, but it did so at the expense of the internal environment that is critical in the implementation stage.

7 **Single-point forecasting was an inappropriate basis for planning in an era of restructuring and uncertainty**. . . . Companies still tended to rely on single-point forecasting. Scenario-based planning was the exception rather than the rule. . . . Plans that relied on [single-point forecasting] suffered increased vulnerability to surprises. . . . [Moreover] because planning assumptions spelled out a single future, one that was almost always some slight variation of an extrapolation of past trends, there was an inherent bias in favor of continuing a 'momentum strategy.' . . .

The fallacies of strategic planning

An expert has been defined as someone who avoids all the many pitfalls on his or her way to the grand fallacy. Here, therefore, we consider the fallacies of strategic planning, three in particular, which, to our mind, blend into that one grand fallacy. We wish to make clear that our critique is not of planning but of *strategic* planning—the idea that *strategy* itself can be developed in a structured, formalized process. (Planning itself has other useful functions in organizations.)

The fallacy of predetermination

To engage in strategic planning, an organization must be able to predict the course of its environment, to control it, or simply to assume its stability. Otherwise, it makes no sense to set the inflexible course of action that constitutes a strategic plan.

Igor Ansoff wrote in *Corporate Strategy* in 1965 that 'We shall refer to the period for which the firm is able to construct forecasts with an accuracy of, say, plus or minus 20 percent as the planning horizon of the firm' (44). A most extraordinary statement in such a famous book! For how in the world can predictability be predicted?

The evidence on forecasting is, in fact, quite to the contrary. While certain repetitive patterns (e.g., seasonal) may be predictable, the forecasting of discontinuities, such as technological breakthroughs or price increases, is, according to Spiro Makridakis, a leading expert in the field, 'practically impossible.' (See Box 3.3: 'Forecasting: Whoops!') In his opinion, 'very little, or nothing' can be done, 'other than to be prepared, in a general way, to . . . react quickly once a discontinuity has occurred' (1990: 115). The only hope for planning, therefore, is to extrapolate the present trends and hope for the best. Unfortunately that 'best' may be rare: 'Long-range forecasting (two years or longer) is notoriously inaccurate' (Hogarth and Makridakis, 1981: 122).

> **❝ long-range forecasting is notoriously inaccurate ❞**

Strategic planning requires not only predictability following, but also stability during, strategy making. The world has to hold still while

---

box 3.3

Forecasting: Whoops!

■ 'Atomic energy might be as good as our present-day explosives, but it is unlikely to produce anything more dangerous.' (Winston Churchill, 1939)

■ 'I think there is a world market for about five computers.' (Thomas J. Watson, President of IBM, 1948)

■ 'X-rays are a hoax.' (Lord Kelvin, 1900)

■ 'Not within a thousand years will man ever fly.' (Wilbur Wright, 1901) (from Coffey, 1983)

Item in a South African newspaper: 'A weather forecast should be obtained before leaving, as weather conditions are extremely unpredictable' (in Gimpl and Dakin, 1984: 125).

Researcher in the British Foreign Office from 1903 to 1950: 'Year after year the worriers and fretters would come to me with awful predictions of the outbreak of war. I denied it each time. I was only wrong twice.'

---

the planning process unfolds. Remember those lockstep schedules that have strategies appearing on, say, the fifteenth of each June? One can just picture the competitors waiting for the sixteenth (especially if they don't much believe in such planning).

Responsive strategies do not appear on schedule, immaculately conceived. They can happen at any time and at any place in an adaptive organization. If strategy means stability (as a plan into the future or a pattern out of the past), then strategy making means unexpected interference.

The fallacy of detachment

As mentioned earlier, Marianne Jelinek developed the interesting point in her book, called *Institutionalizing Innovation*, that strategic planning has been to the executive suite what Frederick Taylor's work study was to the factory floor. Both set out to circumvent human idiosyncrasies in order to systematize behaviour. 'It is through administrative systems that planning and policy are made possible, because the systems capture knowledge about the task. . . .' Thus 'true management by exception, and true policy direction are now possible, solely because management is no longer wholly immersed in the details of the task itself' (1979: 139). Put differently, if the system does the thinking, then thought has to be detached from action, strategy from operations (or 'tactics'), formulation from implementation, thinkers from doers, and so strategists from the objects of their strategies. Managers must, in other words, manage by *remote* control.

> **" it turns out that hard data can have a decidedly soft underbelly "**

The trick, of course, is to get the relevant information up there, so that those senior managers 'on high' can be informed about the consequences of those details 'down below,' without having to enmesh themselves in them. And that is supposed to be accomplished by 'hard data'—quantitative aggregates of the detailed 'facts' about the organization and its context, neatly packaged for immediate use. That way, the 'head'—executives and planners—can formulate so that all the hands can get on with the implementation.

We maintain that all of this is dangerously fallacious. Detached managers together with abstracted planners do not so much make bad strategies; mostly they do not make strategies at all. Look inside all those organizations where people are searching for a vision, amidst all their strategic planning, and you will mostly find executives doing exactly what planning tells them to do—sit there disconnected from the details. Effective strategists, in contrast, are not people who abstract themselves from the daily detail, but who *immerse* themselves in it while being able to abstract the strategic *messages* from it.

---

box 3.4

The soft underbelly of hard data

(adapted from Mintzberg, 1994: 257–66)

The belief that strategic managers and their planning systems can be detached from the subject of their efforts is predicated on one fundamental assumption: that they can be informed in a formal way. The messy world of random noise, gossip, inference, impression, and fact must be reduced to firm data, hardened and aggregated so that they can be supplied regularly in digestible form. In other words, systems must do it, whether they go by the name of (reading back over the years) 'information technology,' 'strategic information systems,' 'expert systems,' 'total systems,' or just plain so-called 'management information systems' (MIS). Unfortunately, the hard data on which such systems depend often proves to have a decidedly soft underbelly:

1 **Hard information is often limited in scope, lacking richness and often failing to encompass important noneconomic and nonquantitative factors.** Much information important for strategy making never does become hard fact. The expression on a customer's face, the mood in the factory, the tone of voice of a government official, all of this can be information for the manager but not for the formal system. That is why managers generally spend a great deal of time developing their own *personal* information systems, comprising networks of contacts and informers of all kinds.

2 **Much hard information is too aggregated for effective use in strategy making.** The obvious solution for a manager overloaded with information and pressed for the time necessary to process it is to have the information aggregated. General Electric before 1980 provided an excellent example of this type of thinking. First it introduced 'Strategic Business Units' (SBUs) over the divisions and departments and then 'Sectors' over the SBUs, each time seeking to increase the level of aggregation to enable top management to comprehend the necessary information quickly. The problem is that a great deal is lost in such aggregating, often the essence of the information itself. How much could aggregated data on six sectors really tell the GE chief executives about the complex organization they headed? It is fine to see forests, but only so long as nothing is going on among the trees. As Richard Neustadt, who studied the information-collecting habits of several presidents of the United States, commented: 'It is not information of a general sort that helps a President see personal stakes; not summaries, not surveys, not the *bland amalgams*. Rather . . . it is the odds and ends of *tangible detail* that pieced together in his mind illuminate the underside of issues put before him. . . . He must become his own director of his own central intelligence' (1960: 153–54, italics added).

3 **Much hard information arrives too late to be of use in strategy making.** Information takes time to 'harden': time is required for trends and events and performance to appear as 'facts,' more time for these facts to be aggregated into reports, even more time if these reports have to be presented on a predetermined schedule. But strategy making has to be an active, dynamic process, often unfolding quickly in reaction to immediate stimuli; managers cannot wait for information to harden while competitors are running off with valued customers.

> 4 **Finally, a surprising amount of hard information is unreliable.** Soft information is supposed to be unreliable, subject to all kinds of biases. Hard information, in contrast, is supposed to be concrete and precise; it is, after all, transmitted and stored electronically. In fact, hard information can be far worse than soft information. Something is always lost in the process of quantification—before those electrons are activated. Anyone who has ever produced a quantitative measure—whether a reject count in a factory or a publication count in a university—knows just how much distortion is possible, intentional as well as unintentional. As Eli Devons (1950:Ch. 7) described in his fascinating account of planning for British aircraft production in World War II, despite the 'arbitrary assumptions made' in the collection of some data, 'once a figure was put forward . . . it soon became accepted as the "agreed figure," since no one was able by rational argument to demonstrate that it was wrong. . . . And once the figures were called "statistics", they acquired the authority and sanctity of Holy Writ' (155).
>
> Of course, soft information can be speculative, and distorted too. But what marketing manager faced with a choice between today's rumor that a major customer was seen lunching with a competitor and tomorrow's fact that the business was lost would hesitate to act on the former? Moreover, a single story from one disgruntled customer may be worth more than all those reams of market research data simply because, while the latter may identify a problem, it is the former that can suggest the solution. Overall, in our opinion, while hard data may inform the intellect, it is largely soft data that builds wisdom.

It turns out that hard data can have a decidedly soft underbelly. As specified in the accompanying box, such data are often late, thin, and excessively aggregated. This may explain why managers who rely primarily on such formalized information (accounting statements, marketing research reports in business, opinion polls in government, etc.), often have so much trouble coming up with good strategies.

Effective strategy making connects acting to thinking which in turn connects implementation to formulation. We think in order to act, to be sure, but we also act in order to think. We try things, and the ones that work gradually converge into patterns that become strategies. This is not some quirky behaviour of disorganized people but the very essence of strategic learning as we shall see in Chapter 7. (See De Geus (1988), who headed up the planning function at Shell, on 'Planning as Learning.')

Such strategy making breaks down the classic dichotomy by allowing implementation to inform formulation. As noted in the last chapter, either the formulator must implement or else the implementers must formulate. As we shall see, one fits the entrepreneurial school, the other, the learning school. Either way, the process of strategy making becomes more richly interactive. Hence we would do well to drop the term strategic planning altogether and talk instead about strategic thinking connected to acting.

The fallacy of formalization

Can the system in fact do it? Can strategic planning, in the words of a Stanford Research Institute economist, 'recreate' the processes of the 'genius entrepreneur'? (McConnell, 1971: 2). Can innovation really be institutionalized? Above all, can such analysis provide the necessary synthesis?

Bear in mind that strategic planning has not been presented as an *aid* to strategy making, as some kind of *support* for natural managerial processes (including intuition), but as strategy making itself and *in place of* intuition. Proponents of this school have long claimed this to be the 'one best way' to create strategy. Yet, unlike Frederick Taylor, who coined the phrase, planners never studied the very process they sought to change. Best practice was simply assumed to be *their* practice. The CEO 'can seriously jeopardize or even destroy the prospects of strategic thinking by not consistently following the discipline of strategic planning . . .' wrote Lorange in 1980, without offering any supporting evidence.

Indeed, go back to all those popular strategic planning charts and look for the box that explains how strategies are actually created. You will not find it, because the writers never explained this. Amidst all that hype about having to develop strategy in a planned process, no one ever explained how the thinking of those genius entrepreneurs, or even ordinary competent strategists, could be recreated. At best— or perhaps at worst—they inserted boxes with labels such as 'apprehend inputs' and 'add insights' (Malmlow, 1972). Very helpful! A phenomenon is not captured simply because it has been labelled in a box on a piece of paper.

Research (as we shall see in subsequent chapters) tells us that strategy making is an immensely complex process involving the most sophisticated, subtle, and at times subconscious of human cognitive and social processes. These draw on all kinds of informational inputs, many of them nonquantifiable and accessible only to strategists with their feet on the ground. Such processes follow no predetermined schedules nor fall on to any preset tracks. Effective strategies inevitably exhibit some emergent qualities and, even when significantly deliberate, often appear to be less formally planned than informally visionary. Above all, learning, in the form of fits and starts, discoveries based on serendipitous events, and the recognition of unexpected patterns, plays a key role, if not the key role, in the development of strategies that are novel. Accordingly, we know that the process requires insight, creativity, and synthesis, the very things that the formalization of planning discourages. Lorange might well be asked to entertain the proposition that CEOs can seriously jeopardize the prospects of strategic thinking by following the discipline of strategic planning.

The failure of strategic planning is the failure of formalization—of systems expected to do better at such tasks than flesh and blood human beings. It is the failure of forecasting to predict discontinuities, of institutionalization to provide innovation, of hard data to substitute for soft, of lockstep schedules to respond to the dynamic factors. The formal systems could certainly process more information, at least hard information, consolidate it, aggregate it, move it about. But they could never *internalize* it, *comprehend* it, *synthesize* it.

There is something strange about formalization, something that can cause the very essence of an activity to be lost simply in its specification. As human beings, we often believe that we have captured a process simply because we have broken it into component parts, and specified procedures for each. Yet all too often, that just breeds a certain mindlessness. For some kinds of processes involving learning, innovating, and the like, that only seems to drive them over some kind of edge. We illustrate a *formalization edge* in Figure 3.6.

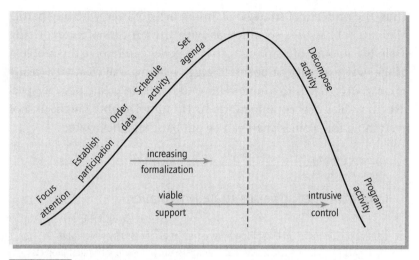

figure 3.6 The formalization edge   Source: From Mintzberg, 1994.

Planners and managers need to be very sensitive to just where that formalization edge may appear. They may have to formalize the time and participation at a particular meeting about strategy, to ensure that the appropriate people appear together. But how about specifying the agenda, so that precious time will not be lost? Seems sensible enough. And the procedures to ensure order in the discussion? Well At what point do we realize that everything went according to plan but no strategic thinking came about? Decomposing the strategy-making process so that, for example, goals are discussed from 9–10:30 and strengths and weaknesses from 10:30–12, can stifle creative discussion. The object of the exercise, to repeat, is not analysis but synthesis. Efforts to force a loose process into a tight sequence can kill it.

Zan has distinguished between 'systems that facilitate thinking' and 'systems that (try to) do it' (1987: 191). To quote one Texas Instruments executive on that company's systems, 'We made 'em bureaucratic. We used the system as a control tool, rather than a facilitating tool. That's the difference' (in Jelinek and Schoonhoven, 1990: 411). Box 3.5 shows how capital budgeting fell into much the same trap, emerging as a technique that in some ways impeded strategic thinking.

Thus, the problem of strategic planning has not been with any particular category it uses so much as with the process of categorizing itself. No amount of rearranging of the boxes can resolve the problem of the very existence of boxes. Strategy making, like creativity (really as creativity), needs to function beyond boxes, to create new perspectives as well as new combinations. As Humpty Dumpty taught us, not everything that comes apart can be put back together again.

---

box 3.5

Capital budgeting versus strategy formation

(adapted from Mintzberg, 1994: 122–33)

Capital budgeting is an established procedure in businesses by which unit managers (division heads, functional managers, etc.) propose individual projects up the hierarchy for approval. These are supposed to be assessed in terms of their costs and benefits (combined to indicate return on investment) so that the senior managers can compare and rank them, and accept only as many as the capital funding available for a given period allows. Because of the impetus of the flow from unit managers to general managers, capital budgeting is sometimes referred to as bottom-up strategic planning.

Evidence on the actual practice of capital budgeting tells a very different story. One of the early studies—an intensive probe into the process in one large divisionalized firm—found that the senior management had a propensity to approve all the projects that reached its level. 'The important question,' wrote the author, 'was whether that group of officers which possessed the power to move proposals through the funding process chose to identify a particular proposal for sponsorship,' because once that happened, proposals had more or less free passage (Bower, 1970: 322).

In a later study, Marsh et al. looked carefully at three firms considered 'sophisticated' in their use of capital budgeting, and found all kinds of problems. The procedure manuals 'proved quite hard to locate!' (1988: 22); the presentation to the divisional board in one firm 'was described as "a con job", in another as 'rubber stamping' (23). 'Hard-to-qualify costs and benefits were excluded from the financial analysis.'

Broms and Gahmberg found evidence of capital projects in some Finnish and Swedish firms 'regularly miss[ing] the mark' (e.g., requiring 25 percent return on investment while consistently getting about 7 percent). These authors referred to 'this self-deception,' these 'mantras' as 'socially accepted fact' (1987: 121).

▶ Capital budgeting, therefore, appears to be a formal means, not to plan strategy, but to structure the consideration of projects and to inform senior management about them. For example, most capital budgeting seems to take place in the context of existing strategies—which means in the absence of any fresh strategy thinking. In other words, it reinforces the strategies already being pursued. Of course, some capital projects may break established patterns and thereby create precedents that change strategy (in emergent fashion). But we suspect that capital budgeting itself may actually work to impede such strategic change and to discourage strategic thinking.

Capital budgeting is a disjointed process, or, more to the point, a *disjointing* one. Projects are expected to be proposed independently, along departmental or divisional lines. Any joint effects across units have to be ignored for the convenience of formal analysis. But since synergy is the very essence of creative strategy—the realization of new, advantageous combinations—then capital budgeting may discourage it. 'If the key players had acted on the rational financial information available at the time, there would have been no xerography . . . no aircraft, no jet engines, no television, no computers . . . and so on ad infinitum' (Quinn, 1980a: 171, 174).

Picture yourself as a senior manager reviewing capital proposals on the basis of financial projections. How are you to think strategically when everything comes to you split into bits and pieces, in concise, numerical, disconnected terms? Now picture yourself as the project sponsor, sitting behind your computer. You are not being asked to conceive strategies, not even to think about the future of your unit. All they want from you is quantitative justification for the moves you wish to make, each one separated into a nice neat package for the convenient comprehension of your superiors, delivered on their schedule.

To conclude, taken seriously, we find that not only is capital budgeting not strategy formation, it most decidedly impedes strategy formation. But taken by its effects, it can sometimes have an inadvertent influence on the strategies that organizations do pursue, in contradiction to the dictates of its own model.

The grand fallacy of 'strategic planning'

Thus we arrive at the grand fallacy of strategic planning, a composite, in fact, of the three fallacies already discussed. *Because analysis is not synthesis, strategic planning has never been strategy making.* Analysis may also precede and support synthesis, by providing certain necessary inputs. Analysis may follow and elaborate synthesis, by decomposing and formalizing its consequences. But analysis can never substitute for synthesis. No amount of elaboration will ever enable formal procedures to forecast discontinuities, to inform detached managers, to create novel strategies. Thus planning, rather than providing new strategies, could not proceed without their prior existence. Richard Rumelt sums up this common misconception as follows (Lovallo and Mendonca, 2007: 56):

Most corporate strategic plans have little to do with strategy. They are simply three-year or five-year rolling resource budgets and some sort of market share projection. Calling this strategic planning creates false expectations that the exercise will somehow produce a coherent strategy. Now, lots of people think the solution to the strategic-planning problem is to inject more strategy into the annual process. But I disagree. I think the annual rolling resource budget should be separate from strategy work. So my basic recommendation is to do two things: avoid the label 'strategic plan'—call those budgets 'long-term resource plans'—and start a separate, nonannual, opportunity-driven process for strategy work.

We conclude that strategic planning has been misnamed. It should have been called *strategic programming*. And it should have been promoted as a process to formalize, *where necessary*, the *consequences* of strategies already developed by other means. Ultimately, the term 'strategic planning' has proved to be an oxymoron.

---

box 3.6

The upside of toolism

(from Rigby, 1993: 15)

1 **Every tool carries a set of strengths and weaknesses**. Success requires understanding the full effects—and side effects—of each tool, then creatively combining the right ones in the right ways at the right times. The secret is . . . in learning which tools to use, how and when.
2 **Tools should be judged by their utility, not by their novelty.**
3 **Tools exist for the benefit of people, not vice versa**. Management tools are credited by their advocates with saving corporations—almost as loudly as they are blamed by their critics for destroying them. The truth is, tools do neither: people make companies succeed or fail.

The context and contribution of the planning school

There is, however, no need to throw out the strategic planner baby with the strategic planning bathwater. Planners have important roles to play around the black box of strategy formation, if not within it. This is shown in Figure 3.7. They can act as analysts, by providing data inputs at the front end, particularly the ones managers are prone to overlook (as shall be elaborated upon in the next chapter). They can also scrutinize the strategies that come out the back end, to assess their viability. Planners can also act as catalysts, not to promote formal planning as some kind of imperative, but to encourage whatever form of strategic behaviour makes sense for a particular organization at a particular time (Glaister and Falshaw, 1999). Hence planners should read this book! As suggested in the accompanying box, by a strategy consultant, organizations need tools, but sensibly applied.

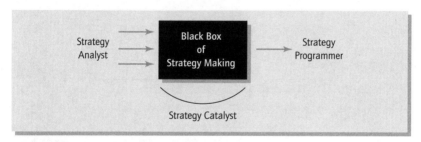

figure 3.7 Planners around strategy making

When necessary, but only then, planners can carry out formal planning too, but as a means to *programme* the strategies that came out of that black box—to codify them, elaborate them, translate them into ad hoc programmes and routine plans and budgets, and use these for purposes of communication and control.

Of course, creative planners can sometimes be strategists too (in other words, enter the black box). But that has more to do with their personal knowledge, creativity, and skills of synthesis than with any formalized technique of planning.

Some of these roles are rather formally analytical, others less so. This means that organizations might do well to distinguish two types of planners, who can be labelled left-handed and right-handed. Left-handed planners encourage creative strategic thinking, they raise all kinds of difficult questions, and they search around for emergent strategies in streams of their organizations' actions. The right-handed planners are concerned with more formal kinds of strategy analysis, and particularly with the strategic programming of clearly intended strategies, which, as we hope this discussion has made clear, suit only a context that is rather *stable*, or at least *predictable* or, what amounts to the same thing, *controllable* by the organization. But when change must be dramatic, and an organization's situation becomes less stable, predictable, and/or controllable, then it is better off to rely on the looser forms of strategy making first and the left-handed planners second, but *not* the precepts of the planning school.

The positioning school: strategy formation as an analytical process

"Send in two eggs and some more butter."

In science, as in love, a concentration on technique is likely to lead to impotence.

—Berger

In the early 1980s, a wind from economics blew through the strategic management field, blowing away, or at least into a corner, much of its traditional prescriptive literature. Although this *positioning* school accepted most of the premises that underlay the planning and design schools, as well as their fundamental model, it added content, in two ways. It did so in the literal sense of emphasizing the importance of strategies themselves, not just the process by which they were to be formulated. And it added substance: after all those years of the general pronouncements of the planning school and the repetition of the design school model, the positioning school, by focusing on the content of strategies, opened up the prescriptive side of the field to substantial investigation.

Scholars and consultants now had something to sink their teeth into: they could study and prescribe the specific strategies available to organizations and the contexts in which each seemed to work best. So the field—which, in fact, adopted the name of 'Strategic Management' in the early 1980s as a result of this thrust—'took off.' Conferences flourished, courses multiplied, journals appeared, and consulting firms—the so-called 'strategy boutiques'—established the 'strategy industry.' Because of the energy of this school, as well as its influence today, we accord it considerable space in this book.

Enter Porter

The watershed year was 1980, when Michael Porter published *Competitive Strategy*. While one book can hardly make a school, this one acted as a stimulant to draw together a good deal of the disenchantment with the design and planning schools, as well as the felt need for substance. Much as a simple disturbance can suddenly freeze a supersaturated liquid, *Competitive Strategy* gelled the interests of a generation of scholars and consultants. A huge wave of activity followed, quickly making this the dominant school in the field.

Of course, Porter's book was not the first on strategy content (nor was it only on content, since much of it proposed technique to do competitive and industry analysis). Earlier work on strategy content had been done especially at the Purdue University Krannert Business School by people like Dan Schendel and Ken Hatten. And Porter himself took his lead from *industrial organization*, a field of economics that had long addressed related issues, albeit with a focus on how industries, rather than individual firms, behave. There were also the earlier writers on military strategy, who for centuries had analyzed the strategic advantages and constraints of forces and terrain during war.

Premises of the positioning school

In fact, the positioning school did not depart radically from the premises of the planning school, or even those of the design school, with one key exception. But even the subtle differences also served to reorient the literature.

Most notable in this school has been one simple and revolutionary idea, for better and for worse. Both the planning and design schools put no limits on the strategies that were possible in any given situation. The positioning school, in contrast, argued that only certain strategies—as *positions* in the economic marketplace—are desirable in any given industry: ones that can be defended against competitors. Ease of defence means that firms which occupy these positions enjoy higher profits than other firms in the industry. And that, in turn, provides a reservoir of resources with which to expand, and so to enlarge as well as consolidate position.

Cumulating that logic across industries, the positioning school ended up with a limited number of basic strategies overall, or at least categories of strategies—for example, product differentiation and focused market scope. These were called *generic*.

By thereby dispensing with one key premise of the design school—that strategies have to be unique, tailor-made for each organization—the positioning school was able to create and hone a set of analytical tools dedicated to matching the right strategy to the conditions at hand— themselves also viewed as generic, such as maturity of, or fragmentation in, an industry. So the key to the new strategic management lay in the use of analysis to identify the right relationships. And thus the search began: academics ran statistical studies from established data bases to find out which generic strategies seemed to work best under what generic conditions, while consultants touted favoured strategies for particular clients, or else promoted frameworks for selecting such strategies.

As in the other two prescriptive schools, strategy making continued to be perceived as a controlled, conscious process that produced full-blown deliberate strategies, to be made explicit before being formally implemented. But here the process focused more narrowly on calculation—to be specific, on the close-ended selection of generic strategic positions rather than on the development of integrated and unusual strategic perspectives (as in the design school) or on the specification of coordinated sets of plans (as in the planning school). The notion that strategy precedes structure was also retained in this school. But another form of 'structure,' that of the industry, was added on top, so that industry structure drove strategic position which drove organizational structure. The process resembled that of the planning school in its formality, particularly in the external appraisal stages, with Porter (1980) being especially detailed about the steps by which to do competitive and industry analyses.

Again, as in planning, the chief executive remained the strategist in principle, while the planner retained the power behind the throne. Except that the positioning school elevated the planner's importance another notch. Here that person became an analyst (often on contract from a consulting firm), a studious calculator who amassed and studied reams of hard data to recommend optimal generic strategies. But, to repeat an important point, that analyst did not *design* strategies (indeed, did not even formulate them) so much as select them. In some sense, strategies were to be plucked off the tree of generic strategic opportunities.[1]

---

1 One of us recalls a conversation with one of the best-known early proponents of this school. He was incredulous at our 'exaggerated' comment that there could be an infinite number of possible strategies. He could not appreciate the idea of strategy as invention, as playing Lego instead of putting together a jigsaw puzzle.

To summarize these premises of the positioning school:

1 Strategies are generic, specifically common, identifiable positions in the marketplace.

2 That marketplace (the context) is economic and competitive.

3 The strategy formation process is therefore one of selection of these generic positions based on analytical calculation.

4 Analysts play a major role in this process, feeding the results of their calculations to managers who officially control the choices.

5 Strategies thus come out from this process full blown and are then articulated and implemented; in effect, market structure drives deliberate positional strategies that drive organizational structure.

The body of this chapter describes three different 'waves' of the positioning school: (1) the early military writings, (2) the 'consulting imperatives' of the 1970s, and (3) the recent work on empirical propositions, especially of the 1980s. We devote considerable space to the third wave before turning to our critique and assessment of the context of this school.

The first wave: origins in the military maxims

If the positioning school truly focuses on the selection of specific strategies, as tangible positions in competitive contexts, then it must be recognized as a good deal older than might otherwise be assumed. Indeed, this makes it by far the oldest school of strategy formation, since the first recorded writings on strategy, which date back over two millennia, dealt with the selection of optimal strategy of literal position in the context of military battle. These writings codified and expressed commonsense wisdom concerning the ideal conditions for attacking an enemy and defending one's own position.

The best of these writings is also among the oldest, for example that of Sun Tzu, who is believed to have written around 400 BC. More recent is the still influential work of von Clausewitz, who wrote in the nineteenth century. In a way, these military writers did what today's business writers of this school do: they delineated types of strategies and matched them to the conditions that seemed most suitable. But their work was not so systematic, at least not in the contemporary sense of statistical data, and so their conclusions tended to be expressed in imperative terms. Hence our use of the label 'maxims.'

Sun-Tzu

Sun Tzu's *The Art of War* (1971) has been particularly influential, especially in East Asia. (There is a current Chinese saying that the 'marketplace is a battlefield' (Tung, 1994: 56).) This is a remarkably contemporary book, suggesting that there may really be not much new under the sun. Some of Sun Tzu's maxims are rather general, such as 'To subdue the enemy without fighting is the acme of skill' (77). Others come in the forms of ploys, such as 'When capable, feign incapacity; when active, inactivity,' and 'Offer the enemy a bait to bait him; feign disorder and strike him' (66). But other maxims come rather close to the spirit of today's positioning school.

> **to subdue the enemy without fighting is the acme of skill**

Much as this school places emphasis on the study of the industry in which the company operates, so too did Sun Tzu emphasize the importance of being informed about the enemy and the place of battle. He devoted a good deal of attention to specific position strategies, for example locating armies with respect to mountains and rivers, fighting downhill, and occupying level or high ground. He also identified a variety of generic conditions, for example, dispersive, frontier, focal, and difficult. He then presented maxims linking generic strategies to each of these generic conditions, for example:

- . . . do not fight in dispersive ground; do not stop in frontier borderlands.

- In focal ground, ally with neighboring states; in deep ground, plunder. (131)

  As for numerical strength:

- When ten to the enemy's one, surround him . . . When five times his strength, attack him . . . If double his strength, divide him . . . If equally matched, you may engage him . . . If weaker numerically, be capable of withdrawing . . . And if in all respects unequal, be capable of eluding him. (79–80)

Other maxims anticipate what is called in today's positioning school 'first mover advantage':

■ Generally, he who occupies the field of battle first and awaits his enemy is at ease; he who comes later to the scene and rushes into the fight is weary. (96)

But it is the following passages of Sun Tzu's work that demonstrate just how old is the 'modern' wave of the positioning school:

■ Now the elements of the art of war are first, measurement of space; second, estimation of quantities; third, calculation; fourth, comparisons; and fifth, chances of victory. (88)

■ With many calculations, one can win; with few one cannot. How much less chance of victory has one who makes none at all! (71)

Yet Sun Tzu also recognized the limits of generic thinking, something that is less common today.

■ The musical notes are only five in number but their melodies are so numerous that we cannot hear them all. (91)

■ As water has not constant form, there are in war no constant conditions. (101)

■ When I have won a victory I do not repeat my tactics but respond to circumstances in an infinite variety of ways. (100)

Clausewitz

The west has never lacked for military thinkers. But none achieved the stature of Carl von Clausewitz (1780–1831), whose work bears the unmistakable stamp of the German proclivity for grand systems of thought.

Clausewitz wrote in the aftermath of the Napoleonic Wars. During the late seventeenth and eighteenth centuries, war had settled into a familiar pattern. Armies in most countries were made up of rather unmotivated recruits, commanded by officers drawn from the aristocracy. They used the same frameworks, with armies that were practically the same in organization and tactics. The difference between victory and defeat was often relatively small. One side attacked and the other retreated. At the end of the day, the diplomats met and some territory exchanged hands. It was a game with few surprises, in which strategy was a variation on themes that all sides knew and accepted.

Napoleon changed all that. In one battle after another, the French armies under his command destroyed forces that were numerically superior. His victories were not only military, they were also intellectual. He demonstrated the obsolescence of traditional ideas about organization and strategy. As a Prussian officer on the opposing side of battles, and at one time taken prisoner by the French, Clausewitz experienced Napoleon's methods firsthand.

In his masterwork *On War*, Clausewitz (1989) sought to replace the established view of military strategy with a set of flexible principles to govern thinking about war. While his predecessors saw strategy as a problem-solving activity, he argued—here more in the spirit of the design school—that it was open-ended and creative, due to tensions and contradictions inherent in war as a human and social activity. Yet it also called for organization in a situation riddled with chaos and confusion. Strategy seeks to shape the future, yet intentions are likely to be frustrated by chance and ignorance—by what Clausewitz called 'friction.' To make strategy happen, it is necessary to put together an organization with a formal chain of command in which orders are executed without question. Yet this organization must tap the initiative of its members. It does so by defining the mission, and then giving the person in charge total control over execution – the so called 'unity of command' principle.

On War contains chapters on attack and defence, manoeuvring, intelligence gathering, and night operations. The book is long and frequently discursive, but periodically illuminated by maxims containing powerful metaphors and vivid imagery.

In view of the insidious influence of friction on action, how is strategy possible? Closer to the positioning school, Clausewitz argued that strategy depends on basic building blocks, which are used in attack, defence, and manoeuvre. Strategy making relies on finding and executing new combinations of these blocks. In every age, technology and social organization limit the combination. After some time, these limits seem inevitable and hence natural. Strategists cease to question received wisdom and confine themselves to variations on accepted themes. It is therefore left to the great commanders, such as Napoleon, to innovate strategically by recognizing and bringing about new combinations. Such people are few because:

It takes more strength of will to make an important decision in strategy than in tactics. In the latter, one is carried away by the pressures of the moment . . . In strategy . . . there is ample room for apprehension, one's own and those of others; for objections and remonstrations and in consequence, for premature regret. In a tactical situation one is able to see at least half the problem with the naked eye, whereas in strategy everything has to be guessed at and presumed. Conviction is therefore weaker. Consequently, most generals, when they ought to act, are paralyzed by unnecessary doubts. (1989:179)

Clauswitz today

Clausewitz's influence on military thinking in more recent times is reflected in a book by the American Colonel Harry Summers (1981), called *On Strategy: The Vietnam War in Context.* What the Pentagon planners ignored in that arena, argued Summers, were the fundamentals of strategy that Clausewitz outlined. The first of these was the insistence that 'War is merely the continuation of policy by other means' (87). This frequently cited dictum is often interpreted as an affirmation of the subordination of military to civilian authority. But it is a warning that strategy should not become dominated by the short term; that transient success should not be confused with enduring performance. Summers also borrowed from Clausewitz the notion of friction, applying it to the resilience, energy, firmness, belief in the cause, and devotion to duty of the enemy. Pentagon planners misperceived the Vietnamese ability to take terrible punishment and continue to fight.

❝ pentagon planners misperceived the Vietnamese ability to take terrible punishment and continue to fight ❞

Summers's book updates Clausewitz's insights for the late twentieth century. Taking Clausewitz as his point of departure, he analyzed the Vietnam conflict in terms of the 'principles of war,' as they were stated in the 1962 ('Vietnam-era') Field Service Regulations of the US Army. These are reproduced in Box 4.1.

Note the consistency of these principles with the prescriptive schools of strategic management in general, notably the need for clear deliberate strategy, the centrality of authority to develop or at least execute that strategy, the need to keep strategy simple, and the presumed proactive nature of strategic management. Yet, as in the planning school as well as in Clausewitz's own urgings, flexibility is presumed to coexist somehow with these characteristics.

The rediscovery of Clausewitz by the American military, coincided with his discovery by American managers (*Economist*, 2002). For the founder of Federal Express, Fred Smith, Clausewitz speaks to fundamental truths about the pitfalls of planning. As he puts it (*Fortune*, 2004): 'As you get older, what you get is simply a greater appreciation for what the war expert Carl von Clausewitz called "friction." Stuff happens. You think you're on one timeline, but you have to recognize that decisions will take longer and the road will be more difficult.'

In the case of Jack Welch, the ideas of Clausewitz seemed to have had direct impact on his approach to strategy. In 1981, upon his ascent to the position of CEO at General Electric, Welch gave a speech in which he outlined his views of strategy. The speech explicitly cited Clausewitz as his inspiration for how he was going to transform General Electric (Mink, 2004):

Clausewitz summed up what it had all been about in his classic *On War*. Men could not reduce strategy to a formula. Detailed planning necessarily failed, due to the inevitable frictions encountered: chance events, imperfections in execution, and the independent will of the opposition. Instead, the human elements were paramount: leadership, morale, and the almost instinctive savvy of the best generals.

---

box 4.1

United States principles of war, based on Clausewitz

Circa 1962 (from Summers, 1981: 59–97)

The Objective. Every military operation must be directed toward a clearly defined, decisive, and attainable objective. The ultimate military objective of war is the destruction of the enemy's armed forces and his will to fight . . .

> **The Offensive**. Offensive action is necessary to achieve decisive results and to maintain freedom of action. It permits the commander to exercise initiative and impose his will upon the enemy . . . The defensive may be forced on the commander, but it should be deliberately adopted only as a temporary expedient . . .
>
> **Mass [sometimes called Concentration]**. Superior combat power must be concentrated at the critical time and place for a decisive purpose . . .
>
> **Economy of Force**. Skillful and prudent use of combat power will enable the commander to accomplish the mission with minimum expenditure of resources. This principle . . . does not imply husbanding but rather the measured allocation of available combat power . . .
>
> **Manoeuvre [or Flexibility]**. . . . The object of manoeuvre is to dispose a force in such a manner as to place the enemy at a relative disadvantage. . . . Successful manoeuvre requires flexibility in organization, administrative support, and command and control . . .
>
> **Unity of Command** . . . Unity of command obtains unity of effort by the coordinated action of all forces toward a common goal. While coordination may be attained by cooperation, it is best achieved by vesting a single commander with the requisite authority.
>
> **Security** . . . Security is achieved by measures taken to prevent surprise, preserve freedom of action, and deny the enemy information of friendly forces . . .
>
> **Surprise** . . . Surprise results from striking an enemy at a time, place, and in a manner for which he is not prepared . . .
>
> **Simplicity** . . . Direct, simple plans and clear, concise orders minimize misunderstanding and confusion. If other factors are equal, the simplest plan is preferred.

Fighting corporate battles

Jack Welch was by no means the first to explore the analogy between strategy in war and in business, although arguably he put this analogy into practice more explicitly than most (see Lampel and Shamsie, 2000). Some picked up on the spirit, even the letter, of the military maxims. James, for example, described the 'military experience [as] a veritable goldmine of competitive strategies all well tested under combat positions' (1985: 56). He saw 'remarkable similarities' with business, 'in terms of deterrence, offense, defense, and alliance,' as well as in the use of 'intelligence, weaponry, logistics and communications, all designed for one purpose—to fight' (45–46). In his corporate strategy textbook, Robert Katz discussed maxims such as 'always lead from strength' and 'the basic strategy for all companies should be to concentrate resources where the company has (or can develop readily) a meaningful competitive advantage' (1970: 349–350). He added that:

For the large company:
A. Planning is crucial.
B. Give up the crumbs.
C. Preserve company strength and stability.

For the small company:
A. Attack when the enemy retreats.
B. Do not take full advantage of all opportunities.
C. Be as inconspicuous as possible.
D. Respond quickly. (1970: 302–3)

Perhaps most sophisticated has been James Brian Quinn's use of the military experience in business (see especially 1980a: 155–68). To Quinn, 'effective strategy develops around a few key concepts and thrusts, which give them cohesion, balance, and focus,' and also a 'sense of positioning against an intelligent opponent' (162, 164). Such a strategy 'first probes and withdraws to determine opponents' strengths, forces opponents to stretch their commitments, then concentrates resources, attacks a clear exposure, overwhelms a selected market segment, builds a bridgehead in that market, and then regroups and expands from that base to dominate a wider field' (160–1). Table 4.1 lists some of the terms of military strategy that Quinn employed in his book.

Maxims about maxims

There is something interesting and helpful in these military maxims. Yet there is something to be careful of as well: a language that is both obvious and obscure. Hence, in their own spirit, we offer our own maxims about maxims:

- Most maxims are obvious.
- Obvious maxims can be meaningless.
- Some obvious maxims are contradicted by other obvious maxims (such as to concentrate force and to remain flexible).

So

- Beware of maxims.

table 4.1 Military maxim terminology: A listing of some of the terms from military strategy

Attack and overwhelm	Feint, cunning, nerve
Surround and destroy	Deceptive manoeuvres
Attack opponent's weakness	Using misleading messages
Concentrated attack	
Major focused thrust	
Establish dominance	Mobility, surprise fast manoeuvres
Indirect approach	Planned flexibility
Flanking manoeuvres	
Planned withdrawal	Points of domination
Planned counterattack	Fortify a key base
Conceding early losses	Form a bridgehead
Stretch opponent's resources	Consolidate forces
Lure away from defensive positions	Fallback
Soften enemy's political and psychological will	

Source: Quinn (1980: 150–6)

The second wave: the search for consulting imperatives

The positioning school has been tailor-made for consultants. They can arrive cold, with no particular knowledge of a business, analyze the data, juggle a set of generic strategies (basic building blocks) on a chart, write a report, drop an invoice, and leave. So, beginning in the 1960s, but really accelerating in the 1970s and 1980s, the strategy boutiques arose, each with some niche in the conceptual marketplace to promote positioning concepts of its own.

In one sense, these writers were systematic students of experience, but they often interpreted that experience narrowly. Indeed, for marketing purposes, they often turned maxims into *imperatives* (perhaps we should say *maximums*).

For some, the quest for market share became the overriding imperative. The Boston Consulting Group (BCG), perhaps in this period the most successful of the new strategy boutiques, championed market share as the Holy Grail. It focused on two techniques in particular: the *growth-share matrix* and the *experience curve*.

BCG: the growth-share matrix

The growth-share matrix was part of 'portfolio planning,' which addressed the question of how to allocate funds to the different businesses of a diversified company. Before its appearance, corporations depended on capital budgeting and the like to assess return on investment of different proposals. The growth-share matrix sought to embed these choices in a systematic framework. The intent was nothing short of an attempt to overhaul strategic analysis—the 'killer strategy application,' to paraphrase a term that became popular subsequently. Use the BCG matrix, insists Bruce Henderson, founder of BCG and the inventor of the matrix, and you will not need much else: 'Such a single chart, with a projected position for five years out, is sufficient alone to tell a company's profitability, debt capacity, growth potential and competitive strength' (Henderson, 1973: 3). So what are the key elements of this wonderful chart? Below and in Figure 4.1 we present this technique in the words of Bruce Henderson.

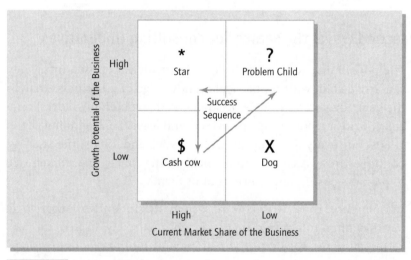

figure 4.1 **BCG growth-share matrix**   Source: Henderson (1979).

To be successful, a company should have a portfolio of products with different growth rates and different market shares. The portfolio composition is a function of the balance between cash flows. High-growth products require cash inputs to grow. Low-growth products should generate excess cash. Both kinds are needed simultaneously.

Four rules determine the cash flow of a product:

- Margins and cash generated are a function of market share. High margins and high market share go together. This is a matter of common observation, explained by the experience curve effect.
- Growth requires cash input to finance added assets. The added cash required to hold share is a function of growth rates.
- High market share must be earned or bought. Buying market share requires additional investment.
- No product market can grow indefinitely. The payoff from growth must come when the growth slows, or it will not come at all. The payoff is cash that cannot be reinvested in that product.

Products with high market share and slow growth are 'cash cows.' [see Figure 4.1.] Characteristically, they generate large amounts of cash, in excess of the reinvestment required to maintain share. This excess need not, and should not, be reinvested in those products. In fact, if the rate of return exceeds growth rate, the cash *cannot* be reinvested indefinitely, except by depressing returns.

❝ the BCG growth-share matrix was considered a 'killer strategy application' ❞

Products with low market share and slow growth are 'dogs.' They may show an accounting profit, but the profit must be reinvested to maintain share, leaving no cash throwoff. The product is essentially worthless, except in liquidation.

All products eventually become either a 'cash cow' or a 'dog.' The value of a product is completely dependent upon obtaining a leading share of its market before the growth slows.

Low-market-share, high-growth products are the 'problem children.' They almost always require far more cash than they can generate. If cash is not supplied, they fall behind and die. Even when the cash is supplied, if they only hold their share, they are still dogs when the growth stops. The 'problem children' require large added cash investment for market share to be purchased. The low-market-share, high-growth product is a liability unless it becomes a leader. It requires very large cash inputs that it cannot generate itself. The high-share, high-growth product is the 'star.' It nearly always shows reported profits, but it may or may not generate all of its own cash. If it stays a leader, however, it will become a large cash generator when growth slows and its reinvestment requirements diminish. The star eventually becomes the cash cow—providing high volume, high margin, high stability, security—and cash throwoff for reinvestment elsewhere . . .

The need for a portfolio of businesses becomes obvious. Every company needs products in which to invest cash. Every company needs products that generate cash. And every product should eventually be a cash generator; otherwise, it is worthless.

Only a diversified company with a balanced portfolio can use its strengths to truly capitalize on its growth opportunities. [See success sequence in Figure 4.1.] The balanced portfolio has

- 'stars,' whose high share and high growth assure the future.
- 'cash cows,' that supply funds for that future growth.
- 'problem children,' to be converted into 'stars' with the added funds.
- 'Dogs' are not necessary; they are evidence of failure either to obtain a leadership position during the growth phase, or to get out and cut the losses. (Henderson, 1979:163–6)

> Note the reductionist nature of this technique. BCG took the two major categories of the classic design school model (external environment and internal capabilities), selected one key dimension for each (market growth and relative market share), arranged these along the two axes of a matrix, divided into high and low, and then inserted into each of the boxes labels for the four resulting generic strategies. Then, presumably, all a company had to do was plot its condition and select its strategy, or, at least, sequence its strategies as it went around the matrix, passing money from one business to another in the prescribed way. Really rather simple—better even than a cookbook, which usually requires many different ingredients.

> As John Seeger (1984) pointed out in a colourful critique of this, however, what looks like a star might already be a black hole, while a dog can be a corporation's best friend. And cows can give new products called calves as well as the old one called milk—but, in both cases, only so long as the farmer is willing to invest the attention of a bull periodically. To extend its own mixture of metaphors, the BCG of those heady days may have mixed up the ordinary milk cow with the goose that laid the golden eggs.

BCG: exploiting experience

The BCG *experience curve* dates back to some research done in 1936 (see Yelle, 1979) that suggested that as the cumulative production of a product doubles, the cost of producing it decreases by a constant percentage (generally 10 to 30 percent). In other words, if the first widget ever made cost $10 to produce, then the second (assuming 20 percent) should cost about $8, the fourth $6.40, etc., and the ten millionth, 20 percent less than the five millionth. In brief, firms learn from experience—at a constant rate. Figure 4.2 shows an example from a BCG publication.

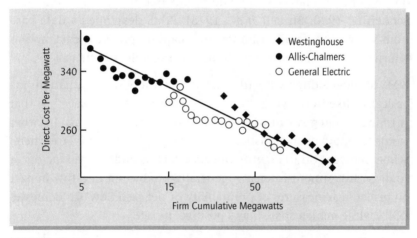

figure 4.2 Experience curve for steam turbine generators (1946–63)

Source: The Boston Consulting Group (1975).

The idea is interesting. It suggests that, all other things being equal, the first firm in a new market can rev up its volume quickly to gain a cost advantage over its competitors. Of course, the essence of strategy is that all other things are rarely equal. In fact, the widespread application of the experience curve often led to an emphasis on volume as an end in itself. Scale became all important: firms were encouraged to manage experience directly—for example, by cutting prices to grab market share early, so as to ride down the experience curve ahead of everyone else. As a result of the popularity of this technique as well as the growth-share matrix, being the market leader became an obsession in American business for a time (Alberts, 1989).

PIMS: from data to dicta

PIMS stands for Profit Impact of Market Strategies. It too was all the rage for a time, likewise built on an empirical base, to find that 'one best way'.

Developed in 1972 for General Electric, later to become a stand-alone data base for sale, the PIMS model identified a number of strategy variables—such as investment intensity, market position, and quality of products and service—and used them to estimate expected return on investment, market share, and profits (see Schoeffler *et al.*, 1974; Schoeffler, 1980; Buzzell *et al.*, 1975). PIMS developed a data base from several thousand businesses that paid in, provided data, and in return could compare their positions with samples of others.

PIMS founder Sidney Schoeffler stated that 'All business situations are basically alike in obeying the same laws of the marketplace,' so that 'a trained strategist can usefully function in any business.' In other words 'product characteristics don't matter' (1980: 2, 5). From here, Schoeffler went on to identify the good factors and the bad factors of strategy. Investment intensity 'generally produces a negative impact on percentage measures of profitability or net cash flow' (it 'depresses ROI'), while market share 'has a positive impact.'

But finding a *correlation* between variables (such as market share and profit, not *'profitability'*) is one thing; assuming causation, and turning that into an imperative, is quite another. Data are not dicta. Does high market share bring profit, or does high profit bring market share (since big firms can afford to 'buy' market share)? Or, more likely, does something else (such as serving customers well) bring both? Market share is a reward, not a strategy!

With their obvious biases toward the big established firms (which had the money to buy into the data bases and pay the consulting contracts), both PIMS and BCG seemed unable to distinguish 'getting there' from 'being there' (or 'staying there'). Perhaps the young, aggressive firms, which were pursuing rather different strategies of rapid growth, may have been too busy to fill out the PIMS forms, while those in the emerging industries, with a messy collection of new products coming and going, may have been unable to tell BCG which firms had which market shares, or even what their 'businesses' really were.

The overall result of much of this was that, like that proverbial swimmer who drowned in a lake that averaged six inches in depth, a number of companies went down following the simple imperatives of the positioning school's second wave (see Hamermesh, 1986).

The third wave: the development of empirical propositions

What we are calling the third wave of the positioning school, which began as a trickle in the mid-1970s, exploded into prominence after 1980, dominating the whole literature and practice of strategic management. This wave consisted of the systematic empirical search for relationships between external conditions and internal strategies, discussed at the outset of this chapter. Gone was the faith in homilies and imperatives, at least about the *content* of strategies (if not the process by which to make them). Instead it was believed that systematic study could uncover the ideal strategies to be pursued under given sets of conditions.

Porter's *Competitive Strategy*, published in 1980, really set this work on its course. He wedged a doctorate in Harvard's economics department between an MBA and a teaching career in its business school. From that, he drew on the branch of economics called industrial organization which provides, as he put it: 'a systematic and relatively rigorous ["approach to industry analysis"] backed by empirical tests' (1981: 611). Turning it around, he extended its implications for the corporate strategist. Business strategy, in Porter's view, should be based on the market structure in which firms operate.

In essence, Porter took the basic approach of the design school and applied it to the external, or industry environment. (Eventually, as we shall see in a later chapter, this gave rise to a countermovement, based on the internal situation, called the 'resource-based view' of the firm.) Porter was thus able to build on the already widespread acceptance of strategy as design, although the procedures he promoted were very much more in the spirit of the planning school. To this he added the established body of knowledge from industrial organization. The combination was powerful, and it was an instant hit in both academic and business circles.

Porter's work, particularly his 1980 book followed by another, called *Competitive Advantage* in 1985, offered a foundation rather than a framework; in other words, it provided a set of concepts on which to build rather than an integrated structure in its own right. Most prominent among these concepts have been his model of competitive analysis, his set of generic strategies, and his notion of the value chain.

Porter's model of competitive analysis

Porter's model of competitive analysis identifies five forces in an organization's environment that influence competition. These are described below and shown with their elements in Figure 4.3.

- **Threat of new entrants.** An industry is like a club in which firms gain admittance by overcoming certain 'barriers to entry,' such as economies of scale, basic capital requirements, and customer loyalty to established brands. High barriers encourage a cosy club in which competition is friendly; low barriers lead to a highly competitive group in which little can be taken for granted.

- **Bargaining power of firm's suppliers.** Since suppliers wish to charge the highest prices for their products, a power struggle naturally arises between firms and their suppliers. The advantage goes to the side which has more choices as well as less to lose if the relationship ends—for example, the firm that need not sell the bulk of its output to one customer, or the one that makes a unique product with no close substitutes.

- **Bargaining power of firm's customers.** A firm's customers wish to get prices down or quality up. Their ability to do so depends on how much they buy, how well informed they are, their willingness to experiment with alternatives, and so on.

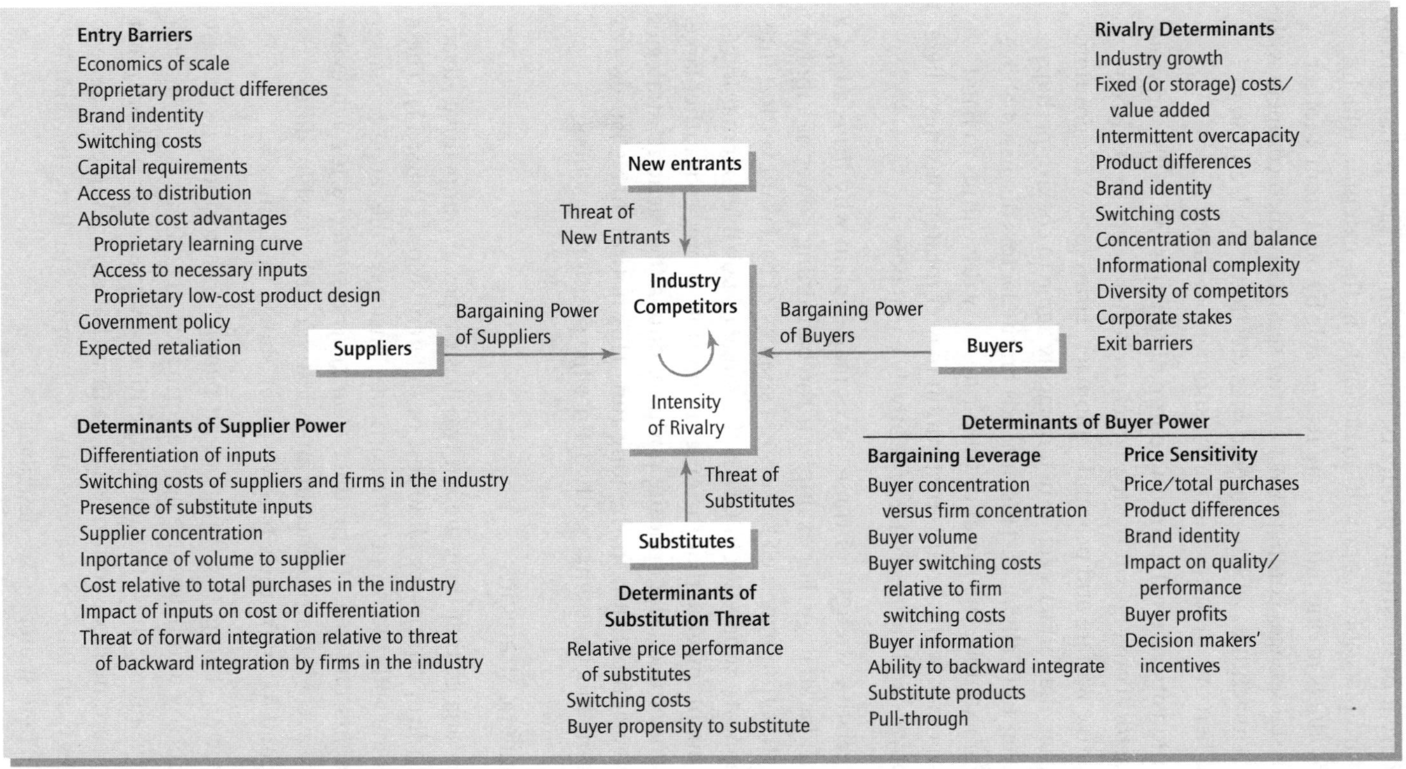

Entry Barriers
Economics of scale
Proprietary product differences
Brand indentity
Switching costs
Capital requirements
Access to distribution
Absolute cost advantages
 Proprietary learning curve
 Access to necessary inputs
 Proprietary low-cost product design
Government policy
Expected retaliation

Determinants of Supplier Power
Differentiation of inputs
Switching costs of suppliers and firms in the industry
Presence of substitute inputs
Supplier concentration
Inportance of volume to supplier
Cost relative to total purchases in the industry
Impact of inputs on cost or differentiation
Threat of forward integration relative to threat
 of backward integration by firms in the industry

Rivalry Determinants
Industry growth
Fixed (or storage) costs/
 value added
Intermittent overcapacity
Product differences
Brand identity
Switching costs
Concentration and balance
Informational complexity
Diversity of competitors
Corporate stakes
Exit barriers

Determinants of Buyer Power

Bargaining Leverage
Buyer concentration
 versus firm concentration
Buyer volume
Buyer switching costs
 relative to firm
 switching costs
Buyer information
Ability to backward integrate
Substitute products
Pull-through

Price Sensitivity
Price/total purchases
Product differences
Brand identity
Impact on quality/
 performance
Buyer profits
Decision makers'
 incentives

Determinants of Substitution Threat
Relative price performance
 of substitutes
Switching costs
Buyer propensity to substitute

New entrants

Suppliers

Industry Competitors
Intensity of Rivalry

Buyers

Substitutes

Threat of New Entrants

Bargaining Power of Suppliers

Bargaining Power of Buyers

Threat of Substitutes

figure 4.3 Elements of industry structure

Source: Reprinted with the permission of The Free Press, a Division of Simon & Schuster Adult Publishing Group, from COMPETITIVE STRATEGY: Techniques for Analyzing Industries and Competitors by Michael E. Porter. Copyright © 1980, 1998 by The Free Press, All rights reserved.

■ **Threat of substitute products.** There is an old saying that nobody is irreplaceable. Competition depends on the extent to which products in one industry are replaceable by ones from another. Postal services compete with courier services, which compete with fax machines, which compete with electronic mail, and so on. When one industry innovates, another can suffer.

■ **Intensity of rivalry among competing firms.** All of the previous factors converge on rivalry, which to Porter is a cross between active warfare and peaceful diplomacy. Firms jockey for position. They may attack each other, or tacitly agree to coexist, perhaps even form alliances. This depends on the factors discussed above. For example, the threat of substitutes may drive firms to band together, while severe competition may erupt in industries where buyers and suppliers are of relatively equal power.

The relative strength of these forces may explain why firms adopt a particular strategy. For example, if the bargaining power of suppliers is high, a firm may seek to pursue a strategy of backward vertical integration—to supply itself. Given the range of possible external forces, one might imagine that the range of possible strategies is rather large. But Porter takes the opposite position: only a few 'generic' strategies survive competition in the long run. This notion, like Clausewitz's building blocks, is what really defines the positioning school.

Porter's generic strategies

Porter argued that there are but two 'basic types of competitive advantage a firm can possess: low cost or differentiation' (1985: 11). These combine with the 'scope' of a particular business—the range of market segments targeted—to produce '*four generic strategies* for achieving above-average performance in an industry: cost leadership, differentiation, and focus' (namely narrow scope), shown in Figure 4.4.

To Porter, 'being "all things to all people" is a recipe for strategic mediocrity and below-average performance' (12); firms must 'make a choice' among these to gain competitive advantage. Or, in words that have become more controversial, 'a firm that engages in each generic strategy but fails to achieve any of them is "stuck in the middle"' (16). These strategies are described:

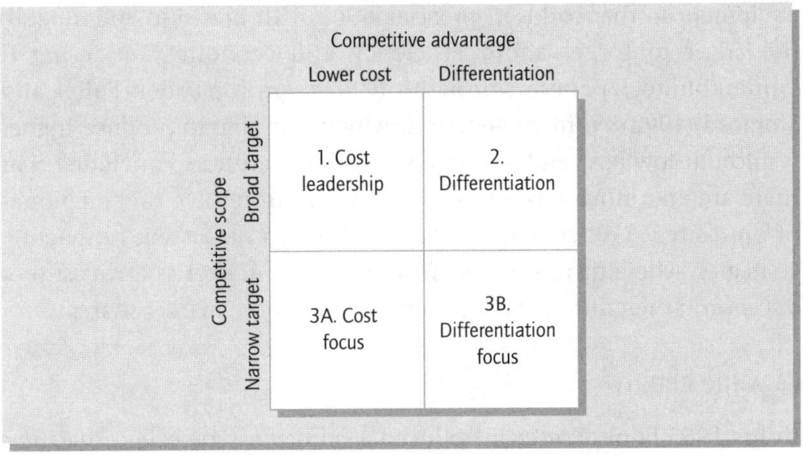

Competitive advantage

	Lower cost	Differentiation
Broad target	1. Cost leadership	2. Differentiation
Narrow target	3A. Cost focus	3B. Differentiation focus

(Competitive scope)

figure 4.4 **Porter's generic strategies**

Source: Reprinted with the permission of The Free Press, a Division of Simon & Schuster Adult Publishing Group, from *COMPETITIVE ADVAN-TAGE: Creating and Sustaining Superior Performance* by Michael E. Porter. Copyright © 1985, 1998 by Michael E. Porter, All rights reserved.

1 **Cost leadership.** This strategy aims at being the low-cost producer in an industry. The cost leadership strategy is realized through gaining experience, investing in large-scale production facilities, using economies of scale, and carefully monitoring overall operating costs (through programmes such as downsizing and total quality management).

2 **Differentiation.** This strategy involves the development of unique products or services, relying on brand/customer loyalty. A firm can offer higher quality, better performance, or unique features, any of which can justify higher prices.

3 **Focus.** This strategy seeks to serve narrow market segments. A firm can 'focus' on particular customer groups, product lines, or geographic markets. The strategy may be one of either 'differentiation focus,' whereby the offerings are differentiated in the focal market, or 'overall cost leadership focus,' whereby the firm sells at low cost in the focal market. This allows the firm to concentrate on developing its knowledge and competences.

Among many others, Miller (1992) has questioned Porter's notion of having to pursue one strategy or else be caught 'in the middle.' Might such strategic specialization not 'cause inflexibility and narrow an organization's vision' (37)? Miller cited the example of Caterpillar, Inc., which differentiated itself by making the highest quality earth-moving equipment in the world. Its preoccupation with precision and durability led it to forget about efficiency and economy, rendering it vulnerable to Japanese competition. In contrast, Baden-Fuller and Stopford (1992) point to Benetton, which was able to produce higher fashion at low cost and on large scale. These authors concluded that there are enormous rewards for those who can resolve the 'dilemmas of opposites.' Gilbert and Strebel (1988) also discussed 'outpacing' strategies, where firms (such as Toyota) enter a market as low-cost producers and then differentiate to capture even more market share.

Porter's value chain

In his 1985 book, Porter introduced a framework he called the *value chain*. It suggests that a firm can be disaggregated into primary and support activities, as shown in Figure 4.5. *Primary activities* are directly involved in the flow of product to the customer, and include inbound logistics (receiving, storing, etc.), operations (or transformation), outbound logistics (order processing, physical distribution, etc.), marketing and sales, and service (installation, repair, etc.). *Support activities* exist to support primary activities. They include procurement, technology development, human resource management, and provision of the firm's infrastructure (including finance, accounting, general management, etc.).

❝ the value chain helps to identify sources of strategic advantage ❞

The word 'margin' on the right side of Porter's figure indicates that firms achieve profit margins based on how the value chain is managed. The dotted lines of the figure are meant to demonstrate that all the support activities (with one exception) can be associated with each of the primary activities and also support the entire chain. The exception is firm infrastructure, which is shown to apply to the complete chain instead of to any one part of it. For Porter, the value chain 'provides a systematic way of examining all the activities a firm performs and how they interact' with one another (33). But the totality of the value chain must be considered, in his view. For example, being best at marketing may not be a strategic advantage if this is poorly matched with operations.

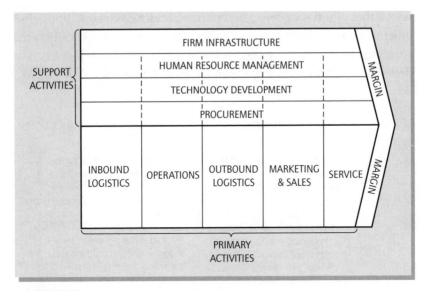

figure 4.5 **Porter's generic value chain**

Source: Reprinted with the permission of The Free Press, a Division of Simon & Schuster Adult Publishing Group, from *COMPETITIVE ADVAN-TAGE: Creating and Sustaining Superior Performance* by Michael E. Porter. Copyright © 1985, 1998 by Michael E. Porter, All rights reserved.

From Porter, as noted above, the literature of strategic positioning mushroomed. We have not the space here to attempt any thorough review of this. Rather, we seek to offer synthesis, by presenting a structure to consider the nature of this work, as it developed increasing sophistication.

Four kinds of positioning school research

One possible means by which to link the various research activities of this school—in effect a way to position the efforts of the positioning school—is shown in the matrix of Figure 4.6. Research is divided into that concerned with single factors as opposed to clusters of factors and that concerned with static conditions as opposed to dynamic ones. The activity of this school can then be found to take place in all four of the resulting boxes, although the tendency has been to favour the simpler forms of research.

Single static research

Probably the greater part of the research fits into the *single static* cell. Some of this focuses on particular generic strategies (such as outsourcing or product bundling) and seeks to find the industry conditions that favour them (or the strategies best pursued under given conditions). But other work, more in the spirit of the second wave, simply considers the effectiveness of different strategies per se (for example, 'Does diversification pay?', on which there has been an enormous amount of research).

	Single Factors	Clusters of Factors
Static conditions	Linking particular strategies to particular conditions (e.g., diversification to industry maturity)	Delineating clusters of strategies (e.g., strategic groups) and/or clusters of conditions (e.g., generic industries) and their linkages
Dynamic conditions	Determining particular strategic responses (e.g., turnarounds, signalling) to external changes (e.g., technological threats, competitive attacks)	Tracking sequences of clusters of strategies and/or conditions over time (e.g., industry life cycles)

figure 4.6 A matrix of strategy content research

Cluster static research

The strategist's job involves not only selecting individual strategic positions but also weaving these into integrated strategies. Accordingly, research in this second cell focuses on clusters of factors, but still in a static context. For example, Porter (1980) used the term *strategic group* to describe a collection of firms within an industry that pursue similar combinations of strategies and other factors (such as the fast-food hamburger chains within the restaurant industry). Research in this cell, for example, seeks to match such strategic groups with clusters of industry conditions (for example, that render them 'fragmented' or 'mature').[2]

Strategic groups research itself experienced something of a miniboom in the mid-1980s. It was Hunt (1972) who first coined the term, to help explain competitive rivalry in the home appliance industry. He observed a puzzling phenomenon: although industry concentration

---

2 Generic strategies and strategic groups should not be confused. Generic strategies describe internal consistencies; strategic groups reflect the possible diversity of positions in an industry (McGee and Thomas, 1986).

was high (meaning relatively few competitors), industry profitability was poor. His explanation was that within the same industry various subsets of firms (strategic groups) appeared to be pursuing fundamentally different strategies. Some of these strategies were highly profitable, and others were far less so, with average profitability as a result being low.

Later Porter (1980) introduced the idea of *mobility barriers*—essentially a downsized version of entry barriers—to help explain this. So while entry barriers may define the boundaries of the industry, mobility barriers create distinct competitive spaces within the industry in which groups of firms can sustain dissimilar strategies. For example, a regional firm that serves local markets may not have the advertising and distribution resources of a national firm. But it will often have intimate understanding of the idiosyncrasies of local consumers, not to mention their loyalty. The firm thus gets drawn into a particular strategy group (which can be labelled 'regional players'). By contrast, firms that pursue a 'national' strategy will target common consumer preferences across the entire country, and sustain their position using national advertising and distribution. The two groups compete with each other, but mobility barriers allow each group to operate successfully in its own competitive space.

Of course, strategic groups can be generic in the sense that the same types can be found in multiple industries. (For example, we can find firms that pursue regional or national strategy in many different industries.) This clustering of *types* of strategic groups is described in Box 4.2.

Single dynamic research

Research in the two remaining cells of our matrix, about dynamic change, is more difficult to do and so has been less common. Work in this third cell considers the effect of a single change (for example, a breakthrough in technology or a new competitive attack). Researchers here have been interested not only in substantive responses, such as to divest or to differentiate, but also in *signalling* ones (again following the lead of Porter, 1980, Chapters 4 and 5), for example announcing the construction of a factory that will never be built in order to ward off a competitor. Here, therefore, we see strategy as ploy. (But because of the political nature of such maneuvering, we shall discuss it in Chapter 8.)

Studies of turnaround strategies are also common here, as are ones of 'mover advantage': the benefits to be gained and costs to be incurred by moving first into a new market, as opposed to waiting (being a 'fast second' or a 'late mover').

Popular of late among some of the more theoretical strategy researchers has been so-called *game theory*. We review it in Box 4.2, concluding that it may help to order some strategic thinking, particularly under conditions of competitive manoeuvring, rather than providing any answers to strategic issues.

---

box 4.2

Generic strategic groups

by Henry Mintzberg

- **Niche players**: highly differentiated, usually by quality or design, with narrow scope core businesses, such as the *Economist* magazine
- **Pioneers**: very focused scope and highly innovative designs, first movers, as in the origins of Amazon.com (books), Travelocity (airline tickets), and eBay (online auctions)
- **Local producers**: undifferentiated strategies in particular geographic niches, such as corner gas station or the national post office
- **Dominant firms**: 'heavy' cost leaders, whether resource producers upstream or mass marketers further down, with wide scope and often vertically integrated, like Alcan or General Motors
- **Me-too firms**: like the dominant firms but not dominant, with copycat strategies, as in the case of many mobile phone operators
- **Worldwide replicators**: heavy on marketing, producing, and selling in individual markets around the world, according to formula, like Coca-Cola or McDonald's
- **Professionals**: providing established professional services to customers, such as the consulting, engineering, and accounting firms
- **Thin producers**: filling huge, occasional contracts for customers, usually anywhere in the world, involving extensive design innovation and complex technology, like a Boeing or an Airbus
- **Rationalizers**: so-called 'global firms' that distribute production 'mandates' around the world while selling to large segments on a wide geographic basis, such as Starbucks or Berlitz

> - **Crystalline diversifiers or network firms**: highly diversified, with wide scope and many products differentiated by design, mostly created through internal development around core competences, as in a 3M or Canon
> - **Conglomerates**: often made up of unrelated diversification by acquisition of dominant firms.

Cluster dynamics research

Our final cell considers clusters of relationships in a dynamic setting. This is obviously the most comprehensive and therefore the most difficult form of research, so it is not surprising that it has probably received the least attention. Issues considered here include the dynamics of strategic groups (how they rise and develop over time), the evolution of industries (including 'life cycles'), and the rise and fall of competition. In Chapter 11, we shall discuss Alfred Chandler's work on stages in the evolution of the large American corporation, which has both positioning and configuration aspects.

---

box 4.3

Game theory and strategy

by Joseph Lampel

The positioning school owes considerable intellectual debt to economic theory, in particular the field of industrial organization. More recently, strategy researchers have sought to draw on another field that has become popular in economics, called game theory. This theory, developed by von Neumann and Morgenstern (1947), was originally applied to the analysis of the nuclear standoff between the superpowers during the Cold War. In economics, game theory has been used to examine competition and cooperation within small groups of firms. From here, it was but a small step to strategy.

Game theory provides a rigorous approach to modelling what rational actors behaving in self-interest are likely to do in well-defined situations. Perhaps the best known example of this is the so-called 'Prisoner's Dilemma.'

Two individuals are detained by the police on suspicion of having committed a serious crime. The police have sufficient evidence to convict on a lesser charge; what they lack is the additional evidence needed to convict on the more serious charges. A confession is therefore highly desirable for a successful prosecution.

The chief investigator approaches one of the individuals and makes him the following offer: 'We have enough evidence to convict you on a charge that normally carries a three-year prison term. Confess and you will receive a one-year sentence. If you do not confess and your partner does, you will be charged with the more serious offence which carries a mandatory ten-year sentence. However, I have to warn you that, by law, if you both confess you will each receive a seven-year sentence.'

If the two suspects could talk to each other and strike a binding agreement not to confess, they would both be assured of a three-year sentence. But the police keep them apart, so each must make his decision based on how the partner is likely to behave. As rational actors, they should both assume that the other will act in his own best interest and confess. Each is therefore left with little choice but to confess. As a result, they both go to prison for seven years, even though they would have been better off to have kept silent.

It is the perverse contrast between good intentions and bad outcomes that makes the Prisoner's Dilemma relevant to a wide range of business situations. Firms are often in situations where competition without limits would produce results detrimental to everybody. Cooperation in such cases is objectively preferable to cutthroat competition. Yet transforming the 'zero-sum game' of competition (what one side wins the other loses) into a 'positive-sum game' of cooperation (so-called 'win-win') does not take place unless other strategies can be found.

In an article intended to popularize the use of game theory in strategy, Brandenburger and Nalebuff (1995) described a number of instances where firms have done just that. In the 1990s, for example, the US automobile industry was locked into cycles of price wars which eroded everybody's margins. General Motors decided to break the vicious cycle by issuing a credit card which gave users discounts on future purchases of GM cars. Other car makers followed suit. As a result, price competition was curbed and the industry moved from a 'lose-lose' situation to one of 'win-win.' There was also little chance of a return to price wars: the high costs of launching a major credit card constituted what game theorists call 'credible commitments' to mutual cooperation. In this case, the commitment was to compete for customer loyalty rather than for short-term sales increases.

Game theory provides valuable insights when it deals with situations that permit simple questions. For example, should an airline maximize operating economies by purchasing all its aircraft from one powerful supplier such as Boeing, or would it be wiser to balance Boeing's power by also buying from Airbus? Game theory does not necessarily provide yes or no answers to such questions. Instead, it systematically examines various permutations and combinations of conditions that can alter the situation.

> Unfortunately, most real-world strategic issues give rise to large numbers of possibilities. There is rarely what game theorists call a 'dominant strategy,' one preferable to all others. So the approach should not be thought of as one to resolve strategic issues so much as to help order the strategist's thinking, providing especially a set of concepts to help understand dynamic strategic manoeuvring against competitors.

Critique of the positioning school

The positioning school can be critiqued on the same grounds as the design and planning schools, since it carries their predispositions even further. As we discussed in the design school, the separation of thinking from acting—formulation done at the 'top,' through conscious thought, here based on formal analysis, implementation to follow lower down, through action—can render the strategy-making process excessively deliberate and so undermine strategic learning. And as we discussed in the planning school, there are dangers in looking to the future by extrapolating the trends of the present, in relying excessively on hard data, and in overformalizing the strategy-making process.

Ultimately we return to that grand fallacy of the last chapter: that analysis can produce synthesis. Porter, in fact, claimed in a 1987 article in *The Economist* that 'I favor a set of analytic techniques to develop strategy.' In our view, no one has ever developed a strategy through analytical technique. Technique has certainly fed useful information into the strategy-making process. But it has never developed a strategy. As Hamel commented in an article in *Fortune* magazine, as applicable to positioning as to planning: 'The dirty little secret of the strategy industry is that it doesn't have any theory of strategy creation' (1997: 80). Techniques do not create strategies; people do.

❝ the strategy industry doesn't have any theory of strategy creation ❞

Our critique of this school will focus on concerns about focus, context, process, and strategies themselves.

Concerns about focus

Like the other prescriptive schools, the approach of the positioning school has not been wrong so much as narrow. First the *focus* has been narrow. It is oriented to the economic and especially the quantifiable but the social and the political, or even the nonquantifiable economic. Even the selection of strategies can thereby be biased simply because cost leadership strategies generally have more hard data to back them up than, say, strategies of quality differentiation. This came out most clearly in the second wave of this school, notably in the BCG obsessive emphasis on market share, and in some other consulting firms' virtual obsession with perceiving strategy in terms of managing costs.

This school's bias in favour of the economic over the political is especially noteworthy. For example, the words 'political' and 'politics' do not appear in the table of contents or the index of Porter's main book *Competitive Strategy* (1980); yet this book can be taken as a primer for political action. If profit really does lie in market power, then there are clearly more than economic ways to generate it. Think of all the possible 'barriers to entry.' It does not take a great deal of imagination to read between the lines of sentences such as 'Government can limit or even foreclose entry into industries with such controls as licensing requirements and limits on access to raw materials' (13). In fact, Porter occasionally stepped across that fine line between competitive economics and political manoeuvring:

For large firms suing smaller firms, private antitrust suits can be thinly veiled devices to inflict penalties. Suits force the weaker firm to bear extremely high legal costs over a long period of time and also divert its attention from competing in the market. (86)

In fact, the political implications of using market power got Porter into some difficulties when, some years later, he was asked by the management of the National Football League (NFL) to suggest tactics that would counter the threat of the recently formed US Football League (USFL). Porter's presentation and notes to a meeting of NFL management figured prominently as evidence in the private antitrust suite that the USFL launched against the NFL in 1984. The jury found the NFL guilty of using monopoly power to damage the younger league (Kennedy and Pomerantz, 1986).

Concerns about context

A second concern is the narrow *context* of the positioning school. For one thing, there is a bias toward traditional big business—which, not incidentally, is where market power can be greatest, competition least effective, and the potential for political manipulation most pronounced. There have been studies of niche strategies and fragmented industries, but these are far outnumbered by those of mainline strategies in mature industries. That, of course, is where the hard data are, and the positioning school—in practice as well as in research—is dependent on large quantities of such data.

We already made this point about BCG and PIMS in the second wave, especially in the attention given to market share. In his chapter on fragmented industries in *Competitive Strategy*, Porter discussed at some length strategies to consolidate fragmented industries. But nowhere did he balance this with discussion of strategies to fragment consolidated industries (which, of course, is a favourite trick of small firms). In one section, he also discussed 'industries that are "stuck"' in a fragmented situation, but nowhere did he consider ones that are stuck in a consolidated situation.

The bias toward the big, the established, and the mature also reflects itself in a bias toward conditions of stability, much as in the design and planning schools. Instability encourages fragmentation; it also breaks down barriers of various kinds (entry, mobility, exit). But that does not help the positioning analyst: how can one tell who has what market share in an unstable industry?

Indeed, it is interesting that amidst this focus on formal analysis under conditions of relative stability, another side of this school considers the dynamic aspects of strategic positioning by the use of signalling, posturing, first and later mover advantage, and the like. That this side requires a very different orientation, both in practice (quick manoeuvring, based on scant hard data, with little time for analysis) and in research (the need for softer concepts and more imagination to understand the use of surprise, etc.), is never discussed in the positioning literature. The result is a conceptual schism in this school. It tells the practitioner, on the one hand to study carefully and move generically, and on the other hand to move fast and unexpectedly. Take your pick, in some sense, between 'paralysis by analysis' and 'extinction by instinct'! (Langley, 1995).

Overall, much of the problem may stem from a bias in this school toward the external conditions, especially of industry and competition, at the expense of internal capabilities. The balance between the two, so carefully maintained by the design school, was thrown off once the positioning school became popular, and so later, as we shall see, the field of strategic management was pulled the other way—not into balance, but out of it on the other side.

In a controversial paper entitled 'How Much Does Industry Matter?,' UCLA professor Richard Rumelt (1991) used government statistics to examine the performance of manufacturing firms for the years 1974–77. His working hypothesis was relatively simple: if industry is truly the most important aspect of strategy formation, then differences in the performance of business units across industries should far exceed performance differences among business units within the same industry. What Rumelt found was exactly the opposite.

McGahan and Porter (1997) responded six years later, in an article entitled 'How Much Does Industry Matter, Really?' Using a more sophisticated statistical technique, they analyzed the performance of manufacturing and service business segments for the years 1981–94. They concluded that being in a particular industry contributes substantially to performance, while admitting that differences among firms within the same industry may still be more important than differences among industries.

This is just the kind of controversy that hard-nosed researchers love, since the question is so well defined, the data so statistical, and the possible techniques of such unending sophistication. But we might do well to return to some basics, to put not just this debate but the whole positioning school into perspective. How are industries defined and classified in the first place? This is generally done by outsiders, usually economists in government or research jobs. But those industries are created—and destroyed, as well as combined and unbundled—by managers who use complex cognitive and social processes (see Anand and Peterson, 2000). So if industry does matter, it may not be in the way asserted by the positioning school.

Concerns about process

The third concern relates to *process*. The message of the positioning school is not to get out there and learn, but to stay home and calculate. 'Massaging the numbers' is what is expected in the managerial offices no less than the MBA classrooms. The strategist is supposed to deal in abstractions on paper, detached from the tangible world of making products and closing sales. Clausewitz argued in the nineteenth century that 'calculation' is 'the most essential thing to . . . the end' of attaining superiority. Yet he also acknowledged that 'an infinity of petty circumstances' produce 'unexpected incidents upon which it [is] impossible to calculate' (1968: 164, 165). That is the dilemma for all of the positioning school.

Calculation, as already suggested in our critique of the planning school, can impede not only learning and creativity but also personal commitment. With the planners sequestered in the central offices feeding reports to the top managers, everyone else gets slighted as a mere implementer. These people may be forced to pursue strategies dictated, not by the nuanced appreciation of a complex business, but by pat numerical calculations carried out by analysts who may know little about the 'petty' details of the business. 'Opportunities for innovative strategy don't emerge from sterile analysis and number crunching—they emerge from novel experiences that can create opportunities for novel insights' (Hamel, 1997: 32).

> 6 6 a successful strategy is one that committed people infuse with energy: they *make* it good by making it real 9 9

Brunsson has compared a 'commitment building type behavior,' more an act of will than a cognitive process, with a 'critically scrutinizing type behavior,' which disregards 'emotional involvement' and is 'more apt to reject than to accept' (1976: 12). In other words, the calculation of the analyst can displace the commitment of the actor. Hence there is no such thing as an optimal strategy, worked out in advance. A successful strategy is one that committed people infuse with energy: they *make* it good by making it real—perhaps because they made it themselves. That is not quite the same thing as claiming, as Porter did later, that 'factors (assets, people) can and must be assembled and accumulated' (1997: 162).

Concerns about strategies

Finally, *strategy* itself tends to have a narrow focus in the positioning school. It is seen as generic position, not unique perspective. At the limit, the process can reduce to a formula, whereby such a position is selected from a restricted list of conditions. Or else, in the case of strategic groups, the company joins one club or another, which itself dictates the generic portfolio of strategies to be pursued.

The design school promoted strategy as perspective and encouraged its creative design. By focusing on strategies as generic, the effect of the positioning school may have been exactly the opposite. Companies can be drawn toward behaviours that are generic in their detail as well as in their orientation. One need only look at all the copycatting and 'bench-marking' going on in business these days (Knuf, 2000; Denrell, 2005). The same problem seems to occur in the academic research, when it favours boxing strategies into particular categories rather than studying their nuanced differences.

The boxes are, of course, based on existing behaviours. And so, managers and researchers alike are tempted to become codifiers of the past rather than inventors of the future. Hence the bias in this school, discussed earlier, toward 'staying there' rather than 'getting there.' Richard Rumelt has been sympathetic to the positioning approach, at least its deliberate, analytic side. But he has also been articulate in recognizing its problems. We reproduce Box 4.4, one of his favourite transparencies.

Some of the most famous battles in business and war have been won, not by doing things correctly, following the accepted wisdom, but by breaking the established patterns—by *creating* the categories in the first place, as we saw earlier in the case of Napoleon. Burger King might have joined the 'fast-food hamburger group,' but it was McDonald's that created the initial vision and wrote the rules for the group. Some firms stay home and do 'competitive analysis'; others go out and create their own positions (perhaps leaving them with no competition to analyze!). The positioning school focuses its attention on strategies that are generic, on industries that are established, on groups that have formed, and on data that has hardened. Studying the established categories discourages the creation of new ones.

---

box 4.4

But how do you deal with the 'Honda question'?

(used with the permission of Richard Rumelt)

- ■ In 1977 my MBA final exam on the Honda Motorcycle case asked 'Should Honda enter the global automobile business?'
- ■ It was a 'giveaway' question. Anyone who said 'yes' flunked.
  - – Markets were saturated
  - – Efficient competitors existed in Japan, the US, and Europe
  - – Honda had little or no experience in automobiles
  - – Honda had no auto distribution system
- ■ In 1985 my wife drove a Honda.

BCG would have had to call Honda a 'dog' when it entered the US motorcycle market in 1959. The market was established—big machines for black-leather tough guys—and Honda was an insignificant player. It should have stayed away. But partly by creating a new market for small motorcycles driven by ordinary Americans, the dog became a star: it took a huge share of a new growth business created by itself. (Ironically, years later a BCG report extolled this as exemplary positioning behaviour. This is the 'case' Rumelt refers to in the box. But, as we shall see in Chapter 7, Honda's success had a great deal more to do with learning than with positioning.)

On its dynamic side, the positioning school may have a category called 'first mover advantage.' But its own orientation to the strategic analysis of hard data in existing categories discourages taking such advantage. By the time a firm is through analyzing, the first movers may be out of sight.

It is another interesting irony that the positioning school, so proactive in tone, is in fact among the most deterministic of all the schools of thought on strategy formation. While proclaiming managerial choice, it delineates boxes into which organizations should fit if they are to survive. This school's first wave promoted maxims; its second wave, imperatives. Market share was good per se, as was mass production experience; capital intensity was bad. Its third wave offers options and contingencies, but still not full choices. All of these prescriptions are presented in the belief that there is a best generic strategy for a given set of conditions: ignore it at your peril.

Why Porter's 'What is Strategy' may not be

In a 1996 *Harvard Business Review* article entitled 'What is Strategy?,' Michael Porter responded to his critics. He emphasized the importance of strategy, referring in contrast to 'constant improvement in operational effectiveness' as a 'necessary . . . but not usually sufficient' condition for 'superior profitability.'

While such a conclusion can hardly be disputed, Porter went on to list six points for 'sustainable competitive advantage,' the first five of which pertain to strategy and overall organizational issues, while the sixth reads 'operational effectiveness as given' (74). But would any manager who struggles with this last point every day accept such a dismissive role for it?

Moreover, improvements in operating effectiveness can be a kind of strategy (as, perhaps, in the role of innovation at 3M). Indeed, such improvements often produce the breakthroughs that induce key changes in strategy. But in this article, Porter continued to see strategy as necessarily deductive and deliberate, as if strategic learning and emergent strategy do not exist. As he commented in response to letters in the March/April 1997 of the *Harvard Business Review*:

If strategy is stretched to include employees and organizational arrangements, it becomes virtually everything a company does or consists of. Not only does this complicate matters, but it obscures the chain of causality that runs from competitive environment to position to activities to employee skills and organization. (162)

But what is wrong with seeing strategy in 'everything a company does or consists of'? That is simply strategy as perspective (rather than position). And why must there be any such chain of causality at all, let alone having to run in one direction?

Indeed, Porter's narrow view of the strategy process led him to an astonishing conclusion, namely that Japanese companies 'rarely have strategies,' that they 'will have to learn strategy' (1996: 63). Were this true, and given the performance of so many Japanese companies, not least Toyota's astounding success at this juncture, how could strategy be a necessary condition for corporate success?! In our opinion, however, it is not true at all. Rather than having to learn strategy, the Japanese might better teach Michael Porter about strategic learning.

Porter argued strongly throughout this article for distinctiveness of strategy and for 'creativity and insight' in 'finding' strategic position; he railed against the benchmarking, herding, and imitating he saw as so common in corporations. This was a welcome commentary. But the question must be raised as to how many of these practices have been encouraged by the very procedures Porter so long advocated. (At one point, he criticized activities that become too 'generic' as a result of outsourcing! [64])

Porter used the words 'choice' of strategy and 'choosing' strategy often in this article. At one point he defended his three generic strategies with the comment that this 'framework introduced the need to choose in order to avoid being caught between what I [earlier] described as the inherent contradictions of different strategies' (67). But are 'creativity and insight' promoted by 'finding' and 'choosing' generic strategic positions, as opposed to inducing and inventing novel strategic perspectives?

> " the Japanese don't need to study strategy; Porter needs a lesson in strategic learning "

Porter's basic model indicates what writers of military strategy call a 'come as you are' approach to strategy: once the strategic confrontation begins, you are stuck with what you've got. You can change only before or after. But in business, there is usually no before, during, or after. (One exception, those discrete strategic moves in diversification, may explain why Porter has been so fond of analyzing them.) Organization building and people development, which some other people see as intricately tied up with strategy, require ongoing processes rather than distinct moves. This seems to include the Japanese, who tend not to view time as some kind of broken up linear succession of before, during, and after.

In our view, Porter called for many of the right things in this article, but suggested going about them in a number of wrong ways. Or, at least we should say, in overly restricted ways, because what Porter really did in this article was retreat back into the positioning school, dismissing or ignoring other important points of view. Perhaps academics and consultants can grab hold of one part or other of the strategy elephant. Managers, however, must deal with the entire beast.

Bill Andrews, as a doctoral student at the University of Georgia, used an earlier version of this manuscript in a course. He proposed an additional stanza to our opening poem, which serves as an ideal conclusion to this critique.

> The Tenth as an economist
> At once the problem saw,
> And having never touched the beast
> Avoided empirical flaw.
> Saith he, 'The elephant with all its strength and verve
> Is best depicted on a graph, and similar to a curve.'

Contribution and context of the positioning school

We conclude that, with its emphasis on analysis and calculation, the positioning school has reduced its role from the formulation of strategy to the conducting of strategic analyses in support of that process (as it proceeds in other ways). Strategy making, as we continue to describe it in this book, is a far richer as well as messier and more dynamic process than the rather orderly and static one depicted in this school. Thus, the role of positioning is to *support* that process, not to *be* it. This school has added content to the planning school—no small achievement—while shifting the role of planner to that of analyst. In practice, of course, the techniques of planning never really worked for creating strategy, while those of analysis have been able to inform the process significantly. For this reason, researchers such as Cynthia Montgomery (2008) believe that the positioning school would do well to bring back the CEO as the chief strategist, in effect going back to the design school (see Box 4.5).

box 4.5

Back to design school?

(Excerpted from Montgomery, 2008: 54-60)

Strategy is not what it used to be—or what it could be. In the past 25 years it has been presented as an analytical problem to be solved, a left-brain exercise of sorts. This perception has led to an era of specialists eager to help managers analyze their industries or position their firms for strategic advantage.

We now know more than before about the role market forces play in industry profitability and importance of differentiating a firm from its competitors. These gains have come in large part from the infusion of economics into the study of strategy. A host of unintended consequences have developed from what in its own right could be a very good thing.

Most notably, strategy has been narrowed to a competitive game plan, divorcing it from the firm's larger sense of purpose; the CEO's unique role as arbiter and steward of strategy has been eclipsed; and the exaggerated emphasis on sustainable competitive advantage has drawn attention away form the fact that strategy must be a dynamic tool for guiding the development of a company over time.

Fifty years ago strategy was taught as part of the general management curriculum in business schools. Although strategy had considerable breadth then, it didn't have much rigor. Advances over the next few decades not only refined tools but spawned a new industry around strategy.

It has been a heady period, and the strategy tool kit is far richer because of it. That said, something has been lost along the way. While gaining depth, strategy has lost breadth and stature. It has become more about formulation than implementation, and more about getting the idea right at the outset than living with a strategy over time.

What we have lost sight of is that strategy is not just a plan, not just an idea; it is a way of life for a company. Strategy doesn't just position a firm in its external land-scape; it defines what a firm will be. As strategy has striven to become a science, we have allowed this fundamental point to slip away. We need to reinstate it.

In the strategy portion of the Owner/President Management executive program at Harvard Business School, the notion of added value is core to everything we do. Early in the module, executives are asked to respond to the following:

- ▇ If your company were shuttered, to whom would it matter and why?
- ▇ Which of your customers would miss you the most and why?
- ▇ How long would it take for another firm to step into that void?

> When the questions are presented, classrooms that minutes earlier were bursting with conversation fall silent. Managers long accustomed to describing their companies by the industries they are in and the products they make often find themselves unable to say what is truly distinctive about their firm.
>
> At heart, most strategies, like most people, involve some mystery. Interpreting that mystery is an abiding responsibility of the chief strategist, the CEO. The CEO is the one who chooses a company's identity, who has responsibility for declining certain opportunities and pursing others. In this sense he or she serves as the guardian of organizational purpose.
>
> The need to create and re-create reasons for a company's continued existence sets the strategist apart from every other individual in the company. He or she must keep an eye on how the company is currently adding value and the other eye on changes, both inside and outside the company, that either threaten its position or present some new opportunity for adding value. Guiding this never-ending process, bringing perspective to the midst of action and purpose to the flow – not solving the strategy puzzle once—is the crowning responsibility of the CEO.

Strategy analysis would appear to be appropriate for strategy making where conditions are sufficiently *established* and *stable* to offer appropriate data which can be analyzed at a single centre. Such analysis should, however, never be allowed to dominate the process. A host of soft factors always have to be considered alongside the hard ones. In other words, no Gresham-like law of strategy analysis can be allowed to operate, in practice or in research, whereby the hard data inputs drive out the soft ones, and whereby a portfolio of positions drives out thinking about integrated perspective. Where analyzing the numbers or even reading the results have stopped strategists and researchers, from getting into the tangible world of products and customers, then the positioning school has done strategic management a disservice.

Otherwise, the positioning school must be counted as having made a major contribution to strategic management. This school has opened up tremendous avenues for research and has provided a powerful set of concepts for practice. It is gaining strength as it combines with other perspectives.

Two efforts illustrate the direction in which the positioning school is evolving. Brandenburger and Nalebuff (1996) argue that firms should look beyond competition as a driving force to include 'co-option': the possibility of cooperative interaction with 'complementors' such as buyers, suppliers, and substitutors. In the same spirit, Iansiti and Levien (2004) have suggested that the concept of industry, with its emphasis on competition and rivalry, should be transformed into a 'business ecosystem' in which interdependence is more varied and complex.

The positioning school originally saw strategy formation as a process that consists of finding the position that can best withstand existing and potential competition. But it turns out that focusing on competition narrows vision and curtails strategic creativity. It can also be counterproductive: one aggressive competitive move tends to beget another in an escalating cycle that leaves no one better off. The thinking that currently informs research in this school regards competition and cooperation not as opposites, but as two poles that span a range of choices. The metaphor of war yields to the metaphor of international relations: today's competitors are tomorrow's collaborators, competition and cooperation are practised simultaneously.

The entrepreneurial school: strategy formation as a visionary process

"Before we talk about direction, let's spend a minute on mission and vision."

The soul . . . never thinks without a picture.

—Aristotle

F rom the schools of *prescription*, we now move toward those of *description*, which seek to understand the process of strategy formation as it unfolds. We begin, however, with a school that stands in between, and takes a view not entirely different from that of the design school.

The design school, if not the planning and positioning schools, took formal leadership seriously, rooting strategy formation in the mental processes of the chief executive. That person is the 'architect' of strategy. But the design school stopped short of building a cult around that leadership. Indeed, by stressing the need for a conceptual framework, and by dismissing intuition, it specifically sought to avoid the softer, more personalized and idiosyncratic elements of leadership.

The *entrepreneurial school* has done exactly the opposite. Not only has this school focused the strategy formation process exclusively on the single leader, but it has also stressed the most innate of mental states and processes—intuition, judgment, wisdom, experience, insight. This promotes a view of strategy as *perspective*, associated with image and sense of direction, namely *vision*. In our Strategy Safari, we might think of this school as the rider on the elephant.

Here, however, the strategic perspective is not so much collective or cultural, as in some of the other schools to be discussed, as personal, the construct of the leader. Consequently, in this school the organization becomes responsive to the dictates of that individual—subservient to his or her leadership. And the environment, if not exactly subservient, becomes the terrain on which the leader manoeuvres with some ease, at least in terms of directing the organization into a protective niche.

The most central concept of this school is *vision*: a mental representation of strategy, created or at least expressed in the head of the leader. That vision serves as both an inspiration and a sense of what needs to be done—a guiding idea, if you like. True to its label, vision often tends to be a kind of image more than a fully articulated plan (in words and numbers). That leaves it flexible, so that the leader can adapt it to his or her experiences. This suggests that entrepreneurial strategy is both deliberate and emergent: deliberate in its broad lines and sense of direction, emergent in its details so that these can be adapted en route. The accompanying Box 5.1 (on following page) develops the metaphor of strategic thinking as 'seeing.'

Origins in economics

In one sense, the entrepreneurial school, like the positioning school, grew out of economics. The entrepreneur figures prominently in neo-classical economic theory. His or her role, however, was confined to deciding what quantities to produce and at what prices. Competitive dynamics took care of the rest. The rise of large companies forced economists to modify economic theory, giving birth to oligopoly theory (which forms the foundation of the positioning school). But even here, the entrepreneur still had little more to do than calculate prices and quantities.

There were economists, however, who considered this narrow view of the entrepreneur to be a major failure of economics. Karl Marx, oddly enough, was one of them. He lavished praise on entrepreneurs as agents of economic and technological change, but was highly critical of their impact on society at large. The seminal figure who brought the entrepreneur into prominence in economic thought was Joseph Schumpeter. To him, it was not maximization of profits that explained corporate behaviour so much as attempts

to deal with a situation that is sure to change presently—an attempt by these firms to keep on their feet, on ground that is slipping away from under them. In other words, the problem that is usually being visualized is how capitalism administers existing structures, whereas the relevant problem is how it creates and destroys them. (1950: 84)

Accordingly, Schumpeter introduced his famous notion of *creative destruction*. This is the engine that keeps capitalism moving forward, and the driver of that engine is the entrepreneur. For Schumpeter, the entrepreneur is not necessarily somebody who puts up the initial capital or invents the new product, but the person with the business idea. Ideas are elusive, but in the hands of entrepreneurs, they become powerful as well as profitable. For those, like economists, who focus on the tangible parts of business, such as money, machinery, and land, the contribution of the entrepreneurs may seem baffling. Vision and creativity are less evident. Schumpeter sought to clarify this:

What have [the entrepreneurs] done? They have not accumulated any kind of goods, they have created no original means of production, but have employed existing means of production differently, more appropriately, more advantageously. They have 'carried out new combinations.' . . . And their profit, the surplus, to which no liability corresponds, is an entrepreneurial profit. (1934: 132)

---

box 5.1

Strategic thinking as 'seeing'

(by Henry Mintzberg, adapted Mintzberg, 1991)

If strategies are visions, then what role does seeing play in strategic thinking? Three pairs of factors are presented below, together with a seventh that knits them together into a framework of strategic thinking.

Almost everyone would agree that strategic thinking means *seeing ahead*. But, you cannot see ahead unless you can *see behind*, because any good vision of the future has to be rooted in an understanding of the past.

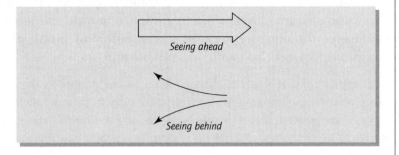

Seeing ahead

Seeing behind

Many people also claim that strategic thinking is *seeing above*. It is as if strategists should take helicopters, to be able to see the 'big picture,' to distinguish 'the forest from the trees.' But can anyone really get the big picture just by seeing above? The forest looks like a rug from a helicopter. Anyone who has taken a walk in a forest knows that it doesn't look much like that on the ground. Forestry people who stay in helicopters don't understand much more than strategists who stay in offices.

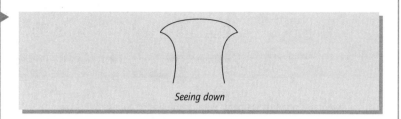

Seeing down

Finding the diamond in the rough might be a better metaphor. Strategic thinkers have to find the gem of an idea that changes their organization. And that comes from a lot of hard and messy digging. There is no big picture ready for the seeing; each strategist has to construct his or her own. Thus, strategic thinking is also inductive thinking: seeing above must be supported by *seeing below*.

Seeing below

You can, however, see ahead by seeing behind and see above by seeing below and still not be a strategic thinker. That takes more—creativity for one thing.

Strategic thinkers see differently from other people; they pick out the precious gems that others miss. They challenge conventional wisdom—the industry recipe, the traditional strategy—and thereby distinguish their organizations. Since creative thinking has been referred to as lateral thinking, this could be called *seeing beside*.

Seeing beside

But there are many creative ideas in this world, far more than it can handle—just visit any art gallery. And so, beside seeing beside, strategic thinkers have to *see beyond*. Creative ideas have to be placed into context, to be seen in a world that is to unfold. Seeing beyond is different from seeing ahead. Seeing ahead foresees an expected future by constructing a framework out of the events of the past—it intuitively forecasts discontinuities. Seeing beyond constructs the future—it invents a world that would not otherwise be.

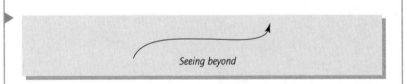

Seeing beyond

But there remains one last element. What is the use of doing all this seeing—ahead and behind, above and below, beside and beyond—if nothing gets done? In other words, for a thinker to deserve the label *strategic*, he or she must also *see it through.*

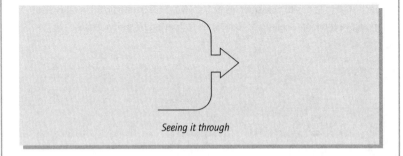

Seeing it through

Put this all together and you get *strategic thinking as seeing.*

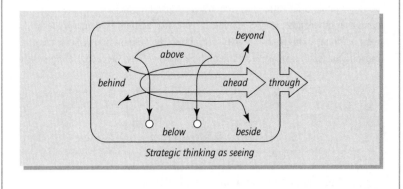

Strategic thinking as seeing

For Schumpeter, 'new combinations,' including 'the doing of new things or the doing of things that are already being done in a new way' (1947: 151), was key. The capitalist bore the risk. Moreover, although a founder may remain at the helm of his or her organization, in Schumpeter's view this person ceases to perform an entrepreneurial function as soon as he or she stops innovating.

But not everyone agreed with this interpretation. Knight (1967) saw entrepreneurship as synonymous with heavy risk and the handling of uncertainty. And outside of economics, Peter Drucker took this further, identifying entrepreneurship with management itself. 'Central to business enterprise is . . . the entrepreneurial act, an act of economic risk-taking. And business enterprise is an entrepreneurial institution.' (1970: 10).

Thus, depending on one's point of view, an entrepreneur can be (a) the founder of an organization (whether that is an act of innovation or not, and whether or not he or she is an opportunist or a strategist), (b) the manager of a self-owned business, or (c) the innovative leader of an organization owned by others. Cole (1959), another economist, who popularized the phrase 'bold stroke' to capture the act of entrepreneurship, mentioned four types of entrepreneurs: the calculating inventor, the inspirational innovator, the overoptimistic promoter, and the builder of a strong enterprise. Box 5.2 presents the views of one famous entrepreneur, Richard Branson of the Virgin Group in Britain, who perhaps reflects characteristics of all four.

Regrettably, aside from Cole and some others, few economists (such as Kirzner (1997) and Casson (2005)) followed in the footsteps of Schumpeter. Mainstream economics always preferred the abstractions of the competitive market and the predictabilities of the skeletal manager to the vagaries of strategic vision and the uniqueness of the market niche.

The literature of the entrepreneurial school

And so it really fell to the field of management to develop the entrepreneurial school. Proponents of this school saw personalized leadership, based on strategic vision, as the key to organizational success. They noted this especially in business, but also in other sectors, and not only in starting up and building new organizations, but also in 'turning around' faltering established ones.

box 5.2

Reflections of an entrepreneur

Quotes from Richard Branson (1986: 13–18)

- 'The biggest risk any of us can take is to invest money in a business that we don't know. Very few of the businesses that Virgin has set up have been in completely new fields.'
- 'I have not depended on others to do surveys or market research, or to develop grand strategies. I have taken the view that the risk to the company is best reduced by my own involvement in the nitty-gritty of the new business.'
- 'There is always another deal. Deals are like London buses—there's always another one coming along.'
- 'Reduce the scale of . . . risk through joint ventures . . . [and] have a way out of a high risk venture.'
- 'As businesses grow, watch out for management losing touch with the basics— normally the customer.'
- '[Our] "keep it small" rule enables . . . more than usual numbers of managers the challenge and excitement of running their own businesses.'
- 'Pursue a "buy, don't make" strategy.'
- 'Having evaluated an investment . . . and having decided to make an investment, don't pussyfoot around. Go for it!'

Therefore, although 'entrepreneurship' was originally associated with the creators of their own businesses, the word has gradually been extended to describe various forms of personalized, proactive, single-minded leadership in organizations. For reasons to be discussed shortly here, we use the label less broadly, restricting it to visionary leadership at the helm of an organization. Another term, 'intrapreneurship' (Pinchot, 1985), describes those people who take strategic initiatives *within* large organizations—internal entrepreneurs, if you like. But since this really describes how organizations learn from the bottom up, we discuss it in the chapter on the learning school.

In this section, we review the literature of the entrepreneurial school. We then discuss some of our own research before summarizing the key premises of this school. We close with consideration of the contribution, limitations, and context of the entrepreneurial school.

The great leader in the popular press

Of all the writings about entrepreneurship, the vast majority has been popular—in the spirit of the 'great leader' view of management—and can be found in the popular press or in the biographies and autobiographies of famous tycoons of industry and other notable leaders. Entrepreneurship can, for example, be followed biweekly in *Fortune*, a magazine that tends to attribute business success to the vision and personal behaviour of the heroic leader. 'CEO Jack Smith didn't just stop the bleeding,' reported a *Fortune* headline on 17 October 1994. 'With a boost from rising auto sales, he made GM healthy again' (54). All by himself!

The entrepreneurial personality

A second body of literature on entrepreneurship, probably the largest in terms of empirical content, focuses on the entrepreneurial personality. Manfred Kets de Vries, for example, referred to the entrepreneur as 'the last lone ranger' in a 1977 article (34), and published another in 1985 on 'The Dark Side of Entrepreneurship.' Almost 30 years later, John Gartner (2005) was struck by the similarity between the textbook description of 'hypomanic' patients in psychiatry and the descriptions of internet entrepreneurs in the press. He culled the basic traits of hypomania, and then asked ten internet CEOs if these accurately described the typical entrepreneur in their field. Respondents in general agreed that the clinical traits describing hypomanics are entrepreneurs. For instance, both hypomanics and entrepreneurs are often charismatic and persuasive; they are filled with energy; they need little sleep; and they channel their energy into wildly grand ambitions which they believe will change the world. Gartner's (2005) survey, however, suggests that hypomanics and entrepreneurs share a number of less attractive features. For instance, they are reckless, easily irritated by minor obstacles, prone to act impulsively with poor judgment, and as a rule are oblivious to the negative reactions their actions justifiably elicit. Instead of recognizing that there can be honest differences of opinion, they often feel prosecuted by those who do not agree with them.

Of course, although entrepreneurs often display unattractive traits (as do most people), what is of greater interest to researchers is where these traits come from. In a book called *The Organization Makers*, Collins and Moore (1970) presented a fascinating picture of the independent entrepreneur, based on a study of 150 of them. The authors traced their lives from childhood through formal and informal education to the steps they took to create their enterprises. Data from psychological tests reinforced their analysis. What emerged is a picture of tough, pragmatic people driven from early childhood by powerful needs for achievement and independence. At some point in their lives, each entrepreneur faced disruption ('role deterioration'), and it was here that they set out on their own:

> ❝ entrepreneurs are driven by powerful needs for achievement and independence ❞

What sets them apart is that during this time of role deterioration they interwove their dilemmas into the projection of a business. In moments of crisis, they did not seek a situation of security. They went on into deeper insecurity. (134)

Among the various characteristics attributed to the entrepreneurial personality have been strong needs for control, for independence, and for achievement, a resentment of authority, and a tendency to accept moderate risks. As Baumol summarized McClelland's (1961) well-known study, the entrepreneur is not a 'gambler' or a 'speculator,' 'not essentially a man who chooses to bear risks,' but a 'calculator' (1968: 70). (As we shall soon see, however, not all observers have accepted this point.)

In looking into the 'entrepreneurial' personality, a number of writers have contrasted it with the 'administrative' one. Stevenson and Gumpert have suggested, for example, that 'in making decisions, administrators and entrepreneurs often proceed with a very different order of questions.'

The typical administrator asks: What resources do I control? What structure determines our organization's relationship to its market? How can I minimize the impact of others on my ability to perform? What opportunity is appropriate? The entrepreneur . . . tends to ask: Where is the opportunity? How do I capitalize on it? What resources do I need? How do I gain control over them? What structure is best? (1985: 86, 87)

With respect to 'strategic orientation,' Stevenson and Gumpert describe the entrepreneur as 'constantly attuned to environmental changes that may suggest a favorable chance, while the [administrator] . . . wants to preserve resources and reacts defensively to possible threats to deplete them' (87). Moreover, entrepreneurs 'move quickly past the identification of opportunity to its pursuit. They are the hawkers with umbrellas who materialize from nowhere on Manhattan street corners at the first rumbles of thunder overhead' (88). Hence their actions tend to be 'revolutionary, with short direction,' in contrast to the administrators' 'evolutionary' actions, 'with long duration' (89).

The search for entrepreneurial 'personality' has its detractors. Mitchell *et al.* (2002) describe efforts to find psychological or demographic characteristics that are common and unique to entrepreneurs as a failure. Conceding the unique entrepreneurial personality may be non-existent, many writers have turned their attention to how entrepreneurs think.

Research by Busenitz and Barney (1997: 10) concludes that while entrepreneurs are prone to 'overconfidence,' this 'may be particularly beneficial in implementing a specific decision and persuading others to be enthusiastic about it.' Indeed 'the window of opportunity would often be gone by the time all the necessary information became available for more rational decision making' (10). Palich and Bagby (1995: 426) also found that 'entrepreneurs categorized scenarios significantly more positively than did [their] other subjects . . . i.e., entrepreneurs perceived more strengths versus weaknesses, opportunities versus threats, and potential for performance improvement versus deterioration.'

What then become the chief characteristics of the approach of such personalities to strategy making? Some years ago, Mintzberg (1973) suggested four:

1 **In the entrepreneurial mode, strategy making is dominated by the active search for new opportunities**. The entrepreneurial organization focuses on opportunities; problems are secondary. As Drucker wrote: 'Entrepreneurship requires that the few available good people be deployed on opportunities rather than frittered away on "solving problems"' (1970: 10).

2 **In the entrepreneurial organization, power is centralized in the hands of the chief executive.** Collins and Moore wrote of the founder-entrepreneur as 'characterized by an unwillingness to "submit" to authority, an inability to work with it, and a consequential need to escape from it' (1970: 45). Power here is believed to rest with one person capable of committing the organization to bold courses of action. In one Egyptian firm described years ago, but characteristic of today's entrepreneurial firms nonetheless: 'There is no charted plan of organization, no formalized procedures for selection and development of managerial personnel, no publicized system of wage and salary classifications . . . . Authority is associated exclusively with an individual' (Harbison and Myers, 1959: 40–1).

3 **Strategy making in the entrepreneurial mode is characterized by dramatic leaps forward in the face of uncertainty.** Strategy moves forward in the entrepreneurial organization by the taking of large decisions—those 'bold strokes.' The chief executive seeks out and thrives in conditions of uncertainty, where the organization can make dramatic gains.

---

box 5.3

Entrepreneurship and planning

(from Amar Bhide, 1994: 152)

Interviews with the founders of 100 companies on the 1989 Inc. '500' list of the fastest growing companies in the United States revealed that entrepreneurs spent little effort on their initial business plan:

- 41 percent had no business plan at all
- 26 percent had just a rudimentary, back-of-the-envelope type of plan
- 5 percent worked up financial projections for investors
- 28 percent wrote up a full-blown plan

Many entrepreneurs, the interview suggested, don't bother with well-formulated plans for good reasons. They thrive in rapidly changing industries and niches that tend to deter established companies. And under these fluid conditions, an ability to roll with the punches is much more important than careful planning.

4 **Growth is the dominant goal of the entrepreneurial organization**. According to psychologist David McClelland (1961), the entrepreneur is motivated above all by the need for achievement. Since the organization's goals are simply the extension of the entrepreneur's own, the dominant goal of the organization operating in the entrepreneurial mode would seem to be growth, the most tangible manifestation of achievement. *Fortune* magazine came to this conclusion in an article years ago about the Young Presidents' Organization, entitled 'The Entrepreneurial Ego':

Most of the young presidents have the urge to build rather than manipulate. 'Expansion is a sort of disease with us,' says one president. 'Let's face it,' says another. 'We're empire builders. The tremendous compulsion and obsession is not to make money, but to build an empire.' (1956: 143)

Visionary leadership

As organizations grow larger the leader as the entrepreneur; the person who single handedly directs the organization, seems less relevant. A new role therefore emerges for the leader: developing and articulating vision for the organization. But what is true vision? Perhaps the simplest answer is that a true *vision* is something you can see in your mind's eye. Being the biggest or earning 42 percent return on investment would hardly count. A vision has to distinguish an organization, set it apart as a unique institution. Warren Bennis perhaps put it best with the comment that 'if it is really a vision, you'll never forget it.' In other words, you don't have to write it down. Wouldn't this make a wonderful test for all those banal statements labelled 'the vision'!

❝ if it is really a vision, you'll never forget it ❞

In their book on leadership, Bennis and Namus devote a good deal of attention to vision. We reprint various excerpts below:

■ To choose a direction, a leader must first have developed a mental image of a possible and desirable future state of the organization. This image, which we call a *vision*, may be as vague as a dream or as precise as a goal or mission statement. The critical point is that a vision articulates a view of a realistic, credible, attractive future for the organization, a condition that is better in some important ways than what now exists.

- A vision is a target that beckons . . . . Note also that a vision always refers to a *future* state, a condition that does not presently exist and never existed before. With a vision, the leader provides the all-important bridge from the present to the future of the organization.

- By focusing attention on a vision, the leader operates on the *emotional and spiritual resources* of the organization, on its values, commitment, and aspirations.

- If there is a spark of genius in the leadership function at all, it must lie in this transcending ability, a kind of magic, to assemble—out of the variety of images, signals, forecasts and alternatives—a clearly articulated vision of the future that is at once simple, easily understood, clearly desirable, and energizing. (1985: 89, 90, 92, 103)

Below, we draw on a number of studies conducted at McGill University that probe into the role of vision and help to describe where it comes from.

---

box 5.4

Successful habits of visionary companies

(from Collins and Porras, 1997: 220-1, 237)

James Collins and Jerry Porras' book *Built to Last: Successful Habits of Visionary Companies* suggest that firms should develop a 'vision' which both 'preserves the core' while at the same time 'stimulate progress'. In this best best selling business book, they argue that the 'fundamental distinguishing characteristic of the most enduring and successful corporations is that they '. . . preserve a cherished core ideology while simultaneously stimulating progress in everything that is not part of the core ideology' (1997: 220). Firms should develop a vision which consists of two major components – 'core ideology' and an 'envisioned future'. The core ideology defines 'the enduring characteristic of an organization' while the envisioned future sets forth what the firm '. . . aspires to become, to achieve, to create.'

The core ideology consists of both 'core values' and 'core purpose'. Core values are '. . . the organization's essential and enduring tenents.'

> Core purpose is '. . . the fundamental reason for being.'
>
> The envisioned future also consists of two components; '. . . a ten-to thirty-year "Big Hairy Audacious Goal"' (BHAG) and a 'vivid description' of what it would be like when the organization achieves the BHAG.
>
> Collins and Porras provide Sony's 'vision' as an example, as follows (1997: 237):
>
> ## Sony 1950s
>
> **Core Values**: Elevation of Japanese national culture and status. . .
>
> **Core Purpose**: To experience the sheer joy of innovation and the application of technology for the benefit and pleasure of the general public. . . .
>
> **BHAG**: Become the company most known for changing the worldwide image of Japanese products as being of poor quality. . . .
>
> **Vivid Description**: We will create products which will become pervasive around the world.

Vision as drama

A paper co-authored by Frances Westley and Henry Mintzberg (1989) contrasted two views of visionary leadership. One, more traditional, is likened to a hypodermic needle. The active ingredient (vision) is loaded into a syringe (words), which is injected into the employees. That causes them to jump up and down with great energy.

There is some truth to this, but these authors preferred a rather different image. Drawing from a book on theatre by Peter Brook (1968: 154), the legendary director of the Royal Shakespeare Company, the authors conceived strategic vision, like drama, as beginning in that magical moment when fiction and life blend together. Brook argued that, in theatre, the magic is the result of endless 'rehearsal,' followed by the 'performance' itself, supported by the 'attendance' of the audience. But Brook introduced a lovely touch here, translating these three words into their more dynamic French counterparts—'repetition,' 'representation,' and 'assistance'—and then using their equivalent meanings back in English. Westley and Mintzberg followed suit in applying Brook's ideas to visionary management.

■ **Repetition** (rehearsal) suggests that success comes from deep knowledge of the subject at hand. Just as Sir Laurence Olivier would repeat his lines again and again until he had trained his tongue muscles to say them effortlessly, so too the visionary leader's inspiration stems not so much from luck, although chance encounters certainly play a role, as from endless experience in a particular context.

■ **Representation** (performance) means not just to perform but to make the past live again, giving it immediacy, vitality. To the strategist, that is vision articulated, in words and actions, but of a particular kind: the words are pictures. What distinguishes visionary leaders is their profound ability to use language in symbolic form—as metaphor. They do not just 'see' things from a new perspective; they get others to so see them too. Hence 'vision.' For example, Edwin Land, who built a great company around the Polaroid camera he invented, claimed that 'it's not merely the camera you are focusing: you are focusing yourself . . . when you touch the button, what is inside of you comes out' (1972: 84). But vision goes beyond words, into actions. The vision has to be brought to life. And, again, that is not so much through formal plans and programmes as by informal actions—the rolling up of sleeves and getting in there with everyone else. As the modern dancer Isadora Duncan described her art: 'If I could say it, I wouldn't have to dance it.'

■ **Assistance** (attendance) means that the audience of the drama, whether in the theatre or the organization, empowers the actor no less than the actor empowers the audience. Leaders become visionary because they appeal powerfully to specific constituencies at specific periods of time. When Steve Jobs unveiled his much anticipated NeXT computer in front of 3,000 invited guests the atmosphere in the hall was more like that of a religious revival than product demonstration:

They have come to hear the word according to the prophet Steve. He is the evangelist, the visionary, the Zen priest of the personal computer. And this is his second coming. He is one of them. As young people, they were mocked and castigated as nerds, propeller heads and techno-turkies. But they clung to their beliefs . . . And now, their time has come. And Steve Jobs is the light. He showed the rest of the world that nerds knew all along. That the nerds were right (Kennedy and Pomerantz (1986)).

Stephen Downing (2005) suggests that power of visionary leadership resides in the use of dramatic narratives to turn constituencies into stakeholders. It therefore follows that when the narratives take a disastrous turn, or simply run their course, the visionaries often fall from grace. This happened to Winston Churchill. His narrative of blood, sweat, and tears which served Britain so well, became increasingly irrelevant as the Second World War was drawing to a close. Steve Jobs, on the other hand, was drummed out of Apple at one point because he was not sufficiently business minded, but came back to run Apple once again, thus proving that some narratives can endure.

Of course, management is not theatre. The leader who becomes a stage actor, playing a part he or she does not live, is destined to fall from grace. It is genuine feeling behind what the leader says and does that renders leadership visionary, and that is what makes it impossible to translate such leadership into any formula.

So visionary leadership is style and strategy coupled together. It is drama, but not play-acting. Such leadership is born *and* made, the product of a historical moment.

Entrepreneurial strategy in a supermarket chain[1]

Let us probe into visionary leadership through a study that tracked the behaviour of one rather visionary entrepreneur over a long period of time. His company was Steinberg's, a Canadian retail chain that began with a tiny food store in Montreal in 1917 and grew to sales of several billion dollars, most of it in supermarket operations, during the sixty-year reign of its leader.

In many ways Steinberg's fits the entrepreneurial model quite well. Sam Steinberg, who joined his mother in that little store at the age of eleven and personally made a quick decision to expand it two years later, maintained complete formal control of the firm (including every single voting share) to the day of his death in 1978. He also exercised close managerial control over all of its major decisions, at least until the firm began to diversify after 1960, primarily into other forms of retailing.

---

1 Adapted from Mintzberg and Waters (1982).

In terms of Cole's 'bold stroke' of the entrepreneur, in Steinberg's we saw only two major reorientations of strategy in the sixty years: a move into self-service in the 1930s and one into the shopping centre business in the 1950s. But these strokes were not so much bold as tested. The story of the move into self-service is indicative.

In 1933, one of the company's eight stores 'struck it bad,' in Sam Steinberg's words, incurring 'unacceptable' losses ($125 a week). He closed that store one Friday evening, converted it to self-service (a new concept then), changed its name from 'Steinberg's Service Stores' to 'Wholesale Groceteria,' slashed its prices by 15–20 percent, printed handbills, stuffed them into neighbourhood mailboxes, and reopened on Monday morning. That's strategic change! But only once these changes proved successful did he convert the other seven stores. Then, in his words, 'We grew like Topsy.'

It would appear, therefore, that 'controlled boldness' might be a better expression. The ideas were bold, the execution careful. Sam Steinberg could simply have closed that one unprofitable store. Instead he used it to create a new vision, which he tested before leaping.

Absolutely central to this entrepreneurship was intimate, detailed knowledge of the business, that 'repetition' discussed earlier. The leader as conventional strategist—the so-called architect of strategy— seems to sit on a pedestal and is fed aggregate data that is used to formulate strategies that others are supposed to implement. But the history of Steinberg's belies that image. 'Nobody knew the grocery business like we did. Everything has to do with your knowledge.' He added: 'I knew merchandise, I knew cost, I knew selling, I knew customers, I knew everything . . . and I passed on all my knowledge; I kept teaching my people. That's the advantage we had. They couldn't touch us.'

> ❝'controlled boldness' is key to entrepreneurial success❞

Such concentrated knowledge can be incredibly effective so long as the business is simple and focused enough to be comprehended in one head, so moves can be fast and focused. That is why entrepreneurship is at the centre of so many of the most glorious corporate successes.

But in its strength lies its weakness. The metaphors and dances become difficult to sustain after the leader departs (or simply loses energy). Then another form of management may have to take over, if it can. (After Sam Steinberg died, his three daughters eventually inherited control of the voting stock. They quarrelled, and subsequently sold the company to a financial operator with no experience in the supermarket business. The firm later went into bankruptcy.)

Conceiving a new vision in a garment firm[2]

Where does vision come from? How do entrepreneurial leaders pick up signals in the environment that allow them to trigger major shifts in strategic perspective? Another study provides some clues.

Canadelle produced women's undergarments, primarily brassieres and girdles. It too was a highly successful organization, although not on the same scale as Steinberg's. Things were going well for the company in the late 1960s, under the personal leadership of Larry Nadler, the son of its founder, when suddenly everything changed. A sexual revolution of sorts was accompanying broader social upheaval, with bra-burning a symbol of resistance. For a manufacturer of brassieres, the threat was obvious. Moreover, the miniskirt had just come to dominate the fashion scene, giving rise to pantyhose. The girdle market was declining at 30 percent a year. ('The bottom fell out of the girdle business,' they liked to say.) The whole environment—long so receptive to the company's strategies—seemed to turn on it all at once.

At the time, a French company had entered the Quebec market with a light, moulded garment called 'Huit,' using the theme, 'just like not wearing a bra.' Their target market was fifteen- to twenty-year-olds. The product was expensive, but it sold well. Nadler flew to France in an attempt to license it for manufacture in Canada. The French firm refused, but, in Nadler's words, what he learned in 'that one hour in their offices made the trip worthwhile.' He suddenly realized what it was that women wanted, especially younger women: a more natural look, not no bra but less bra.

---

2 Adapted from Mintzberg and Waters (1984).

This led to a major shift in strategic vision. 'All of a sudden the idea forms,' Nadler said. Canadelle reconfirmed its commitment to the brassiere business, and sought greater market share while its competitors were cutting back. It introduced a new line of more natural brassieres for younger customers, which required the firm to work out the new moulding technology as well as a new approach to promotion.

We can draw on Kurt Lewin's (1951) three-stage model of change—unfreezing, changing, and refreezing—to explain such a gestalt shift in vision. The process of *unfreezing* is essentially one of overcoming the natural defence mechanisms, getting past the established 'mental set' of how an industry is supposed to operate. The old 'industry recipe' (Grinyer and Spender, 1979; Spender, 1989) no longer holds. 'There is a period of confusion,' Nadler told us. 'You sleep on it . . . start looking for patterns . . . become an information hound, searching for [explanations] everywhere.'

Change of this magnitude seems to require a shift in mindset before a new strategic vision can be conceived. If this story is indicative, just one or two key insights—even trivial ones—seem necessary to stimulate the creation of a new concept. Continuous bombardment of information may prepare the mind for the shift, but it is those sudden insights that seem to crystallize it—to bring all the disparate elements into one 'eureka'-type flash.

Once the strategist's mind is set, then the *refreezing* process begins. Here the object is not to read the situation, at least not in a global sense, but in effect to block it out. It is a time to work out the consequences of the new strategic vision.

Tom Peters (1980: 12–16) has claimed that obsession is an ingredient in effective organizations. That certainly seems to be the case in this period of refreezing, when the organization must pursue the new orientation—the new mindset—with full vigour. The organization now knows where it is going; the object of the exercise is to get there using all the skills at its command, many of them necessarily formal and analytic.

Of course, not everyone accepts the new vision. Those steeped in old strategies may resist it (as was the case at Canadelle). Then the refreezing of the leader's mindset has to be followed by the unfreezing, changing, and refreezing of the organization. But when the structure is simple, as it usually is in the entrepreneurial organization, that problem is relatively minor. Not so in the big bureaucracy, as we shall see in Chapter 11, where the job of the visionary leader is 'turnaround.'

Premises of the entrepreneurial school

We summarize the premises that underlie the entrepreneurial view of strategy formation briefly below.

1 Strategy exists especially in the mind of the leader, as perspective, specifically a sense of long-term direction, a vision of the organization's future.

2 The process of strategy formation is semiconscious at best, rooted in the experience and intuition of the leader, whether he or she actually conceives the strategy or adopts it from others and then internalizes it in his or her own behaviour. While the mental process of 'intuition' remains a mysterious process, E. Dane and M. Pratt's (2007) review of the various literatures on intuition suggest that it converges on four characteristics as outlined in Box 5.5.

3 The leader promotes the vision single-mindedly, even obsessionally, maintaining close personal control of the implementation in order to be able to reformulate specific aspects as necessary.

4 The strategic vision is thus malleable, and so entrepreneurial strategy tends to be deliberate and emergent—deliberate in overall vision, as perspective and emergent in how the details of the vision unfold, including specific strategic positions.

5 The organization is likewise malleable, a simple structure responsive to the leader's directives, whether an actual startup, a company owned by an individual, or a turnaround in a large established organization many of whose procedures and power relationships are suspended to allow the visionary leader considerable latitude for manoeuvre.

6 Entrepreneurial strategy tends to take the form of niche, one or more pockets of market position protected from the forces of outright competition.

---

box 5.5

Intuition

(from Dane and Pratt, 2007: 33–54)

Intuiting is non-conscious

One of the defining characteristics of intuitive processing is that it is non-conscious—it occurs outside of conscious thought. . . . While the outcome of intuiting is accessible to conscious thinking, how one arrives at them is not. Hence, there is 'no awareness of the rules on knowledge used for inference' during intuiting (Shapiro and Spence, 1997: 64) . . . [T]his quality differentiates intuition from insight.

Intuiting involves making holistic associations

A second characteristic of intuiting is that it involves a process in which environmental stimuli are matched with some deeply held (non-conscious) category, pattern, or features. . . . This linking together of elements is why many refer to intuiting as being *associative*. . . . Further, because intuiting involves recognizing features or patterns . . ., rather than making connections through logical considerations, it has also been conceptualized as *holistic*. . . .

All told, it comes as little surprise that intuiting is perhaps better suited than rational methods to integrate wide ranging stimuli into usable categories of information. . . .

Intuiting is fast

A third characteristic of the human intuition process, and the one that has seemed to spark the most interest among both managers and academics, is its speed. . . .

Intuiting results in affectively charged judgments

Intuitive judgments often involve emotions. . . . Synonyms for intuition, such as 'gut feelings' and 'gut instincts', . . . as well as '*feeling* in our marrow' (Barnard, 1938: 306), reflect an affective component to intuitive judgments. . . . For example, Agor (1986) notes that as executives make intuitive judgments, they often experience excitement and harmony. . . . [R]ationality is often associated with the 'head' and intuition with the 'heart'—a common divide in philosophy. However, recent research suggests other possibilities. To begin with, intuitive judgments may be *triggered* by emotions and affect. Positive mood, for example, has been linked to an increase in the use of intuition and a decrease in more rational approaches to decision making . . .

Contribution, critique, and context of the entrepreneurial school

The entrepreneurial school has highlighted critical aspects of strategy formation, most notably its proactive nature and the role of personalized leadership and strategic vision. It is especially in their early years that organizations benefit from such a sense of direction and integration, or 'gestalt.' Visionary strategies stand in sharp contrast to the all-too-common 'me-too' strategies that result from uncreative or detached managements.

But the entrepreneurial school also exhibits some serious deficiencies. It presents strategy formation as all wrapped up in the behaviour of a single individual, yet can never really say much about what the process is. This has remained largely a black box, buried in human cognition. So for the organization that runs into difficulty, this school's central prescription can be all too obvious and facile: find a new visionary leader.

Moreover, the entrepreneurial school has never really come to grips with the fact that behaviours described as glorious and energizing by some of its writers have been seen as pathological and demotivating to others. Are these simply differences among writers, the pessimists who see the glass of entrepreneurship as half empty, the optimists as half full? Also, as discussed, many entrepreneurial leaders, especially visionaries, go over the edge. Is it merely some personal excess that does this? Or do conditions change so that what functioned so well before suddenly becomes dysfunctional—in other words that the organization simply has to move on, get past its obsession with 'the great one'? Clearly we can answer all of the above questions in the affirmative. What we really have to know is when entrepreneurial and visionary leadership is needed and how do we get it.

Under entrepreneurship, key decisions concerning strategy and operations are together centralized in the office of the chief executive. Such centralization can ensure that strategic response reflects full knowledge of the operations. It also encourages flexibility and adaptability: only one person need take the initiative. On the other hand, the chief can get so enmeshed in operating details on the ground that he or she loses sight of strategic considerations. Alternatively, the leader may end up in the clouds, enamoured of a vision that has lost its roots. The more routine operations may then wither for lack of attention and eventually pull down the whole organization. Both problems occur frequently in entrepreneurial situations.

Stacey (1992) has pointed to a number of 'harmful consequences of vision.' First, 'the advice to form a vision is neither concrete enough to be useful, nor is it possible when the future is unknowable.' Second, visions can fix managers too tightly in one direction: 'If you insist that managers should all share a common view of their future without question, you invite them to persist with what they already know how to do. Or, you encourage them to pursue what could be a disastrous new idea in a lemming-like dash to destruction, and while they are doing this, they will inevitably overlook other changes.'

Third, Stacey believes that the current quests for vision place 'a tremendous and unrealistic burden on the "leader".' A vision-driven philosophy perpetuates the myth that organizations have to rely on one or two unusually gifted individuals to decide what to do, while the rest enthusiastically follow. This advice perpetuates 'cultures of dependence and conformity that actually obstruct the questioning and complex learning which encourages innovative action.'

Finally, Stacey suggests that the advice about vision 'distracts attention from what people are really doing when they successfully handle unknowable futures—learning and political interaction' (44–6).

As suggested in these and earlier comments, the entrepreneurial approach is risky, hinging on the health and whims of one individual. One heart attack can literally wipe out the organization's key strategist. It is partly for this reason that Collins and Porras, in their popular book *Built to Last*, suggest that it is better to build a visionary organization than to rely on a leader with vision. They develop this difference in an imaginative way:

> ❝ one heart attack can literally wipe out the organization's key strategist ❞

Imagine you met a remarkable person who could look at the sun or stars at any time of day or night and state the exact time and date: 'It's April 23, 1401, 2:36 A.M., and 12 seconds.' This person would be an amazing time teller, and we'd probably revere that person for the ability to tell time. But wouldn't that person be even more amazing if, instead of telling the time, he or she *built* a clock that could tell time forever, even after he or she was dead and gone?

Having a great idea or being a charismatic visionary leader is 'time telling'; building a company that can prosper far beyond the presence of any single leader and through multiple product life cycles is 'clock building.' The builders of visionary companies tend to be clock builders, not time tellers. They concentrate primarily on building an organization—building a ticking clock—rather than on hitting a market just right with a visionary product . . . . And instead of concentrating on acquiring the individual personality traits of visionary leadership, they take an architectural approach and concentrate on building the organizational traits of visionary companies. The primary output of their efforts is not the tangible implementation of a great idea, the expression of a charismatic personality, the gratification of their ego, or the accumulation of personal wealth. Their greatest creation is *the company itself* and what it stands for. (1994: 22–3)

> Collins and Porras suggest from their study that the role of charisma in establishing vision is very much overrated, and that attempts to substitute charisma for substance are often destructive (1991: 51).
>
> This is one point of view, albeit provocative and interesting. What we need are more such studies on the positive and negative effects of entrepreneurship and vision, including where they seem to function most effectively and how they really do work. Perhaps entrepreneurship is less glorious than typically described, but also more functional, at least to get interesting ideas and (in the spirit of Collins and Porras) to get interesting organizations up and running. Obsessiveness does have a role to play in contemporary organizations!
>
> In spite of the shortage of such research, we do have some indication of the appropriate contexts of the entrepreneurial school. Clearly, as already noted, *startup* is one situation in need of forceful leadership and rich vision, since direction must be set and niches secured. (This tends to be equally true in the startup of government agencies and not-for-profit organizations.) Likewise, organizations in trouble—even

❝ organizations in trouble often have to defer to visionary leaders ❞

the largest, in business as well as nonbusiness—often have to defer to visionary leaders who can render dramatic changes through *turnaround*.

Also, many ongoing *small* organizations require this strong personalized leadership in perpetuity. Retailing may be the best example. In fact, probably the most commonly occurring strategy by far, yet one almost totally ignored in strategic management, is that of the 'local producer' (mentioned in the last chapter)—the organization that pursues a standard industry recipe in a clearly defined geographic niche. In other words, there are organizations distinguished strategically only by their locations: for example, pumping gas on a particular corner, bottling Coke in a particular town, collecting taxes in a particular nation. A great many of these organizations, at least at the corner and town level, would seem to be owner-managed. Clearly there are important pockets of organized society that still have great need for the kind of strategy formation promoted by the entrepreneurial school.

The cognitive school:
strategy formation as a mental process

"Miss Demby, bring my rose-coloured glasses.
I don't like the looks of this projection."

© 2008 Robert Mankoff from cartoonbank.com. All Rights Reserved.

'I'll see it when I believe it'

—Anonymous

If we are really serious about understanding strategic vision as well as how strategies form under other circumstances, then we had better probe into the mind of the strategist. That is the job of the cognitive school: to get at what this process means in the sphere of human cognition, drawing especially on the field of cognitive psychology.

This school has attracted a number of prominent researchers in the past ten or fifteen years, sometimes working in association with other schools (for example Tripsas and Gavetti (2000); Reger and Huff, 1993; Bogner and Thomas, 1993; see Lyles's survey of 1990). The body of work that we shall be discussing forms not so much a tight school of thought as a loose collection of research, which seems, nonetheless, to be growing into such a school. If it can deliver on its intentions, it could very well transform the teaching and practice of strategy as we know it today.

Prior to this surge of work, what took place in the minds of managers was largely terra incognita. Investigators were more concerned with the requisites for thinking than with thinking itself—for example with what a strategist needs to know. The focus has changed but we remain far from understanding the complex and creative thoughts that give rise to strategies.

Hence, strategists are largely self-taught: they develop their knowledge structures and thinking processes mainly through direct experience. That experience shapes what they know, which in turn shapes what they do, which then shapes their subsequent experience. This interplay of reflection and action plays a central role in the cognitive school, giving rise to two rather different wings.

One wing, more positivistic, treats the processing and structuring of knowledge as an effort to produce some kind of *objective vision* of the world. The mind's eye is seen as a kind of video camera: it scans the world, zooming in and out in response to its owner's will, although the pictures it takes are considered in this school to be rather distorted.

The other wing sees all of this as *subjective*: strategy is some kind of *interpretation* of the world. Here the mind's eye turns inward, on how the mind does its 'take' on what it sees out there—the events, the symbols, the behaviour of customers, and so on. So while the previous wing seeks to understand cognition as some kind of *re-creation* of the world, this wing drops the prefix and instead believes that cognition *creates* the world.

Notice where this chapter sits in this book: as a kind of bridge between the more objective schools of design, planning, positioning, and entrepreneurial, and the more subjective schools of learning, culture, power, etc. In line with this, we begin with the objectivist wing, first the research on cognitive biases, namely what research tells us about the mental limitations of the strategist, next on an information-processing view of strategic cognition, and finally on how the mind maps the structures of knowledge. Then we turn to the subjectivist wing, of strategic cognition as a process of construction. We conclude with observations about the limits of the cognitive approach as a framework for explaining strategic thinking.

Cognition as confusion

Scholars have long been fascinated by the peculiarities of how individuals process information to make decisions, especially the biases and distortions that they exhibit. Management researchers have been especially stimulated by the brilliant work of Herbert Simon (1947, 1957; see also March and Simon, 1958), a political scientist who spent most of his career at the business school and then the psychology department of Carnegie Mellon University. In 1978, he was awarded the Bank of Sweden Prize in Economics (named for Alfred Nobel). Simon popularized the notion that the world is large and complex, while human brains and their information-processing capacities are highly limited in comparison. Decision making thus becomes not so much rational as a vain effort to be rational.

A large research literature on judgmental biases followed. The work by the psychologists Tversky and Khaneman (1974)—the latter also received that prize in 2002, generally referred to as 'prospect theory', broke new ground in our understanding of how biases influence decision making. Some of the key results of this literature have been summarized by Makridakis (1990), and reproduced in Table 6.1, have obvious consequences for strategy making. These include the search for evidence that supports rather than denies beliefs, the favouring of more easily remembered recent information over earlier information, the tendency to see causal effect between two variables that may simply be correlated, and the power of wishful thinking. Makridakis also devoted considerable attention to what he called 'unfounded beliefs or conventional wisdom,' commenting:

> " we need an understanding of how biases influence decision making "

We have grown up in a culture where we accept certain statements as true, though they may not be. For instance, we believe that the more information we have, the more accurate our decisions will be. Empirical evidence does not support such a belief. Instead, more information merely seems to increase our confidence that we are right without necessarily improving the accuracy of our decisions. . . . In reality, the information found is usually redundant and provides little additional value. (38)

Moreover, analogies and metaphors, which as we saw in the last chapter can open up thinking, may also work in the opposite way, by oversimplifying and so narrowing the range of solutions we consider (Schwenk, 1988, and Steinbruner, 1974). Duhaime and Schwenk (1985) have probed into how these and other distortions can affect acquisition and divestment decisions:

1 **Reasoning by analogy**. The authors cite an example where an 'acquisition candidate was seen by management as "the third leg of a stool" supporting the company's high rates of return. This image or analogy suggested to company managers that they enter a line of business not closely related . . . to current businesses.' (289).

table 6.1 Biases in decision making

Type of bias	Description of bias
Search for supportive evidence	Willingness to gather facts which lead toward certain conclusions and to disregard other facts which threaten them
Inconsistency	Inability to apply the same decision criteria in similar situations
Conservatism	Failure to change (or changing slowly) one's own mind in light of new information/evidence
Recency	The most recent events dominate those in the less recent past, which are downgraded or ignored
Availability	Reliance upon specific events easily recalled from memory, to the exclusion of other pertinent information
Anchoring	Predictions are unduly influenced by initial information which is given more weight in the forecasting process
Illusory correlations	Belief that patterns are evident and/or two variables are causally related when they are not
Selective perception	People tend to see problems in terms of their own background and experience
Regression effects	Persistent increases [in some phenomenon] might be due to random reasons which, if true, would [raise] the chance of a [subsequent] decrease. Alternatively, persistent decreases might [raise] the chances of [subsequent] increases
Attribution of success and failure	Success is attributed to one's skills while failure to bad luck, or someone else's error. This inhibits learning as it does not allow recognition of one's mistakes
Optimism, wishful thinking	People's preferences for future outcomes affect their forecasts of such outcomes
Underestimating uncertainty	Excessive optimism, illusory correlation, and the need to reduce anxiety result in underestimating future uncertainty

Source: Reprinted with the permission of The Free Press, a Division of Simon & Schuster Adult Publishing Group, from FORCASTING, PLANNING, AND STRATEGY FOR THE 21st CENTURY by Spyros G. Makridakis. Copyright © 1990 by Spyros G. Makridakis, All rights reserved.

2 **Illusion of control.** 'Decision makers may overestimate the extent to which the outcomes of an acquisition are under their personal control and may assume that they can make the business succeed should problems arise' (289). This can reduce anxiety about a decision, but lead to problems as well.

3 **Escalating commitment**. This 'involves continued and increasing investment in the face of poor and declining outcomes of performance' (291). Staw (1976) popularized this concept in an article entitled 'Knee Deep in the Big Muddy,' about the escalating commitment of the United States government to the Vietnam War in the face of repeated failures.

4 **Single outcome calculation**. 'Some evidence suggests that once divestment is considered as a way of dealing with a failing unit, it may quickly become the *only* alternative considered. . . . This process allows decision makers to deny the unpleasant value trade-offs that are always present in a choice between alternatives, and it significantly reduces the stress associated with ill-structured decision making' (292).

With so many different biases confronting decision makers, creating strategies that are not distorted by biases seem hopelessly difficult. Das and Teng (1999) suggest that in practice one way that decision makers can tackle this problem is by consciously neutralizing biases that are associated with their particular approach to the strategy process. For example, managers who follow rational and systematic decision processes should be aware that are likely to fall prey to the illusion of control. By contrast, managers who are comfortable with ill-structured decision making processes should be conscious of their susceptibility to single outcome calculation. In other words, they are not only less likely to explore alternatives, but also to display relative disregard to the probability of outcomes when making decisions.

Das and Teng's (1999) review demonstrates that there is no shortage of evidence about organizations that got locked into set ways of doing things, based on set ways of *seeing* things, and then spiralled downward as the world around them changed (see Bazerman, 2005). Put differently, to use our opening quotation, 'I'll see it when I believe it' could well be the motto of the cognitive school (both wings, as we shall soon see).

Indeed, the doing can influence the seeing too. Recall the laboratory finding by Kiesler (1971) cited in Chapter 2, that having people articulate their approach to solving a problem created a resistance to changing that approach, compared with people who did not discuss what they were doing. In other words, making a strategy explicit can create psychological resistance to changing strategy. And Kiesler's was a study of single minds; imagine what happens in the collection of minds that constitute an organization. Hence the popular term 'groupthink' (Janis, 1972). Even 'beneficial change is often resisted by loyal members who sincerely want what is best for the organization' (Reger *et al.*, 1994: 567).

Of course, strategists differ in their *cognitive styles*. So psychologists who study such style characteristics as 'cognitive complexity' and 'openness' help to inform strategy making too. Best known in this regard is probably the Myers-Briggs instrument (Myers, 1962), based on the work of Karl Jung. They propose four sets of opposite dimensions:

Extroversion (E) (energized by the outside world)	— Introversion (I) (energized by the world inside one's own head)
Sensing (S) (information comes from relying on the senses)	— Intuition (N) (information comes from trying to grasp the essential patterns)
Thinking (T) (relying on analysis for decision)	— Feeling (F) (relying on feelings for decision)
Judgment (J) (to live in a planned, orderly, controlled way)	— Perception (P) (to live in a flexible, spontaneous way)

Combining these leads to sixteen possible types or styles. For example, the ESTJs ('Extroverted Thinking Sensing Judging') are 'logical, analytical, objective, critical, and not likely to be convinced by anything but reasoning. . . . They like to organize facts', but 'run the risk of deciding too quickly before they have fully examined the situation' (10). In contrast, the ESFPs ('Extroverted Sensing Feeling Perceiving') are 'friendly, adaptable realists . . . relying on what they can see, hear, and know first hand. . . . They solve problems by being adaptable . . . [but] are not necessarily bound by a need to follow standard procedures or preferred methods' (19). If these two styles sound like the strategists of our positioning and learning schools respectively, then we can see how these researchers can help us get inside the different schools of strategy making.

Cognition as information processing

Beyond the biases in individual cognition are the effects of working in the collective entities for processing information that we call organizations. Managers are information workers. They serve their own needs for information as well as that of their colleagues and others around them. In large organizations especially, this creates all sorts of well-known problems. For example, senior managers have limited time to oversee vast arrays of activities, hence much of the information they receive has to be aggregated, which can pile distortions upon distortions. If the original inputs have been subjected to the biases discussed above, then think about what happens when all of this gets combined and presented to the 'boss.' No wonder so many senior managers become the captives of their information-processing organizations.

In what they call a 'parallel' information-processing model, Corner *et al.*, (1994) argue that individuals and organizations operate along essentially the same principles. Information processing begins with attention, continues with encoding, turns to storage and retrieval, culminates in choice, and concludes by the assessment of outcomes. This is illustrated in Figure 6.1 and described below.

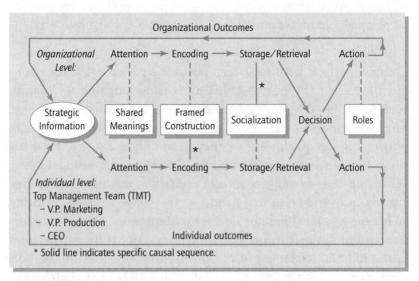

figure 6.1   A parallel process model of strategic decision making

Source: Corner, Kinicki, and Keats (1994:296).

Attention

Attention determines what information will be processed and what will be ignored, acting much like a receptionist who screens callers according to certain priorities, blocking out some and rushing others in.

Encoding

Encoding gives information meaning, by looking for its fit with existing categories, for example, that someone calling is a 'customer.' Such categories can, however, be the source of bias, by driving out nuance. Whatever gets put into a category risks becoming a stereotype.

Storage/Retrieval

Cognition begins with memory. In the case of individuals, memory is a web of associations between different items of information. In the case of organizations, the associations are also embodied in forms, rules, procedures, conventions, and technologies. The link between the two is socialization: the organization works on the individual to accept existing routines. Then these routines become part of the individual's own memory, thus attuning cognition to organization.

Decision

What organizations in retrospect call 'decisions' are choices embedded and enmeshed in cognitive processes. In most organizations strategic choices are collective in the sense that different levels of the organization participate and exert influence, for example by directing attention to certain problems, or making available previously encoded information. Cognitive processes do not produce 'decisions,' but they often create and reinforce a need to resolve issues. When the resolution takes the form of a 'decision' there is a tendency to see the outcome as the end product of rational analysis, but in fact the process is emergent. The notion of a definitive category called 'decision' may help to undertake action as well as to gather further information, but that category too cannot be viewed as some isolated event. (See Box 6.2, 'Does Decision Get in the Way?')

Outcomes

Outcomes herald the beginning of the feedback process. Individuals and organizations make sense of their choices and feed this understanding into the ongoing processing of information—namely back to attention, encoding, storage, and retrieval. But this process is sometimes hampered by past learning which must be unlearned. William Starbuck outlines some strategies for 'unlearning' current beliefs and methods in Box 6.1.

---

box 6.1

Unlearning

(Excerpted from William H. Starbuck, 1996, 11: 725–37).

Since the essential requirement for unlearning is doubt, any event or message that engenders doubt about current beliefs and methods can become a stimulus for unlearning. There are at least eight viewpoints that can help people turn events and messages into such stimuli.

'It isn't good enough.'

Dissatisfaction is probably the most common reason for doubting current beliefs and methods. . . .

'It's only an experiment.'

People who see themselves as experimenting are willing to deviate temporarily from practices they consider optimal in order to test their assumptions. When they deviate, they create opportunities to surprise themselves. . . . They find it easier to alter their beliefs and methods to allow for new insights

'Surprises should be question marks.'

Events that violate expectations, both unpleasant disruptions and pleasant surprises, can become opportunities for unlearning. For instance, the Allies developed the tank during World War I, and most army officers viewed the tank as lethargic support for the infantry. . . .

'All dissents and warnings have some validity.'

Listeners need to guard against hasty rejections of bad news or unfamiliar ideas. At a minimum, dissents and warnings can remind people that diverse viewpoints exist and that their own beliefs and methods may be wrong. . . .

▶ ## 'Collaborators who disagree are both right.'

Beliefs held by qualified observers nearly always have foundations in some sort of truth. The most common problem is not to prove that one set of beliefs is wrong but to reconcile apparent contradictions by showing that they are not contradictions at all. These efforts can lead everyone to new conceptualizations. They can also produce some strange inversions. . . .

'What does a stranger think strange?'

It is usually easier to respect the views of collaborators than those of strangers. Unfamiliar with current methods and unacquainted with recent efforts, strangers are likely to make suggestions that seem naïve or ignorant or foolish. Yet, new people often introduce new perspectives. Although the newcomers may be less expert than their predecessors, they are also free of some expectations that their predecessors took for granted. Thus, strangers may be able to see peculiarities that the indoctrinated cannot see or they may be able to offer breakthrough suggestions.

'All causal arrows have two heads.'

People can use thought processes that tend to disclose and challenge their tacit assumptions. One useful heuristic is to insist that all causal paths carry influence in both directions: Whenever one perceives that A affects B, one should also look for ways in which B feeds back and affects A. There are some causal paths that do not carry influence in both directions. However, one-directional causation is rare because systems that can converge toward equilibrium have to entail feed-backs. Searching carefully for these feedback paths can lead one to see previously overlooked causal paths.

'The converse of every proposition is equally valid.'

Dialectic reasoning is a generalization of two-directional causation. Starting from a proposition (A affects B), one states the converse proposition (B affects A) and then one insists that both the original proposition and its converse are valid. The philosopher Georg Hegel, who advocated this mode of reasoning, called the original proposition the thesis, its converse the antithesis, and their union, the synthesis. As with causal paths, not every thesis has a valid antithesis and not every thesis can be synthesized with its antithesis. But it is possible to apply dialectic reasoning to almost all situations and the process of applying it helps one to break free of tacit assumptions.

Cognition as mapping

In spite of the diversity of views in the cognitive school, on one point there is widespread agreement: an essential prerequisite for strategic cognition is the existence of mental structures to organize knowledge. These are the 'frames' referred to above, although a host of other labels have been used over the years, including schema, concept, script, plan, mental model, and map.

---

box 6.2

Does decision get in the way?

(from Mintzberg and Waters, 1990, as adapted in Langley *et al.*, 1995)

Most of the research [on decision making] has proceeded initially, not from decision so much as action, for example, the purchase of a computer or the acquisition of a firm. It then assumed decision: that some identifiable moment of commitment inevitably preceded action. In other words, if an organization *did* something, it must have previously *decided* to do so.

... In fact, the relationship between decision and action can be far more tenuous than almost all of the literature ... suggests.

For one thing, action can occur without commitment to act. The doctor who strikes your knee knows that and so does the judge who accepts that when a murder is planned and deliberate, it is called first degree, otherwise it is second degree. In other words, in law, people can murder without deciding.

Transferring to the organizational context, consider the following comment by an executive of the then world's largest corporation:

It is often difficult to say who decided something and when—or even who originated a decision. . . . I frequently don't know when a decision is made in General Motors. I don't remember being in a committee meeting when things came to a vote. Usually someone will simply summarize a developing position. Everyone else either nods or states his particular terms of consensus. (Quoted in Quinn, 1980a: 134)

But organizations can act even without explicit consensus. The story circulated in Europe several years ago that the top management of another large automobile firm had hired consultants to find out who in their company 'decided' to introduce a major new model. Perhaps someone really did decide; but conceivably no one did. Someone may have just produced a clay model of a speculative design, someone else may have perceived the engineering implications of this, and, like a

> rolling snowball, thousands of 'decisions' and actions later—concerning bumpers and assembly lines and advertising campaigns—a new automobile appeared. . . .
>
> Must there always be a clear *point* as well as a clear *place* of decision? . . . Consider the example of a company that announces the 'decision' to build a new factory. Tracing back, one might find a minute of a board meeting in which the 'decision' was 'made,' which really means recorded. But perhaps the real commitment preceded that minute by six months, when the owner-president visited the site and made up his or her mind.
>
> It is, in fact, a precept of one particular form of organization—the machine-like bureaucracy—that explicit commitment must precede all action. Administrators are supposed to decide formally, and then have that choice formally 'authorized' in the hierarchy 'above,' before others are expected to implement the choice 'below. . . .'
>
> The important conclusion to be drawn from all this is that decision, like so many other concepts in organization theory, is sometimes an artificial construct, a psychological one that imputes commitment to action. For individuals as well as for organizations, commitment need not precede action, or, perhaps more commonly, whatever commitment does precede action can be vague and confusing.

Map is a currently popular label, perhaps because of its metaphoric value. It implies the navigation through confusing terrain with some kind of representative model. Karl Weick likes to recount a story about a Hungarian military unit on manoeuvres in the Alps that did not return after two days in a snowstorm. On the third day, the soldiers appeared, and explained:

Yes, they said, we considered ourselves lost and waited for the end. And one of us found a map in his pocket. That calmed us down. We pitched camp, lasted out the snowstorm, and through the map we discovered our bearings. And here we are. The lieutenant [who had dispatched the unit] borrowed this remarkable map and had a good look at it. He discovered to his astonishment that it was not a map of the Alps, but a map of the Pyrenees. (1995: 54)

❝ the map prefigures their perceptions, and they see what they expect to see ❞

The moral of the story is clear: when you are lost, any map will do! In other words, a wrong mental representation is better than no representation at all, for at least it gives encouragement, and so can stimulate action. As Weick explained:

With the map in hand, no matter how crude it is, people encode what they see to conform as closely as possible to what is on the map. The map prefigures their perceptions, and they see what they expect to see. But, as discrepancies accumulate, they pay closer attention to what is in their immediate experience, look for patterns in it, and pay less attention to the map. The map in hand then becomes more metaphorical but, ironically, only because it was the means by which other, more current maps were formed. (1990: 5)[1]

> There are, of course, all kinds of maps, in management, just as in geography, each with its own uses. Ann Huff (1990), one of the most active writers in the cognitive school, has distinguished descriptive cognitive maps that simply identify the factors that are important to managers (for example, a profile of important competitors) from causal cognitive maps that show the cause/effect relationships among these different factors (for example, how important competitors will respond to price cuts).

> Maps of the first type are often referred to as *schemas*, a term borrowed from cognitive psychology. Everyone is bombarded with data. The problem is how to store it and make it available on a moment's notice. Schemas do this by representing knowledge at different levels. This enables people to create full pictures from rudimentary data—to fill in the blanks. For example, when one reads about the possibility of another 'oil crisis,' the mind likely triggers a schema with knowledge at the political, economic, and technological levels. Certain implicit assumptions go with this schema. At the political level the assumption may be that an oil crisis is caused by some sort of war or military aggression. At the economic level, one may think about cartels and higher gasoline prices, while at the technological level, thoughts may turn to tradeoffs between heating oil and natural gas.

---

1 Without disputing Weick's basic point, experience in the Alps suggests to one of the authors that this particular analogy may be unfortunate. The possible safe routes in such rugged terrain can be so few and so obscure that the odds of getting out with the wrong map—as opposed to being led over a cliff—may be low indeed. In other words, content does count, not only process, in the positions and patterns of strategy no less than the details of a map, especially in rugged terrain.

Schemas, in other words, drive expectations of what decision makers notice. Noticing adds details to schemas which in turn produces new questions. How are prices likely to climb? Will people turn to natural gas instead of oil to heat their houses? Note that these questions can emerge almost automatically from the schema. This is what makes schemas efficient from an information-processing point of view. Yet that also means that evidence inconsistent with the schema is ignored. Following the 1973 oil crisis, governments around the world invested in expensive alternate technologies, ignoring evidence that higher oil prices were due to temporary supply constraints. When prices fell, alternative technology programmes were abandoned. Thirty years later the world is once again facing higher oil prices, but this time the push to develop alternate technologies is shaped by climate change schemas rather than concern about economics.

Of course, activating a schema is one thing, deciding whether or not to act is another. Here, causal cognitive maps which detail relationships between supply, demand, price, timing, etc., play an important role. All experienced managers carry around in their heads schemas that describe causal relationships. And their impact on behaviour can be profound. For example, Barr *et al.*, (1992) compared two railroads, Rock Island and C&NW, over a twenty-five-year period (1949–73). They were similar to begin with, but one eventually went bankrupt while the other survived. The researchers attributed this to their managers' causal maps about the environment. Initially, both firms ascribed poor performance to bad weather, government programmes, and regulations. Then one firm's maps shifted to a focus on the relationships between costs, productivity, and management style, and that provoked the necessary changes.

Cognition as concept attainment

Managers are, of course, map makers as well as map users. How they create their cognitive maps is key to our understanding of strategy making. Indeed, in the most fundamental sense, this *is* strategy making. A strategy is a *concept*, and so, to draw on an old term from cognitive psychology, strategy making is 'concept attainment.'

On this important issue, despite an early start (e.g., Bruner and his colleagues, 1956), cognitive psychology has not been terribly helpful. Perhaps the problem lies with its long-favoured research methodology—the elicitation of 'protocols,' or verbal accounts by decision makers as they go about making decisions. The really interesting mental processes related to the development of strategy—visual perception, synthesis, so-called intuition, the parallel processing of data—may be buried deep in our subconscious minds. In other words, much of our crucial knowledge may be 'tacit' (Polanyi, 1966): we may know far more than we can tell.

As noted earlier, especially influential in how we view the cognition of managerial decision making has been the work of Herbert Simon. Simon argued repeatedly and forcefully that words such as 'judgment, intuition, and creativity' are not mysterious at all:

The first thing we have learned—and the evidence for this is by now substantial—is that these human processes can be explained *without* postulating mechanisms at subconscious levels that are different from those that are partly verbalized. Much of the iceberg is, indeed, below the surface and inaccessible to verbalization, but its concealed bulk is made of the same kind of ice as the part we can see. . . . The secret of problem solving is that there is no secret. It is accomplished through complex structures of familiar simple elements. (1977: 69)

> **❝ much of the iceberg is, indeed, below the surface ❞**

In a later article, Simon (1987) went on to argue that the essence of intuition lies in the *organization* of knowledge for quick identification ('arranged in terms of recognizable chunks' [60]) and not in the rendering of that knowledge for inspired design. In his words: 'Intuition and judgment—at least good judgment—are simply *analyses frozen into habit* and into the capacity for rapid response through recognition' (1987: 63, italics added). But this view is open to question.

Consider this explanation of one famous exercise of creative synthesis:

One day when we were vacationing in Santa Fe in 1943 my daughter, Jennifer, who was then 3, asked me why she could not see the picture I had just taken of her. As I walked around that charming town, I undertook the task of solving the puzzle she had set for me. Within the hour the camera, the film and the physical chemistry became so clear that with a great sense of excitement I hurried to the place where a friend was staying to describe to him in detail a dry camera which would give a picture immediately after exposure. In my mind it was so real that I spent several hours on the description. (Edwin Land, the inventor of the Polaroid Camera, quoted in *Time* magazine, 1972: 84)

> What 'familiar element' did Land recognize here? Which of his analyses were frozen into what kind of habit? Indeed, how exactly did his rationality bound him? Land claimed elsewhere that during his periods of creative insight, 'atavistic competencies seem to come welling up. You are handling so many variables at a barely conscious level that you can't afford to be interrupted' (in Bello, 1959: 158), least of all by a researcher demanding verbal protocols!
>
> The source of insights may be mysterious, but their appearance is not, whether they be Land's revelation or even Kohler's (1925) famous ape, who realized quite suddenly that he could get the banana hanging high in his cage if he put the box sitting in the corner under it (see also Hadamard, 1949).
>
> In reference to the Japanese executive, Shimizu (1980) has referred to insight as 'intuitive sensibility,' an 'ability to grasp instantly an understanding of the whole structure of new information.' He mentioned the 'sixth sense or *kan*' which, in contrast to the 'sequential steps of logical thinking,' entails the 'fitting together of memory fragments that had until then been mere accumulation of various connected information' (23). *In*-sight, seeing inside, seems to come to the decision maker when he or she sees beyond given facts to understand the deeper meaning of an issue.

A great deal of the behavior of organizations . . . is determined by those occasional insights that restructure thinking, as in Land's idea for a camera that created a major corporation and reconfigured a major market. If the soldier's lot is months of boredom interrupted by moments of terror, to cite an old adage, then the lot of organizations may likewise be described as years of routine reconfigured by flashes of insight, those of their competitors if not their own. How, then, can the adjective 'strategic' possibly be applied to any theory of decision making that does not take account of such insights? (Langley *et al.*, 1995: 268)

Careful study of the strategy making process in organizations repeatedly bears witness to phenomena of this nature—at the very heart of the process. We need to understand, therefore, how it is that strategists are sometimes able to synthesize vast arrays of soft information into new perspectives. Perhaps this will require less study of words and other 'recognizable chunks' and more recognition of images. Drawing on the famous story of Nassruden, who looked for his lost keys under the lamppost, where the light was better, rather than where he actually lost them, have the cognitive psychologists been looking for clues to mental behaviour in the light of verbal protocols while the answers have been lost in the darkness of the processes we label intuition and insight?

If so, then perhaps cognitive psychology may prove less helpful than the harder science of physiology. The work of Roger Sperry (1974), which gained him a Nobel Prize in physiology suggests the existence of two very different sets of processes operating within the human brain. One, accessible to verbalization, is usually associated with the left hemisphere, while the other, more spatial, is apparently often found in the mute right hemisphere. Have we, therefore, focused too much of our research and technique of strategic management on the wrong side of the human brain?

Overall, we have a long way to go in understanding the critical mental processes of strategy making as concept attainment. Dane and Pratt's (2007) analysis of 'intuition', as outlined in Box 6.3, is a useful contribution. But notwithstanding recent research, we must conclude that the cognitive school, while potentially the most important of the ten, practically may well now be the least.

---

box 6.3

Intuition

(Excerped from Dane and Pratt, 2007: 33–54)

Intuiting is non-conscious

One of the defining characteristics of intuitive processing is that it is non-conscious—it occurs outside of conscious thought. . . . While the outcome of intuiting is accessible to conscious thinking, how one arrives at them is not. Hence, there is 'no awareness of the rules on knowledge used for inference' during intuiting (Shapiro and Spence, 1997: 64) . . . [T]his quality differentiates intuition from insight.

▶ ## Intuiting involves making holistic associations

A second characteristic of intuiting is that it involves a process in which environmental stimuli are matched with some deeply held (non-conscious) category, pattern, or feature. . . . This linking together of elements is why many refer to intuiting as being associative. . . . Further, because intuiting involves recognizing features or patterns . . ., rather than making connections through logical considerations, it has also been conceptualized as *holistic*. . . .

All told, it comes as little surprise that intuiting is perhaps better suited than rational methods to integrate wide ranging stimuli into usable categories of information. . . .

Intuiting is fast

A third characteristic of the human intuition process, and the one that has seemed to spark the most interest among both managers and academics, is its speed. . . .

Intuiting results in affectively charged judgments

Intuitive judgments often involve emotions. . . . Synonyms for intuition, such as 'gut feelings' and 'gut instincts,' . . . as well as 'feeling in our *marrow*' (Barnard, 1938: 306), reflect an affective component to intuitive judgments. . . . For example, Agor (1986) notes that as executives make intuitive judgments, they often experience excitement and harmony. . . .

[R]ationality is often associated with the 'head' and intuition with the 'heart'—a common divide in philosophy. However, recent research suggests other possibilities. To begin with, intuitive judgments may be *triggered* by emotions and affect. Positive mood, for example, has been linked to an increase in the use of intuition and a decrease in more rational approaches to decision making.

Cognition as construction

There is another side to the cognitive school (at least as we interpret it), very different and potentially, perhaps, more fruitful. This views strategy as interpretation, based on cognition as construction.[2]

---

2 Chaffee (1985) has in fact identified this alongside the 'rational' view (our first three schools) and the 'adaptive' view (our learning school) as one of three major approaches of strategy formation. See also Johnson (1987: 56–7), who links the two main wings of the cognitive school with that of the cultural school.

To proponents of this view, the world 'out there' does not simply drive behavior 'in here'. Cognition is therefore much more than an effort to mirror reality by removing distortion, bias, and simplification. For if it was, these people point out, how would we explain strategies that change the world? Where do they come from?

For this *interpretative,* or *constructionist,* view, what is inside the human mind is not a reproduction of the external world. All that information flowing in through those filters, supposedly to be decoded by those cognitive maps, in fact interacts with cognition and is shaped by it. The mind, in other words, imposes some interpretation on the environment—it constructs its world. In a sense, the mind has a mind of its own—it marches to its own cognitive drummer. Or perhaps we might better say *they* march, because there is a collective dimension to this too: people interact to create their mental worlds. (Of course, there is a collective dimension to the other wing of the cognitive school too, as is evident, for example, in 'groupthink.' We shall delve more deeply into collective perception in the cultural school.)

This view has radical implications. Researchers who subscribe to it fully, called 'social constructionists,' break decisively with the pervasive tendency to accept what we see as a given, that is to ascribe to the status quo a logical inevitability. To them, outside reality with all its rich details actually exists inside our heads.

Social constructionists owe much to the philosophical revolution that swept Europe after the Second World War. This revolution crossed over to psychology in the unusual work of Gregory Bateson. Observing monkeys playing with each other in a zoo started him thinking about how animals that cannot communicate directly nevertheless seem to 'understand' each other.

❝the mind constructs its own world❞

In an essay titled 'A Theory of Play and Fantasy,' which he wrote in 1955, Bateson suggested that the answer to this conundrum in both animals and humans lies in the ubiquity of what he called *frames*. For example, the frame 'this is play' allows the monkey to distinguish gestures that are playful from those that are not.

Monkeys do not negotiate an agreement to play; their social life has taught them the frame 'play.' The same principle holds for humans, except that we have enormous numbers of frames which are generally more complex and have many different levels of interpretation.

The psychological frame, Bateson argued, performs a function not dissimilar to that of a picture frame: it resolves the ambiguity of what is 'inside' and what is 'outside,' what is 'real' within the context of interaction between viewer and situation and what is not. More generally, a psychological frame, according to Bateson, has the following properties:

1 Psychological frames are exclusive, i.e., by including certain messages (or meaningful actions) within a frame, certain other messages are excluded.

2 Psychological frames are inclusive, i.e., by excluding certain messages certain others are included. The frame around a picture, if we consider the perception of the viewer, says, 'Attend to what is within and do not attend to what is outside.'

3 Psychological frames are related to 'premises.' The picture frame tells the viewer that he or she is not to use the same sort of thinking in interpreting the picture that might be used in interpreting the wallpaper outside the frame.

4 [Thus] a frame is metacommunicative. Any message, which either explicitly or implicitly defines a frame, *ipso facto* gives the receiver instructions or aids in any attempt to understand the messages included within the frame. (1972: 187)

Whereas the concept of schemas has been widely used by researchers, that of frame is only beginning to get the attention it deserves. One of the earliest, and probably still the best research of the use of frames by managers was done by El Sawy and Pauchant (1988). They studied how seventeen professionals and managers working as a group dealt with information about strategic opportunities in the emerging cellular telephone market. The group met regularly over a period of three months. They began with discussion of initial information about the market and the technology. A consensus gradually emerged on two frames: the potential cellular phone market and the potential applications for cellular phones. Further information, mostly from media and trade journals, was fed to the group during the rest of the study.

Of primary interest to El Sawy and Pauchant was the interaction between the initial frames and the subsequent information. When frames and information were at odds with each other, was the frame modified or the information reinterpreted? This came up when information that the use of the cellular phone could be dangerous while driving led one group member to declare that the frame defining the potential for cellular phone applications had to be drastically modified. In defence of the initial frame, the other group members offered the following pieces of information: (a) owners of cellular phones were safer drivers than nonowners; (b) 'no-hands' operation capabilities for cellular phones were being developed, and (c) having a cellular phone allows drivers to call for help in case of accident. The group member was thus 'persuaded' that the frame was correct, and so the threat to the shared constructed reality passed, and subsequent information continued to be interpreted along the same lines as before.

This study points to a distinction between the schema which essentially belongs to the individual, and the frames which belong to the group. The schema depends on what the individual sees and believes. The frame, on the other hand, depends on group dynamics—on the relationships of individuals to each other and to the group. Indeed, when it comes to groups, individuals 'see' the market or 'perceive' the competition because they share information with others who have the same schema. Of course, this can lead to the groupthink we discussed earlier: the dependence on an interpretation of reality that resists contrary evidence.

One obvious conclusion is that to avoid this problem managers need a rich repertoire of frames—alternate views of their world, so as not to be imprisoned by any one. Hence the success of books such as Gareth Morgan's *Images of Organizations* (1986), which offers chapters on seeing organizations as machines, as organisms, as brains, and so on. Bolman and Deal's *Reframing Organizations* (1997) suggests that managerial insight hinges on a willingness to use multiple lenses, which they too present. (A book on different schools of thought on strategy formation might be considered a companion of these two.)

The problem, of course, is that the practice of management requires focus, sometimes (as we saw in the last chapter) even obsession. 'On the one hand, on the other hand' is hardly the best route to decisive action. On the other hand, opening up perspectives is also critical for effective management.

Is the 'environment' constructed?

The social constructionist view begins with a strong premise: no one in an organization 'sees' the environment. Instead, organizations construct it from rich and ambiguous information in which even such basic categories as 'inside' and 'outside' can be very fuzzy. While this premise is strongly supported by evidence, what the social constructionists do with it is more controversial. They argue that since environments are constructed within the organization, they are little more than the product of managerial beliefs. Harking back to Figure 2.1 of the design school, the big box that deals with the environment, of which the positioning school made so much of—here gets relegated to a minor role (as, of course does the whole positioning school). And in its place appears that most obscure box on the chart—the beliefs of the managers.

Many people baulk at this conclusion. Surely, they say, there is an environment out there. Markets are, after all, littered with the debris of companies that got them wrong, regardless (or some would say because) of what their managers believed. To this social constructionists reply: this objection itself represents a simplistic assumption about the meaning of 'environment.' Smircich and Stubbart (1985) help to clarify this by describing three competing conceptions of the environment. Historically, our understanding has moved from the first, through the second, and now toward the third:

1 **The Objective Environment.** . . . [This] assumes that an 'organization' is embedded within an 'environment' that has an external and independent existence. . . . Terms that seem to capture this sense of 'environment' include concrete, objective, independent, given, imminent, out there. . . . Nearly all strategic management research and writing incorporates [this] assumption. . . . Environmental analysis thus entails *discovery*, or finding

things that are *already somewhere* waiting to be found . . . [and then] to delineate a strategy that will meet [them].

2 **The Perceived Environment.** . . . [This does not mean] a change in the conception of environment (which remains real, material, and external). Instead, the difference . . . involves a distinction about strategists. Strategists are permanently trapped by bounded rationality . . . and by their incomplete and imperfect perceptions of the 'environment.' . . . From a practical standpoint, the challenge . . . is minimizing the gap between [their] flawed perceptions and the reality of their environment.

3 **The Enacted Environment.** . . . From an interpretative worldview, *separate objective* 'environments' simply do not exist. . . . Instead, organizations and environments are convenient labels for patterns of activity. What people refer to as their environment is generated by human actions and accompanying intellectual efforts to make sense out of their actions. . . . The world is essentially an ambiguous field of experience. There are no threats or opportunities out there in the environment, just material and symbolic records of action. But a strategist—determined to find meaning—makes relationships by bringing connections and patterns to action. . . . [For example] there is

" strategists create imaginary lines between events, objects, and situations "

really no Big Dipper in the sky, although people find it useful to imagine that there is. People see the Big Dipper when they furnish imaginary lines to cluster and make sense of the stars . . . astronomers [use] their own imaginations to produce a symbolic reality (Orion, the Lion, etc.). The same is true for strategists. . . . By themselves . . . automobiles, oil wells, and missiles are meaningless, and they appear as random as the stars appear to an untrained eye. Strategists create imaginary lines between events, objects, and situations so that [they] become meaningful for the members of an organizational world. (725–6)

While the first conception is clearly favoured by our three prescriptive schools, especially that of positioning, the second and third conceptions represent, respectively, the views of the two wings of the cognitive school. But these two are wholly different. What one sees as the basis for distortion, the other takes as the opportunity for creation.

Under this constructionist perspective, strategy making takes on a whole new colour. Metaphors become important, as do symbolic actions and communications (Chaffee, 1985: 94), all based on the manager's total life experience (Hellgren and Melin, 1993). And vision emerges as more than an instrument for guidance: it becomes the leader's interpretation of the world made into a collective reality. Smircich and Stubbart's implications of this for managerial action are outlined in the accompanying box.

Competition and cognition

Competition presents an intriguing challenge to the cognitive school. At first sight, there is nothing more objective than competition: If your rivals make better products and offer lower prices you must respond, or else you will eventually be out of business. You surely cannot 'construct' you way out of this situation. All you can do is strive to correctly perceive the competitive signals that your competitors are sending out, and act accordingly.

But hold on, say some scholars, the story is not that simple. Interpreting what your rivals are doing is objective only in retrospect. While you are engaged in the competitive struggle there is usually considerable ambiguity about what they are attempting to do. This is not simply because you lack information, but because the information that comes your way is complex and contradictory (see Lampel and Shapira, 2001). To make sense of this information, you have to engage in a complex process of interpretation in which imagination and evidence are inseparable and play equally important roles.

It is lack of conscious effort while engaging in this process, argue the same scholars, which makes competition appear objective. Experienced managers are adept at transforming ambiguous information into clear mental images. But this has less to do with objectivity than with stability. In many, if not most industries, competition is relatively predictable. There are 'rules of the game' so to speak. As managers are socialized into their business they learn these rules, and come to see them as an objective aspect of the competitive environment. When everybody behaves according to what they believe are the rules it is but a small step to believing that the rules, reflect objective reality to which firms must conform if they are to survive.

But this view of how managers make sense of competition is increasingly being questioned by researchers who argue that managerial cognition changes when regular competition becomes what Richard D'Aveni (1994) has called 'hypercompetition.' In hypercompetition, rivalry is aggressive, without boundaries or rules; it is 'characterized by intense and rapid competitive moves, in which competitors must move quickly to build advantage and erode the advantage of their rivals' (pp. 217–18). Seeking sustainable competitive advantage in this environment is pointless. The primary goal of strategy is 'disruption of the status quo, to seize the initiative through creating a series of temporary advantages' (p. 10).

When the status quo breaks down, the veneer of objectively ordered environments likewise begins to disintegrate. Under these conditions, we would expect managers to seek powerful and sophisticated explanations that reduce the ensuing uncertainty. But in reality, the exact opposite takes place. Based on their research on the microcomputer industry, Eisenhardt and Sull (2001) suggested that when technological change is constant and rapid, managers tend to 'pick a small number of strategically significant processes and craft a few simple rules to guide them.'

Bogner and Barr (2000) developed this line of inquiry further, arguing that under the pressures of hypercompetition managers abandon efforts to make sense of the competitive moves of their rivals all together, and instead focus on improving the process of strategic decision making. They become increasingly preoccupied by the '"hows" of strategy, and not the "whats"'. Remarkably, this preoccupation produces what may be described as 'group think' at the industry level. In an effort to stay ahead of the competition, firms imitate their rivals' decision making approach. Thus, paradoxically, without intending to, firms drive industry instability to higher levels: 'the very sensemaking actions that managers undertake to build new frameworks can result in industry-level beliefs that perpetuate competitive turbulence and, in effect, institutionalize hypercompetition' (Bogner and Barr, 2000: 213).

Premises of the cognitive school

The cognitive school is, at best, an evolving school of thought on strategy formation. Hence we present its premises here, as induced from its literature, to conclude our review of its work:

1 Strategy formation is a cognitive process that takes place in the mind of the strategist.

2 Strategies thus emerge as perspectives—in the form of concepts, maps, schemas, and frames—that shape how people deal with inputs from the environment.

3 These inputs (according to the 'objective' wing of this school) flow through all sorts of distorting filters before they are decoded by the cognitive maps, or else (according to the 'subjective' wing) are merely interpretations of a world that exists only in terms of how it is perceived. The seen world, in other words, can be modelled, it can be framed, and it can be constructed.

4 As concepts, strategies are difficult to attain in the first place, considerably less than optimal when actually attained, and subsequently difficult to change when no longer viable.

---

box 6.4

Using the constructionist approach

(from Smircich and Stubbart, 1985: 728–732)

Abandoning the prescription that organizations should adapt to their environments. . . . The executives in an industry cannot simply stand outside the action and adjust themselves to trends; their actions make the trends. Thus, if every firm rushes to take advantage of an opportunity, the opportunity vanishes. . . . The facts *never* speak for themselves. If facts seem to 'go without saying,' it is only because observers happen to be saying very similar things. . . .

Rethinking constraints, threats, opportunities. Managers face a tidal wave of situations, events, pressures, and uncertainties. . . . [Thus, they] must look first to themselves and their actions and inactions, and not to 'the environment' for explanations of their situations. . . .

Thinking differently about the role of strategic managers. The interpretative perspective . . . defines a strategist's task as an imaginative one, a creative one, an art. . . . The best work of strategic managers inspires splendid meanings. . . .

> **Managerial analysis**. . . . One's own actions and the actions of others make an 'organization' and its 'environment.' Because of this sequence, environmental analysis is much less critical than managerial analysis. Managerial analysis means challenging the assumptions on which managers act and improving managers' capacity for self-reflection. . . .
>
> **Creation of context**. The answers to such questions as Who are we? What is important to us? What do we do? and What don't we do? set the stage for strategy formulation. . . .
>
> **Encouraging multiple realities**. . . . Successful strategists have often contemplated the same facts that everyone knew, and they have invented startling insights (e.g., Ray Kroc and the hamburger restaurant chain). . . . Interesting enactments blossom when strategists draw out novel interpretations from prosaic facts.
>
> **Testing and experimenting**. Every industry is saddled with a long list of dos and don'ts. These stipulated limits should be tested periodically . . . Organizational wisdom may require continuous unlearning. . . .

Critique, contribution, and context of the cognitive school

As noted at the outset, this school is characterized more by its potential than by its contribution. The central idea is valid—that the strategy-formation process is also fundamentally one of cognition, particularly in the attainment of strategies as concepts. But strategic management, in practice if not in theory, has yet to gain sufficiently from cognitive psychology. Or, perhaps more accurately, cognitive psychology has yet to address adequately the questions of prime interest to strategic management, especially how concepts form in the mind of a strategist.

It would be especially useful to know not just how the mind distorts, but also how it is sometimes able to integrate such a diversity of complex inputs. For despite all the strange strategic behaviour that does take place, including the 'strategic lethargy' of overwhelmed managers who simply give up trying to develop strategy, some managers do manage to make remarkable leaps of cognition. And so, however interesting it may be to learn about distortions in decision making, our understanding itself risks becoming distorted when phenomena such as experiential wisdom, creative insight, and intuitive synthesis are slighted, or downright ignored.

The constructionist wing of this school has hardly answered these questions. But at least it has recognized them, bringing front and centre phenomena that may help in these explanations. It has also given a boost to the creative side of strategy making, something to be very much welcomed after all the attention that has been given to the limitations of human cognition, not to mention the limited procedures of planning and the constrained analyses of positioning.

In spite of its shortcomings, the subjective wing reminds us that strategy formation is also a mental process, and that funny things can happen on the way to a strategy. It further reminds us that strategists vary in their cognitive styles, with important consequence for the strategies pursued. In this sense, the cognitive school is less deterministic than the positioning school, and more personalized than the planning school. It is also the first of the five schools so far discussed to recognize that there is an interesting environment out there: that strategists don't just pluck strategies from some tree of environmental opportunity, or else slot passively into set conditions when their entrepreneurial leaders cannot magically direct them into visionary market niches. Instead, they get buffeted around by a nasty world that, in the view of one side of this school at least, is too complicated to be fully understood. Yet, interestingly enough, the other side of this school says, in effect: so what? Good strategists are creative, which means that they construct their world in their collective heads and then (as we shall see in the next chapter) make it happen—'enact' it.

As for context, the work of the objective wing of this school would seem to apply best to strategy formation as an individual rather than a collective process. We do not mean to imply that cognition is not relevant to the collective context, only that the interaction of different cognitions has to be orders of magnitude more difficult to study, and so has hardly been embraced by a research community that has had its hands full with individual cognition. The interpretative wing has, of course, been more open to social process, perhaps because its agenda has been less ambitious: it seeks to probe less deeply inside cognition.

This school also draws attention to particular stages in the strategy making process, notably periods of the *original* conception of strategy, periods of the *reconception* of existing strategies, and periods of the *clinging* by organizations to existing strategies, due to cognitive fixations.

Above all, the cognitive school tells us that we had better understand the human mind as well as the human brain if we are to understand strategy formation. But this may have more important implications for cognitive psychology as a supplier of theory than for strategic management as a consumer of it. In other words, much of this chapter could be considered a customer's lament!

The learning school: strategy formation as an emergent process

This is the course in advanced physics. That means the instructor finds the subject confusing. If he didn't, the course would be called elementary physics.

—Luis Alvarez, Nobel laureate, 1964

I f the world of strategy is really as complex as implied by the cognitive school, and thus overwhelms the prescriptions of the design, planning, and positioning schools, then how are strategists supposed to proceed? Our sixth school suggests an answer: they *learn* over time.

This is a simple enough idea. Putting it into practice is another matter—mammoth, in fact. According to this school, strategies emerge as people, sometimes acting individually but more often collectively, come to learn about a situation as well as their organization's capability of dealing with it. Eventually they converge on patterns of behaviour that work. Lapierre has put it well: strategic management becomes 'no longer just the management of change but management by change' (1980: 9).

It was the publication of Charles Lindblom's (1959) provocative article 'The Science of "Muddling Through"' that, in some sense, initiated this school. Lindblom suggested that policy making (in government) is not a neat, orderly, controlled process, but a messy one in which policymakers try to cope with a world they know is too complicated for them. Lindblom's notions may have violated virtually every premise of 'rational' management. But they struck a chord by describing behaviour with which everyone was familiar, and in business no less than government.

Some related publications followed, for example H. Edward Wrapp's (1967) article 'Good Managers Don't Make Policy Decisions.' But it was James Brian Quinn's book of 1980, *Strategies for Change: Logical Incrementalism*, that signalled the takeoff of what we are calling the learning school. A steady flow of literature has followed and subsequently entered the mainstream (or at least formed a major current) of strategic management.

While other schools have questioned specific aspects of the 'rational' traditions of the design, planning, and positioning schools, the learning school did so most broadly and forcefully, turning on their heads most of their basic assumptions and premises. That set up a disturbing debate within the field of strategic management, which continues today. *Who* really is the architect of strategy and *where* in the organization does strategy formation actually take place? How deliberate and conscious can the process really be? Is the separation of formulation and implementation really sacrosanct? At the limit, the learning school suggests that the traditional image of strategy formulation has been a fantasy, one which may have been attractive to certain managers but did not correspond to what actually happens in organizations.

Formation vs formulation

Key to the learning school is its foundation in description rather than prescription. Its proponents keep asking the simple but important question: how do strategies *actually* form in organizations? Not how are they are supposed to be formulated, but how do they actually form.

Walter Kiechel (1984: 8), who wrote about strategy for *Fortune* magazine, once pointed to a study suggesting that only 10 percent of formulated strategies actually got implemented (a figure Tom Peters called 'wildly inflated'). Such concerns have led to huge efforts by senior executives to clean up implementation. 'Manage culture' or 'tighten up your control systems' they were told by a generation of management consultants. After all, the problem could not possibly reside in their own brilliant formulations.

So when a strategy failed, the thinkers blamed the doers. 'If only you dumbbells appreciated our beautiful strategy . . .' But if the dumbbells were smart, they would have replied: 'If *you* are so smart, why didn't you formulate a strategy that we dumbbells were capable of implementing?' In other words, every failure of implementation is also, by definition, a failure of formulation. But the real problem may lie beyond that: in the very separation between formulation and implementation, the disassociation of thinking from acting. As suggested in Box 7.1, maybe we need a little less cleverness in strategic management.

Researchers sympathetic to the learning approach found that when significant strategic redirection did take place, it rarely originated from a formal planning effort, indeed often not even in the offices of the senior management. Instead strategies could be traced back to a variety of little actions and decisions made by all sorts of different people (sometimes accidentally or serendipitously, with no thought of their strategic consequences). Taken together over time, these small changes often produced major shifts in direction.

In other words, informed individuals anywhere in an organization can contribute to the strategy process A strategist can be a mad scientist working in a far-flung research laboratory who comes up with a better product. A group of salespeople who decide to flog one product and not others can redirect a company's market positions. Who better to influence strategy than the foot soldier on the firing line, closest to the action.

> ❝ who better to influence strategy than the foot soldier on the firing line ❞

---

box 7.1

More effective, less clever strategies

If you place in a bottle half a dozen bees and the same number of flies, and lay the bottle horizontally, with its base [the closed end] to the window, you will find that the bees will persist, till they die of exhaustion or hunger, in their endeavor to discover an [opening] through the glass; while the flies, in less than two minutes, will all have sallied forth through the neck on the opposite side. . . . It is [the bees'] love of flight, it is their very intelligence, that is their undoing in this experiment. They evidently imagine that the issue from every prison must be where the light shines clearest; and they act in accordance, and persist in too-logical action. To [bees] glass is a supernatural mystery . . . and, the greater their intelligence, the more inadmissible, more incomprehensible, will the strange obstacle appear. Whereas the featherbrained flies, careless of logic . . . flutter wildly hither and thither, and meeting here the good fortune that often waits on the simple . . . necessarily end up by discovering the friendly opening that restores their liberty to them. (Gordon Siu, in Peters and Waterman, 1982: 108)

Do we have too many bees making strategy and not enough flies?

We open our discussion with a sequence of ideas that together, perhaps in the same unplanned way, ended up converging in a kind of learning model of strategy formation. This we summarize in the premises of the learning school. Then we consider new directions for strategic learning—the learning organization, evolutionary theory, knowledge creation, the dynamic capabilities approach, and chaos theory. As usual, we close with the critique, context, and contribution of the learning school.

Emergence of a learning model

We can trace the evolution of the learning school—how it itself actually learned, if you like—through several phases. These represent fairly distinct bodies of literature that converged around the central themes of this school.

Disjointed incrementalism

In an early 1960s book with a colleague, Charles Lindblom, a political science professor at Yale University, elaborated a set of ideas at length, under the label of 'disjointed incrementalism' (Braybrooke and Lindblom, 1963). He described 'policy making' (the label in government) as a 'serial,' 'remedial,' and 'fragmented' process, in which decisions are made at the margin, more to solve problems than to exploit opportunities, with little regard for ultimate goals or even for connections between different decisions. Lindblom argued that many actors get involved in the process, but they are hardly coordinated by any central authority. 'Various aspects of public policy and even various aspects of any one problem or problem area are analyzed at various points in time with no apparent coordination,' he wrote (105). At best, the different actors engage in an informal process of 'mutual adjustment.'

❝ continual nibbling is a substitute for a good bite ❞

In a later book, Lindblom summarized his theory with the statement that 'policy making is typically a never-ending process of successive steps in which continual nibbling is a substitute for a good bite' (1968: 25–6). He argued further that 'the piecemealing remedial incrementalist or satisficer may not look like an heroic figure. He is, nevertheless, a shrewd, resourceful problem-solver who is wrestling bravely with a universe that he is wise enough to know is too big for him' (27).

But questions remained. Could this incrementalist be called a strategist? Did anything come out of such a process that could rightly be labelled strategy? Was there deliberate direction or even emergent convergence that defined common positions or a collective perspective? Because the evident answers were no (Bower and Doz, 1979: 155), or at least because these issues were not addressed, Lindblom's theory stopped short of being one of strategy formation. True he sought to describe public policy-making, especially in the US congressional system of government. But even there, strategies can be discerned as patterns. (Consider, for example, the overall consistency in US foreign policy with regard to the Soviet Union for so many years.) Lindblom did, nonetheless, point the way toward a new school of thought on strategy formation.

Logical incrementalism

James Brian Quinn (1980a, b) of the Amos Tuck School of Business at Dartmouth College picked up some years later where Lindblom left off. Quinn agreed with Lindblom on the incremental nature of the process but not on its disjointedness. Instead he felt that in the business corporation at least, central actors pulled it together and directed it toward a final strategy.

Quinn started his investigation with the belief that organizations do arrive at strategies as integrated conceptions. To find out how, he interviewed the chief executives of several large, successful corporations. He concluded that while planning did not describe how they formulated their strategies, incrementalism did—but an incrementalism with an underlying logic that knit the pieces together. Hence Quinn called this process 'logical incrementalism':

The real strategy tends to evolve as internal decisions and external events flow together to create a new, widely shared consensus for action among key members of the top management team. In well-run organizations, managers pro-actively guide these streams of actions and events incrementally toward conscious strategies (1980a: 15)

The organization, for Quinn, consists of a series of 'subsystems'—for example, ones for diversification, reorganization, and external relations. And so strategic management means trying 'to develop or maintain in [the top executives'] minds a consistent pattern among the decisions made in each subsystem' (1980a: 52). Reading Quinn, one gets the impression of strategic management done on the run.

But there was an interesting ambiguity in Quinn's theory. Incrementalism can be interpreted in two ways, on one hand as a process for developing the strategic vision itself, and on the other, as a process for bringing to life a vision already in the strategist's mind. In the first case, the central strategist learns incrementally; in the second, the strategist manoeuvres tactically, almost politically, in incremental fashion, through a complex organization. This maintains the separation between formulation and implementation, consistent with the separation between *the* strategists and everyone else.

Either way, the central actor—in Quinn's view, the team of top executives led by the chief executive—remains the architect of strategy, as in the design school. Except that here, the organization is less obedient; it has a mind of its own, so to speak. Thus Quinn wrote about top executives 'selectively moving people toward a broadly conceived organizational goal' (1980a: 32), and he devoted a large part of his book (1980a: 97–152) to what might be called 'political implementation,' which includes discussions of 'building credibility,' 'broadening support,' 'systematic waiting,' and 'managing coalitions.'

Ultimately Quinn sought to marry the two interpretations by arguing that strategists have to promote strategic visions that are themselves changing and improving. Thus he referred to the process as 'continuous, pulsing dynamic' and concluded that:

. . . successful managers who operate with logical incrementalism build the seeds of understanding, identity, and commitment into the very processes that create their strategies. By the time the strategy begins to crystallize in focus, pieces of it are already being implemented. Through their strategic formulation processes, they have built a momentum and psychological commitment to the strategy, which causes it to flow toward flexible implementation. Constantly integrating the simultaneous incremental processes of strategy formulation and implementation is the central art of effective strategic management. (145)

Did Quinn describe all of strategy formation or one particular kind of it? To be true to the different schools of thought, we should place the various relationships between formulation and implementation along a continuum. At one end, the two are thoroughly intertwined, as in the learning school. At the other end is the implementation of a well-formulated strategy, as in the three prescriptive schools. Quinn really places himself somewhere in between, which means that he cannot be considered to stand squarely in the learning school so much as to straddle this and the prescriptive (especially design) schools (with a toe or two in the political school).[1] This is especially evident in the dominant role he gave the top management team in strategy formation, relegating other people to bit parts.

But the foot Quinn did place in the learning school proved important for its development, since it gave incrementalism a prominent place in the literature of strategic management. It also shifted its role from the just plain adapting of Lindblom to one of conscious learning. The prescriptive flavour of Quinn's own recommendations (which also show a blending of learning with designing) are presented in the accompanying box, drawn from his work.

Evolutionary theory

Related to Quinn's work is so-called *evolutionary* theory, first developed by the economists Nelson and Winter (1982). They describe similar subsystems, but see change as deriving from their interaction rather than leadership per se.

According to Nelson and Winter, organizations are not governed by global rationality, and no single consistent framework that guides change. Change emerges from the cumulative interaction among basic action systems, called 'routines.' Routines are repetitive patterns of activity that underpin and control the smooth functioning of the organization. They cover areas such as hiring, firing, promotion, and budgeting. Organizations are composed of hierarchies of routines, stretching from the most basic one on the factory floor to ones used by managers to control other activities. Routines impart stability to the organization much as gyroscopes maintain aircraft on stable courses.

---

1 As he himself noted with reference to 'formal strategy formulation models' (namely the prescriptive schools), as well as to 'the political or power-behavior approaches . . . logical incrementaism does not become subservient to any one model' (1980a: 58)

box 7.2

Prescriptions for logical incrementalism

(adapted from Quinn, 1982)

1 **Lead the formal information system**. Rarely do the earliest signs for strategic change come from the company's format horizon scanning or reporting systems. Instead, initial sensing of needs for major strategic changes is often described as 'something you feel uneasy about,' 'inconsistencies' or 'anomalies' (Normann, 1977) . . . Effective managers . . . use . . . networks . . . to short circuit all the careful screens their organizations build up. . . .

2 **Build organizational awareness**. At early stages [of strategy formation], management processes are rarely directive. Instead they are likely to involve studying, challenging, questioning, listening, talking to creative people outside ordinary decision channels, generating options, but purposively avoiding irreversible commitments. . . .

3 **Build credibility change symbols**. Knowing they cannot communicate directly with the thousands who must carry out a strategy, many executives purposively undertake a few highly visible symbolic actions which wordlessly convey complex messages they could never communicate as well, or as credibly, in verbal terms.

4 **Legitimize new view points**. . . . Top managers may purposely create discussion forums or allow slack time [so that] their organizations can talk through threatening issues, work out the implications of new solutions, or gain an improved information base that permits new options to be evaluated objectively in comparison with more familiar alternatives.

5 **Pursue tactical shifts and partial solutions**. Executives can often obtain agreement to a series of small programs when a broad objective change would encounter too much opposition. . . . As events unfurl, the solutions to several initially unrelated problems tend to flow together into a new synthesis.

6 **Broaden political support**. Broadening political support for emerging new thrusts is frequently an essential and consciously proactive step in major strategy changes. Committees, task forces, or retreats tend to be favored mechanisms.

7 **Overcome opposition**. [Careful managers] persuade individuals toward new concepts whenever possible, coopt or neutralize serious opposition if necessary. . . . People selection and coalition management are the ultimate controls top executives have in guiding and coordinating their companies' strategies.

8 **Consciously, structure flexibility**. One cannot possibly predict the precise form or timing of all important threats and opportunities [a] firm may encounter. Logic dictates therefore that managers purposely design flexibility into their organizations and have resources ready to deploy

> incrementally as events demand. This requires . . . creating sufficient
> resource buffers, or slacks, to respond as events actually do unfurl . . .
> developing and positioning 'champions' who will be motivated to take
> advantage of specific opportunities as they occur, [and] shortening decision
> lines between such persons and the top for rapid system response.
>
> 9 **Develop trial balloons and pockets of commitment**. Executives may also
>   consciously launch trial balloons . . . in order to attract options and concrete
>   proposals.
>
> 10 **Crystallize focus and formalize commitment**. . . . Guiding executives often
>   purposely keep early goal statements vague and commitments broad and
>   tentative. . . . Then as they develop information or consensus on desirable
>   thrusts, they may use their prestige or power to push or crystallize a
>   particular formulation.
>
> 11 **Engage in continuous change**. Even as the organization arrives at its new
>   consensus, guiding executives must move to ensure that this too does not
>   become inflexible. Effective strategic managers therefore immediately
>   introduce new foc[i] and stimuli at the top to begin mutating the very
>   strategic thrusts they have just solidified—a most difficult but essential
>   psychological state.
>
> 12 **Recognize strategy not as a linear process**. The validity of strategy lies not
>   in its pristine clarity or rigorously maintained structure, but in its capacity to
>   capture the initiative, to deal with unknowable events, to redeploy and
>   concentrate resources as new opportunities and thrusts emerge, and thus to
>   use resources most effectively when selected.

In an ingenious twist, evolutionary theorists argue that routines are also responsible for creating change, however inadvertently. The interaction between established routines and novel situations is an important source of learning. As routines are changed to deal with new situations, larger changes come about. This happens because the routines are interlinked, so that change in one set will impact on others, creating a cascading effect. For those who query how routines, the epitome of repetition and constancy, can also produce change, Feldman and Rafaeli (2002) have an interesting analogy that illustrates how this contradiction can be achieved. The term 'routine' they point out, is also defined as 'a series of steps in a dance' (Webster, 1984: 1241). Let us consider ballroom dances as a metaphor for an organization, they write (p. 324):

In such dances individual actions are scripted, but not to the point of inflexibility. The dance specifies which connections will be made, when and how. Dancing requires adapting to the context (is there an object in the middle of the dance floor? Are you going to bump into the other dancers?) and to

> ❝ like ballroom dancing, new organizational routines arise and others disappear ❞

variability in the behaviours of participants (is my partner near or far, on tempo or not?). The connection between the two bodies enables the dancers to communicate with one another and adjust to the context. The resulting behaviour will be similar in many ways but is unlikely to be repeated exactly. Some variations are likely because

individuals need to adapt to other individuals to whom they are connected through the routine and to the context in which they perform the routine. Taking action in an organizational routine is very similar, though the connection is not usually direct bodily contact, but some other form of communication.

Just as in the case of ballroom dancing, new organizational routines arise and others disappear. But unlike dancing, effectiveness plays a role. Management can influence the process by phasing out ineffective routines, transferring effective ones from one part of the organization to another, and inserting new routines into the organization, whether by imitation—borrowing what appears the best practice from other organizations, or by experimentation—seeing how innovation on a small scale will affect the rest of the organization.

So, while this approach parallels Quinn's emphasis on the role of sub-systems, it gives them more emphasis in the strategy process and *the* strategist less emphasis, as does the next approach.

Strategic venturing

Meanwhile, on another front, other parts of the organization were being heard from—in their role in championing strategic initiatives. Quinn mentioned championing (in point 8 of Box 7.2) but really focused on the driving and integrating role of top management. Other writers, however, have focused on this key element in describing how the ideas for strategic change arise initially. This is seen to happen in the proposals or ventures 'championed' by individual strategic actors, not necessarily—or even perhaps commonly—in positions of senior management.

The first hints of what this process might look like came from work on innovation in large established corporations. The traditional picture of innovation emphasized the creation of new firms by dynamic entrepreneurs (as discussed in Chapter 5). But some large firms continue to be innovative beyond their nascent period. Their people are given the freedom to pursue promising ideas and develop new products. Support is provided without the need to run the gauntlet of a rigid system of resource allocation.

All of this depends on the initiative and skills of people who act deep within the corporate hierarchy, as internal entrepreneurs (hence the term 'intrapreneurship' (Pinchot, 1985)). As in the case of external entrepreneurs who operate in the marketplace, these people must compete for resources with others who are busy promoting their own ventures. But they have to persuade their own senior management, not outside venture capitalists. Although these senior managers use a variety of formal administrative systems to evaluate internal ventures (such as the capital budgeting procedures discussed in Chapter 3), much depends on their judgment, based on past experience. In other words, their own learning may be more important than any formal analysis.

Work on internal venturing dates back to Joseph Bower's (1970) classic description of the resource allocation process. Critical of traditional capital budgeting, Bower found resource allocation to be 'more complex than most managers seem to believe . . . a process of study, bargaining, persuasion and choice spread over many levels of the organization and over long periods of time.' Bower found 'substantially separate processes at work' (320–21) here, an idea that was advanced by a number of his doctoral students at Harvard and then especially by Robert Burgelman's thesis at Columbia University on corporate venturing (1980, see also 1983a, b, 1988, 1996; Burgelman and Sayles, 1986).

The overall conclusion was that strategic *initiatives* often develop deep in the hierarchy and are then championed, or given *impetus*, by middle-level managers who seek the *authorization* of senior executives. In a later paper, Noda and Bower (1996) summarize the 'Bower-Burgelman Process Model of Strategy Making' as involving 'multiple, simultaneous, interlocking, and sequential managerial activities over three levels of organizational hierarchy' (160). In conventional terms, these levels normally refer to front-line, middle, and top managers. But in Burgelman's model, as shown in Figure 7.1, the hierarchy locates the group leader or venture manager at the bottom, middle managers who are charged with new venture development are one level above, and at the very top is corporate management which oversees every aspect of the strategy, including new venture development. The other axis of the model deals respectively with two processes, each of which are in turn divided into two subprocesses. Noda and Bower describe these processes as follows (161):

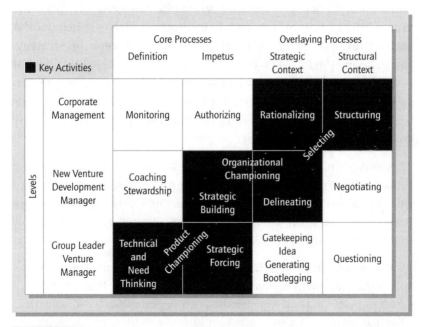

figure 7.1 Burgelman's process model of internal corporate venturing (ICV)

Source: Burgelman (1983a).

1 **Definition** – The cognitive processes that front-line managers use to transform ambiguous information about technologies and markets into explicit data for decision making by middle managers.

2 **Impetus** – The sociopolitical processes that front-line and middle-managers use to champion and promote strategic initiatives.

3 **Strategic context** – The political processes that middle managers use to convince top managers of the new fields of business that the firm should enter and develop.

4 **Structural context** – The various administrative mechanisms such as information and measurement systems, rewards and punishing systems that top managers use to shape the context in which front-line managers make decisions.

Burgelman stresses the first stage as key to creating entrepreneurship at the operational level of organizations. But transforming entrepreneurship at the operational level into full-fledged ventures at the corporate level depends crucially on middle managers who play 'the crucial role of linking successful autonomous strategic behavior at the operational level with the corporate concept of strategy' (Burgelman, 1983a: 241). Performing this role successfully calls for politics and subterfuge. Middle managers must do their best to persuade their superiors that the venture will further corporate goals while at the same time keeping the venture alive, if necessary by covertly finding the resources.

This notion of 'venturing' seems to sit squarely in the learning school, with regard to both the learning process itself and the role of multiple actors in it. This is made clear in the following passage from Burgelman (1988) on the implications of 'internal corporate venturing' for management practice:

First, this view of strategy making . . . draw[s] the attention of top management to the role of internal entrepreneurs in organizational learning. They are the driving force in perceiving and apprehending new opportunities based on new capabilities that are not as yet recognized as distinctive to the firm. . . . Second . . . top management should establish mechanisms for capturing and leveraging the learning that results from experiments engaged in by individual participants at operational and middle levels in the organization. . . . Assessing, decomposing, and rewarding entrepreneurial success and failure may therefore be critical to sustaining strategy making as a social learning process. (83, 84)

But, with this important work, we were not at a full learning model of strategy formation quite yet. The internal venturing process may culminate in strategic movement, but not necessarily in coordinated effort or patterning, namely strategy. Corporate ventures act largely on their own; they break away from the rest of the organization rather than blend into it. As one CEO put it, 'there's only a fine line between entrepreneurship and insubordination' (Garvin and Levesque, 2006: 104). Furthermore, the care

❝ there's only a fine line between entrepreneurship and insubordination ❞ and feeding of new ideas cannot be left to an internal competitive process that resembles the functioning of markets. There has to be coherence in action too. Taking creative sparks and integrating them into new strategic perspectives is a fundamental challenge that preoccupies many organizations (and, therefore, the learning school). And that seems to depend on two other concepts developed in the spirit of the learning school. One is emergent strategy and the other is retrospective sense making.

Emergent strategy

In work carried out at McGill University's Faculty of Management,[2] in which strategy was defined as pattern or consistency in action, *deliberate* strategy was distinguished from *emergent* strategy (as we noted in Chapter 1).

Deliberate strategy focuses on *control*—making sure that managerial intentions are realized in action—while emergent strategy emphasizes *learning*—coming to understand through the taking of actions what those intentions should be in the first place. Only deliberate strategy has been recognized in the three prescriptive schools of strategic management, which, as noted, emphasize control almost to the exclusion of learning. In these schools, organizational attention is riveted on the realization of explicit intentions (meaning 'implementation'), not on adapting those intentions to new understandings.

The concept of emergent strategy, however, opens the door to strategic learning, because it acknowledges the organization's capacity to

---

2 This includes a whole string of empirical studies that tracked the strategies of different organizations, as some conceptual articles. See Mintzberg (1972, 1978); Mintzberg and McHugh (1985); Mintzberg and Waters (1982, 1984); Mintzberg, Taylor, and Waters (1984); Mintzberg, Brunet and Waters (1986); Mintzberg, Otis, Shamsie and Waters (1988); and Mintzberg and Austin (1996). All of these are reported in Mintzberg (2007).

experiment. A single action can be taken, feedback can be received, and the process can continue until the organization converges on the pattern that becomes its strategy. Put differently, to make use of Lindblom's metaphor, organizations need not nibble haphazardly. Each nibble can influence the next, leading eventually to a rather well defined set of recipes, so that it all ends up in one great big feast!

Emergent strategy can, of course, result from the efforts of an individual leader or a small executive team, as Quinn has suggested. But it often goes well beyond that, as suggested in Table 7.1, which lists a range of possible forms strategies can take, from the rather purely deliberate to the rather unconventionally emergent. For example, the prime actor may be a clandestine player who conceives a strategic vision and then conveys it to the chief as if the latter invented it, or who simply foists it upon an unsuspecting organization. (In that case, the strategy is deliberate for the actor but emergent for the organization.) And the 'strategist' can be the collectivity too. Various people can interact and so develop a pattern, even inadvertently, that becomes a strategy.

This collective process of emergence can be rather simple. For example, the salespeople of a firm may find themselves favouring one type of customer over another (perhaps because the former are easier to sell to). So the firm's market simply shifts through no intention of the management. But the process can also be more complex. Consider the venturing process we have just described, with initiatives on the firing line, champions in middle management who give them impetus, and senior managers who seek to create a context for all this. Then superimpose on this the notion of convergence, that somehow the consequences of these initiatives lead to some kind of integration, or pattern. That can happen in all sorts of ways, as people interact, conflict and mutually adjust, learn from each other, and eventually develop consensus. Box 7.3 describes one view of this—by which strategy emerges in the professional organization, such as a university or a hospital, maybe even an accounting or consulting firm. Notice how everything we supposedly know and cherish about strategy gets turned on its head in this description.

table 7.1 Of strategy, deliberate and emergent

Kind of strategy	Major features
Planned	Strategies originate in formal plans; precise intentions exist, formulated and articulated by central leadership, backed up by formal controls to ensure surprise-free implementation in benign, controllable, or predictable environment; strategies most deliberate
Entrepreneurial	Strategies originate in central vision: intentions exist as personal vision of single leader, and so are adaptable to new opportunities; organization under personal control of leader and located in protected niche in environment; strategies broadly deliberate but can emerge in detail and even orientation
Ideological	Strategies originate in shared beliefs: intentions exist as collective vision of all actors, in inspirational form and relatively immutable, controlled normatively through indoctrination and/or socialization; organization often proactive *vis-à-vis* environment; strategies rather deliberate
Umbrella	Strategies originate in constraints; leadership, in partial control of organizational actions, defines strategic boundaries or targets within which other actors respond to own experiences or preferences; perspective is deliberate, positions, etc. can be emergent; strategy can also be described as deliberately emergent
Process	Strategies originate in process: leadership controls process aspects of strategy (hiring, structure, etc.), leaving content aspects to other actors; strategies partly deliberate, partly emergent (and, again, deliberately emergent)
Unconnected	Strategies originate in enclaves and ventures: actor(s) loosely coupled to rest of organization produce(s) patterns in own actions in absence of, or in direct contradiction to, central or common intentions; strategies organizationally emergent whether or not deliberate for actor(s)
Consensus	Strategies originate in consensus: through mutual adjustment, actors converge on patterns that become pervasive in absence of central or common intentions; strategies rather emergent
Imposed	Strategies originate in environment: environment dictates patterns in actions either through direct imposition or through implicitly preempting or bounding organizational choice; strategies most emergent, although may be internalized by organization and made deliberate

Source: Adapted from Mintzberg and Waters (1985: 270).

box 7.3

Learning strategy in the professional organization

(adapted from Hardy et al. 1983)

Using the definition of strategy as pattern in action opens up a whole new view of strategy formation in the professional organization. Rather than simply throwing up our hands at its resistance to strategic planning or, at the other extreme, dismissing these places as 'organized anarchies' whose decision-making processes are mere 'garbage cans' (March and Olsen, 1976, with special references to universities), we can focus on how decisions and actions in such organizations order themselves into patterns over time.

In these organizations, many key strategic issues come under the direct control of individual professionals, while others can be decided neither by individual professionals nor by central managers, but instead require the participation of a variety of people in a complex interactive process. As illustrated in the accompanying figure, we examine in turn the decisions controlled by individual professionals, by central managers, and by the collectivity.

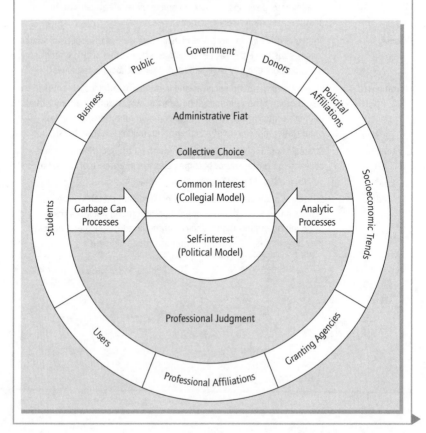

▶ Decisions made by professional judgment

Professional organizations are distinguished by the fact that the determination of the basic mission—the specific services to be offered and to whom—is in good part left to the judgment of professionals as individuals. In the university, for example, each professor has a good deal of control over what is taught and how, as well as what is researched and how. Thus the overall product-market strategy of a university must be seen as the composite of the individual teaching and research postures of all its professors. There is, however, a subtle but not insignificant constraint on this power. Professionals are left to decide on their own only because years of training have ensured that they will decide in ways generally accepted in their professions. Pushed to the limit, then, individual freedom becomes professional control.

Decisions made by administrative fiat

Professional autonomy sharply circumscribes the capacity of central managers to manage the professionals in the ways of conventional hierarchy. But certain types of activities do fall into the realm of what can be called administrative fiat. They include some financial decisions, for example to buy and sell facilities as well as control over many of the nonprofessional workers. Central managers may also play a prominent role in determining the procedures by which the collective process functions: what committees exist, who gets nominated to them, and so on, which can lead to considerable influence. Moreover, in times of crisis, managers may acquire more extensive powers, as the professionals defer to a leadership that must act decisively.

Decisions made by collective choice

Many decisions are handled in interactive processes that combine professionals with managers from a variety of levels and units. Included are decisions related to the creation and discontinuation of the activities and units of various kinds. Other important decisions here include the hiring and promotion of the professionals. Proposed changes in activities may require a professional or managerial 'champion,' but development and final approval of them often ends up with task forces and layers of standing committees, composed of professionals and managers, and sometimes outsiders as well. Our figure shows four models by which such collective processes operate: a *collegial* model based on a *common interest*; a *political* model based on *self-interest*; a *garbage-can* model, based on a kind of *disinterest* (characterized by 'collections of choices looking for problems, issues and feelings looking for decision situations in which they may be aired, solutions looking for issues to which they might be an answer, and decision makers looking for work' [Cohen *et al.* 1972: 1]); and an *analytical* model, based

> too on *self-interest*, because champions use analysis to promote their own strategic candidates, or to block those of others.

Strategies in the professional organization

While it may seem difficult to create strategies here, due to the fragmentation, the politics, and the garbage can phenomenon, in fact the professional organization is inundated with strategies (meaning patterns in its actions). After all, the professionals all carry out rather standardized activities. That means the presence of product-market strategies galore—sometimes one or more for each and every professional! Decisions made by professional fiat can obviously lead to strategies, but even the collective processes can lead to consistent patterns. What is collegiality after all, but cooperative behavior. And just think of the forces of habit and tradition in professional organizations.

Overall, the strategies of the professional organization tend to exhibit a remarkable degree of stability. Major reorientations in strategy—'strategic revolutions'—are discouraged by the fragmentation of activity and the power of individual professionals as well as of their outside associations. But at a narrower level, change is ubiquitous. Individual programs are continually being altered, procedures redesigned, and clientele shifted. Thus, paradoxically, overall the professional organization is extremely stable yet in its operating practices in a state of perpetual change. Slightly overstated, the organization never changes while its operations never stop changing.

At the limit of the learning school, a kind of 'grassroots' model of strategy making appears (Mintzberg and McHugh, 1985, based on a study of the National Film Board of Canada): strategies grow initially like weeds in a garden, taking root in all kinds of strange places. Some proliferate, to become broadly organizational, sometimes without even being recognized as such, let alone being consciously managed to do so. Box 7.4 presents this 'grassroots' model, in its full flowering, so to speak. Box 7.5 is the alternate, 'hothouse' model, propagated by the design, planning, and positioning schools. These two models face each other to make the point that they are extremes, that real strategic behaviour falls somewhere in between. We particularly wish to emphasize that while the grass roots model is obviously overstated, the hothouse model, despite being much more widely accepted, is no less overstated. Only by juxtaposing each against the other can it be made clear that all real strategic behaviour has to combine deliberate control with emergent learning.

We have associated emergent strategy with learning. But this is not quite right. If emergent strategy means, literally, unintended order, then patterns may just form, driven by external forces or internal needs rather than the conscious thoughts of any actors. Real learning takes place at the interface of thought and action, as actors reflect on what they have done. In other words, strategic learning must combine reflection with result. Accordingly, we add another element to our model, turning now to the ideas of Karl Weick.

Retrospective sense making

Karl Weick has long described a process that proves key for the learning school (even though for many years the word *strategy* did not figure in his writings). Weick argues that management is inextricably bound up with the process of imposing sense on past experience. We try things, see the consequences, then explain them, and continue along. It all sounds sensible enough. Yet it breaks with decades of tradition in strategic management, which has insisted that thinking must end before action begins—that formulation must be followed by implementation.

---

box 7.4

A grassroots model of strategy formation

(from Mintzberg, 1989: 214–16)

1 **Strategies grow initially like weeds in a garden, they are not cultivated like tomatoes in a hothouse.** In other words, the process of strategy formation can be overmanaged; sometimes it is more important to let patterns emerge than to force an artificial consistency upon an organization prematurely. The hothouse, if needed, can come later.

2 **These strategies can take root in all kinds of places, virtually anywhere people have the capacity to learn and the resources to support that capacity.** Sometimes an individual or unit in touch with a particular opportunity creates his, her, or its own pattern. This may happen inadvertently, when an initial action sets a precedent. . . . At other times, a variety of actions converge on a strategic theme through the mutual adjustment of various people, whether gradually or spontaneously. And . . . the external environment can impose a pattern on an unsuspecting organization. The point is that organizations cannot always plan where their strategies will emerge, let alone plan the strategies themselves.

▶ 3 **Such strategies become organizational when they become collective, that is, when the patterns proliferate to pervade the behavior of the organization at large.** Weeds can proliferate and encompass a whole garden; then the conventional plants may look out of place. Likewise, emergent strategies can sometimes displace the existing deliberate ones. But, of course, what is a weed but a plant that wasn't expected? With a change of perspective, the emergent strategy, like the weed, can become what is valued (just as Europeans enjoy salads of the leaves of America's most notorious weed, the dandelion!).

4 **The processes of proliferation may be conscious but need not be; likewise they may be managed but need not be.** The processes by which the initial patterns work their way through the organization need not be consciously intended, by formal leaders or even informal ones. Patterns may simply spread by collective action, much as plants proliferate. Of course, once strategies are recognized as valuable, the processes by which they proliferate can be managed, just as plants can be selectively propagated.

5 **New strategies, which may be emerging continuously, tend to pervade the organization during periods of change, which punctuate periods of more integrated continuity.** Put more simply, organizations, like gardens, may accept the biblical maxim of a time to sow and a time to reap (even though they can sometimes reap what they did not mean to sow). Periods of convergence, during which the organization exploits its prevalent, established strategies, tend to be interrupted by periods of divergence, during which the organization experiments with and subsequently accepts new strategic themes. . . .

6 **To manage this process is not to preconceive strategies but to recognize their emergence and intervene when appropriate.** A destructive weed, once noticed, is best uprooted immediately. But one that seems capable of bearing fruit is worth watching, indeed sometimes even worth building a hothouse around. To manage in this context is to create the climate within which a wide variety of strategies can grow . . . and then to watch what does in fact come up. But [management] must not be too quick to cut off the unexpected. . . . Moreover, management must know when to resist change for the sake of internal efficiency and when to promote it for the sake of external adaptation. In other words, it must sense when to exploit an established crop of strategies and when to encourage new strains to displace them. . . .

---

box 7.5

The hothouse model of strategy formation

Henry Mintzberg

1 There is only one strategist, and that person is the chief executive officer (other managers may participate; planners provide support).
2 The CEO formulates strategies through a conscious, controlled process of thought, much as tomatoes are cultivated in a hothouse.
3 These strategies come out of this process fully developed, then to be made formally explicit, much as ripe tomatoes are picked and sent to the market.
4 These explicit strategies are then formally implemented (which includes the development of the necessary budgets and programs as well as the design of the appropriate structure).
5 To manage this process is to analyze the appropriate data, preconceive insightful strategies, and then plant them carefully, caring for them and watching them as they grow on schedule.

There is no sequence of analysis first and integration later because, as described by the constructionist wing of the cognitive school, the world is not some stable entity 'out there,' to be analyzed and put together into a final picture. Rather, as Weick puts it, the world is *enacted*. Reality emerges from a constant interpreting and updating of our past experience. We need order, but that gives rise to anomalies, and these in turn cause us to rearrange our order.

Using the ecology model of *enactment* (or variation), *selection*, and *retention*, Weick has described a form of learning behaviour as: first act ('do something'), as did his Hungarian soldiers from the last chapter, once they found the map. Then find out and select what works—in other words, make sense of those actions in retrospect. Finally, retain only those behaviours that appear desirable. The important implication of this for managers is that they need a wide range of experiences and the competences with which to deal with them in order to create novel, robust strategies. To Weick: 'all understanding originates in reflection and looking backward' (1979:194).

Normally it is believed that learning should stop before acting begins. If you want to diversify, *analyze* your strengths and weaknesses so that you can establish what markets you belong in. Then go get them. This sounds highly efficient. The problem is that, all too often, it just does not work. In Weick's view, learning is not possible without acting. As we concluded in our critique of the design school, organizations have to *discover* their strengths and weaknesses.

Thus a firm bent on diversifying might enter a variety of different markets to find out what it can do best (learn about its strengths and weaknesses). It continues only in those that have worked out. Gradually, by seeking to make sense out of all this, it converges on a diversification strategy suited to itself. Box 7.6 describes how the tobacco companies really did go about diversifying their product lines—a learning process that took almost two decades!

Emergent sense making

Combining these notions of emergence and sense making raises all sorts of fascinating possibilities. For example, organizations may learn by recognizing patterns in their own behaviours, thereby converting emergent strategies out of the past into deliberate ones for their future. Thus behaviour that seems to be the very antithesis of planning can, under certain circumstances, inform it, by providing creative new strategies to programme. Or else learning can take place within a broad vision—the *umbrella strategy* described in Table 7.1, that is deliberate in its overall perspective yet emergent in its specific positions. People adapt under the umbrella. Similarly, an organization can use a *process strategy*, where the central leadership manages the process (for example, by encouraging venturing and strategic initiatives) while leaving the content (what these strategies are to be) to others.

The interplay between thought and action also leads to all sorts of interesting questions. For example, how do strategic intentions diffuse through an organization, not just down its hierarchy, but up it, and across different activities? And what about that wonderfully elusive concept of the 'organization's mind'? What happens when many people in a system act with one mind, so to speak? Where does this 'collective cognition' come from? Interestingly, as we shall see in Chapter 9, the cultural school may provide better clues here than the cognitive school.

This discussion suggests that a learning model of strategy formation is now itself emerging, out of the lower right-hand corner of the matrix shown in Figure 7.2, which lays different processes against our main definitions of strategy.

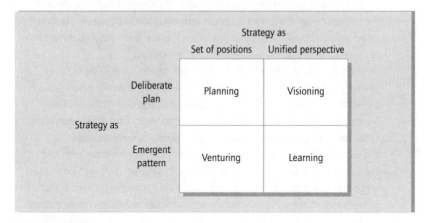

figure 7.2 Strategy processes by strategies

---

box 7.6

Learning from diversifying

(drawn from Miles, 1982: 186–9)

Drawing on the diversification experiences of Philip Morris, especially its legendary acquisition and turnaround of Miller Brewery, as well as those of R. J. Reynolds and Liggett and Meyers, Robert H. Miles in his book *Coffin Nails and Corporate Strategies* developed a number of conclusions about 'learning from diversifying,' including the following:

■ Decisions made early in the strategy-formation process, although appropriate given the initial learning situation, later served to constrain the range of strategic choices. All three companies approached the initiation of their diversification strategies with appropriate caution. They began tentatively, experimentally, and conservatively by developing or acquiring small businesses that were closely tied or related to their traditional business and that led them into the fields of packaging or consumer packaged goods. . . . Based on these early experiments, senior managers in all three companies were able to learn some early lessons that would help them refine the future development of their diversification strategies. . . .

■ The meaning of business 'relatedness' became clarified only after experience in new business domains. The apparent similarities between traditional and new businesses at the time the diversification strategy was initiated proved to

▶ be more illusory than expected. Although all three companies moved into repetitive-purchase, packaged consumer-goods fields, a domain also populated by the cigarette market each had traditionally served, all discovered that their 'distinctive competence' was not always applied with equal success. Business practices varied widely, technologies were difficult to assimilate, and volatilities in market price, demand, and supply were greater than anticipated. . . .

■ More accurate knowledge of 'other' and of 'self' came with experience in new businesses. Hindsight revealed to these companies that diversification required a more thorough assessment of the context and critical success factor of new businesses than originally anticipated. In the beginning, most senior managers in the three companies were not in the best position to make accurate assessments of acquisition candidates because their business experience had been confined largely to the tobacco industry. In addition, the conditions under which potential acquisitions became available did not encourage systematic, in-depth industry analysis prior to takeover. Attractive acquisitions came on the market rather suddenly and were taken out of the running just as quickly. Therefore, acquisitive executives had to act fast if they wanted their bids to be considered favorably. With time and experience, however, our companies learned what to look for in the markets, management, and product lines of acquisition candidates. . . . Just as important, diversification required a more thorough assessment of the strengths and weaknesses of the parent organization than anticipated initially. . . . In all three histories it is evident that an appreciation of the strengths and weaknesses of both acquisition candidates and the parents themselves developed out of the actual enactment of the diversification strategy and the process by which new businesses were assimilated, organized, and managed. . . .

■ After 15–20 years of experience with a diversification strategy, senior executives in these companies had acquired a substantial base of knowledge that was now firmly established in the management belief system and institutionalized in the formal planning documents that guided each firm's future development.

Source: Robert H. Miles, *Coffin Nails and Corporate Strategies* (Englewood Cliffs, New Jersey: Prentice-Hall/Pearson), 1982. Reprinted in abbreviated form by permission.

Learning by mistake(s) at Honda

Richard T. Pascale's (1984) account of how Honda really entered the American motorcycle market compared with claims by the Boston Consulting Group (1975) provides a stunning juxtaposition of the positioning and learning schools, and serves as an ideal conclusion to this discussion. We review Pascale's comparison of the two stories, followed by a debate over them that erupted in the strategic management literature.

The BCG account

Some years ago, the British Government hired the Boston Consulting Group (BCG) to help explain how it was that the Japanese firms, especially Honda, so dramatically outperformed those of the UK in the markets for motorcycles in the United States. (In 1959, the British had 49 percent of the import market; by 1966, Honda alone had captured a 63 percent share of the entire market.) The BCG report was issued in 1975 and it was vintage BCG of the time, and classic rational positioning—so much so that the report became the basis for well-known case studies written at Harvard and elsewhere. The report was about experience curves and high market shares and carefully thought-out deliberate strategies, especially how a firm dedicated to low cost, using the scale of its domestic production base, attacked the American market by forcing entry through a new segment—the sale of small motorcycles to middle-class consumers. To quote from the BCG report:

The Japanese motorcycle industry, and in particular Honda, the market leader, present a [consistent] picture. The basic philosophy of the Japanese manufacturers is that high volumes per model provide the potential for high productivity as a result of using capital intensive and highly automated techniques. Their marketing strategies are, therefore, directed towards developing these high model volumes, hence the careful attention that we have observed them giving to growth and market share. (1975: 59)

The Honda managers' account

Wondering about all this, Richard Pascale, co-author with Anthony Athos of *The Art of Japanese Management* (1981), flew to Japan and interviewed the managers who had done all this in America. They told a rather different story (from Pascale, 1984).

'In truth, we had no strategy other than the idea of seeing if we could sell something in the United States.' Honda had to obtain a currency allocation from the Japanese Ministry of Finance, part of a government famous for supporting the competitiveness of its industry abroad. 'They were extraordinarily skeptical,' said the managers; they finally granted Honda the right to invest $250,000 in the United States, but only $110,000 in cash!

'Mr Honda was especially confident of the 250 cc and 305 cc machines,' the managers continued about their leader. 'The shape of the handlebars on these larger machines looked like the eyebrow of Buddha, which he felt was a strong selling point.' (Bear in mind that motorcycles in America at the time were driven by black leather jacket types. No market existed for them as regular commuter transportation.)

The managers rented a cheap apartment in Los Angeles; two of them slept on the floor. In their warehouse in a rundown section of town, they swept the floors themselves and stacked the motorcycles by hand, to save money. Their arrival in America coincided with the closing of the 1959 motorcycle season.

The next year, a few of the larger bikes began to sell. Then, as they put it, 'disaster struck.' Because motorcycles are driven longer and faster in the United States, the Hondas begun to break down. 'But in the meantime,' they said, 'events had taken a surprising turn':

Throughout our first eight months, following Mr Honda's and our own instincts, we had not attempted to move the 50 cc Supercubs. While they were a smash success in Japan (and manufacturing couldn't keep up with demand there), they seemed wholly unsuitable for the US market where everything was bigger and more luxurious. As a clincher, we had our sights on the import market—and the Europeans, like the American manufacturers, emphasized the larger machines.

We used the Honda 50s ourselves to ride around Los Angeles on errands. They attracted a lot of attention. One day we had a call from a Sears buyer. While persisting in our refusal to sell through an intermediary, we took note of Sears' interest. But we still hesitated to push the 50 cc bikes out of fear they might harm our image in a heavily macho market. But when the larger bikes started breaking, we had no choice. We let the 50 cc bikes move.

The rest is history. Sales rose dramatically. Middle-class Americans began to ride on Hondas, first the Supercubs, later the larger bikes. Even the famous ad campaign—'You meet the nicest people on a Honda'—was serendipitous. Conceived by a UCLA undergraduate for a class project, it was shown to the Honda managers. But still trying to straddle the market and not antagonize the black leather jacket types, they were split. Eventually the sales director talked his more senior colleagues into accepting it.

Disputed accounts

After Mintzberg (1990) used this story in an article in the *Strategic Management Journal* to critique the design school and make some points about strategic learning, Michael Goold, who has published extensively from a planning and positioning perspective (cited in Chapter 3), published a reply (1992: 169–70). Goold identified himself as a co-author of the BCG report, and commented on it as follows:

The report does not dwell on how the Honda strategy was evolved and on the learning that took place. However, the report was commissioned for an industry in crisis, with the brief of identifying commercially viable alternatives. The perspective required was managerial ('what should we do now?'), not historical ('how did this situation arise?'). And for most executives concerned with strategic management the primary interest will always be 'what should we do now?'

Given such an interest, [a learning approach would presumably recommend] 'try something, see if it works and learn from your experience.' Indeed there is some suggestion that one should specifically try 'probable nonstarters.' For the manager, such advice would be unhelpful, even irritating. 'Of course, we should learn from experience,' he will say, 'but we have neither the time nor the money to experiment with endless, fruitless nonstarters.' Where the manager needs help is with what he should try to make work. This, surely, is exactly where strategic management thinking should endeavor to be useful.

In this context, the BCG analysis of Honda's success is much more valid. . . . Its purpose was to discern what lay behind and accounted for Honda's success, in a way that would help others to think through what strategies would be likely to work. (169)

Figure 7.3 graphs the figures of US imports of motorcycles and parts from Great Britain and from Japan before and after the 1975 publication of the BCG report. British imports plummeted after that year, while those of the Japanese began a dramatic rise in the next, passing the one billion dollar mark in the same year that British imports fell close to one million dollars! The BCG report, therefore, hardly stands as a model of successful consulting intervention.

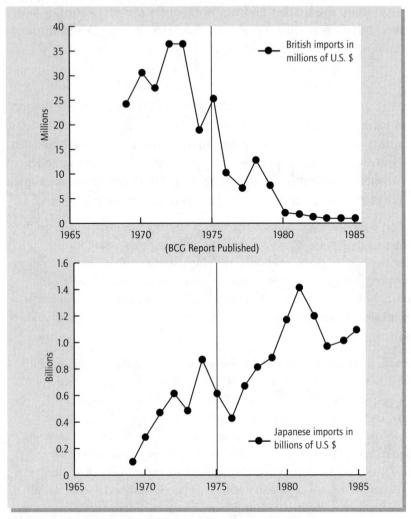

figure 7.3 United States imports of motorcycles and parts

Source: Commodity trade statistics

In his reply to Goold, Mintzberg (1996a: 96–9) published these figures and added the following comments:

To argue that being managerial means the need to ignore the history is exactly the problem. The BCG report erred in its inferences about how Honda developed its strategy, and so misled any manager who read it. Read that report and the implication is that you should lock yourself in your office and do clever competitive analysis. Honda never would have produced its strategy that way. Read, instead, Pascale's account of the Honda executives' own story and you get the impression you should sell your Rolls Royce, buy a pair of jeans, and start riding motorcycles around Des Moines, Iowa. There is a critical difference between doing 'random experiments' and exposing oneself to the chance to be surprised by the marketplace and so to learn.

> ❝ sell your Rolls Royce, buy a pair of jeans, and start riding motorcycles ❞

Reading Pascale's account, one has to ask: What makes the Japanese so smart? This is a story of success, not failure, yet they seemed to do everything wrong. True they were persistent, their managers were devoted to their company, and they were allowed the responsibility to make the important decisions on site. But when it came to strategic thinking, they hardly appear to be geniuses. Indeed, the story violates everything we believe about effective strategic management (and much that BCG imputed to those clever Japanese). Just consider the passive tone of the Japanese managers' comments ('events took a surprising turn,' 'we had no choice,' and so on) compared with the proactive vocabulary of the BCG report.

If this story is any indication, then the Japanese advantage lies not in their cleverness at all, but in our own stupidity. While we run around being 'rational,' they use their common sense. The Honda people avoided being too rational. Rather than believing they could work it all out in Tokyo, they came to America prepared to learn. Sure they used their experience and their cost position based on production volumes in Japan. But only after they learned what they had to do. The BCG people's crucial mistake was in skipping that critically necessary period of learning. . . .

[In contrast] managers who 'have neither the time nor the money to experiment' are destined to go the route of the British motorcycle industry. How in the world can anyone identify those 'endless, fruitless nonstarters' in advance? To assume such an ability is simple arrogance, and would, in fact, have eliminated many, if not most, of the really innovative products we have come to know. (Procter & Gamble apparently never dreamed that people would use Pampers other than for traveling; Thomas Watson Sr. apparently claimed in 1948: 'I think there is a world market for about five computers.') Analysis doesn't see ahead at all; mostly it looks behind (but not far behind).

And then, all too often, it extrapolates the identifiable trends of the past into the future. That is how great innovations end up as 'nonstarters' for a time.[3]

In a reply to this (1996: 100), Michael Goold wrote, among other things: 'Despite its analytical power, the BCG Report was not able to come up with a strategy for saving the industry.'[4]

Premises of the learning school

We can now conclude this discussion by inferring the premises from the evolving collection of writings we call the learning school.

---

3 Or forever: In a book called *Whatever Happened to the British Motorcycle Industry?* Bert Hopwood, a long-time executive with BSA, the British motorcycle firm, commented:

At this stage in the history of BSA, the early 1960s, this huge slice of the total British motorcycle industry was busy embarking on a madness of management consultancy, rather than getting on with the real job of work. It was this disaster of academic business thinking that finally crucified a British industry which was respected throughout the world. I would think that the great and highly successful Japanese motorcycle industry looked on and studied our capers with unbelieving eyes. (1981: 173)

Hopwood discusses one of those nonstarters, a scooter that was ruined because 'during this period we had been invaded by hordes of management consultants. When these experts had doctored the industry, the large volume scooter market had disappeared.' Hopwood also mentions the executive who said 'there could be no profit for us in very small motorcycles and there was no point in our entering that section of the market.' This executive, in fact, publicly thanked the Japanese for introducing people to the product so that they could trade up to the large British machines (p. 183)! This led Hopwood to make his most stunning statement of all:

In the early 1960s the Chief Executive of a world famous group of management consultants tried hard to convince me that it is ideal that top level management executives should have as little knowledge as possible relative to the product. This great man really believed that this qualification enabled them to deal efficiently with all business matters in a detached and uninhibited way. (171)

4 A full account of this debate, including an exchange between Ansoff and Mintzberg before the Goold reply, is contained in the *California Management Review* (Summer 1996: 78–117). The initial Mintzberg paper, as well as a resulting exchange between him and Ansoff, can be found in the *Strategic Management Journal* (1990: 171–95; 1991: 449–61; 1991: 463–66).

1 The complex and unpredictable nature of the organization's environment, often coupled with the diffusion of knowledge bases necessary for strategy, precludes deliberate control; strategy making must above all take the form of a process of learning over time, in which, at the limit, formulation and implementation become indistinguishable.

2 While the leader must learn too, and sometimes can be the main learner, more commonly it is the collective system that learns: there are many potential strategists in most organizations.

3 This learning proceeds in emergent fashion, through behaviour that stimulates thinking retrospectively, so that sense can be made of action. Strategic initiatives are taken by whoever has the capacity and the resources to be able to learn. This means that strategies can arise in all kinds of strange places and unusual ways. Some initiatives are left to develop by themselves or to flounder, while others are picked up by managerial champions who promote them around the organization and/or to the senior management, giving them impetus. Either way, the successful initiatives create streams of experiences that can converge into patterns that become emergent strategies. Once recognized, these may be made formally deliberate.

4 The role of leadership thus becomes not to preconceive deliberate strategies, but to manage the process of strategic learning, whereby novel strategies can emerge. Ultimately, then, strategic management involves crafting the subtle relationships between thought and action, control and learning, stability and change.

5 Accordingly, strategies appear first as patterns out of the past, only later, perhaps, as plans for the future, and ultimately, as perspectives to guide overall behaviour.

New directions for the learning school

The learning school encouraged managers to see strategy as intimately related to learning, in one form or another. C. K. Prahalad and Gary Hamel have developed this line of thinking in a number of highly influential articles in the *Harvard Business Review*, including 'The Core Competence of the Corporation' (1990) and 'Strategy as

Stretch and Leverage' (1993), as well as a book published in 1994 called *Competing for the Future*. We discuss the three most influential concepts that came out of these publications—core competency, strategic intent, and stretch and leverage. Note that these have more to do with the characteristic of organizations than with the processes they use.

Core competency

The origins of these ideas should really be traced back to a significant little book published by Hiroyuki Itami in 1987 called *Mobilizing Invisible Assets*. There he argued that 'the essence of successful strategy lies in . . . *dynamic strategic fit*,' the match of external and internal factors and the content of strategy itself. 'A firm achieves strategic fit through the effective use and efficient accumulation of its invisible assets, such as technological know-how or customer loyalty' (1).

Invisible assets, which 'serve as the focal point of strategy development and growth' (31), are 'hard to accumulate, they are capable of simultaneous multiple uses, and they are both inputs and outputs of business activities,' meaning that they feed into strategy but can also further accumulate as a consequence of it (12–13).

Itami also discussed 'dynamic unbalanced growth,' to 'transcend [the] current level of invisible assets': the firm should 'overextend' itself, its 'strategy sometimes should require stretching its invisible assets' (159):

Resources accumulated in these difficult conditions tend to be sturdy, like plants that have survived the strong winter winds. The human invisible assets of the firm must be well rooted and strong to survive the harsh winds of competition. You do not find such hardy plants very often in a nursery; the same goes for hardy invisible assets. . . . The resources must be exposed to the harsh competitive environment to grow strong, and an overextension strategy can be the best way to do this. (162)

Prahalad and Hamel elaborated upon a similar set of notions. For them, the 'roots' of competitive advantage can be found in the *core competencies* of a firm. In developing this idea, the authors used the image of a 'competency tree':

The diversified corporation is a large tree. The trunk and major limbs are core products, the smaller branches are business units; the leaves, flowers, and fruit are end products. The root system that provides nourishment, sustenance, and stability is the core competence. You can miss the strength of competitors by looking only at their end products, in the same way you miss the strength of a tree if you look only at its leaves. (1990: 82)

Prahalad and Hamel pointed to Casio and Canon as examples of the tree in action. Canon, for example, had a core competence in optics which was 'spread across businesses as diverse as cameras, copiers, and semiconductor lithographic equipment' (90).

Thus Prahalad and Hamel believed that competitive advantage derives from deeply rooted abilities which lie behind the products that a firm produces. They allow the firm to diversify into new markets by reapplying and reconfiguring what it does best. Moreover, because these competencies are 'hidden' (like the root of a tree), they cannot easily be imitated. Hence the secret to success lies not with great products but with a unique set of abilities that allow a firm to create great products. Managers are thus encouraged to look at their business as a portfolio of resources and capabilities which can be combined in various ways, not as a collection of products or business divisions.

> **" competitive advantage derives from deeply rooted abilities "**

These authors saw core competency as the consequence of the 'collective learning of the organization, especially how to coordinate diverse production skills and integrate multiple streams of technology' (1990: 82). This requires 'communication, involvement, and a deep commitment to working across organizational boundaries. . . . Competencies are the glue that binds existing businesses. They are also the engine for new business development' (1990: 82).[5]

---

5 In a sense, we could have added core competence to our steps in the development of our learning school model. Once sense has been made of behaviour, as described by Weick, then the competencies that are core can he recognized and built upon to enhance the learning and pursue the strategies that have emerged.

Strategic intent

Strategic intent is another important concept for Hamel and Prahalad:

On the one hand, strategic intent envisions a desired leadership position and establishes the criterion the organization will use to chart its progress. Komatsu set out to 'Encircle Caterpillar.' Canon sought to 'Beat Xerox.' Honda strove to become a second Ford—an automotive pioneer. All are expressions of strategic intent.

At the same time, strategic intent is more than simply unfettered ambition. (Many companies possess an ambitious strategic intent yet fall short of their goals.) The concept also encompasses an active management process that includes: focusing the organization's attention on the essence of winning; motivating people by communicating the value of the target; leaving room for individual and team contributions; sustaining enthusiasm by providing new operational definitions as circumstances change; and using intent consistently to guide resource allocations. (1989: 64)

> Thus strategic intent sets general direction, defines emerging market opportunities, and provides a rallying cry for employees. Boisot saw particular value in this concept in situations of environmental uncertainty: '. . . strategic intent relies on an intuitively formed pattern or *gestalt*—some would call it a vision—to give it unity and coherence. . . . [This] yields a simple yet robust orientation, intuitively accessible to all the firm's employees, an orientation which, on account of its clarity, can be pursued with some consistency over the long term in spite of the presence of turbulence.' (1995: 36).

Stretch and leverage

> Subsequently, Hamel and Prahalad added the dual concepts of 'stretch' and 'leverage.' They defined *stretch* literally as 'a misfit between [a firm's] resources and [its] aspirations' (1993: 78). On one hand, there are many firms that are well endowed with resources but lack sufficient 'stretch' in their aspirations—often a complacency associated with being 'number one.' On the other hand, there are firms that have meagre resource bases but are driven by very high ambition—that is, by an abundance of *stretch in aspirations*. This is what allows the small Davids to take on the big Goliaths.

But stretch is not enough: firms also need to learn how to *leverage* a limited resource base. This can be done in various ways (78):

1 **Concentrating** resources more effectively around a strategic focal point (e.g., Walt Disney's dream of an amusement park the likes of which the world had never seen).

2 **Accumulating** resources more efficiently, by extracting knowledge from experience plus borrowing the resources of other companies, such as securing links with critical suppliers to exploit their innovations.

3 **Complementing** one kind of resource with another to create higher value, by blending them and balancing product development, product or service production, and widespread delivery, marketing, and service infrastructure.

4 **Conserving** resources wherever possible, by recycling, and by coopting the resources of other companies (for example, by enticing a competitor into a fight with a common enemy).

5 **Recovering** resources from the marketplace in the shortest possible time.

In later writings (1996, 1997), Hamel argued for 'strategy as revolution.' Companies can no longer simply play by the rules of the game; instead they must radically change 'the basis of competition in their industries' (1997: 72). Hamel pointed to IKEA, the Body Shop, Charles Schwab, Dell Computer, Swatch, and Southwest Airlines as rule breakers that are 'overturning the industrial order' (1996: 70). In a 1998 article in *Sloan Management Review* magazine, Hamel proposes fives ways organizations can rethink their missions, reproduced in Box 7.7.

---

box 7.7

How Does Strategy Emerge?

(from Hamel, 1998: 12-13)

Let me ask a question of those who've ever sat through a business school case study: Have you ever gotten halfway through a brilliant exposition of a company's strategy and thought to yourself, 'Did they really have this thing figured out ahead of time? Isn't this just luck? Isn't this 20/20 hindsight? What about all the failures?' Sure, you have. These impertinent questions lie at the heart of our search for a theory of strategy creation. Is a great strategy luck, or is it foresight? Of course, the answer is that it is both. The question is, how can we increase the odds that new wealth-creating strategies emerge? How can we make serendipity happen? How can we prompt emergence?

My experience suggests that there are five preconditions for the emergence of strategy.

1. New voices. Bringing new 'genetic material' into the strategy process always serves to illuminate unconventional strategies. Top management must give up its monopoly on strategy creation, and previously underrepresented constituencies must be given a larger share of voice in the strategy creation process Specifically, I believe that young people, newcomers, and those at the geographic periphery of the organization deserve a larger share of voice. It is in these constituencies where diversity lurks. So strategy creation must be a pluralistic process, a deeply participative undertaking.

2. New conversations. Creating a dialogue about strategy that cuts across all the usual organizational and industry boundaries substantially increases the odds that new strategy insights will emerge. All too often, in large organizations, conversations become hard-wired over time, with the same people talking to the same people about the same issues year after year. After a while, individuals have little left to learn from each other. Opportunities fiat new insights are created when one juxtaposes previously isolated knowledge in new ways.

3. New passions. Unleashing the deep sense of discovery that resides in almost every human being, and focusing that sense of discovery on the search for new wealth-creating strategies is another prerequisite. I believe the widespread assumption that individuals are against change is flat wrong. People are against change when it doesn't offer the prospect of new opportunity. There is much talk today about return on investment, but I like to think in terms of return on emotional investment. Individuals will not invest emotionally in a firm and its success unless they believe they will get a return on that investment. All my experience suggests that individuals will eagerly embrace change when given the chance to have a share of voice in inventing the future of their company. They will invest when there's a chance to create a unique and exciting future in which they can share.

4. New perspectives. New conceptual lenses that allow individuals to reconceive their industry, their company's capabilities, customer needs, and so on substantially aid the process of strategy innovation. To increase the probability of strategy innovation, managers must become the merchants of new perspective. They must search constantly for new lenses that help companies reconceive themselves, their customers, their competitors, and, thereby, their opportunities.

5. New experiments. Launching a series of small, risk-avoiding experiments in the market serves to maximize a company's rate of learning about just which new

> strategies will work and which won't. The insights that come from a broad-based strategy dialogue will never be perfect. While much tradition al analysis can be done to reline those insights into viable strategies, there is much that can be learned only in the marketplace.
>
> So where does this leave us? We should spend less time working on strategy as a 'thing' and more time working to understand the preconditions that give rise to the thing' Executives, consultants, and business school professors must rebalance the attention given to context, content, and conduct in favor of conduct.
>
> In focusing on the conduct of strategy, not only are we trying to *discover* something – the hidden properties of strategy emergence – we are also trying to *invent* something. Like those long-ago Neanderthals trying to figure out the principles of cooking ('Why can't we have pork every night, rather than only after electrical storms?'), we need to invent an oven – a *strategy oven*.
>
> In Our quest for the strategy oven, our most valuable insights will probably come from far beyond the traditional strategy disciplines. Personally, I believe we will discover the strategy oven at the juncture of concepts like emergence, self-organization, cognition, and organizational learning. Science is closing in on the deep secrets of life. And we, as strategists, are finally beginning to close in on the deep secrets of corporate vitality.
>
> Source: Copyright 1998 by Massachusetts Institute of Technology. All rights reserved. Distributed by Tribune Media Services

From organizational learning to the learning organization

There has, of course, been a long and somewhat active literature on organizations as learning systems, dating back at least to Cyert and March's landmark book on *A Behavioral Theory of the Firm* (1963) and including the works of Richard Normann (1977), Chris Argyris (1976), and Donald Schön (1983).[6] Subsequently, interest in the 'learning organization' burgeoned, especially after the publication of Peter Senge's book, *The Fifth Discipline* (1990).

Most of this literature looked at learning from a process point of view, with its main focus on the management of change rather than on strategy per se. As Schultz (2001) noted, research on organizational learning is saturated with dynamic notions that seek to explain every facet of decision making and change. For this reason, it is

---

6 See Shrivastava (1983) for a review of this literature; also Hedberg's (1981) handbook review article.

useful to map the basic process of organizational learning. A starting point is a distinction that is often made between what Argyris and Schön (1978) have called *single-loop* and *double-loop* learning. Single-loop learning is more conservative, its main purpose being to detect errors and keep organizational activities on track. Double-loop learning is learning about single-loop learning: learning about how to learn, if you like.

A thermostat that automatically turns on the heat whenever the temperature in a room drops below 68 degrees is a good example of single-loop learning. A thermostat that could ask, 'Why am I set at 68 degrees?' and then explore whether or not some other temperature might more economically achieve the goal of heating the room would be engaging in double-loop learning. (Argyris, 1991: 100)

This means that managers 'need to reflect critically on their own behavior, identify the ways they often inadvertently contribute to the organization's problems, and then change how they act. . . . Teaching people how to reason about their behavior in new and more effective ways breaks down the defenses that block learning' (100).

In the pages that follow, we review three more recent major thrusts related to organizational learning that help to inform strategy formation: learning as knowledge creation, the dynamic capabilities approach of Hamel and Prahalad, and chaos theory.

Learning as knowledge creation

An important recent thrust in the literature concerns work on 'knowledge creation.' This has been popular of late, really a fad when companies designate positions of Chief Learning Officer. After all, which manager in any organization, including the chief executive officer, should not be concerned with learning?

One book of considerable substance on this subject is *The Knowledge-Creating Company* by Nonaka and Takeuchi (1995). Managers in the west, they argue:

need to get out of the old mode of thinking that knowledge can be acquired, taught, and trained through manuals, books, or lectures. Instead, they need to pay more attention to the less formal and systematic side of knowledge and start focusing on highly subjective insights, intuitions, and hunches that are gained through the use of metaphors, pictures, or experiences. (11)

To do this, Nonaka and Takeuchi believe that managers must recognize the importance of *tacit* knowledge—what we know implicitly, inside, and how it differs from *explicit knowledge*—what we know formally. The former suggests that 'we can know more than we can tell' (citing Polanyi, 1966, who first introduced the idea of tacit knowledge). 'Tacit knowledge is personal, context-specific, and therefore hard to formalize and communicate. Explicit or "codified" knowledge, on the other hand, refers to knowledge that is transmittable in formal, systematic language' (59).

Particularly crucial is the conversion of tacit knowledge into explicit knowledge, for which middle managers 'play a key role.' These are the people who 'synthesize the tacit knowledge of both front-line employees and senior executives, make it explicit, and incorporate it into new products and technologies' (16).

The book is built around what its authors call 'four modes of knowledge conversion,' shown in Figure 7.4 and described below.

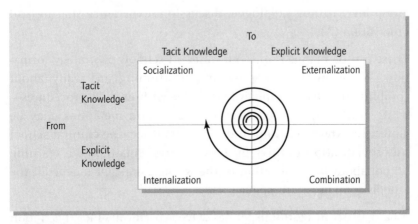

figure 7.4 The knowledge spiral   Source: *The Knowledge-Creating Company* by Nonaka I & Takeuchi H (OUP, 1995) reprinted by permission of Oxford University Press Inc.

■ **Socialization** describes the implicit sharing of tacit knowledge, often even without the use of language—for example, through experience. It is prevalent in Japanese corporate behaviour.

- **Externalization** converts tacit to explicit knowledge, often through the use of metaphors and analysis—special uses of language.

- **Combination**, favoured in western corporations, combines and passes formally codified knowledge from one person to another. 'An MBA education is one of the best examples of this kind' (67); though interestingly there is almost no MBA education in Japan.

- **Internalization** takes explicit knowledge back to the tacit form, as people internalize it, as in 'learning by doing.' Learning must therefore take place with the body as much as in the mind (239).

Key to all learning is, therefore, the 'knowledge spiral,' shown in the figure, by which these four processes interact in a dynamic way. 'The essence of strategy lies in developing the organizational capability to acquire, create, accumulate, and exploit knowledge' (74). But since 'knowledge is created only by individuals,' the role of the organization is to facilitate this learning, by supporting and stimulating individual learning, amplifying it, and crystallizing and synthesizing it at the group level through dialogue, discussion, experience sharing and observation (239).

> the role of the organization is to facilitate this learning

These can be mapped onto our different schools of strategy formation. For example, planning and positioning are really about combination—using explicit knowledge with explicit procedures—while entrepreneurship, based on vision and metaphor, may be closest to externalization. And, as we shall see, the cultural school uses socialization to drive in the strategies. Finally, is our learning school about internalization or the whole spiral? Or maybe all the schools combine in the spiral.

A particularly insightful paper has delved specifically into this notion of how individual learning fosters learning at the collective level. Mary Crossan, Henry Lane, and Roderick White (1999) of the University of Western Ontario set out to build a **comprehensive framework** of organizational learning. Organizational learning, they maintain, 'involves a tension between assimilating new learning (exploration) and using what has been learned (exploitation).' Like

Nonaka and Takeuchi, they argue that this takes places on the individual, group, and organizational levels, each one feeding the other. The three levels are linked by social and psychological processes they label intuiting, interpreting, integrating, and institutionalizing, as shown in Figure 7.5 (523).

Intuiting is a subconscious process that occurs at the level of the individual. It is the start of learning and must happen in a single mind. *Interpreting* then picks up on the conscious elements of this individual learning and shares it at the group level. *Integrating* follows to change collective understanding at the group level and bridges to the level of the whole organization. Finally, *institutionalizing* incorporates that learning across the organization by imbedding it in its systems, structures, routines, and practices. Sequenced in terms of our schools, this suggests that cognitive understanding comes first, then learning (as emergent strategies pervade the organization), followed by the entrepreneurial and the cultural aspects to express and internalize the understanding, with completion coming via the planning that formalizes all this.

Level	Process	Inputs/Outcomes
Individual	*Intuiting*	Experiences Images Metaphors
Group	*Interpreting*	Language Cognitive Map Conversation/Dialogue
Organization	*Integrating*	Shared Understandings Mutual Adjustment Interactive Systems
	Institutionalizing	Routines Diagnostic Systems Rules and Procedures

figure 7.5 Crossan, Lane and White's unifying framework for organizational learning (1999)

To close this discussion, Box 7.8 presents suggestions on how to move toward the learning organization.

---

box 7.8

Towards the learning organization

by Joseph Lampel

For many students of strategy, the Holy Grail is an organization capable of cumulative learning and constant self-renewal. Such an organization combines flexibility with effectiveness; it is able to learn from experience, without being trapped by this experience; and it can leverage this learning in the marketplace. This so-called 'learning organization' represents the fullest expression of the learning school. It strives to make organizational learning a central rather than an accidental activity which often goes unused. The basic character of the learning organization can be expressed in the following principles:

1 **Learning from failure** – Learning organizations fight the natural tendency of all organizations to bury failure and forget it as soon as possible. They recognize that improvements often begin with a detailed examination of failings. And they also recognize that for this to happen, the learning process must be open and free of recriminations and blame.

2 **Continuous re-examination** – Learning organizations are constantly reflecting on the effectiveness and efficiency of their processes. They explicitly reject the old adage 'that if it ain't broken, don't fix it.' Managers in a learning organization know that even apparently smoothly functioning processes can be improved. But because the source of the improvements is often buried deep within existing ways of doing things, it is important to periodically examine the organization's systems, routines, and procedures. The payoff is new knowledge and better practices which in turn improve key processes.

3 **First-hand learning** – Learning organizations recognize that front-line workers often have the best grasp of operational processes (their strengths as well as their weaknesses). A key managerial skill therefore is tapping this knowledge and making it work for the organization. Walking around and interacting with subordinates in their work settings is one of the most effective methods of tapping knowledge. Another is practising an open-door policy that encourages workers and supervisors to bring problems to the attention of top managers.

4 **Keeping knowledge mobile** – In learning organizations people at every level exchange and pool their knowledge. Managers in learning organizations are aware that knowledge tends to accumulate in relatively autonomous areas of business that only communicate with each other on a need-to-work basis. This compartmentalisation of knowledge constrains improvement and stifles change. A learning organization actively therefore seeks to move knowledge

▶ from one part of the organization to another. That means encouraging informal interaction, through social gatherings, rotation of personnel between units, and creation of multifunctional or multiunit project teams.

5 **Searching outside for knowledge** – Learning organizations recognize the importance of looking beyond their own boundaries for new knowledge. They know that much can be learned from customers, suppliers, and competitors. But doing this effectively requires a mindset that treats customers as partners rather than as a source of statistical data. It means making suppliers part of the development and design process. And it also means benchmarking against competitors not merely to keep track of who is ahead, but as a way of engaging in critical and honest self-assessment.

The learning organization is the antithesis of the old bureaucratic organization: it is decentralized, encourages open communications and motivates individuals to work in teams. Collaboration replaces hierarchy, and the predominant values are those of risk taking, honesty, and trust. Indeed, the picture that emerges has an uncanny resemblance to the utopian visions of social reformers at the turn of the twentieth century, and may prove just as difficult to create and sustain in practice. The difficulty, however, should not disguise an important aspect of the learning organization that is often lost in the hype that surrounds this concept since it was made popular by the work of Peter Senge (1990): Organizations that are capable of learning from their experience do better than organizations that simply adapt to their environments. In short, the improved capabilities conferred by such organizational learning do not result merely in better products and higher profits; they also increase the ability of the organization to take advantage of rapidly changing external conditions. Strategies that emerge from learning are sufficiently open-ended not only to respond but also take advantage of the unexpected.

The dynamics of dynamic capabilities

The learning school focuses attention on internal organizational processes, especially those that deal with innovation and change. The external environment loses the dominant role it plays in the design, planning, and positioning schools, and instead is seen as backdrop for how organizations manage their internal resources. At first sight, therefore, the key challenge for strategy is to discover which bundle of resources delivers sustainable advantage. But in a dynamic environment sustaining competitive advantage calls for combining, arranging, and rearranging resources. Doing this effectively depends on learning. More precisely, as organizations learn which bundles deliver competitive advantage and which do not, they build up knowledge that improves the bundling and rebundling process. This knowledge is a crucial capability at the heart of strategy, hence the term 'dynamic capabilities,' defined broadly by Eisenhardt and Martin (2003: 343) as:

The firm's processes that use resources – specifically the processes to integrate, reconfigure, gain and release resources – to match and even create market change. Dynamic capabilities thus are the organizational and strategic routines by which firms achieve resource configurations as markets emerge, collide, split, evolve, and die.

Because dynamic capabilities are essentially the organization's 'collective learning' this approach fits naturally into our learning school (see Volberda and Elfring, 2001). It does, however, share in spirit some of the characteristics of the design school, especially an emphasis on the role senior management as responsible for 'orchestrating' the selection and flow of resources (Helfat *et al.*, 2007: 25). Taking this idea one step further, a recent publication by Sirmon, Hitt, and Ireland (2007) argues that top management should pursue a deliberate 'resource management programme':

. . . top-level managers should view their firm as a system of resources and capabilities, developing leveraging strategies that match their capabilities to the market and environmental context in order to create value for customers and owners [p. 273]. . . . In particular, managers need to be able to acquire, accumulate, and divest resources to have the most effective resource portfolio at any given time. Managers should also have the skills necessary to bundle resources to create effective capabilities. [And they] must also effectively manage the feedback and learning processes necessary to continuously update capabilities and adjust the resource portfolio. (p. 288)

The increasing popularity of dynamic capabilities is a product of the so called 'new economy' which emerged in the 1990s. Proponents of the new economy argued that technology and globalization were increasingly making the standard strategy prescriptions irrelevant. Hamel and Prahalad framed this perception in a commentary published in 1996:

As we careen from the machine age into the information age, the more questionable become the traditional practices and precepts of management. A horse-drawn plow is useless on a factory floor. Management tools developed in the machine age may turn out to be as irrelevant in the information age as agrarian tools were in the machine age.

Dynamic capabilities seemed to answer the call for radical rethinking of the strategy process. What also made this concept attractive was the way it combined the design and learning schools (with a dose of the entrepreneurial school as well). If you like, a contemporary view of adaptive strategy as a process of conceptual design.

Of course, such a combination can begin to make a mess of the nice, neat categories of our ten schools. But we welcome such combinations, because they suggest that the field is becoming more sophisticated: growing beyond the pat categories of the past. As we build up to our last schools, we shall see a number of such hybrids of the earlier ones.

Beyond learning to chaos

There are those who claim that even the learning organization is constrained, since it tends to emphasize what is constant and persistent rather than what is innovative and revolutionary. These people look to theories of chaotic or disorderly systems as an alternative approach.

Chaos theory was originally developed in the physical sciences to better understand complex, nonlinear, dynamic systems, such as turbulence in liquids and gases. This represented an attempt to shift from a traditional scientific outlook, based on decomposing complex phenomena into simple and predictable elements, to one in which the system is seen as holistic and dynamic. That way scientists could better understand 'the swirls and vortices that characterize turbulent flow . . .' (Levy, 1994: 168).

A central tenet of chaos theory is that simple sets of deterministic relationships can produce patterned yet unpredictable outcomes (168). Put differently, 'order can produce chaos and chaos can lead to new order . . .' (Stacey, 1992: 98–99). Recall that 'for want of a nail the shoe was lost; for want of a shoe, the horse was lost,' and so on through the rider and the battle to the kingdom.

These days the popular metaphor, first presented by Edward Lorenz in a famous speech of 1972, is the butterfly that, flapping its wings in Brazil, might just have set off a tornado in Texas (1993: 181–4). Who can know in these systems what 'are not random but look random . . . that appear to proceed according to chance even though their behavior is in fact controlled by precise laws' (4). (Recall also our flies at the beginning of this chapter who, flapping their wings rather randomly, did better than the organized flapping of the bees.)

The traditional approach to management has led to an emphasis on control, order, and predictability. Chaos and disorder have been seen as inimical to the very notion of organization, destructive forces to be constrained. Even the learning process, which may seem initially disorderly, is ultimately expected to be institutionalized in the routine of the organization.

However, people such as Nonaka (1988), Stacey (1992), and Brown and Eisenhardt (1998), argue that disorder and chaos are intrinsic rather than alien properties of organizations. The constant disturbances that managers fight contain important creative opportunities, which can be harnessed to produce learning that can transcend established ways of strategic thinking. Thus organizations, say those sympathetic to chaos theory, should be seen as dynamic systems in a permanent state of disequilibrium. Indeed, their own managers should deliberately inject disturbances into the operations so that the resulting inconsistencies can generate new knowledge. A chaotically run organization, in other words, is self-subversive: it welcomes instability and seeks to create crisis as a means of transcending its limits. It is in a state of permanent revolution.

These ideas may be overstated, but they do contain an interesting grain of truth. Stacey (1992: 99–100) has discussed the assumptions of conventional management that are undermined by chaos theory, for example, that 'long-term futures are knowable,' that 'the environment is a given' to which 'the successful business adapts' by understanding the 'clear cause and effect relationships.' In contrast, chaos theory suggests that almost anything can happen, that irregularity is a fundamental property of the organization, in which 'small, chance disturbances' can have large effects. Therefore, managers cannot rely on structures, systems, rules and procedures, but must instead be prepared to adapt continually in novel ways.

Of course, all of this seems to preempt managerial choice altogether: how can anyone possibly do anything under such conditions? In fact, much like the rest of the learning school, this really grants great choice, at least to the shrewd strategist. As suggested in the accompanying box, which contains Levy's suggested lessons of chaos theory for strategic management, things are so chaotic, so disorderly, that those who are flexible and quick moving can grab opportunities all over the place. It is the bureaucrats and the planners who really suffer.

Critique of the learning school

One should not expect a harsh condemnation of the learning school from authors who are among its enthusiastic adherents. We support it because we feel it offers a counterbalancing force to the 'rational' deliberateness that has for so long dominated the literature and practice of strategic management. Our support, however, is not unqualified. There is always the danger of going to the opposite extreme. 'Learning,' after all, is currently very much in vogue. Yet it can lead to the very disintegration of strategy. Let us consider, in turn, the problems of no strategy, of lost strategy, and of wrong strategy.

---

box 7.9

Chaos theory for strategic management

(from Levy, 1994:170–173)

1 **Long-term planning is very difficult**. . . . In chaotic systems, small disturbances multiply over time because of nonlinear relationships and the dynamic, repetitive nature of [the system]. As a result, such systems are extremely sensitive to initial conditions, which make forecasting very difficult. . . . The payoff in terms of better forecasts of building more complex and more accurate models may be small. . . .

> 2 **Industries do not reach a stable equilibrium**. . . . Chaotic systems do not
> reach a stable equilibrium; indeed, they can never pass through the same
> exact state more than once. . . . The implication is that industries do not 'settle
> down' and any apparent stability . . . is likely to be short lived. . . .
>
> 3 **Dramatic change can occur unexpectedly**. . . . The entry of one new competi-
> tor or the development of a seemingly minor technology can have a
> substantial impact on competition in an industry . . .
>
> 4 **Short-term forecasts and predictions of patterns can be made**. . . . There is a
> surprising degree of order in chaotic systems. . . . If we imagine that strategic
> decisions in companies are made on a monthly or even annual cycle, then
> industry simulation models might be able to make useful predictions over a
> time horizon of several months or possibly years. . . .
>
> 5 **Guidelines are needed to cope with complexity and uncertainty**. . . . It is the
> complexity of strategic interactions, whether in chess, soccer, or in business,
> that makes it essential to adopt simplifying strategies to guide decisions; even
> the most powerful computers are unable to track all possible moves and coun-
> termoves in a chess game.

No strategy

Andrews (1980) has referred to Lindblom's 'muddling through'
organization as 'purposeless' and to Wrapp's related (1967) article
about good managers not making policy decisions as 'anti-strategic.'
While this may be an unjust characterization of the more recent
work in this school, which goes beyond disjointed incrementalism to
convergent learning, it is true that under incrementalism—that constant nibbling instead of a good bite—central direction can dissolve
into tactical manoeuvring. A series of rational moves can belie the
rationality of the whole activity. To quote the Canadian humourist,
Stephen Leacock: 'He flung himself from the room, flung himself
upon his horse and rode madly off in all directions.' Thus Hayes and
Jaikumar (1988) refer to an 'irrational incrementalism,' where companies innovate piecemeal thereby producing a hodgepodge of
technologies and systems that collectively end up as less than the
sum of their parts. A pile of tusks does not an elephant make.

Of course, as we argued in our critique of the design school, organizations do not always need clear strategies (just as poachers get rich on

piles of tusks). But it is also true that a great many organizations suffer from the lack of clearly articulated strategy (just as casual hunters often come home empty-handed). Gaddis (1997), for example, has written about the assumption of the 'super-organization [that] can continuously develop, increment by increment, its own strategic direction to a prosperous (undefined) future.' He mentions the Roman general Varro, 'an early incrementalist . . . who "did not need any strategy."' He took his superior force into battle against Hannibal (who had a strategy of the 'weak centre') and suffered a devastating defeat. Gaddis concludes (with more than a touch of sarcasm): 'Apparently a suitable strategy for the superior Roman army failed to "emerge" as the battle wore on.'

This is hardly a fair test: we hope this chapter has made clear that strategies do not emerge on convenient schedules, let alone in the heat of a battle. (We might add too that Hannibal ultimately had to quit Italy, having been worn down by Roman incrementalism.) But there are conditions under which patient learning cannot be relied upon, crisis being the most obvious. Here the organization may require a forceful leader who already has a strategic vision to save it. Even under more stable conditions, some organizations need the strong strategic visions that come from centralized entrepreneurship more than decentralized learning. An organization can have loads of venturing and thousands of flowers blooming all over the place, yet have no coherence at all—no strategy.

If this organization is in the toy business, its managers may well respond: 'Who cares? The products are coming out, the customers are buying. So what? Performance is what counts, not strategy.' But if it is nuclear reactors that an organization builds, or assembly lines that it runs, or even foreign policy that it makes, then coherence may be critical for performance. In other words, what matters in these organizations is not just learning but collective learning.

Take the case of foreign policy. The signals coming into a government vary widely, reflecting all sorts of pressures and special interests groups. The government nevertheless has to have the means of choosing some and ignoring others. A strategic perspective does this.

Without it, people can manoeuvre at will, riding off in all directions. The government can end up being buffeted every which way, wasting resources while leaving everyone confused. Of course, the opposite danger is no less serious nor any less evident in foreign affairs ministries around the world: perfect coherence which fails repeatedly because it allows no one to get the messages that times are changing.

Lost strategy

An overemphasis on learning can also work to undermine a coherent and perfectly viable strategy. People run around learning *away* from what works, championing initiatives simply because they are new or more interesting. Bear in mind that having no discipline ultimately means having no organization.

The result may be *Strategic drift* (Johnson, 1987: 244–247). Gradually, incrementally, perhaps imperceptibly, the organization drifts away from its established strategies, perhaps to everyone's eventual regret. The well-known story of the boiled frog applies here. Put a frog into boiling water and it jumps out. Put it in cold water that is slowly brought to a boil and it apparently remains to die. The frog does not want to die; it just does not notice until it is too late.

The learning school should not be about learning as some kind of Holy Grail. Mostly it should be about learning as a discipline for elaborating a valued sense of direction—an established strategic perspective—and occasionally about changing that sense of direction, when necessary learning a new one. That may require continuous experimentation, to know when something better has come along, as well as to help bring that something better along.

But constant change is another matter. As we shall discuss in Chapter 11, the trick is not to change everything all the time, but to know what to change when. And that means balancing change with continuity. Effective management means to sustain learning while pursuing the strategies that work. There may be, as we noted earlier in this chapter, a time to sow strategies and a time to reap them.

The tricky part concerns learning at the edges of that strategic umbrella: when to cut off initiatives that venture beyond the umbrella as opposed to when to enlarge the umbrella to recognize their benefits. Managers cannot be constantly doing the latter—enlarging the organization's strategic perspective—but neither can they fix it so that it can never be allowed to change.

Wrong strategy

Besides the lack of strategies and the *un*learning of good strategies, learning in an incremental way can also encourage the emergence of strategies that no one ever wanted, let alone intended. The organization is lured, one step at a time, into an undesirable position.

We already discussed the 'foot in the door' technique, whereby incremental steps are used to attain what might have been unacceptable overall. But here the assumption is that of the clandestine strategist in some corner who fools an unsuspecting central management. There need not, however, be any strategist at all: little decisions sometimes just lead to big undesired strategies, as in that automobile company we mentioned earlier that woke up to find itself with a new model no one ever decided upon: like the nail in the horse's shoe that lost the war, so a mock-up of a design may have produced a new car. Connolly has generalized about such things in a most pointed way: 'Nuclear wars and childbearing decisions are poor settings for a strategy of "try a little one and see how it goes"' (1982: 45)! Learning tends to be about trying the little ones; so we have to be careful about learning too.

Careful of learning

The learning organization is all the rage right now, and mostly for good reason. But it is no panacea for anything. People have to learn, but they also have to get on with doing the regular work efficiently. (Horses wear blinders for good reason.) There can be a time to learn and a time to exploit previous learning. Moreover, as we saw in the last chapter, there can be superstitious learning too, and 'groupthink,' which means learning into a collective corner, if you like. There is also negative learning, as we saw in Staw's (1976) notion of 'escalating commitment': as you fail, you keep investing more in the hope of recouping your losses, not recognizing that the situation may be hopeless.[7] So learning is wonderful, but there can be too much of any wonderful thing!

Finally, learning can be expensive. It takes time, sometimes resulting in endless meetings and floods of electronic mail; it goes off in all sorts of funny directions; resources must be invested in false starts; people have to be convinced of the benefits of one initiative over another; and the organization may be forced to bounce around repeatedly, and so pay the price of not settling down quickly enough to concentrate its resources. Managers have to focus their learning; they need to know 'learning about *what?*' A real learning organization also worries about unnecessary learning.

Given all this, is it any wonder that so many organizations find it more convenient to look for a leader at the helm pronouncing a clear vision for all to follow, or, better still, to be handed an optimal strategy from the computers of the positioning school?

Contribution and context of the learning school

The previous sentence, of course, also suggests the contribution of the learning school. Visionaries cannot always be found, sometimes because a situation is too unstable to 'envision.' Likewise, the positioning school computers often come up short, offering standard solutions to complex problems (recall the Honda story). Then the organization in need of a new strategy may have no choice but to learn collectively.

Such learning seems particularly necessary in *professional*-type organizations (for example, hospitals), that operate in highly *complex* environments, where the knowledge required to create strategy is widely diffused. (Of course, organizations decentralize for other reasons as well—for example, because power rests legally in the hands of

---

7 Staw actually labelled his main article about the US experience in Vietnam 'Knee Deep in the Big Muddy.' But could he have used that title if the American forces had stopped the Viet Cong? In other words, how can we ever be sure, before the fact, that a situation is hopeless?

many people, as in the US Congress, about which Lindblom [1959, 1968] wrote.) Here, strategy formation may have to be a process of collective learning simply because *no central authority* has the power to impose strategy on the whole organization. The various actors have to work it out by mutual adjustment, if they can. Quinn's (1980a) corporations are like this to a degree: the central managers may be able to formulate strategy but the political realities require that implementation be a process of collective agreement, if not collective learning.

Also, any organization that faces a *truly novel* situation usually has to engage in a process of learning, in order to figure out what is taking place. (That process may be individual or collective, depending on the organization's ability to bring the relevant information to a central place.) For example, when a company in a mature industry is subjected to an unprecedented discontinuity, say a technological breakthrough that upsets established practices, it has to engage in a process of learning in order to develop viable new strategies.

Some organizations face perpetual novelty. In other words, their environments are *dynamic* and *unpredictable*, which makes it difficult to converge on a clear strategy at all. In this case, the structure tends to take the form of adhocracy, or project organization, and the learning approach becomes almost mandatory—the means to work things out in a flexible manner. At the very least, it allows the organization to do *something*—to respond to an evolving reality in individual steps instead of having to wait for a fully determined strategy.

To conclude, the learning school brings a reality to the study of strategy formation that has been lacking in the other schools so far discussed. Based largely on descriptive research, it tells us not so much what organizations are supposed to do as what they actually do when faced with complex and dynamic conditions. But good description can be prescriptive too, indeed, sometimes it can reveal exemplary behaviour under particular circumstances.

Just as we can get good prescription from description, so perhaps might we get voluntarism from what seems like determinism. The prescriptive schools, especially that of positioning, seem to be all about free will. But as we saw in critiquing them, they are rather more deterministic than their proponents would have people believe.

The learning school may be the opposite. Within what appear to be passive or reactive responses to outside forces, the organization actually learns and creates—it comes up with novel and interesting strategies. Nowhere is this better revealed than in Pascale's story of how Honda did everything wrong to emerge as the market leader in the American motorcycle industry.

Grabbing initiative, no matter how serendipitous the circumstances, no matter how messy the process, no matter how initially confused the actors, is ultimately voluntaristic. In contrast, slotting an organization into a supposedly optimal strategy dictated by the formal analysis of its industry is ultimately deterministic. Much as setting out to maximize profit may undermine profitability (because it is so compulsive), so too setting out to be in control may in fact forfeit control (because it can be no less compulsive). Perhaps it is the playful who ultimately inherit the earth.

Our personal (and perhaps biased) belief is that the learning school has served us well. Its research has been based on simple methods that seem well suited to explaining complex phenomena, better perhaps than the sophisticated techniques of so much social science—from the protocols of the cognitive psychologists to the mathematics of the game theorists. In practice too, learning approaches to strategy are hardly fancy or sophisticated. Indeed, they might be seen as naive—the strategist as waif who bounces around, trying one thing and another until, lo and behold, the concept emerges. But don't be fooled by the messiness of the process: this requires a great deal of sophistication. These people have to have an innate sense of trying things that just might work—or better still, encouraging others to do so. And then they have to recognize something good when it appears.

It is important that we come to understand strategy as a learning process, both individual and collective. The learning school, whose literature is small compared with that of the planning and positioning schools (yet whose real practice may be far larger), has made a major contribution in this regard. And it will likely continue to do so.

The power school: strategy formation as a process of negotiation

"They can't find their hidden agenda!"

Fancy what a game of chess would be if all the chessmen had passions and intellects, more or less small and cunning; if you were not only uncertain about your adversary's men, but a little uncertain also about your own; if your knight could shuffle himself on to a new square by the sly; if your bishop, in disgust at your castling, could wheedle your pawns out of their places; and if your pawns, hating you because they are pawns, could make away from their appointed posts that you might get checkmate on a sudden. You might be the longest-headed of deductive reasoners, and yet you might be beaten by your own pawns. You would be especially likely to be beaten, if you depended arrogantly on your mathematical imagination, and regarded your passionate pieces with contempt.

—George Eliot, *Felix Holt, The Radical* (1980: 237)

The learning school, especially in the writings of Quinn and Lindblom, has already introduced power and politics into this discussion, in contrast to the first four schools, which ignore it. What is here labelled the power school takes off the gloves altogether, and characterizes strategy formation as an overt process of influence, emphasizing the use of power and politics to negotiate strategies favourable to particular interests.

We are using the word *power* here to describe the exercise of influence beyond the purely economic (which includes economic power used beyond conventional, marketplace competition). This brings it close to politics, a term we use rather broadly in this chapter. In a sense, in so doing, we reverse the position of the positioning school: if the purpose of a commercial organization is to compete 'legitimately' in an economic marketplace, then the label 'political' can be used for behaviour that is not legitimate in that way. In other words, it is illegitimate or a legitimate (i.e., not expressly legitimate). Politics thus becomes synonymous with the exploitation of power in other than purely economic ways. This would obviously include clandestine moves to subvert competition (such as establishing a cartel), but it could also include cooperative arrangements designed for the same effect (such as certain alliances).

This means, as noted earlier, that strategies that are generic for the positioning school can, with a slight twist of perception, become political here. (At what point does expansion of a market position become subversion of the competition?) Likewise, we could use Porter's own concepts to talk about political strategic groups and political generic strategies. We can do this because the line between economic goals and political intent is both fine and subtle. With the positioning school having so carefully situated itself on one side, the power school is able to take its place on the other. But such a distinction must be considered artificial: real behaviour spans the continuum of the two, with distinctions impossible to make at the margins.

Power relations surround organizations; they can also infuse them. Therefore, we shall make a distinction between two branches of this school. What we call *micro* power deals with the play of politics—of illegitimate and legitimate power—*inside* an organization, in this book specifically within the processes of strategic management. *Macro* power concerns the use of power *by* the organization. An example of the former might be the conflicts that revolve around the divestiture of a division, an example of the latter, an organization on the verge of bankruptcy that pressures a government for loan guarantees. One focuses on internal actors conflicting with their colleagues, usually out of self-interest; the other sees the organization acting out of its own self-interest, in conflict, or cooperation, with other organizations.

The literature of strategic management that falls into the power school is rather small, hardly more than a trickle since the early 1970s, although it later grew somewhat.[1] Power used to be viewed as a kind of fifth column in this field. Everyone knew about it but researchers rarely studied it. That has changed.

Of course, in practice power and politics have never been absent from organizations, especially large ones, nor from their strategy making processes. It just took time for all of this to get formally acknowledged in print. And so, some publications appeared in the late 1970s, such as Macmillan's text (1978) on *Strategy Formulation: Political Concepts*; Sarrazin's study (1975, 1977–8) of the political side of planning; and Pettigrew's (1977); and Bower and Doz's (1979)

---

1 See Bigley and Wiersema (2002); Clark (2004); Davenport and Leitch (2005); Greve and Mitsuhashi (2004); Greve and Mitsuhashi (2007); Lawrence *et al.* (2005).

works on strategy formulation as a political process. However, when we add to this the associated work from political science on public policy-making, the literature of this school becomes quite large.

We divide this chapter into three major sections, the first on micro power, the second on macro power, the third on critique, context, and contribution of the power school.

Micro power

The intention of people writing in the power school has been to wake strategic management up to a basic reality of organizational life: that organizations consist of individuals with dreams, hopes, jealousies, interests, and fears. This may seem like an obvious point, but much of the literature for a long time gave the impression that senior managers were rational actors who defined strategies that everyone else embraced, being the compliant and loyal 'human resources' that they were. In contrast to this, let us consider strategy making as a political process, and then strategies themselves as political, before we conclude with the positive benefits of micro politics.

Strategy making as a political process

If strategy making can be a process of planning and analysis, cognition and learning, so too can it be one of bargaining and compromise among conflicting individuals, groups, and coalitions. Introduce any form of ambiguity—environmental uncertainty, competing goals, varied perceptions, scarcity of resources—and politics arises. Accordingly, proponents of this school argue that it is not possible to formulate, let alone implement, optimal strategies: the competing goals of individuals and coalitions ensure that any intended strategy will be disturbed and distorted every step of the way. People play all sorts of 'political games' in organizations, some of which are described in Box 8.1.

Zald and Berger (1978) have described 'Social Movements in Organizations,' three in particular. *Coup d'état* is the seizure of power from within, where the objective is to displace the holders of authority while keeping the system of authority intact. (833). *Insurgency* seeks not to replace the leadership, but to 'change some aspect of organizational function'—some programme or key decision, for example—but from outside the conventional political channels (837, 838). And *mass movements*, which range 'from protest to rebellion,' are 'collective attempts to express grievances and discontent and/or to promote or resist change' (841). These are more visible and involve more people than the other two movements.

---

box 8.1

Political games in organizations

(from Mintzberg, 1989: 238–40)

Insurgency game: usually played to resist authority, or else to effect change in the organization; is usually played by 'lower participants' (Mechanic, 1962), those who feel the greatest weight of formal authority.

Counterinsurgency game: played by those in authority who fight back with political means, perhaps legitimate ones as well (such as excommunication in the church).

Sponsorship game: played to build power base, in this case by using superiors; individual attaches self to someone with more status, professing loyalty in return for power.

Alliance-building game: played among peers—often line managers, sometimes experts—who negotiate implicit contracts of support for each other in order to build power bases to advance selves in the organization.

Empire-building game: played by line managers, in particular, to build power bases, not cooperatively with peers but individually with subordinates.

Budgeting game: played overtly and with rather clearly defined rules to build power base; similar to the last game, but less divisive, since prize is resources, not positions or units per se, at least not those of rivals.

Expertise game: nonsanctioned use of expertise to build power base, either by flaunting it or by feigning it; true experts play by exploiting technical skills and knowledge, emphasizing the uniqueness, criticality, and irreplaceability of the expertise, also by keeping knowledge to selves; non-experts play by attempting to have their work viewed as expert, ideally to have it declared professional so that they alone can control it.

Lording game: played to build power base by 'lording' legitimate power over those without it or with less of it (i.e., using legitimate power in illegitimate ways); manager can lord formal authority over subordinate or public servant over a citizen, etc.

Line versus staff game: a game of sibling-type rivalry, played not just to enhance personal power but to defeat a rival; pits line managers with formal decision-

▶ making authority against staff advisers with specialized expertise; each side
tends to exploit legitimate power in illegitimate ways.

Rival camps game: again played to defeat a rival; typically occurs when alliance or
empire-building games result in two major power blocs; can be most divisive
game of all; conflict can be between units (e.g., between marketing and
production in manufacturing firm), between rival personalities, or between two
competing missions (as in prisons split by conflict between some people who
favor custody and others who favor rehabilitation of the prisoners).

Strategic candidates game: played to effect change in an organization;
individuals or groups seek to promote through political means their own
favored changes of a strategic nature.

Whistle-blowing game: a typically brief and simple game, also played to effect
organizational change; privileged information is used by an insider, usually a
lower participant, to 'blow the whistle' to an influential outsider on
questionable or illegal behavior by the organization.

Young Turks game: played for highest stakes of all; a small group of 'young
Turks,' close to but not at the center of power, seeks to reorient organization's
basic strategy, displace a major body of its expertise, replace its culture, or rid
it of its leadership.

Bolman and Deal (1997) have set out the following propositions
about the world of organizational politics.

1 Organizations are *coalitions* of various individuals and interest
  groups.

2 There are *enduring differences* among coalition members in values,
  beliefs, information, interests, and perceptions of reality.

3 Most important decisions involve the allocation of *scarce
  resources*—who gets what.

4 Scarce resources and enduring differences give *conflict* a central
  role in organizational dynamics and make *power* the most
  important resource.

5 Goals and decisions emerge from *bargaining, negotiation*, and
  jockeying for position among different stakeholders. (163)

These propositions invite us to move away from the idea of strategy
formation as the product of a single 'architect' or homogeneous
'strategy' team. Instead, various actors and coalitions of actors pursue
their own interests and agendas. The power school warns us that

there are 'dangers of attributing the idea of managerial strategy to management as a collectivity . . . the internal cohesion of management is itself a matter for investigation . . . [and] may shift from issue to issue' (Cressey *et al.*, 1985: 141).

> **the internal cohesion of management is itself a matter for investigation**

Moreover, subordinate groups can enter into the processes of determining and distorting strategies. Thus the power school presses for better understanding of the role of organized and unorganized individuals in shaping or reshaping behaviours.

Policy making in government

As noted earlier, strategy formation in business goes under the label of policy-making in government. Here there is a rather significant literature. Much of it is about specific policies (such as foreign affairs or police reform) and so is not really of much help to strategic management at large. There are also significant bodies of work related to our other schools, especially planning, and some to learning (such as Lindblom, cited in the last chapter) and cognition (e.g., Steinbruner, 1974), etc. But there are important works related to this school too, obviously.

Probably best known is Graham Allison's (1971) model of 'government politics' (based on a study of the Cuban missile crisis), likely the most comprehensive description of policy-making or strategy formation as a process of internal politics. Other interesting work in political science has been done on 'policy slippage' and 'policy drift' (Majone and Wildavksy, 1978: 105; Kress *et al.*, 1980; Lipsky, 1978). *Slippage* means that intentions get distorted somewhat in implementation, *drift* (mentioned in the last chapter) that, as time goes by, a series of 'more or less "reasonable" accommodations . . . cumulatively bring changes which fundamentally alter' the original intentions (Kress *et al.*, 1980: 1101). In the terms we introduced in Chapter 1, the first is about partly unrealized strategies, the second about partly emergent ones. In their discussion of public sector implementation, Majone and Wildavsky (1978) are critical of the notion that public servants are looked upon as mere 'robots' who implement the strategies that spring 'fully armed from the forehead of an omniscient policymaker' (113). Just like the chess pieces of our opening quotation!

Almost all imaginable organizations, private as well as public, are at least mildly and occasionally political. Only the smallest or most autocratically run might be able to avoid overt politics altogether for a time. On the other hand, some organizations become entirely captured by pervasive politics, so that every strategic decision becomes a battlefield. The place becomes an outright 'political arena,' not unlike government legislatures in their most acrimonious form. We have seen this, for example, even in a small family firm where two brothers, one of whom ran marketing and sales, the other production, were not on speaking terms. Of course, it is difficult for a small company to last long under such conditions, although large ones in secure markets can sometimes go on like this for years.

It is in times of difficult change, when power inevitably gets realigned in unpredictable ways, that political arenas arise in otherwise healthy organizations. Under these conditions, many things go up for grabs, and people get to feeling particularly insecure. All of this breeds political conflict, especially in strategy making, where the stakes are high. Robert Greene and Joost Elffers published a best-selling book entitled *The 48 Laws of Power*. These are derived from a review of the great political philosophers, conmen and notorious figures of all time. In the box below, we present some of these which have the greatest relevance to strategy.

---

box 8.2

Laws of power

(from Robert Greene and Joost Elffers, 1998)

Conceal your intentions

Keep people off balance and in the dark by never revealing the purpose behind your actions. Without a clue about what you are up to, they cannot prepare a defense. Guide them far enough down the wrong path, envelop them in enough smoke, and by the time they realize your intentions, it will be too late.

Win through your actions, never through argument

Any momentary triumph you think you have gained through argument is really a Pyrrhic victory: The resentment and ill will you stir up is stronger and lasts longer than any momentary change of opinion. It is much more powerful to get others to agree with you through your actions, without saying a word. Demonstrate; do not explicate.

Crush your enemy totally

All great leaders since Moses have known that a feared enemy must be crushed completely. (Sometimes they have learned this the hard way.) If one ember is left alight, no matter how dimly it smolders, a fire will eventually break out. More is lost through stopping halfway than through total annihilation: The enemy will recover, and will seek revenge. Crush him, not only in body but also in spirit.

Keep others in suspense—cultivate an air of unpredictability

Humans are creatures of habit with an insatiable need to see familiarity in other people's actions. Your predictability gives them a sense of control. Turn the tables; be deliberately unpredictable. Behavior that seems to have no consistency or purpose will keep them off balance, and they will wear themselves out trying to explain your moves. Taken to an extreme, this strategy can intimidate and terrorize.

Use the surrender tactic—transform weakness into power

When you are weaker, never fight for honor's sake: choose surrender instead. Surrender gives you time to recover, time to torment and irritate your conqueror, time to wait for his power to wane. Do not give him the satisfaction of fighting and defeating you. By turning the other cheek you infuriate and unsettle him.

Make surrender a tool of power.

Concentrate your forces

Conserve your forces and energies by concentrating them at their strongest point. You gain more by finding a rich mine and mining it deeper than by flitting from one shallow mine to another, intensity defeats extensity every time. . . .

Re-create yourself

Do not accept the roles that society foists on you. Re-create yourself by forging a new identity, one that commands attention and never bores the audience. Be the master of your own image rather than letting others define it for you. Incorporate dramatic devices into your public gestures and actions. Your power will be enhanced and your character will seem larger than life.

Plan all the way to the end

The ending is everything. Plan all the way to it, taking into account all the possible consequences, obstacles, and twists of fortune that might reverse your hard work and give the glory to others. By planning to the end you will not be

▶ overwhelmed by circumstances and you will know when to stop. Gently guide fortune and help determine the future by thinking far ahead.

Control the options—get others to play with the cards you deal

The best deceptions are the ones that seem to give the other person a choice: Your victims feel they are in control, but are actually your puppets. Give people options that come out in your favor whichever one they choose. Force them to make choices between the lesser of two evils, both of which serve your purpose. Put them on the horns of a dilemma: They will be gored wherever they turn.

Master the art of timing

Never seem to be in a hurry: Hurrying betrays a lack of control over yourself, and over time. Always seem patient, as if you know that everything will come to you eventually. Become a detective of the right moment; sniff out the spirit of the times, the trends that will carry you to power. Learn to stand back when the time is not yet ripe, and to strike fiercely when it has reached fruition.

Stir up waters to catch fish

Anger and emotion are strategically counterproductive. You must always stay calm and objective. But if you can make your enemies angry while staying calm yourself, you gain a decided advantage.

Throw your enemies off balance: Find the chink in their vanity through which you can rattle them and you hold the strings.

Disarm and infuriate with the mirror effect

The mirror reflects reality, but it is also the perfect tool for deception: When you mirror your enemies, doing exactly as they do, they cannot figure out your strategy. The mirror effect mocks and humiliates them, making them overreact. By holding up a mirror to their psyches, you seduce them with the illusion that you share their values; by holding up a mirror to their actions, you teach them a lesson. Few can resist the power of the mirror effect.

Preach the need for change, but never reform too much at once

Everyone understands the need for change in the abstract, but on the day-to-day level people are creatures of habit. Too much innovation is traumatic and will lead to revolt. If you are new to a position of power, or an outsider trying to build a power base, make a show of respecting the old way of doing things. If change is necessary, make it feel like a gentle improvement on the past.

> ▶ Do not go past the mark you aimed for; in victory, learn when to stop

The moment of victory is often the moment of greatest peril. In the heat of victory, arrogance and overconfidence can push you past the goal you aimed for, and by going too far, you make more enemies than you defeat. Do not allow success to go to your head. There is no substitute for strategy and careful planning. Set a goal, and when you reach it, stop.

Assume formlessness

By taking a shape, by having a visible plan, you open yourself to attack. Instead of taking a form for your enemy to grasp, keep yourself adaptable and on the move. Accept the fact that nothing is certain and no law is fixed. The best way to protect yourself is to be as fluid and formless as water; never bet on stability or lasting order. Everything changes.

"Table of Contents", from THE 48 LAWS OF POWER by Robert Greene and Joost Elffers, copyright © 1998 by Robert Greene and Joost Elffers. Use by permission Viking Penguin, a division of Penguin Group (USA) Inc.

The emergence of political strategies

New intended strategies are not just guides to action; they are also signals of shifts in power relationships. The more significant the strategy and the more decentralized the organization, the more likely are these to be accompanied by political manoeuvring. Indeed, such manoeuvres can make it difficult for an organization to arrive at strategies at all—whether deliberate or emergent.

Deliberate strategy means the collective realization of intentions—by the organization as a whole. But how can this happen when perceptions and interests are disputed rather than shared? As for emergent strategy, how is there to be consistency in action when the haphazards of bargaining take over the strategy-making process? Cyert and March explained this very well back in 1963, with their notion of 'sequential attention to goals':

❝organizations resolve conflict among goals by attending to different goals at different times❞

Organizations resolve conflict among goals, in part, by attending to different goals at different times. Just as the political organization is likely to resolve conflicting pressures to 'go left' and 'go right' by first doing one and then the other, the business firm is likely to resolve conflicting pressures to 'smooth production' and 'satisfy customers' by first doing one and then the other. (1963: 118)

In other words, the organization is able to make decisions but it cannot seem to make strategies.

Yet we believe that strategies can and do emerge from political processes. Sometimes a single decision arrived at politically can set a precedent and thereby establish a pattern. For example, a sales department may get its way on lowering the price of a product to one customer and, next thing you know, the prices on all products are being lowered. This is reminiscent of the 'foot-in-the-door' technique, discussed in the last chapter: to mix our metaphors, this pries open a window of opportunity on the way to a strategy. Or some group outside the formal leadership can be powerful enough to impose its intentions politically on the whole organization—for example, an IT group in a bank on whom everyone else is dependent for services. Also, when rival camps arise over a major change in strategy—for example, between the 'young Turks' promoting a new technology and the 'old guard' resisting it—whoever wins sets strategy.

Our suspicion is that when strategies do appear out of political processes, they tend to be more emergent than deliberate and more likely in the form of positions than perspective. To have arrived at a strategy politically usually means to have done so step by step through processes of bargaining and the like. The particular actors may have had the most deliberate of intentions, but the result is likely to be emergent for the organization—in other words, not intended overall, indeed maybe not expected in quite that way by its protagonists. Moreover, while the emergence of a set of distinct strategic positions is imaginable—as goals are attended to sequentially, each faction gets its position, so to speak—the achievement of strategy as an integrated perspective, a single shared vision, seems unlikely under political circumstances. But perhaps most commonly, in such political circumstances we should expect no shortage of strategies as ploys.

The benefits of politics

Little space need be devoted to the dysfunctional effects of politics on organizations. This is divisive and costly; it burns up energies that could otherwise go into serving customers. It can also lead to all sorts of aberrations: the retention of outmoded centres of power or the introduction of new ones that are unjustified, even to paralysis to the point where effective functioning comes to a halt. The purpose of an organization, after all, is to produce goods and services, not to provide an arena in which people can fight with each other.

What does deserve more space, however, because they are less widely appreciated, are those conditions under which politics serves a functional role in organizations.

There are three systems in almost all organizations whose means can be described as *legitimate*, meaning that their power is officially acknowledged: formal authority, established culture, and certified expertise. But these means are sometimes used to pursue *ends* that are illegitimate (for example, by resisting changes that are necessary). Then a fourth system, politics, whose *means* are (by our definition) not formally legitimate, can be used to pursue *ends* that are in fact legitimate. This is evident, for example, in the whistle-blowing and young Turks games, where political pressures can be used to correct the irresponsible or ineffective behaviours of people in formal authority. We can elaborate on this general point in four specific ones.

First, politics as a system of influence can act in a Darwinian way to ensure that the strongest members of an organization are brought into positions of leadership. Authority favours a single chain of command; weak leaders can suppress strong followers. Politics, on the other hand, can provide alternate channels of information and promotion, as when the sponsorship game enables someone to leap over a weak boss. Moreover, since effective leaders have been shown to exhibit a need for power, political games can demonstrate leadership potential. The second-string players may suffice for the scrimmages, but only the stars can be allowed to meet the competition. Political games not only help suggest who those stars are, but also help to remove their weaker rivals from contention.

Second, politics can ensure that all sides of an issue are fully debated, whereas the other systems of influence may promote only one. The system of authority, by aggregating information up a central hierarchy, tends to advance only a single point of view, often the one already known to be favoured above. So, too, does a strong culture, which interprets every issue in terms of 'the word'—the prevailing set of beliefs. And established experts can be closed to new ideas, especially if these developed after the professionals received their training. Politics, however, by obliging people to fight for their preferred ideas, encourages a variety of voices to be heard on any issue. And, because of attacks by opponents, each voice, no matter how self-serving, is forced to justify its conclusions in terms of the broader good—the interests of the organization at large. As Cornford has commented in his amusing 'Guide for the Young Academic Politician':

[Jobs] fall into two classes, My Jobs and Your Jobs. My Jobs are public-spirited proposals, which happen (much to my regret) to involve the advancement of a personal friend, or (still more to my regret) of myself. Your Jobs are insidious intrigues for the advancement of yourself and your friends, spuriously disguised as public-spirited proposals. (1993: 39)

Third, politics may be required to stimulate necessary change that is blocked by the more legitimate systems of influence. Authority concentrates power up the hierarchy, often in the hands of those responsible for the existing strategies. Expertise concentrates power in the hands of senior experts, not junior ones who may possess the newer skills. Likewise, culture tends to be rooted in the past, in tradition, and so likewise can act as a deterrent to change. In the face of these resistances, politics can work as a kind of 'invisible underhand' to promote necessary change.

Fourth, politics can ease the path for the execution of change. Senior managers, for example, often use politics to gain acceptance for their decisions, by building alliances to smooth their path (as we saw in Quinn's work on logical implementation in the last chapter).

Thus, politics may irritate us, but it can also serve us. Box 8.3 summarizes the advice that Macmillan and Guth offer to managers in this regard.

box 8.3

Using politics to get strategies accepted

(from Macmillan and Guth, 1985: 247–53)

A. Recognize the political realities and manage them

Political activity in organizations, such as coalition behavior, is the natural and spontaneous result of competing demands from inside and outside the organization on the allocation of its resources. . . . Since coalition processes exist in organizations, perform a necessary function, and influence decision outcomes, general management must recognize them, understand them, and learn to manage them.

B. Recognize the essentiality of middle management commitment

General management is not omnipotent. It is, in varying degrees, dependent on middle management for technical knowledge and functional skills. . . . If general management decides to go ahead and impose its decisions in spite of commitment, resistance by middle management coalitions will drastically lower the efficiency with which the decisions are implemented, if it does not completely stop them from being implemented. . . . As the Japanese have taught us, spending time on building commitment is worth the investment.

C. Learn to use classical political tools

. . . The following political management tools, used by politicians for centuries, can be helpful to general management in its own organization. . . .

1 **Equifinality**. Since it is often possible to achieve very similar results using different means or paths, general management should recognize that achieving a successful outcome is more important than imposing the method of achieving it. . . .

2 **Satisficing**. Politicians soon learn that achieving satisfactory results is far better than failing to achieve 'optimal' results via an unpopular strategy. . . .

3 **Generalization**. Shifting focus from specific issues to more general ones [for example, from cost cutting to productivity improvement] may increase general management's options in its search for strategy and related policies that are both effective and capable of gaining organizational commitment. . . .

4 **Focus on higher-order issues**. By raising the issue to a higher level, many of the shorter-term interests can be postponed in favor of longer-term but more fundamental interests. For instance, the automobile and steel industries, by focusing on issues of survival, were able to persuade unions to make concessions on wage increases.

▶ **5 Anticipate coalition behavior**. Coalitions form around the current issues that the organization faces. General managers should be prepared to spend some time on thinking through current and recent issues[,] identifying the participants in the coalitions that formed in relation to each issue, [and then analyzing] the apparent reasons why different members joined the coalitions. . . .

D. Manage coalition behavior

What can general management realistically expect to accomplish when confronted with a current or anticipated coalition in opposition to a strategy alternative it finds attractive? It has two major options:

1 To manage the coalition structure of the organization to reduce the influence of coalition opposition. . . .
2 To revise its strategy and/or related policy so that it no longer confronts the coalition opposition. . . .

The major options available to general management [under the first] are discussed below.

1 Manage the sequence in which issues are addressed. This can cause very different coalitions to form. . . .
2 Increase the visibility of certain issues. Doing this in meetings, written communications, or ceremonies, and so forth can be useful in creating coalition structures which are more amenable to general management handling. Once coalitions are formed and positions taken, it is hard for the members to back off from these original positions. . . .
3 Unbundle issues into similar subissues. This may reduce coalition opposition simply because of the time and energy required to form and hold together a coalition. The smaller the issue, the less important the fight and the less the motivation to form or join a coalition. Smaller issues focused in rapid succession also make it more difficult to maintain coalition stability.

E. Take direct action against the opposing coalition

1 Form a preemptive coalition. If general management can anticipate that a coalition is likely to form in opposition to its strategy, it can itself form a coalition by including some middle-level managers in support of the strategy prior to making it known in the organization that it is sponsoring the strategy. Preempting potential coalition members reduces the chances of forming a successful countercoalition. . . .
2 Form a countercoalition after the opposing coalition becomes visible. This option places general management on the other side of a preemptive coalition, and thus it suffers from the reverse of the advantages of the preemptive coalition.

3 **Change the organizational positions of opposing coalition leaders** . . . Information associated with the organizational position and normal interaction patterns associated with the position can contribute to the ease with which a manager can build and manage a coalition . . . Thus, moving or, in serious cases, even demoting an opposing coalition leader could have a significant impact on its potential effectiveness.

4 **Co-opt coalition members**. Appointment of coalition members to boards, committees, or task forces that expose them to new information and new social influence patterns can result in alteration of the views that caused them to form or join the opposing coalition.

5 **Increase communication-persuasion efforts with coalition members**. . . . This option is likely to be particularly effective in organizations where general management typically maintains narrow communication patterns, e.g., with only key subordinates who may not have effectively communicated with others about the sponsored strategy, even though they themselves do not oppose it.

6 **Remove coalition leaders from the organization**. Coalition leaders often have the strongest motivation for rejecting the sponsored strategy. It takes a high degree of motivation to form and lead a coalition. . . . Thus, removing the leader often can be effective in overcoming coalition opposition.

In most of the above options, it is possible that general management may well succeed in overcoming the coalition opposition in the decision-making process, yet still be unable to achieve effective implementation due to low commitment. In this case, general management may have to recognize that it may have to change its strategy.

Upper echelons theory: strategic management at the top

Mastering micro politics calls for considerable skills, but skills alone can only take strategy making so far. Ultimately, when it comes to strategy it helps to have power. And those in the 'Upper Echelons' not only have power, but they also exercise power in a very personal way.

This key point has led researchers to examine more closely the composition and dynamics of top management. As Hambrick (2007: 334) puts it: 'If we want to understand why organizations do the things they do, or why they perform the way they do, we must consider the biases and dispositions of their most powerful actors – their top executives.'

Developed in a seminal article, Hambrick and Mason (1984), 'upper echelons theory' argues that organizations which are remarkably similar in size, technology, and product line, often adopt very different strategies. The 'managerial discretion' at senior levels allow top executives more freedom to influence strategy than managers who operate further down in the organization. As a result, their values, beliefs, and professional experience will shape strategic decision to a greater extent than managers at lower levels.

For example, Finkelstein (1992) has shown that the greater the proportion within the top management teams of executives with finance backgrounds, the more likely the organization to make acquisitions. And Hambrick (2007) has concluded that power dynamics within top management groups may override the normal tendency of groups to coalesce, often ending up with semiautonomous 'barons,' who engage in 'bilateral relations with the CEO but [have] little to do with each other and hardly constituting a team.'

Strategy in the middle-up-down

What is this so called 'top management'? The field of strategic management, especially the design and entrepreneurial schools, conjure an image of the organization divided between a powerful top where 'heads' congregate, and those at the bottom who act as 'hired hands.'

In between, we have the uncharted middle, the so called 'middle managers,' who are neither heads that make strategic decisions, nor hands that perform clearly defined tasks. It is not surprising, therefore, that as large corporations grew in size and scope, middle management came under attack, accused of being less necessary than previously believed. When, in the 1980s, maximizing shareholders' wealth became the overriding concern for top management of publicly-traded companies, they enthusiastically embraced 'downsizing,' slashing middle management jobs left and right. The faddish nature of it all should have raised suspicion about throwing out the babies with the bathwater. How come so many companies discovered the problem all at once? Was senior management asleep before, or overactive after?

In response, a number of publications appeared to redress the negative opinion of middle management, especially with regard to its role in the strategy process. Steven Floyd and Bill Wooldridge, for example, questioned the view of middle managers as 'subversives' and 'drones' (1994: 47–9). They also dismissed the traditional view of middle managers as people who merely 'translate strategies defined at the higher levels into action at operating levels' (1994: 48). They also suggested that because managerial knowledge needs to be put at the forefront of business, 'the middle manager's centrality in the information network' becomes crucial to promote change and learning (1994: 23). Their key roles in this regard are: championing strategic alternatives, synthesizing information, facilitating adaptability, and implementing deliberate strategy. Nonaka argued likewise in an article entitled 'Middle-Up-Down Management' (1988), as did Huy in an article entitled 'In Praise of Middle Management' (2001).

Making strategy in the middle ultimately depends on fruitful communications with top management. As Frances Westley (1990) has pointed out, top managers have a choice: concentrate power and exclude middle managers from the strategy process, or bring middle managers into the process by constructing effective 'strategic conversations.' Such conversations are crucial for what Dutton *et al.* (1997) have described as 'selling issues upward' to top management. But Westley (1990) suggests that the process is sensitive to perceived power disparities. When senior management stands on its authority, it 'de-energizes' the conversation, ensuring compliance but also engendering passivity on the part of middle managers. Whereas when it makes moves to close the power gap, it is more likely to produce a vigorous and constructive engagement (see also research by Balogun and Johnson, 2004).

> ❝ macro power reflects the interdependence between an organization and its environment ❞

Macro power

Macro power reflects the interdependence between an organization and its environment. Organizations have to deal with suppliers and buyers, unions and competitors, investment bankers and government regulators, not to mention a growing list of pressure groups that may target one or another of their activities. Strategy from a macro power perspective consists first of managing the demands of these actors, and second of selectively making use of these actors for the organization's benefit.

External control by organizations

In their groundbreaking book, *The External Control of Organizations*, Pfeffer and Salancik (1978) outlined a theory of macro power (which could really have been called The External Control *by* Organizations). Organizations, they argued, can 'adapt and change to fit environmental requirements, or . . . can attempt to alter the environment so that it fits [their] capabilities' (106). The former view lies behind the environmental school, the latter lies behind this one of macro power—the process of acting upon or negotiating with, rather than reacting to, the external environment.

This second view led Pfeffer and Salancik to describe how some organizations are able to pursue clear, deliberate strategies of a political nature. Indeed, a number of strategies discussed in their book are no less generic than those of the positioning school, and in fact are sometimes the very same ones! For example, whereas merger is seen as an economic strategy in the positioning school, here it is considered a political means pursued for political ends—for power and control. Moulton and Thomas (1987) have even discussed 'bankruptcy as a deliberate strategy.'

The difference comes from what and who Pfeffer and Salancik include in the external context of organizations compared with Porter and his other positioning people. Here *stake*holders get added to *share*holders and the 'market' gets replaced by the 'environment,' thereby opening up the organization to a much wider array of actors and forces.

Pfeffer and Salancik argue that the traditional picture of the marketplace as an open arena where, to use Porter's expression, organizations freely 'jockey for position,' has been largely superseded in advanced economies by organizational, regulatory, and professional systems of considerable interdependence and complexity.

Under these conditions, the dominant problem of the organization becomes:

. . . managing its exchanges and its relationships with the diverse interests affected by its actions. Because of the increasing interconnectedness of organizations, interorganizational effects are mediated more by regulation and political negotiation than by impersonal market forces. . . . Negotiation, political strategies, the management of the organization's institutional relationships—these have all become more important. (94)

As a consequence, it has three basic strategies at its disposal:

1 **An organization can simply deal with each demand as it arises.** This is another example of Cyert and March's (1963) sequential attention to goals, but at the level of macro power. Rather than attempting to resolve opposing demands in one fell swoop, the organization deals with them in turn, for example worrying about pressing financial demands and then turning to concerns about market share (96).

2 **An organization can strategically withhold and disclose information.** In this way it can manipulate expectations and shape outcomes. 'A group is satisfied relative to what it expects to get [also] by what the group has obtained in the past and by what competing groups obtained. Thus, employees may be willing to forgo pay increases when the company is near bankruptcy and suppliers, creditors, and owners are also suffering. If the employees found that the owners were really secretly profiting, they would be quite irate. It is in the organization's interests to make each group or organization feel it is getting relatively the best deal. Knowledge of what each group is getting is best kept secret' (96).

3 **An organization can play one group against the other.** For example, 'the demands of public employees for higher wages can be juxtaposed with the demands of local citizens' groups for lower taxes' (97).

Organizations can seek to reduce external dependency relationships, or else come to accommodations with them—to make common cause with their environment. Strategies of the latter include adaptations of structure and information systems, and the like, while strategies to reduce or take control include merger (to absorb the external force), lobbying for favourable government actions (on tariffs, for example, or regulations), and so on. Informal or covert means may be resorted to. At the turn of the twentieth century, many organizations banded together into cartels, to transform competitive interdependence into mutually advantageous arrangements by fixing prices and dividing markets. Many of these practices were subsequently made illegal. Today, related practices persist, albeit more covertly. But as we shall see, they have become more pervasive.

Overall, organizations can end up in different power places, as described by Mintzberg (1982). At one extreme, some become the *instrument* of an external power group, functioning as directed from the outside—for example, by a single external owner. At the other extreme are organizations relatively *closed* to external influence—monopolies, for example, that can be so widely held by shareholders that none has any real influence. In this way, the organization becomes the exerciser rather than the receiver of influence. In between are those subject to several focused groups of influencers, and so find themselves faced with a rather *divided* system of power. The prison split between factions favouring custody and rehabilitation is one example; the corporation with rather concentrated ownership but also facing a strong union and a single key customer would be another. The object of macro power, of course, is to attain that second status, of being closed to most external influence.

" stakeholder analysis is an attempt to cope with political forces through a rational approach "

Some of the more popular applied work in this area of macro power includes stakeholder analysis, strategic manoeuvring, and cooperative strategy making. We discuss each below, noting that all three have a close link with another of our schools, rendering them, in terms of this book at least, hybrid views of the strategy process.

Stakeholder analysis

Stakeholder analysis is an attempt to cope with political forces through a rational approach. In a sense, it is the planning school's solution to the messiness of politics. Freeman (1984) has put some of these ideas together into a model he calls the 'Stakeholder Strategy Formulation Process,' described below.

1 **Stakeholder behaviour analysis.** 'The first step in the construction of strategic programs for stakeholder groups is the analysis of behavior . . . There are at least three categories of behavior for any stakeholder group on each issue . . . *actual* or *observed behavior,* . . . *cooperative potential* . . . behaviors that could be observed in the future that would help the organization achieve its objective on the issue in question . . . [and] *competitive threat* . . . behaviors . . . that would prevent or help to prevent the organization's achieving its goal' (131–2).

2 **Stakeholder behaviour explanation.** 'The second task in beginning the construction of strategic programs for stakeholders is to build a logical explanation for the stakeholder's behavior . . . [This] asks the manager to put himself/herself in the stakeholder's place, and to try and empathize with that stakeholder's position' (133).

3 **Coalition analysis.** 'The final analytical step in constructing strategic programs for stakeholders is to search for possible coalitions among several stakeholders' (131–5).

Freeman suggests that four generic strategies can result from such a stakeholder strategy-formulation process: offensive (such as trying to change the stakeholders' objectives), defensive (such as to link the issue to others that the stakeholder sees more favourably), hold the current position, and change the rules.

While such an analysis may have an appeal to those with a planning inclination, it is difficult to see how corporations can sit back and analyze who has power over them, and then respond in an orderly fashion to balance these pressures. Perhaps, therefore, the next applied theme of macro power is more realistic.

Strategic manoeuvring

Because the most effective way of controlling the power of external actors is to control the behaviour of those actors, there has grown up an interesting literature on how organizations manoeuvre strategically to attain their objectives. Once again, this was stimulated by the work of Michael Porter, who devoted to it several chapters in his books, especially *Competitive Strategy* (1980), with titles such as 'Market Signals' and 'Competitive Moves.'

Our discussion of this could, of course, fit into our chapter on the positioning school, since this is about competitive moves to secure market positions. But it could also get lost there, not only because of the length of that chapter, but also because the flavour of this work is so very different.

Clausewitz wrote that 'war is politics by other means.' The purpose of such politics is to accomplish certain goals without destructive physical confrontation. The moves and countermoves that Porter enumerates are primarily addressed to firms that have established their position and now wish to maintain a relative equilibrium that is to their advantage. Manoeuvring is used to communicate to rivals that it would be wiser to negotiate mutually beneficial arrangements than to fight. It is, if you like, a comparative form of diplomacy, the mixing of threats and promises in order to gain advantage.

❝ strategy here is less position than ploy ❞

Accordingly, strategy here is less position than ploy, played against a background of stable order established at an earlier time. It consists of feints and other schemes, often with the intention of fooling competitors. This literature is very much about how companies 'throw their weight around.' Porter does not use the word *politics* in his books, but despite the fact that the intentions may be economic, this is all about politics—it is the political side of positioning.

---
box 8.4

Excerpts from Porter on strategic manoeuvring
(from 1980: 91–100)

Because in an oligopoly a firm is partly dependent on the behavior of its rivals, selecting the right competitive move involves finding one whose outcome is quickly determined (no protracted or serious battle takes place). . . .

■ One broad approach is to use superior resources and capabilities to *force* an outcome skewed toward the interests of the firm, overcoming and outlasting retaliation—we might call this the *brute force approach*. This sort of approach is possible only if the firm possesses clear superiorities [which it] maintains . . . and as long as competitors do not misread them and incorrectly attempt to change their positions.

■ Moves that do not threaten competitors' goals are a place to begin in searching for ways to improve position. . . .

■ Many moves that would significantly improve a firm's position do threaten competitors, since this is the essence of oligopoly. Thus a key to the success of such moves is predicting and influencing retaliation. . . . In considering threatening moves, the key questions are as follows: (1) How likely is retaliation? (2) How soon will retaliation come? (3) How effective will retaliation potentially be? (4) How tough will retaliation be, where toughness refers to the willingness of the competitor to retaliate strongly even at its own expense? (5) Can retaliation be influenced?

■ . . . The need to deter or fend against moves by competitors can be equally important. . . . Good defense is creating a situation in which competitors . . . will conclude that a move is unwise. As with offensive moves, defense can be achieved by forcing competitors back down after battle. However, the most effective defense is to *prevent the battle altogether*. To prevent a move, it is necessary that competitors expect retaliation with a high degree of certainty and believe that the retaliation will be effective. . . . Once a competitor's move has occurred, the denial of an adequate base for the competitor to meet its goals, coupled with the expectation that this state of affairs will continue, can cause the competitor to withdraw. . . .

■ Perhaps the single most important concept in planning and executing offensive or defensive competitive moves is the concept of commitment. Commitment can guarantee the likelihood, speed, and vigor of retaliation to offensive moves and can be the cornerstone of defensive strategy . . . Establishing commitment is essentially a form of communicating the firm's resources and intentions unequivocally.

Source: Reprinted with the permission of The Free Press, a Division of Simon & Schuster Adult Publishing Group, from *COMPETITIVE STRATEGY: Techniques for Analyzing Industries and Competitors* by Michael E. Porter. Copyright © 1980, 1998 by The Free Press, All rights reserved.

Moreover, strategy making takes on a flavour most unlike what we find in the rest of the positioning school (and in the other chapters of Porter's own books, for that matter). Whereas that emphasis is on systematic analysis, the assessment of hard data, and the careful working out of strategies, here success depends on soft impressions, quick actions, and gut feel for what opponents might do. To three of us authoring this book, this material belongs here. Strategic manoeuvring really does risk getting lost in the positioning school!

This is not to say that strategic manoeuvring is not sometimes cloaked in the mantle of analysis. Consider Porter's words in the box, on the range of moves he believes are available to a firm in an oligopolic situation. Then ask yourself how a firm might actually execute all this careful assessment.

Bruce Henderson, who built up the Boston Consulting Group, also had interesting ideas on strategic manoeuvring, similar to those of Porter but perhaps more aggressive. He emphasized two points: 'The first is that the management of a company must persuade each competitor to stop short of a maximum effort to acquire customers and profits. The second point is that persuasion depends on emotional and intuitive factors rather than on analysis or deduction' (1979: 27). Henderson suggested five rules for prudent competitive manoeuvring, which do, however, imply rather a good deal of analysis:

1 You must know as accurately as possible just what your competition has at stake in his contact with you. It is not what you gain or lose, but what he gains or loses that sets the limit on his ability to compromise with you.

2 The less the competition knows about your stakes, the less advantage he has. Without a reference point, he does not even know whether you are being unreasonable.

3 It is absolutely essential to know the character, attitudes, motives, and habitual behavior of a competitor if you wish to have a negotiating advantage.

4 The more arbitrary your demands are, the better your relative competitive position—provided you do not arouse an emotional reaction.

5 The less arbitrary you seem, the more arbitrary you can in fact be.

These rules make up the art of business brinkmanship. They are guidelines for winning a strategic victory in the minds of competitors. Once this victory has been won, it can be converted into a competitive victory in terms of sales volume, costs and profits. (32–3)

Coming from the sociological rather than economic side, Paul Hirsch (1975) has provided a particularly colourful description of how organizations manoeuvre politically to establish and protect their strategies. Finding profitability differences between firms operating in the pharmaceutical and record industries, despite similarities in product characteristics and means of distribution, Hirsch pointed to the more astute political manoeuvring of the pharmaceutical companies. This involved active management of the industry's 'institutional' environment, including restrictions on product entry, pricing, and promotion (all areas mandated by legislation and regulation). Wherever possible, the pharmaceutical firms 'created' the institutional environment in which they operated, sometimes through complex cooperative and collaborative actions. The perfect example of macro power!

Cooperative strategy making

'Networks,' 'collective strategy,' 'joint ventures' and other 'strategic alliances,' and 'strategic sourcing' are all part of the contemporary vocabulary of strategic management. Indeed, Volberda and Elfring (2001) find this important enough to suggest that it forms a school of its own within strategic management, which they call the 'boundary school.'

With the rapid rise of cooperative relationships, strategy formation leaves the exclusive confines of the single organization and becomes instead a joint process, to be developed with partners. The firm *negotiates* through a *network* of relationships to come up with a *collective* strategy. There are clearly planning and positioning sides to this, but as we shall see, the power and especially the negotiated aspects of strategy loom large. Let us review the various elements of this in turn.

Networks

As companies extended their relationships among themselves, both in breadth and especially in depth, researchers took notice, and a network model was developed (which Hakansson and Snehota [1989: 190] traced back to research at the Swedish University of Uppsala in the mid-1970s). Organizations do not operate in isolation, but in complex webs of interactions with other actors and organizations, including suppliers, competitors, and customers (see Gulati, 1998). This view challenged the more traditional 'lone pioneer' model of strategy formation, in which 'egocentric organizations' are viewed as 'solitary units confronted by faceless environments' (Astley, 1984: 526).

Collective strategy

The term *collective strategy* was coined by Graham Astley and Charles Fombrun (1983) to describe the 'joint' nature of strategy formation among the members of a network. They argued that, in addition to corporate strategies (what business should we be in?) and business strategy (on what grounds should we be competing in each business?), organizations need to develop strategies at the collective level to deal with their complex interdependencies. Astley argued further that 'collaboration' has come to dominate the process of strategy formation over 'competition.'

Interdependence in modern society has grown to such an extent that organizations have become fused into collective units whose very nature does not permit independent action. Here collaboration becomes genuine as organizations develop orientations that gradually eliminate competitive antagonism. [Attention must be paid] to the institutionalization of these collective allegiances, for they play an increasingly important role in today's corporate society. (1984: 533)

> Developments in the banking industry served as an early case in point: 'an awareness of joint interests among different segments of the industry is manifest in the widespread emergence of shared Automatic Teller Machine networks. As banks and thrifts hook into electronic networks, interstate banking becomes a reality limited only in terms of the kinds of transactions regulators are allowing' (Fombrun and Astley, 1983: 137).

> Dollinger (1990) has pointed out that collective strategies can move a once highly fragmented industry towards greater concentration of firms and more standardization of practices. The emergence of standard shipping containers which today underpins global trade is an example of this process. At one time, shipping containers used for moving freight, on rail and by ship, came in a variety of sizes. Moving goods over long distances often required unloading from one container, and reloading it into another – an inefficient practice that raised costs and hampered trade. The advantages of everybody using the same size container were obvious, but it took collective strategic action backed by the International Organization for Standardization to transform the idea into reality.

Strategic alliances

The idea of networks and collective strategies laid the foundation for a flurry of writing and research on a further idea that was racing through practice—that of *strategic alliances*. This refers to a variety of different cooperative arrangements (as in the sharing of R&D skills to develop a joint new product), usually between suppliers and customers as well as partners—who turn out to be, with increasing frequency, competitors in other domains.

" strategic alliances refer to a variety of different cooperative arrangements " 'Joint ventures' are strategic alliances in which partners take equity positions in new businesses that they have created. The term 'cooperative agreements,' on the other hand, refers to *nonequity* forms of cooperation, such as longterm contracting, licensing, franchising, and turnkey arrangements. While joint ventures have been around for a long time, it is these cooperative agreements that have taken off. Every day, some new creative form seems to be invented. Table 8.1 contains a list of various alliances.

table 8.1 Types of strategic alliances

Alliance types	Examples
Collaborative advertising	American Express and Toys 'R' Us (cooperative effort for television advertising and promotion)
R&D partnerships	Cytel and Sumitomo Chemicals (alliance to develop next generation of biotechnology drugs)
Lease service agreements	Cigna and United Motor Works (arrangement to provide financing services for non-US firms and governments)
Shared distribution	Nissan and Volkswagen (Nissan sells Volkswagens in [Japan] and Volkswagen distributes Nissan's cars in Europe)
Technology transfer	IBM and Apple Computers (arrangement to develop next generation of operating system software)
Cooperative bidding	Boeing, General Dynamics, and Lockheed (cooperated together in winning advanced tactical fighter contract)
Cross-manufacturing	Ford and Mazda (design and build similar cars on same manufacturing/assembly line)
Resource venturing	Swift Chemical Co., Texasgulf, RTZ, and US Borax (Canadian-based mining natural resource venture)
Government and industry	DuPont and National Cancer Institute (DuPont worked partnering with NCI in first phase of clinical cancer trial of IL)
Internal spinoffs	Cummins Engine and Toshiba Corporation (created new company to develop/market silicon nitride products)
Cross-licensing	Hoffman-LaRoche and Glaxo (HL and Glaxo agreed for HL to sell Zantac, anti-ulcer drug, in the United States)

(from Pekar and Allio, 1994: 56)

Strategic sourcing

So-called strategic sourcing has become a particularly fashionable form of cooperative agreement. This refers to contracting out what might otherwise have been made 'in house.' We used to hear about the 'make or buy' decision. Now 'outsourcing', and the related term 'offshoring,' have become more widespread.

The original theory, according to Venkatesan, is that companies should 'outsource components where suppliers have a distinct comparative advantage—greater scale, fundamentally lower cost structure, or stronger performance incentives' (1992: 98). In other words, contract out where you lack the core competence. But as Lampel and Bhalla (2008) point out, the current trend towards offshoring activities to countries such as India and China is often motivated by the wish to let others do non-essential core activities, while firms retain control over their key competencies.

Networks, alliances, collective strategies, outsourcing—all of this taken together is making it increasingly difficult to figure out where one organization ends and another begins (Afuah, 2003). In other words, the boundaries of organizations are becoming increasingly blurred as networks replace rigid hierarchies on the inside and open markets on their outside. And that takes a strategy-making process already rather complicated—if the rest of this book is to be believed—and ups its complexity several notches.

Are alliances political?

All of this activity is clearly about strategy formation as a process of negotiation, to use the subtitle of this chapter. But does it belong under the title of this chapter? In other words, can we describe these alliances as about power and politics, as opposed to simple economics?

Much of this seems straightforwardly economic—just another way to go about creating competitive strategies, albeit in much more complicated situations. The accompanying box, from Hamel and colleagues, suggests this. But there may be more here than meets the eye.

Consistent with our earlier discussion about the political side of ostensibly economic strategies, many alliances have a political dimension to them as well, whether or not deliberate. By this we mean that they stand in opposition to purely open competitive forces. Alliances are meant to be cooperative and therefore exclusive. They can thus close down competition, for a time at least, in favour of more established relationships.

Some alliances are, of course, created expressly to reduce competition or to secure markets. There are overtly political alliances, as when established firms get together to undermine the efforts of smaller and newer ones. And what about all those cooperative agreements among otherwise competitors, which Brandenburger and Nalebuff (1995) have labelled *coopetition?* Rivalry may lurk beneath the surface of cooperation, but cooperation also sits over and smoothes out rivalry. Can firms keep these neatly separated, or will we wake up one day to find ourselves locked into one giant straitjacket of some ultimate network (which, many believe, has already become the case among big business and government in places like France)? We simply have to be sensitive to the political consequences of economic moves. This is the real point of the power school.

---

box 8.5

Principles of collaborative advantage

(from Hamel *et al.*, 1989: 134)

■ **Collaboration is competition in a different form**. Successful companies never forget that their new partners may be out to disarm them. They enter alliances with clear strategic objectives, and they also understand how their partners' objectives will affect their success.

■ **Harmony is not the most important measure of success**. Indeed, occasional conflict may be the best evidence of mutually beneficial collaboration. Few alliances remain win-win undertakings forever. A partner may be content even as it unknowingly surrenders core skills.

■ **Cooperation has limits**. Companies must defend against competitive compromise. A strategic alliance is a constantly evolving bargain whose real terms go beyond the legal agreement or the aims of top management. What information gets traded is determined day to day, often by engineers and operating managers. Successful companies inform employees at all levels about what skills and technologies are off-limits to the partner and monitor what the partner requests and receives.

■ **Learning from partners is paramount**. Successful companies view each alliance as a window on their partners' broad capabilities. They use the alliance to build skills in areas outside the formal agreement and systematically diffuse new knowledge throughout their organizations.

Conclusion

Premises of the power school

We introduce the premises of the power school here to draw this discussion together.

1 Strategy formation is shaped by power and politics, whether as a process inside the organization or as the behaviour of the organization itself in its external environment.

2 The strategies that may result from such a process tend to be emergent, and take the form of positions and ploys more than perspectives.

3 Micro power sees strategy making as the interplay, through persuasion, bargaining, and sometimes direct confrontation, in the form of political games, among parochial interests and shifting coalitions, with none dominant for any significant period of time.

4 Macro power sees the organization as promoting its own welfare by controlling or cooperating with other organizations, through the use of strategic manoeuvring as well as collective strategies in various kinds of networks and alliances.

Critique, context, and contribution of the power school

By now, our critiques of each of the different schools are forming their own pattern, at least in one respect. Strategy formation is about power, but it is not *only* about *power*. Clearly, this school, like each of the others, overstates to make its points. The role of integrating forces, such as leadership and culture, tends to get slighted here, as does the notion of strategy itself. By concentrating attention on divisiveness and fractioning, the power school may miss patterns that do form, even in rather conflictive situations.

Moreover, while it is true that the political dimension can have a positive role in organizations (especially in promoting necessary change blocked by the more established and legitimate forms of influence), this can also be the source of a great deal of wastage and distortion in organizations. Yet many who write about it, let alone those who practise it with relish, seem to view it with a certain affection. And this may cloud other issues that need to be addressed too. For example, macro power in the form of alliances can create severe problems of collusion in a society of large organizations. Yet that aspect is hardly addressed in the literature. We are in the midst of a love affair with these concepts.

These concerns aside, it hardly makes sense to describe strategy formation as a process devoid of power and politics. This is especially true (a) during periods of *major change*, when significant shifts in power relationships inevitably occur and so conflicts arise; also (for macro power) in (b) *large, mature organizations*; and (for micro power) in (c) *complex, highly decentralized organizations of experts* (such as universities, research laboratories, and film companies), where many actors have the power and inclination to further their own interests. Political activity also tends to be common (d) during periods of *blockage*, when strategic change is stopped, perhaps because of the intransigence of those in power, and (e) during periods of *flux*, when organizations are unable to establish any clear direction and so decision making tends to become a free-for-all.

The power school has introduced its share of useful vocabulary to the field of strategic management—for example, 'coalition,' 'political games,' and 'collective strategy.' It has also highlighted the importance of politics in promoting strategic change, where established actors seeking to maintain a status quo have to be confronted. Of course, politics is also a factor in the resistance to strategic change, but perhaps not so effective as the force of culture, which we discuss in our next school of thought.

The cultural school: strategy formation as a collective process

*"No wonder he never forgets. He has a bubble memory
with a storage capacity of 360 megabytes"*

"It's all so simple Anjin-san. Just change your concept of the world.'

—Shogun by James Clavell

Hold power up to a mirror and the reverse image you see is culture. Power takes that entity called organization and fragments it; culture knits a collection of individuals into an integrated entity called organization. In effect, one focuses primarily on self-interest, the other on common interest. So too, the literature of what we are calling the cultural school—strategy formation as a process rooted in the social force of culture—mirrors the power school. While one deals with the influence of internal politics in promoting strategic change, the other concerns itself largely with the influence of culture in maintaining strategic stability, indeed sometimes in actively resisting strategic change.

Culture is hardly a new idea. Every field of study has its central concept—market in economics, politics in political science, strategy in strategic management, and so on—and culture has long been the central concept in anthropology. From the vantage point of anthropology, culture is all around us—in the food we drink, the music we listen to, the way we communicate. At the same time, culture is what is unique about the way we do all these things. It is about what differentiates one organization from another, one industry from another, one nation from another. As we shall see, this duality of culture—its pervasiveness yet its uniqueness—has been reflected in its application to strategic management as well.

Culture was 'discovered' in management in the 1980s, thanks to the success of the Japanese corporations. They seemed to do things differently from the Americans, while at the same time unabashedly imitating US technology. All fingers pointed to Japanese culture, and especially how that has been manifested in the large Japanese corporations.

A flood of American literature appeared to explain this, followed by all sorts of consulting interventions to enhance culture. Yet little of this added to our understanding of strategies; it was mostly about organization and worker motivation. The main thrust of the cultural school of strategic management was to come later (while, interestingly enough, the Japanese approach to strategic management has been better explained by the learning school, as suggested there).

Culture can be studied by an outsider looking in or from the perspective of the native inside. (These correspond to the two wings of our cognitive school.) The first takes an objective stand on why people behave as they do, which is explained by their objective social and economic relationships. The second considers culture as a subjective process of interpretation.

While anthropology began with the objective view and later incorporated the subjective one, in a sense strategic management did the opposite. And that will be reflected in this chapter. We begin by considering the notion of culture, followed by a statement of this school's premises. Then we look at the pioneering work of a group of Swedish writers, who in the 1970s developed a whole array of concepts related to the interpretative side of culture. By the 1990s, however, one such approach, the so called 'strategy-as-practice' focused on the way that managers worked, rather than in abstract norms and ideologies. Finally, we discuss another recent perspective, which has come to be known as the 'resource-based' view of the firm, which considers advantages in the marketplace to be sustained by bundles of resources in the organization that are rare, inimitable, and for which competitors cannot find substitutes. In our terms, this comes down to what is unique about an organization as a cultural system. The chapter concludes with a critique and assessment of the contribution and context of the cultural school.

The nature of culture

Anthropologists debate the definition of culture endlessly. Here we need only focus on the main outlines of the concept. Culture is essentially composed of interpretations of a world and the activities and artefacts that reflect these. Beyond cognition these interpretations are shared collectively, in a social process. There are no private cultures. Some activities may be individual, but their significance is collective.

We thus associate *organizational* culture with collective cognition. It becomes the 'organization's mind,' if you like, the shared beliefs that are reflected in traditions and habits as well as more tangible manifestations—stories, symbols, even artefacts, products and buildings.

Pettigrew (1985: 44) put it well when he wrote that organizational culture can be seen as an 'expressive social tissue,' and much like tissue in the human body, it binds the bones of organizational structure to the muscles of organizational processes. In a sense, culture represents the life force of the organization, the soul of its physical body.

> **it binds the bones of organizational structure to the muscles of organizational processes**

The more closely interpretations and activities are woven together, the more deeply rooted is the culture. At a superficial level, there may be obvious links, such as in the informal dress worn in many software companies—an expression of the belief that creativity is not compatible with shirts and ties. At a deeper level, the relationship between interpretations and activities is more difficult to understand, for outsiders of course, but even for those who function in the culture. The managers of a Toyota or a Hewlett Packard can certainly recite the official credos that are supposed to represent their cultures (such as the points of 'HP way'). But could they describe in detail the nature of that culture and how it impacts on their behaviour? Our suspicion is that much of this exists below the level of conscious awareness.

Indeed, the strength of a culture may be proportional to the degree to which it eludes conscious awareness. As Gerry Johnson has pointed out, organizations with strong cultures are characterized by a set of 'taken for granted assumptions,' which are 'protected by a web of cultural artifacts,' including the way people behave towards each other, the stories they tell 'which embed the present in organizational history,' the language they use, and so on (1992: 30).

This flavour of culture is captured perfectly by another stanza of our elephant poem—this one written when the ideas for these schools were first forming (and the poem first used), at a conference held in the south of France. It was contributed by John Edwards (1977: 13) in a paper on the cultural aspects of the strategy process:

A Seventh, a pace behind the rest,
A Step or so away,
Did strive to sense what was the beast?
What rules did he obey?
By smell, by trace, by atmosphere,
To him the Elephant did appear.

In other words, blind men may better be able to sense culture than those who see all too well!

Culture is also an expression of the organization as community. Pursuing this point, Goffee and Jones (1996) in Box 9.1 argue that 'sociability' and 'solidarity' determine the kind of culture that organizations develop. Often communities have shared beliefs, or 'ideology', that holds them together. We shall use the word *ideology* to describe a *rich* culture in an organization—a strong set of beliefs, shared passionately by its members, that distinguishes this organization from all others. Thus, while the *culture* of, say, Burger King may be associated with broiling hamburgers and the like, the *ideology* of McDonald's has long been associated with an almost fetishist belief in efficiency, service, and cleanliness.

---

box 9.1

What holds the modern company together?

(Excerpted from R. Goffee and G. Jones, 1996)

What holds the modern company together? The short answer is culture. . . .
Culture in a word, is a community. It is the outcome of how people relate to one another. . . .

[S]ociology divides community into two types of distinct human relations: sociability and solidarity. [S]ociability is a measure of sincere friendliness among members of a community. Solidarity is a measure of a community's ability to pursue shared objectives quickly and effectively, regardless of personal ties. . . .

In business communities, the benefits of high sociability are clear and numerous. First, most employees agree that working in such an environment is enjoyable, which helps morale and esprit de corps. Sociability is also a boon to creativity because it fosters teamwork, sharing of information, and a spirit of openness to new ideas...Sociability also creates an environment in which individuals are more likely to go beyond the formal requirements of the job. . . .

> Solidarity, [on the other hand], generates a high degree of strategic focus, swift response to competitive threats, and intolerance of poor performance. It can also result in a degree of ruthlessness. If the organization's strategy is correct, this kind of focused intent and action can be devastatingly effective. . . .

To assess your organization's level of sociability, answer the following questions:

1 People here try to make friends and to keep their relationships strong
2 People here get along very well
3 People in our group often socialize outside the office
4 People here really like one another
5 When people leave our group, we stay in touch
6 People here do favors for others because they like one another
7 People here often confide in one another about personal matters

To assess your organization's level of solidarity, answer the following questions:

1 Our group (organization, division, unit, team) understands and shares the same business objectives
2 Work gets done effectively and productively
3 Our group takes strong action to address poor performance
4 Our collective will to win is high
5 When opportunities for competitive advantage arise, we move quickly to capitalize on them
6 We share the same strategic goals
7 We know who the competition is

Of course, political systems have ideologies too (capitalism, socialism), just as societies and ethnic groups have cultures (Japanese, Californian), as do industries (airline, banking). In fact, the idea of 'industrial recipes' (Grinyer and Spender, 1979; Spender, 1989) really describes industry cultures—'how we do things in this industry' to produce and market the products (for example, the fast-food industry as it has formed under the lead of McDonald's).

Obviously, all these levels of culture and ideology, in society, industry, and organization, interact every which way. Japanese culture, for example, is marked by the strong ideologies of Japanese corporations, no less than vice versa. Roth and Ricks (1994) point out how national cultures influence the way the environment is interpreted, creating different strategic responses by the same company in different countries. Thus, Rieger (1987) has demonstrated the impact of national cultures on the structures and decision-making styles of the airlines of various nations.

Premises of the cultural school

Below we summarize the main premises of the cultural school—its own set of beliefs, if you like.[1]

1 Strategy formation is a process of social interaction, based on the beliefs and understandings shared by the members of an organization.

2 An individual acquires these beliefs through a process of acculturation, or socialization, which is largely tacit and nonverbal, although sometimes reinforced by more formal indoctrination.

3 The members of an organization can, therefore, only partially describe the beliefs that underpin their culture, while the origins and explanations may remain obscure.

4 As a result, strategy takes the form of perspective above all, more than positions, rooted in collective intentions (not necessarily made explicit). This is reflected in the patterns by which resources, or capabilities of the organization, are protected and used for competitive advantage. Strategy is therefore best described as deliberate (even if not fully conscious).

5 Culture and especially ideology do not encourage strategic change so much as the perpetuation of existing strategy. At best, they tend to promote shifts in strategic positions within the organization's overall strategic perspective.

Culture and strategy

Outside of Scandinavia, culture was not a big issue in the management literature prior to 1980. Then a small literature began to develop. In England, Andrew Pettigrew (1985) conducted a detailed

---

1 A similar statement, but more elaborate and containing aspects of the cognitive school as well, can be found in Johnson (1987: 50–7)

study of the British chemical company, ICI, that revealed important cultural factors, while in the United States, Feldman (1986) considered the relationship of culture to strategic change and Barney (1986) asked whether culture could be a source of sustained competitive advantage. In Canada, Firsirotu (1985) and Rieger (1987) wrote award-winning doctoral theses, one on 'strategic turnaround as cultural revolution' in a Canadian trucking company (see also Allaire and Firsirotu, 1985), the other (mentioned above) on the influence of national culture on airlines.

Of course, there has long been a literature on how culture can cause resistance to strategic change. And, much like the stakeholder approach to designing power relationships, there is a literature on handy techniques to design culture, which in our opinion belongs in the planning school, as the following quotation should make clear: 'To match your corporate culture and business strategy, something like the procedures outlined above [four steps] should become a part of the corporation's strategic planning process' (Schwartz and Davis, 1981: 41).

The linkages between the concepts of culture and strategy are therefore many and varied. We summarize below some of these as they have been developed in the literature:

Decision-making style

Culture influences the style of decision-making favoured in an organization as well as its use of analysis, and thereby influences the strategy-formation process. Thus, in its early years General Motors was reorganized by Alfred Sloan to temper the freewheeling, entrepreneurial approach to its different businesses (Buick, Oldsmobile, Pontiac, Chevrolet, etc.). The new culture emphasized careful analysis and deliberate decision making. And so, when John DeLorean wrote many years later about life as a top manager at General Motors, he described a culture obsessed with ensuring a smooth flow of decisions. Before meetings, each executive 'was to see in advance the text of any presentation to be given. There were never to be any surprises . . . we'd get the same material at least three times: when we read the text, heard the presentation of it in the meeting and then read the minutes of the meeting' (in Wright, 1979: 27–8).

Culture acts as a perceptual filter or lens which in turn establishes people's decision premises (Snodgrass, 1984). Put differently, it is the

❝ culture acts as a perceptual filter ❞

cultural school that brings the interpretative wing of the cognitive school to life in the collective world of organization. As a result, organizations with different cultures operating in the same environment will interpret that environment in quite different ways. As noted in Chapter 6, they will see those things they want to see. An organization develops a 'dominant logic' that acts as an information filter, leading to a focus on some data for strategy making while ignoring others (Prahalad and Bettis, 1986).

Resistance to strategic change

A shared commitment to beliefs encourages consistency in an organization's behaviour, and thereby discourages changes in strategy. 'Before strategic learning . . . can occur, the old [dominant] logic must in a sense be unlearned by the organization. . . . Before IBM could begin developing a new strategy, the mainframe logic needed to be partially unlearned or forgotten' (Bettis and Prahalad, 1995: 10). It is culture's very deeply held beliefs and tacit assumptions that act as powerful internal barriers to fundamental change. Perhaps Karl Weick put it best when he said that 'A corporation doesn't *have* a culture. A corporation *is* a culture. That is why they're so horribly difficult to change.'

Lorsch has noted that not only can culture act as a prism that blinds managers to changing external conditions, but that 'even when managers can overcome such myopia, they respond to changing events in terms of their culture'—they tend to stick with the beliefs that have worked in the past (1986: 98). And that, of course, means sticking with established strategies too, as perspectives, embedded in the culture. For example, when a firm that has historically offered products at low prices experiences a decline in sales, it will likely respond by lowering prices even more (Yukl, 1989). The same thing tends to happen at the industry level when an industrial recipe is threatened: the blinders stay on at first, even when technological changes have turned everything upside down. As Abrahamson and Fombrun point out, the networks that link organizations together encourage common values and beliefs which can increase their level of inertia and breed similarities in 'strategic postures' (1994: 728–9). Other writers (Halberstam, 1986; Keller, 1989) point to a related tendency amongst US manufacturers to 'benchmark' against each other, which may cause them to disregard threats from producers outside the 'network.'

Overcoming the resistance to strategic change

Attention has also been directed at how to overcome the strategic inertia of organizational culture. Lorsch has suggested that top managers must accept as a major part of any company's culture the importance of flexibility and innovation (1986: 104). He proposed a number of ways to do this, including naming a 'Top Manager Without Portfolio,' whose role is to raise questions, challenge beliefs, and suggest new ideas; using outside directors to 'raise important questions about the appropriateness of these beliefs in changing times'; holding an 'in-company education program for middle managers, with outside experts'; and encouraging 'systematic rotation of managers among functions and businesses' (107–8). Lorsch also believed that major beliefs should be put in writing: 'If managers are aware of the beliefs they share, they are less likely to be blinded by them and are apt to understand more rapidly when changing events obsolete aspects of culture' (105). He felt managers should undertake *cultural* audits, to develop consensus about shared beliefs in their organization. The question, as we discussed earlier, is whether the deep beliefs can really be captured in these ways.

Bjorkman (1989) has pointed to research indicating that radical changes in strategy have to be based on fundamental change in culture. He described this as happening in four phases:

1 **Strategic drift**. In most cases radical changes are preceded by a widening of the gap between the organizational belief systems and the characteristics of the environment; a 'strategic drift' (Johnson, 1987) has developed. . . .

2 **Unfreezing of current belief systems**. Typically, strategic drift eventually leads to financial decline and the perception of an organizational crisis. In this situation previously unquestioned

organizational beliefs are exposed and challenged. The result is growing tension and disunity in the organization, including a breakdown . . . in homogeneous belief systems.

3 **Experimentation and re-formulation**. After former organizational belief systems have been unlearned, the organization often passes through a period of confusion. This period may lead to the development of a new strategic vision, usually mingling new and old ideas, and culminating in experimental, strategic decisions in accordance with the vision. Demonstrations of positive results may then lead to greater commitment to the new way of doing things. . . .

4 **Stabilization**. Positive feedback may gradually increase organization members' commitment to new belief systems which seem to work. (257)

Dominant values

Successful (or 'excellent') companies are said to be 'dominated' by key values, such as service, quality, and innovation, which, in turn, provide competitive advantage. This was a major theme of one of the most widely sold management books ever, *In Search of Excellence*, by Peters and Waterman (1982). Interestingly enough, the book was not about strategy (the word appears only twice in the index, both times in reference to the titles of books), but about how organizations use these competitive advantages to sustain remarkably stable strategic perspectives.

In an earlier paper, these two authors with another colleague (Waterman, Peters, and Phillips, 1980) introduced the famous 7-S framework, which put culture (called 'superordinate goals,' so that it would start with an 's'!) at the centre, around which were arrayed strategy, structure, systems, style, staff, and skills. According to these authors, all these aspects of an organization have to come into a harmonious fit if it is to be successful.

Culture clash

The strategies of merger, acquisition, and joint venture have been examined from the point of view of the confrontation of different cultures. This 'clash of cultures' has, for example, been used to explain why the 1980s merger wave failed to fulfil expectations. While the combination of two firms may make sense from a 'rational' product or market point of view, the less apparent cultural differences may serve to derail the union. The unique culture that shapes each and every organization ensures that such strategies will always be problematic.

The Swedish wing of the cultural school

In 1965, the Swedish organization SIAR—Scandinavian Institutes for Administrative Research—was formed as kind of a consulting firm-cum-research establishment. Its intellectual leaders were Eric Rhenman, who published *Organization Theory for Long Range Planning* (1973), and Richard Normann, who published *Management for Growth* (1977). These two important books introduced a conceptual framework (rooted largely in organizational culture), a style of theorizing (creative and open-ended), and a methodological approach (ambitious inferences from few, intensive case studies) that stimulated a generation of researchers at various Swedish universities, especially Gothenburg, through the 1970s. These people wove intricate theories from intensive field studies, using colourful vocabulary to label some rather woolly concepts.[2] After reading the likes of Michael Porter and George Steiner, to come across 'ghost myth,' 'organizational drama,' and 'misfits' is itself a form of culture shock, although perhaps not unwelcome in the often drab literature of strategic management.

The Swedish group addressed far more than culture. It interwove a rich network of concepts (from some of the other schools we have been discussing), including fit or consonance (in the spirit of our design and configuration schools), values, images or myths, politics, cognition, and organizational learning, around themes of organizational stagnation, decline, crisis, and turnaround. In ambitious efforts rarely seen elsewhere in the field, these writers sought to draw all this

---

2 We include here especially the work of Sten Jonsson (n.d.), Bo Hedberg (1973, 1974, also with Targama 1973, with Jonsson 1977, with Starbuck 1977, and with Starbuck and Greve, 1978), and Rolf Lundin (with Jonsson, 1977, and with Jonsson and Sjoberg, 1977–8).

into an understanding of organizational growth and strategic change (although the word *strategy* did not figure prominently in their writing). We consider this work to fall into the cultural school more than any other because of its overriding concern with adaptation in a collective context, above all the need for collective 'reframing' as a prerequisite to strategic change.

Much of this work focused on the stagnation and decline of organizations, and how cultural as well as political and cognitive forces help to cause this by impeding adaptation. How then to achieve change, the researchers asked. And their answers, not surprisingly from Sweden, were especially embedded in an understanding of the organization as a *collective* social system.

'Fit' played a key role in these studies. Rhenman (1973: 30–6), for example, described four mechanisms for achieving it (which he called consonance): mapping (reflecting the environment), matching (complementing the environment), joint consultation ('supporting and cooperating with the neighboring system with a view to a joint exploration of the common environment'), and dominance ('a system's ability to project a mapping of itself into the environment').

The notion of myth was also prominent in this work. Hedberg and Jonsson, for example, positioned strategy between reality and myth, which they referred to as the 'metasystem' that changes infrequently and then in revolutionary fashion. This would seem to be akin to what we call perspective in this book, also to culture and especially ideology (all of which are, of course, wrapped up in the same notions of belief systems and worldviews).

A myth is . . . a theory of the world. It cannot be tested directly, but only through acting in accordance with the operationalized hypotheses that strategies represent. And even then, the myth is only conditionally put to the test. . . . Myths are stored as constructs in human brains, and they are always simplified and partly wrong. Still, so long as ruling myths remain unchallenged, they provide the interpretations of reality upon which organizations act. . . . However, regardless of whether the theory or the reality is the starting point, it is by perceived misfits between the two that strategy changes are triggered. (1977: 90–2)

Elsewhere, Jonsson elaborated on the myth, which he also referred to as an ideology:

The myth provides the organization with a stable basis for action. It eliminates uncertainty about what has gone wrong, and it substitutes certainty; we can do it, it is up to us. . . . If you are certain about what should be done, action is precipitated. (n.d.: 43)

> ❝ the myth provides the organization with a stable basis for action ❞

By the late 1970s, as the Gothenburg group scattered and SIAR lost its missionary zeal, this Swedish wing, such as it was, petered out, although research in the same spirit continued in Sweden, for example, in the work of Brunsson (1982) and Melin (1982, 1983, 1985).[3]

Strategy-as-practice: digging deeper into the strategy process

In the conventional cultural school the belief that culture guides actions, and actions in turn reinforce culture became suspect by some researchers towards the end of the twentieth century, partly because of the contrasting fortunes of the Japanese and American economies. As Japan entered a period of stagnation in the 1990s, and the United States economy revived thanks to high-technology industries, successful Japanese strategies were seen as managerial innovations that can be divorced from their cultural context.

Moreover, the use of culture to explain strategy fell into disfavour because it was all too often used as a catch-all explanation: A successful organization had the 'right' culture, whereas organizations that performed poorly had the 'wrong' culture. To become successful firms had to develop the 'right culture,' but they did not know if they had done so until they were successful.

To gain a better understanding of the strategic consequences of social features, some researchers felt the need to dig deeper into how how managers make strategy. To do this, they turned to social anthropology, which sees social practices rather than cultural beliefs and norms as key to understanding social systems. They called their efforts

---

3 See Engwall (1996) for a review of Scandinavian research publications from 1981–92.

'strategy-as-practice' (Whittington, 1996; 2006), publishing a *Journal of Management Studies* Special Issue in January 2003, based on the pioneering work of Langley (1990); Brown and Duguid (1991); Whittington (1996); and Johnson and Huff (1998).

Strategy-as-practice researchers believe that to understand strategy, it is necessary to study in detail and in close proximity the everyday reality of managers involved in making strategy—not their cognitive processes but the outcome of activities such as meetings, presentations, and communications.

Managers who are involved in strategy are masters and servants of their practices; the musicians are their instruments – so to speak. It makes no sense to consider strategy separately from the practices that make strategy. Several key ideas underline this movement:

1   Strategy is not 'something that an organization has but something that its members do' (Jarzabkowski *et al.*, 2007: 6)'.

2   'Strategy is a particular type of activity that is connected with particular practices such as strategic planning, annual reviews, strategy workshops and their associated discourses.' (ibid: 8).

3   To get to the heart of strategy as a process, it is necessary to venture among managers and study them much as anthropologists immerse themselves in native cultures. 'A good deal of process research relies on second-hand retrospective reports, given typically by senior executives. Too often it is reminiscent of the early anthropologists' account of tribal customs based on conversations with local chiefs on colonial verandas. Progress in anthropology involved ethnographers directly engaging with—indeed living in—the world of action and practice' (Johnson *et al.*, (2003: 11).'

The last point highlights both the strengths and weaknesses of a central tenet of strategy-as-practice. The movement rightly criticizes large sample studies that insufficiently take into account the nuance and complexity of strategy formation. But going where 'strategy' is claimed to take place (such as a 'strategic planning' retreat), may encourage the fallacy that De Lorean experienced in General Motors: the belief that strategy consists of the machinations and rituals of formal meetings, etc. (see the matrix in Figure 9.1).

	Called 'strategy'	Not called 'strategy'
Is Strategic	Research works	Research misses the boat
Is not Strategic	Research wasteful or misguided	No problem

figure 9.1 Strategy-as-practice predicament

The cell of greatest concern contains all sorts of events and actions, many tacit and some not recognized by strategy–as–practice researchers, that can have great influence on the strategy (examples of this have been discussed in the learning school).

There maybe, for example, pivotal organizational events that took place long before the researcher showed up at the scene. History can be important. Managers must often deal with the consequences of decisions made decades before they joined the organization. A long-term perspective can also throw into sharp relief a strategy that is obscured by present day preoccupations.

Resources as the basis of competitive advantage

Here we move from the softer side of culture to its harder side.

Material culture

Culture is the shared meaning that a group of people create over time. This is done by purely social activities, such as talking, celebrating, and grieving, also when people work together on common tasks, and interact with the resources they employ (Gagliardi, 1992; Rafaeli and Vilnai-Yavetz, 2004; Taylor, 2002).

" culture is the shared meaning that a group of people create over time "

Tangible resources, such as machines and buildings, as well as less intangible resources, such as scientific know-how and budgetary systems, interact with members of an organization to produce what anthropologists call 'material culture' (Prown, 1993: 1). Of course, the relationship is reciprocal: beliefs and values create resources, and resources create and shape beliefs and values. Take for example the automobile. It was invented in Europe as a luxury machine built by skilled artisans for the affluent. The Americans reinvented the automobile as a standardized, low-cost machine built by unskilled labour for the multitudes. This reflects deep differences in culture: the Europeans had a long tradition of craftsmanship, while the Americans compensated for their shortage of skilled workers by learning to standardize products and master the art of mass production. The competition that eventually arose between American and European car manufacturers turned out to be a competition between the two different cultures (and remains significantly so). Many European firms that tried to beat the Americans by imitating their ways found that, while they could borrow this or that piece of the puzzle, the entire system seemed to elude them. The Japanese tried to do the same thing after the Second World War, but gave up, and instead decided to develop their own way of producing automobiles, more congruent with their culture which did eventually challenge American supremacy.

The idea that it is not products which compete in the marketplace but systems of production is not new. Economists have long held that the efficiency of a production system plays a central role in competition. What few economists failed to appreciate, however, is the degree to which such advantage could be not only culture specific, but firm specific, namely rooted in the culture of an organization too —that uniqueness may be at the root of strategic advantage. Edith Penrose was not one of those economists.

Why do firms diversify?

In 1959, Penrose published a major work which examined a central mystery in economics: why do firms diversify? When a firm comes up with a new product that cannot be used in its own market, why does it bother to enter a new market? Why not simply sell the product to the highest bidder? She had an ingenious answer: market failure. Put simply, markets are poor in valuing products, technologies, and ideas that are novel. The established mousetrap companies just cannot believe that your new mousetrap is better, so you have to prove it by producing and marketing the thing yourself.

Penrose argued that many firms choose to do this, and so many large diversified corporations have come into existence. Her answer, however, had deeper significance, which was appreciated by strategy researchers more than by economists: firms derive their advantages from market imperfections. Uniqueness provides the basis for corporate development. In creating unique products, firms also develop unique capabilities, or 'resources.' They invest more in research and development, create extensive capabilities in production and marketing, and learn about their customers.

Resource-based theory

Birger Wernerfelt (1984) was the first in strategy to develop Penrose's insight, in a prize-winning article that gave *resource-based theory* its name (Rugman and Verbeke, 2002). In it, he argued the following propositions:

1 Looking at firms in terms of their resources leads to different insights than the traditional product perspective. In particular, diversified firms are seen in a new light.

2 One can identify types of resources which can lead to high profits. In analogy to entry barriers, these are associated with what we will call resource position barriers.

3 Strategy for a bigger firm involves striking a balance between the exploitation of existing resources and the development of new ones.

4 An acquisition can be seen as a purchase of a bundle of resources in a highly imperfect market. By basing the purchase on a rare resource, one can *ceteris paribus* maximize this imperfection and one's chances of buying cheap and getting good returns. (1984: 172)

Wernerfelt later claimed (1995: 171) that his ideas did not really take hold until 1990, when Prahalad and Hamel popularized their ideas about dynamic capabilities – which we discussed in Chapter 7. In fact, these two views are rather related (as the respective authors acknowledge), with their focus on the sustenance and development of the internal capabilities of firms—the 'inside-out' view, in opposition to positioning's 'outside-in' view.

We have split these views of resource-based theory and dynamic capabilities, however, one in the learning school, the other here, because of what we perceive to be an important difference: while resource-based theory emphasizes the rooting of these capacities in the evolution of the organization (in effect, its culture), the *dynamic* capabilities approach emphasizes their development essentially through a process of strategic learning. And this, reflects the markedly different audiences to which they appeal, the former the subject of vigorous debate in the academic journals, the latter a favourite among consultants and practising managers.

This may seem like splitting hairs on our part, but we think not. People differ in how they view the strategy process, often by tilting one way or the other on some dimension. In this case, with an emphasis on capability for learning compared with one on capabilities rooted in culture.

Jay Barney developed the resource-based view into a full fledged theory. In an overview published in 1991, he began by outlining the notion of resources, the building block of the entire perspective: these include 'all assets, capabilities, organizational processes, information, knowledge, etc. controlled by a firm' that enable it to create and pursue effective strategies. They can be categorized as physical capital resources (physical technology, plant and equipment, geographic location, access to raw materials), human capital resources (training, experience, judgment, intelligence, relationships, etc.), and organizational capital resources (formal systems and structures as well as informal relations among groups) (103).

> the firm is thus a bundle of resources, both tangible and intangible

The firm is thus a bundle of resources, both tangible and intangible. What weaves this bundle into a single system is a web of shared interpretations. That is what maintains, renews, and shapes these resources. And it is what marries the economic with the social—material culture with social culture.

How then can a firm know which resources are strategic, meaning that they offer the greatest sustained benefits in the face of competition? Barney (1991) stipulated four criteria (somewhat reminiscent of Porter):

- **Valuability**. Obviously a resource must be valuable to be strategic—it must have the capacity to improve the organization's efficiency and effectiveness.

- **Rarity**. A resource is strategic to the extent that it is rare and in high demand. Hence a supermarket chain that has tied up the prime locations in a city has an advantage similar to a charismatic Hollywood star with a unique face.

- **Inimitability**. The resource must not only be valuable and rare but also difficult to imitate. Inimitability can derive from historical fact (that supermarket chain's locations), from 'causal ambiguity' (what is the charisma of a movie star anyway?) or from sheer complexity (competitors know it will be costly and time consuming to create a comparable resource).

- **Substitutability**. A resource may be rare and inimitable and yet not strategic if competitors can find a substitute for what it can do. Consider what the internet has been doing to those long-sought after broadcasting licences.

Having resources with these characteristics puts a firm in a better competitive position than its rivals. But does it deliver sustainable competitive advantage—advantage that persists in spite of variable economic and market conditions? Seeking to answer this question, Margaret Peteraf (1993) offered the following four conditions as necessary for transforming resources that are valuable, rare, inimitable, and non-substitutable into sustainable competitive advantage:

1 **Heterogeneity**—The resource based view sees firms as essentially bundles of resources in competition with each other. It is the fact that resource bundles vary from firm to firm, i.e. that they are heterogeneous, that gives rise to the possibility of resources creating sustainable competitive advantage. If all the firms in the same industry have similar bundles of resources then sustainable competitive advantage cannot emerge. Resource bundle variability, due to accidents of history and managerial decisions, provide the basis for managers to develop competitive advantage that can be sustained.

2 **Ex ante limits to competition**—Having a resource bundle that is different than one's industry competitors is a necessary but not

sufficient condition for attaining sustainable competitive advantage. Other firms in the industry can spot the same bundling opportunity and follow suit. Barriers that deter or prevent other firms from attempting to develop the same resource bundle are therefore an important factor in developing sustainability. Examples of these barriers are exclusive licences that allow only some firms to incorporate into their new products highly specialized technology, or restrictions on the number of hockey teams that can locate in a major metropolitan area such as Toronto or New York.

3 **Ex post limits to competition**—If ex ante limits to competition deal with barriers that prevent competitors from developing the same resource bundle, ex post limits on competition concern barriers that make it difficult for competitors to effectively imitate what the pioneer is doing. Example of ex post limits to competition is obtaining retail locations that are strategically placed, thus forcing rivals to build in locations that are less advantageous.

4 **Resource immobility**—A bundle of resources will confer sustainable competitive advantage if it does not depend on continuous support from external resource providers. This often happens when a resource bundle that delivers sustainable advantage requires the employment of individuals with highly specialized skills. Once these individuals recognize their value to the firm, they demand higher salaries, or offer their services to competitors. Both actions reduce the sustainability of the pioneering firm. An example of this is the breakup of the Hollywood studio system in the late 1940s. Prior to the Second World War the movie studios employed their stars under an exclusive seven year contract. Their competitive sustainable advantage depended on developing and holding onto stars. Actors fought what they regarded as forced servitude, ultimately managing to break the system of exclusive contracting in the 1950s. Today, actors negotiate their contracts on a movie-by-movie basis, adjusting their financial remuneration in line with the demand for their services. As a result, studios had to develop different resource bundles to attain sustainable competitive advantage.

Culture as a key resource

The first line of defence for a resource-based advantage is to prevent imitation. Patents and trademarks of course make this easy. Otherwise, and in the long run, perhaps the best protection is afforded by intangible relationships, systems, skills, and knowledge. And this takes us right back to culture.

Thus, in an article entitled 'Organizational Culture: Can It Be a Source of Sustained Competitive Advantage?' Barney (1986) made the case for culture as the most effective and durable barrier to imitation, citing two reasons. First, culture encourages the production of unique outcomes. Second, it is loaded with causal ambiguity (as we noted in the introduction to this chapter), which makes it difficult to understand, let alone reproduce—even by insiders themselves. So, for example, someone who leaves cannot help a competitor replicate what is unique about the organization. Paradoxically, then, an organization's inability to understand and reproduce its own culture may be the best guarantee of its strategic advantage—far better than any security system or legal device ever devised! Of course, that also renders it vulnerable, easily destroyed by any new leader who does not understand it and so makes dramatic moves without being able to assess their impact on the organization.

A debate took up this paradox of understanding. Conner and Prahalad argued that 'a knowledge-based view is the essence of the resource-based perspective' (1996: 477). Thus a firm should be seen, not as an eclectic bundle of tangible resources, but as a hierarchy of intangible knowledge and processes for knowledge creation. For example, the strategic value of a brand such as Coca-Cola is clear enough. But what about the know-how that goes into such branding? And the experience of the people with this know-how? Are 'human resources' then the ultimate source of inimitability?

Kogut and Zander (1996) argued not. Ultimately, they saw the source of inimitablity as coming from the totality of the organization as a 'social community.' This refers to the affiliation system among individuals who have developed a common identity. They have become 'a moral order' of people 'bounded by what they know and by what they value' (515).

Whither goest the resource-based view?

The resource-based view of strategy has enjoyed great success in the research community. But as Barney (2001) ruefully suggests in his ten year retrospective of its development, success attracts closer scrutiny. Some scholars point out that the resource-based view tends to produce circular reasoning: we identify firms as having sustainable competitive advantage, and then look for resources that possess the characteristics identified by the resource-based view as necessary for creating sustainable advantage (see Priem and Butler, 2003: 27–8).

To avoid this circularity it would help if we could identify and measure resources according to whether they are valuable, rare, inimitable, and non-substitutable. But this has proven to be very difficult. The best and most widely cited study to date, by Miller and Shamsie (1996), examined the impact of valuable property-based resources (such as patents and managerial expertise), on the performance of Hollywood film studios prior and subsequent to their breakup as an integrated oligopoly. Their analysis links valuable resources with sustainable competitive advantage, and even goes so far as to suggest that the value of resources declined when the Hollywood studios were dismantled. However, some researchers remain unconvinced, arguing that this study, and others, do not in fact measure the value of resources as defined by the resource-based view (e.g. Priem and Butler, 2003: 36; and Newbert, 2007).

But even researchers that are critical of the resource-based view concede that it has made an important contribution to strategy. For the fact is that since Porter shifted the focus of strategic management to the external environment, a hype has grown up around change and so-called environmental 'turbulence'—better still 'hyperturbulence'—that gives the impression that firms should change, in fact, do so perpetually. For those firms inclined to follow, the resource-based view serves as a correcting device, by swinging the pendulum back to internal capabilities rooted in culture. In effect, SWOT should be alive and well in strategic management, by ensuring that the SWs (strengths and weaknesses) get consideration alongside the external OTs (opportunities and threats)!

But is it a pendulum we need in strategic management or a balance? Should the firm really be urged to swing to one side and then the other? After all, is inside-out better than outside-in, at least for a time? Perhaps the design school had this right back in the mid-1960s, with its emphasis on balanced fit!

Critique, contribution, and context of the cultural school

If the positioning school has been faulted for artificial precision, then the cultural school can be faulted for conceptual vagueness. Not only in its Swedish version do the concepts come and go with remarkable speed, although they are not always that much different from one another. As Richard Rumelt once quipped, 'If two academics have the same idea, one of them is redundant!' (Strategic Management Society conference talk, Montreal, 1982). So the trick is to change the label and hope for the best.

On the other hand, the 'hard' methods of social science are bound to miss the point about a phenomenon as ethereal as culture, much as they have in the study of leadership. And so we should really applaud the imagination of the Swedish researchers and other researchers working here.

One danger of this school is that it can discourage necessary change. It favours the management of consistency, of staying on track, so to speak. Culture is heavy, established, set; resources are installed, rooted. By emphasizing tradition and consensus as well as by characterizing change as complex and difficult, this school can encourage a kind of stagnation. (Of course, its proponents would say that organizational life does this, not their theories. Why shoot the messenger?)

Ironically, however, while culture itself may be difficult to build in the first place, and even more difficult to reconstruct later, it is rather easy to destroy. Give some disconnected 'professional' manager enough authority, and watch what happens (see Box 9.2). On the other hand, as noted above, with all the hype these days about change, we desperately need more messages about some good old-fashioned stability.

Another danger of culture as an explanatory framework is that it equates strategic advantage with organizational uniqueness. Being different is often good, but not in and of itself, for that can breed a certain arrogance. Who will be left to question the reasoning behind the status quo? NIH ('not invented here') is hardly an unknown phenomenon in organizations.

---

box 9.2

Five easy steps to destroying a rich culture

(adapted from Mintzberg, 1996b)

▪ Step 1: Manage the bottom line (as if you make money by managing money).
▪ Step 2: Make a plan for every action: no spontaneity please, no learning.
▪ Step 3: Move managers around to be certain they never get to know anything but management well (and kick the boss upstairs—better to manage a portfolio than a real business).
▪ Step 4: Always be objective, which means to treat people as objects (in particular, hire and fire employees the way you buy and sell machines—everything is a 'portfolio').
▪ Step 5: Do everything in five easy steps.

Paradoxically, theories such as the resource-based one may exacerbate this tendency, by providing managers with a ready-made vocabulary with which to justify the status quo. Any organizational practice that seems incomprehensible can be justified on the grounds of inimitability: it may be seen as tacit, based on resources that are themselves rare. Who, after all, knows what are the real sources of performance?

Resource-based theory generates some interesting insights. But these do not easily translate into strategic management. The ambiguities associated with resources may help to explain why successful strategies can go unchallenged for a long time, but they do not let managers know when and how to go about challenging them. Should the managers try to disentangle the successful strategies— reverse engineer them, so to speak—or should they simply try to create other strategies that are equally ambiguous to other firms?

And then there is the problem raised above about imbalance. It is not corrections we need in this field—a focus on internal resources after an obsession with external competition—but some sense of dynamic balance between all the appropriate factors. That is why we prefer to have the various chapters of this book seen, not just as a portfolio of possible approaches to managing strategy, but also as different dimensions of a single process. All of this is, after all, about a single beast called *strategy formation*.

The problem with the discourse of culture in general as well as with resource-based theory in particular is that they explain too easily what already exists, rather than tackling the tougher questions of what can come into being. This is not to argue that the contributions of the cultural school have been unimportant. Quite the contrary. In comparison with the disjointed conflict of politics, they offer the integrated consensus of ideology. Against the individualism of the design, cognitive, and entrepreneurial schools, they bring in the important collectivist dimension of social process, securing a place for organizational style, alongside personal style and challenging the popular tendency to chop everything up into disconnected part—'agents' as part of 'portfolios,' etc.—in favour of building integrated perspectives. In contrast to the ahistorical tendencies of the planning and positioning schools—change your strategy the way you change your clothing—they root strategy in the rich tapestry of an organization's history. In this school, strategy formation becomes the management of collective cognition—a critically important idea, although hardly an easy one to manage.

Of course, all of this applies especially to certain kinds of organizations—clearly those more 'missionary' in nature, with rich cultures; also to large, established organizations whose stagnant cultures reinforce their long-standing strategies. The cultural school also seems most applicable to particular periods in the lives of organizations. This includes a period of *reinforcement*, in which a rich strategic perspective is pursued vigorously, perhaps eventually into stagnation. This generally leads to a period of *resistance to change*, in which necessary strategic adaptation is blocked by the inertia of established culture, including its associated strategic perspective. And perhaps this school can also help us to understand a period of *reframing*, during which a new perspective develops collectively, and even a period of *cultural revolution* that tends to accompany strategic turnaround.

The environmental school: strategy formation as a reactive process

"Because I've already said all I can say in this particular medium."

© The New Yorker Collection 1995 Mort Gerberg from cartoonbank.com. All Rights Reserved.

Isaac Bashevis Singer, on being asked if he believed in free will or predestination: "We have to believe in free will; we've got no choice."

—Quoted in Fadiman (1985: 510)

Among the actors at centre stage of the schools so far discussed—the chief, the planner, the brain, the organization, and so on—one has been conspicuous by its absence. That is the set of forces outside the organization, what organization theorists like to call (rather loosely) the 'environment.' The other schools see this as a factor; the environmental school sees it as an actor—indeed *the* actor.

Writers who favour this view tend, as a consequence, to consider the organization passive, something that spends its time reacting to an environment that sets the agenda. This reduces strategy making to a kind of mirroring process, which should really take this school beyond the bounds of strategic management (a conclusion we in fact favour). Nevertheless, a literature has grown up to depict strategy making in this way, and it merits at least a detour on our safari, for several reasons.

For one thing, this school helps to bring the overall view of strategy formation into balance, by positioning environment as one of the three central forces in the process, alongside leadership and organization. At the limit, this school has spawned some rather silly debates about whether or not managers really could make 'strategic choices': to deny such choice is no more sensible than to attribute omniscient power to the strategist. But in more moderate form, the views of this school do encourage people in strategic management to consider the range of decisional powers available, given the demands of the external context. Moreover, this school itself has helped to describe different dimensions of the environments facing strategists, and to suggest their possible effects on strategy formation.

Of course, 'environment' has not been absent from our other schools. It was certainly present in the positioning school, but in a rather specific way: as a set of economic forces—representing industry, competition, and market. Indeed, we concluded that the positioning school ends up in a similar position with regard to strategic choice, clothing rather deterministic ideas in the cloak of free will: the rather macho managers depicted in that school had better do what their competitive conditions dictate.

Likewise, the emphasis on bias and distortion in one wing of the cognitive school reflects the influence of environment: this is considered a place that sends out confusing signals, too complex to be fully understood. Our discussion of the learning school also emphasized the complexity of the environment—but as a place not to react to so much as to experience, experiment with, and enact, as well as learn from. In our other schools, however, the environment has tended to be absent, incidental, or at least assumed.

In this chapter, leadership as well as organization becomes subordinate to the external environment. Indeed, as we have moved through the various schools, the power of the central strategist has gradually diminished. In the design and later the entrepreneurial schools, the chief dominated. The planning and positioning schools modified this, by introducing planners and analysts as supporting strategists, while one side of the cognitive school drew attention to the limitations of the strategic thinker in a complex world. (The other side vests that vision with imagination.) Additional strategists were introduced by the learning and then the power schools, and these became the full-blown collectivity in the cultural school. But through all this, the notion of strategist continued to reign supreme, whoever it was— an individual or the collectivity, whether cooperative or conflictive. In this chapter, the environment takes command. Indeed, the organization becomes akin to the environment in some of the other schools—a kind of skeleton or caricature of its real self.

What, then, is this thing called 'environment'? Not much, in fact, even here. It is usually treated as a set of vague forces 'out there'—in effect, everything that is not organization. Usually environment is delineated as a set of abstract dimensions—for example, not an angry customer banging at the door but 'malevolent'; not an unexpected series of technological breakthroughs but 'dynamic'; not the intricacies of transplanting hearts but 'complex.' Sometimes even all this is reduced to one general force that drives the organization into some sort of ecological-type *niche*. But not the niche of the entrepreneurial school—a place protected from competition, where a market can be exploited. Here niche is the very seat of competition, as in ecology, where the organization competes with entities like itself, just as koala bears all go after the same eucalyptus leaves. In effect, niche is to the environmental school what market is to the positioning school—except that here it is *always* competitive.

The environmental school first grew out of so-called 'contingency theory,' which described the relationships between particular dimensions of the environment and specific attributes of the organization—for example, the more stable the external environment, the more formalized the internal structure. Later these ideas were extended to strategy making—for example that stable environments favoured more planning. Then a group of organization theorists calling themselves 'population ecologists' came along, arguing that actions taken in response to a changing external environment will not improve the adaptation of their organizations. True, the choices that entrepreneurs and managers make during the early life of the organizations are real and decisive—for example, the structure it adapts and the technology it uses. But those can later come back to haunt, or benefit, the organization. In other words, once the organization is up and running, most of its strategic choices are considered to have little impact on whether it survives or fails. The key choices are made early, and these choices set the destiny of the organization.

Meanwhile, others, called 'institutional theorists,' have arrived at a somewhat similar conclusion based on a different framework. They argue that political and ideological pressures exerted by the environment dramatically reduce strategic choice. The environment thereby becomes an 'iron cage'. We discuss these different views in turn after summarizing the premises of this school.

Premises of the environmental school

1 The environment, presenting itself to the organization as a set of general forces, is the central actor in the strategy-making process.

2 During its formative period the organization shapes itself in response to the environment, but thereafter is increasingy unable to respond to the environment.

3 The organization's long-term survival depends on the early choices made during the formative period.

4 Over time, leadership becomes progressively less able to influence the performance and survivability of the organization.

5 Organizations that survive selection pressures end up clustering together in distinct ecological-type niches, where they tend to share similar technologies, products, and management styles.

The contingency view

The environmental school has its roots in contingency theory, which grew up to oppose the confident assertions of classical management that there is 'one best way' to run an organization (see Donaldson, 2001, for a comprehensive review). To contingency theorists, 'it all depends': on the size of the organization, its technology, the stability of its context, external competition, and so on.

This satisfied the commonsense realization that different situations give rise to different behaviours—for example, that bakeries function differently in America than in France. But it also made necessary more systematic descriptions of the environment. So work began to identify the dimensions of this environment. This was summarized by Mintzberg in four main groups, as follows:

1 **Stability**. An organization's environment can range from *stable* to *dynamic*, from that of the wood carver whose customers demand the same pine sculptures decade after decade, to that of the detective squad which never knows what to expect next. A variety of factors can make an environment dynamic, including unstable governments; . . . unexpected changes in customer demand. The real problems are caused by changes that occur unexpectedly, for which no patterns could have been discerned in advance. . . .

2 **Complexity**. An organization's environment can range from simple to complex, from that of the manufacturer of folding boxes that produces . . . simple products with simple knowledge, to that of the space agency which must utilize knowledge from a host of the most advanced scientific fields to produce extremely complex outputs. . . . [Note that a complex environment can be

rather stable, as in accounting practice, while a dynamic one can be rather simple, as in betting on the horse races. In Chapter 11, we shall describe forms of organizations suited to all four possible conditions.]

3 **Market diversity**. The markets of an organization can range from *integrated* to *diversified*—from that of an iron mine that sells its one commodity to a single steel mill, to those of a trade commission that seeks to promote all of a nation's industrial products all over the world. . . .

4 **Hostility**. Finally, an organization's environment can range from munificent to hostile—from that of a prestigious surgeon who picks and chooses patients, through that of a construction firm that must bid on all its contracts, to that of an army fighting a war. Hostility is influenced by competition, by the organization's relationships with unions, government, and other outside groups, as well as by the availability of resources to it. (1979: 268–9)

> **❝ different situations give rise to different approaches to strategy ❞**

Contingency theory delineated a set of responses to such dimensions, mostly about structure (see especially Pugh *et al*., 1963–4; 1968, 1969), then later about strategy. Danny Miller, for example, whose main contribution has been in the configurational school, developed the propositions such as:

- ▪ '. . . risk-taking entrepreneurs . . . tend . . . to be associated with dynamic environments.'
- ▪ '. . . strategies will be more comprehensive and multifaceted in environments which pose a large number of challenges and opportunities.' (1979: 302, 304)

We shall not undertake here a comprehensive review of the lessons of contingency theory for strategic management simply because that is what we do after our ten chapters on the schools.

The population ecology view

The environmental school finds its strongest expression in the work of researchers who label their approach *population ecology*. Whereas contingency theorists allow for adaptation, population ecologists like Hannan and Freeman (1977), who published the most widely cited statement of this view in 'The Population Ecology of Organizations,' express their 'doubt that the major features of the world of organizations arise through learning or adaptation' (957; see also Hannan and Freeman, 1984).

If so, then what are we to make of the changes we commonly observe in organizations? Population ecologists argue that most of these are not consequential. The basic structure and character of an organization is fixed shortly after birth. The early actions of managers, for example investments in plant, equipment, and specialized personnel, create inertia that subsequently reduces management's freedom to act. Alongside practical rigidities, the inertia generated by early choices places constraints on the information received by decision makers; and gives rise to political forces within the organization (such as units that resist reorganization). There are also external pressures toward inertia, including legal and fiscal barriers to the entry, and to exit, from markets; constraints on the availability and acquisition of external information; established forms of legitimacy, which breed resistance to change (such as in a university trying to get rid of undergraduate education); and the problem of collective rationality (that organizations lock each other into set ways of behaving—those 'industry recipes' again).

Population ecologists use Darwin's well-known variation-selection-retention model, but not as we saw it in the learning school. Here the process takes place at the level of populations. In effect, population ecologists perceive organizations the way biologists perceive fruit flies—from a distance, in terms of their collective behaviour. To explain change, they look to the interaction between almost fortuitous innovations by individual organizations and the struggle for existence at the population level.

The birth of an individual organization through an innovation introduces variation into a population. This innovation gives the organization an advantage, but survival depends on its ability to acquire an adequate supply of resources. Each environment, however, has a finite amount of resources, or, to use a term population ecologists borrow from biology, a 'fixed carrying capacity.'

In a new industry that is growing rapidly, the carrying capacity may be able to support most existing organizations. But as these grow and more organizations enter, the carrying capacity will be exceeded. Moreover, as the industry matures its carrying capacity may decline and demand for products level off (Durand, 2001). This can create a struggle for resources which drives out the less fit organizations. This is competition, of course, but unlike that of the positioning school, because here organizations do not target each other directly. Rather, it is the environment that sets the criteria of fit. Organizations that meet these criteria survive and those that do not are selected out.

Although population ecology eschews strategy as a process of continuous adaptation, it still lets strategy in through the back door. Organizations, suggest Hannan and Freeman (1977), do have a choice, even if usually accidental: they can seek to make the most of their environment, in effect maximizing fit, or else they can hold certain resources in reserve for future emergencies. The first choices emphasizes efficiency, the other flexibility. The organization has to place a bet on its future by deciding the amount and type of resources to hold back as excess capacity.

Much of the population ecology research in the aftermath of Hannan and Freeman's work has become a search for what factors increase or decrease an organization's chances of survival (Henderson, 1999). In keeping with the basic selection metaphor, organizational properties are often seen in terms of 'liabilities'—for example, the 'liability of smallness,' which predicts that larger organizations are more endowed with resources and thus less likely to fail; the 'liability of newness,' which sees firms new to an industry as more likely to die than firms which have been there longer; and the 'liability of adolescence,' which maintains that the greatest danger is in the transition between infancy and maturity. Birth is accomplished with innovative ideas and entrepreneurial energy, maturity is characterized by considerable resources and power. In between, an organization may have exhausted the former and not established the latter.

Sooner or later organizations go through all these stages. Does this mean that they experience all these liabilities? This need not be the case according to Henderson (1999). Some liabilities will only occur under certain circumstances, whereas in other cases liabilities may actually compete for influence. The interaction of liabilities can therefore be complex and unpredictable, which from a managerial point of view makes population ecology rather limited in usefulness.

Who needs to adapt?

Critiques of the population ecology of organizations have been numerous, and revolve around a number of obvious issues: '[W]here did these variations in the population come from?' asked Van de Ven (1979: 324), suggesting the role of entrepreneurs and inventors, while Astley (1985) noted that environments are often quite open and receptive to whatever variations are imposed on them.

Critics have suggested that organizations are not fruit flies and decisions are not programmed by genetic endowment. Population ecologists may be looking at the world through the wrong end of a telescope. What is nearby seems far away, and so details melt into amorphous blobs.

Consider the issue of change. To make its arguments, population ecology has to take a long time horizon. Indeed, to justify the argument that 'even the largest and most powerful organizations fail to survive over long periods,' Hannan and Freeman found it necessary to go back to the American Revolution! Only twenty of the firms that existed then survived to the time of their research (seven as divisions of other firms). They comment: 'Presumably one needs a longer time perspective to study the population ecology of the largest and most dominant organizations' (1977: 960). But 200 years?!

Moreover, one organization may die because of the aggressive strategic actions of another, not because of some abstraction called environment. In fact, even in biology, debates about the capacity of species to adapt, not by natural selection but by internally induced change, are now common. A good deal of this has been stimulated by Steven Jay Gould's model of 'punctuated equilibrium,' which argues that change has been too fast, in ecological terms at least, to support Darwin's notion of natural selection. 'The geologic record seems to provide as much evidence for cataclysmic as for gradual change,' in other words, for 'sudden appearance . . . "fully formed"' (1980: 180, 187).

Gould also argued that 'extinction is no shame,' pointing out that 'dinosaurs dominated the land for 100 million years, yet a species that measures its own life in but tens of thousands of years has branded dinosaurs as a symbol of failure'! He thus concluded that life 'is a story of intricate branching and wandering, with momentary survivors adapting to change local environments . . .' (1982: 12). In the spirit of this, back in the field of management but also drawing from ecology, Astley has distinguished *individual* and *communal* adaptation, the former possibly genetic but also possibly somatic. This means that 'an individual organism [can meet] local variations in its environment,' sometimes even temporarily (1984: 530)—much as do organizations when they make strategy. This has led to development of 'community ecology', which considers the emergence and decline of organizational forms rather than the birth and death of specific organizations (Ruef, 2000; see also Hannan, 2005).

Institutional pressures to conform

Max Weber, the father of organization theory, saw organizations as being shaped by the relentless march of technical and managerial rationality, which expresses itself in ever-increasing bureaucratization. There is an 'iron cage' of rationality, to use the expression Weber made famous, that shapes what managers confront.

A number of organizational sociologists picked up where Weber left off, creating a point of view which has come to be known as 'institutional theory.' It is concerned with the institutional pressures an organization faces in its environment, from other organizations and from the pressures of just being an organization.

Institutional theory sees the environment as a repository of two types of resources: economic and symbolic. Economic resources are the familiar and tangible: money, land, and machinery. Symbolic resources include, for example, a reputation for efficiency, leaders celebrated for past achievements, and the prestige associated with alliances with well-known firms. Strategy becomes finding ways of acquiring economic resources and converting them into symbolic ones, and vice versa, in order to protect the organization from uncertainty in its environment. Hence, the strategy process moves into the realm of 'impression management.'

> **the strategy process moves into the realm of 'impression management'**

Here the environment consists of the interactions among key suppliers, consumers, regulatory and other government agencies, and, of course, competitors, which over time become a complex and powerful set of norms that dominate practice. To be successful, an organization must meet and master these norms. This drives organizations in the same environment over time to adopt similar structures and practices.

Such imitation, called *institutional isomorphism* by Meyer and Rowan (1977), who introduced the label, suggest that it provides a cover behind which the organization gains protection, for example, 'from having its conduct questioned. The organization becomes, in a word, legitimate' (349).

Institutional theory distinguishes three types of isomorphism. *Coercive* isomorphism represents the pressures to conform, exerted through standards, regulations, and the like. All airlines, for example, have to obey stringent safety rules (see Lampel, 2006). *Mimetic* isomorphism results from borrowing and imitation. Organizations copy the approaches of successful competitors, obviously because they associate it with the success, but also because they want to convince others that they too are at the cutting edge of best practice. The enduring popularity of 'benchmarking' among managers testifies to this pressure (Vorhies and Morgan, 2005). *Normative* isomorphism results from the strong influence of professional expertise. Many organizations are dominated by experts who bring their own shared professional norms into decision making. For example, the wide-spread reliance on lawyers for negotiating contracts tends to increase uniformity among corporations, and also tends to drive out more informal and idiosyncratic ways of doing business (Dobbin and Sutton, 1998).

Institutional theorists are conscious that the combined impact of these various forms constrain organizations to the point where they seem to have little scope for independent decision making (Dacin *et al.*, 2002). Other research has therefore focused on the diversity of organizational response to isomorphic pressures. For instance, Oliver (1991) has suggested that organizations adapt a variety of responding behaviours: (1) acquiescence (giving in fully to institutional pressures); (2) compromise (only partially acceding to such pressures); (3) avoidance (attempting to preclude the necessity of conformity); (4) defiance (actively resisting institutional pressures); and (5) manipulation (attempting to modify or alter the pressures). But note that this does not represent a break with the assumptions of the environmental school, because all of these postures, even defiance or manipulation are responses to institutional pressures.

Critique, contribution, and context of the environmental school

We have already mentioned our concerns with a restricted view of strategic choice. Here we elaborate on this.

Perhaps the greatest weakness of contingency theory for purposes of strategic management is that its dimensions of environment are often so abstract—vague and aggregated. Strategy has to do with the selection of specific positions. An effective strategist can sometimes find a place to stand in a deep lake; alternatively, ineffective ones sometimes drown in lakes that are on average shallow. That is why the strategy of differentiation is such an important concept in this field. It describes how organizations differ in seemingly similar environments.

In reality, no organization faces an 'environment' that is munificent, or complex, or hostile, or dynamic (let alone turbulent). There may be periodic pockets of such things—in one market or another, with regard to some particular technology or customer preference. But it would be foolhardy to manage strategy at such aggregated levels. Strategists need 'fine-grained' probes that provide 'thick' descriptions, nuanced as to time, application, and context. As we shall argue in the next chapter, strategic management may be better served by a rich description of environmental types, which describe in detail what particular organizations experience at particular points in their histories.

No choice but to act

But our real concern here is with 'strategic choice,' as delineated especially, although not exclusively, by the population ecologists. That organizations have no real strategic choice—that there is some sort of 'environmental imperative' out there—has been criticized on a number of grounds. How is it that two organizations can operate successfully in a similar environment with very different strategies? How distinct really is an organization from its 'environment,' especially with the growth of alliances and joint ventures that blur the boundaries? Indeed, do environments 'select' organizations, or do organizations 'enact' environments? After all, what is an 'industry environment' but all the organizations functioning in it? In a monopoly, for example, environment can be one firm, and often there are but a few such players in an industry.

❝ can any living organism really be said to lack choice ❞

Moreover, do environments 'exist' at all, or are these just the perceptions of people—social constructions themselves? And finally, can any living organism really be said to lack choice?

To our mind, to debate whether or not organ-izations make choices is about as useful as to debate whether or not people can be happy. There is a whole range of each, and prophesies here tend to be self-fulfilling: if you believe in happiness or in choice, you will find it everywhere. If not, it may be found nowhere. Besides, engaging in such debates makes people unhappy and takes time away from making choices.

Fruit flies are, of course, the pets of the population ecologists in biology. Viewed from afar, they seem to respect the laws of natural selection. Yet, viewed up close, they are continuously making choices, for example, to go up, down, left or right—the options are infinite! Imagine a fruit fly looking down on a couple of population ecologists on their way to work in the morning rush hour. Much of the time, they can hardly go forward, let alone left, right, up, or down. Indeed, what if that fruit fly followed them to the office: would it conclude that ecological forces have driven these people to write their articles? And make no mistake about it: the choice of which way to fly is as important for a fruit fly as the choice of which article to write (or, for that matter, which theory to criticize) for a university professor. Maybe the world would be a more interesting place if fruit flies could write about university professors too.

Perhaps the point is best made by Hannan and Freeman themselves, in commenting on the effect of 'large dominant organizations [that] can create linkages with other large and powerful ones so as to reduce selection pressures.' In their view, 'the selection pressure is bumped up to a higher level. So instead of individual systems failing, entire networks fail' (1977: 961). True enough, if one is prepared to realize that the ultimate network is society itself. As we all go down together, carrying this argument to its 'natural' conclusion, and so realizing (or perhaps not) that we are all pawns in some larger order, we might wish to ask why anything matters—population ecology, strategic management, or life itself.

Thus the best advice may well come from Isaac Bashevis Singer, as quoted at the outset of this chapter: 'We have to believe in free will; we've got no choice.'

Choice in constraint

The fact is that to serve its own niche, strategic management has to view organizations close up; in the shoes of the strategist so to speak. And here it has to consider, not the *existence* of choice, but the *conditions* that enlarge or restrict its breadth. Hage (1976) has argued, for example, that organizations choose their constraints and thereby constrain their choices.

The McGill group has seen several interesting examples of this in its research on historical patterns in strategy making. For example, the Air Canada of the 1970s was a large, powerful organization, the major player in the secure and regulated markets of Canada. Yet its size restricted its choice: could any 'world class' airline possibly not have ordered jumbo jets when they initially came out? (Mintzberg *et al.*, 1986). Alternately, in the 1930s, Steinberg's was a tiny supermarket chain functioning in a severe depression. Yet because of its competences, it was able to make choices that the big chains could not, for example, moving into the stores that they vacated (Mintzberg and Waters, 1982).

Similarly, William Taylor (1982) studied the responses of four small organizations to what seemed like a rather hostile environment (anglophone institutions in a francophone region of an increasingly nationalistic Quebec). He found that their internal culture—what he labelled 'the will or desire of the organization to change strategy' (343)—was the major factor in adaptation. For example, by all indications, the hospital that Taylor studied should have been the most constrained. But in actual fact it adapted quite well. Taylor concluded that 'external constraints on strategic adaptation found in this research were extremely broad, allowing a great deal of room for organizational maneuver' (342). That is perhaps the central message of strategic management itself!

In our opinion, what makes strategic management an exciting field is that practitioners and researchers alike are (or at least can choose to be) constantly confronted with a rich and nuanced world, full of surprises, a world that favours imaginative action. Strategists who are successful get in close and understand the details, likewise successful researchers.

Thus, what distinguishes this field from some others in management is its very focus on strategic choice: how to find it and where to find it, or else how to create it when it can't be found, and then how to exploit it. Thus, strategic management has no more need for debates over the existence of choice than does population ecology for debates over the existence of populations. Each has to exploit constructively its central concept.

Let us therefore learn from the environmental school about populations of organizations, about the environments of organizations, and especially about the different forms these can take. And then let us consider where the ideas of this school seem most applicable, asking ourselves what types of organizations seem most constrained and when does strategic choice seem most limited—for example, during the *mature* stage of an organization's life cycle. But let us not get sidetracked by excessive overstatement or abstraction, let alone by unresolvable debates.

The configuration school: strategy formation as a process of transformation

"Is that it? Is that the big bang?"

The history of any one part of the earth, like the life of a soldier, consists of long periods of boredom and short periods of terror.

—Stephen Jay Gould

A ll of the above. This is the message of the configuration school, but with a particular angle. Each school at its own time, in its own place. This school, therefore, differs from all the others in one fundamental respect: it offers the possibility of reconciliation, one way to integrate the messages of the other schools.

Configuration and transformation

There are two main sides of this school, reflected in our two labels of the title. One describes states—of the organization and its surrounding context—as *configurations*. The other describes the strategy-making process—as *transformation*.

These are really two sides of the same coin: if an organization adopts states of being, then strategy making becomes a process of leaping from one state to another. In other words, transformation is an inevitable consequence of configuration. There is a time for coherence and a time for change.

This is compatible with that rather curious characteristic of strategic management noted back in our first chapter, that while its literature makes clear that it is about *change*, strategy itself is not about change at all, but about continuity—whether as deliberate plan to establish patterns of behaviour or as emergent pattern by which such patterns get established. In other words, while the process of strategy making may set out to change the direction in which an organization is going, the resulting strategies stabilize that direction. And the configuration school is most true to this: it describes the relative stability of strategy within given states, interrupted by occasional and rather dramatic leaps to new ones.

If positioning is the 'figuring' school, then this is the *'configuring'* school, in two respects. First is how the different dimensions of an organization cluster together under particular conditions, to define 'states,' 'models,' or 'ideal types.' To take one example, startup organizations, especially in emerging industries, tend to depend on entrepreneurial leaders and visionary strategies. Second is how these different states get sequenced over time, to define 'stages,' 'periods,' and organizational 'life cycles.' To continue with the example, as the entrepreneurial organization ages and its industry settles down to maturity, the startup stage may give way to one of more formalized structure under so-called professional managers who depend on planning processes.

States, of course, imply entrenched behaviours. For those who see the world this way, strategy making thus becomes shaking these stages loose so that the organization can make the transition to a new state (as quickly as possible, so as not to be state-less, so to speak). Hence the other side of this school sees the strategy process as one of rather dramatic transformation—'turnaround' or 'revitalization' to use two popular words of this school.

Like the proverbial horse and carriage, or a man and a woman in marriage, while configuration and transformation may go together, they are in fact very different—at least as reflected in the literature and practice of strategic management (Dycke, 1997). Configuration tends to be researched and described by academics (since this is a question of concepts), while transformation tends to be practised by managers and prescribed (especially) by consultants (since this is a very tricky business). In the metaphor of our safari, one side tracks while the other side traps. Either way, they are still looking for elephants. So to return to our other metaphors, there is a marriage here. The horse (process) must from time to time pull the carriage (state) to another place.

> in the metaphor of our safari, one side tracks while the other side traps

Splitters and lumpers

Charles Darwin (1887: 105) once distinguished 'splitters' from 'lumpers.' Environmental school proponents tend to be inveterate splitters: they like to isolate 'variables,' lay them out along continuous scales, and then study the relationships between pairs of them.

Configuration school people are unabashed lumpers: they see the world in terms of nice, neat categories. Nuanced variability is assumed away in favour of overall clustering; statistically speaking, outliers are ignored in favour of central tendencies.

This, of course, also simplifies. In fact, the strongest criticism of the configuration school may well be the sophistication of the work of certain splitters (for example, the Swedish group discussed in Chapter 9) who have managed to weave a wide variety of issues into intricate, nuanced theories. The descriptions of the lumpers, in contrast, tend to be rather more simple—categorical may be a better word—and so easier to understand, which makes them more widely accepted in practice but not necessarily more accurate.

The configuration approach can be found in all of the social sciences, although not always in their academic mainstreams. What often keeps it out is an obsession with being 'scientific,' which favours measuring, and so splitting. The field of history is, however, a notable exception. Here lumping is common, although theorizing is not: historians like to isolate distinct periods in history and study them intensively, but particularly. A historian who studies one revolution, for example, will typically not theorize about revolutions in general. But there are exceptions: Crane Brinton (1938) generalized about revolutions, while Toynbee (1957), Rostow (1971), and Braudel (2002) presented comprehensive periods of history.

This work can, in fact, inform strategic management. After all, it seems but a small step to go from societies to organizations—for example, to see strategic turnaround as analogous to political or cultural revolution (e.g., Firsirotu, 1985). There are also historians who have written about the nature of 'periodization' itself (such as the early work of Gerhard, 1956; Pokora, 1966; and Popescu, 1965). By identifying the bases on which periods in history can be isolated, their work can help us to understand stages in the history of organizations.

In strategic management, lumping has been reasonably common. This may reflect the close links between theory and practice: researchers are encouraged to supply what practitioners might find helpful. Indeed, the origins of the whole field of strategic management, as well as this school, can be traced back to the 1962 path-breaking book by the business historian, Alfred D. Chandler, entitled *Strategy and Structure: Chapters in the History of the Industrial Enterprise*. In the tradition of history, Chandler's book is largely about specifics, namely how strategies and structures developed especially in four of America's most important corporations: Dupont, Sears Roebuck, General Motors, and Standard Oil (New Jersey). But in his last chapter, on those 'chapters' of the title, Chandler laid out a theory of strategy and structure as a sequence of four distinct stages (which we shall describe later). He also drew a widely cited conclusion, that structure follows strategy (which we have already disputed in our chapter on the design school, which adopted it).

We shall begin with the premises of this school, since they have already been indicated. Then we shall focus on the research side of configuration before turning to the more applied work on transformation. Finally, as usual, we shall close with our critique of this school and some words on its context and contribution.

Premises of the configuration school

In one sense, the premises of the configuration school encompass those of the other schools, but each in a well-defined context. It is, however, this very encompassing that distinguishes the configuration school.

1   Most of the time, an organization can be described in terms of some kind of stable configuration of its characteristics: for a distinguishable period of time, it adopts a particular form of structure matched to a particular type of context which causes it to engage in particular behaviours that give rise to a particular set of strategies.

2   These periods of stability are interrupted occasionally by some process of transformation—a quantum leap to another configuration.

3   These successive states of configuration and periods of transformation may order themselves over time into patterned sequences, for example describing life cycles of organizations.

4   The key to strategic management, therefore, is to sustain stability or at least marginally adaptable strategic change most of the time,

but periodically to recognize the need for major transformation and be able to manage this disruptive process without destroying the organization.

5 Accordingly, the process of strategy making can be one of conceptual designing or formal planning, systematic analyzing or leadership visioning, cooperative learning or competitive politicking, focusing on individual cognition, collective socialization, or simple response to the forces of the environment. But each must be found at its own time and in its own context. In other words, the schools of thought on strategy formation themselves represent particular configurations.

6 The resulting strategies take the form of plans or patterns, positions or perspectives, or else ploys, but again, each for its own time and matched to its own situation.

Researching configuration

We begin our discussion of the work on configuration with some of the early research carried out by the management policy group at McGill University. We follow this with discussion of the work of Danny Miller, the first person to receive his doctorate from that group, who has been particularly prolific in the configuration school. We then turn to a review of other research of this nature.

Configuration studies at McGill University

The arrival of Pradip Khandwalla at McGill University's Faculty of Management in the early 1970s stimulated interest there in the configuration approach. In his doctoral thesis at Carnegie-Mellon University, Khandwalla (1970) uncovered what amounted to an empirical justification for this approach. Effectiveness in the organizations he studied related, not to the use of any particular attribute, such as the decentralization of power or a particular approach to planning, but to the intercorrelations among several attributes. In other words, organizations functioned effectively because they put different characteristics together in complementary ways—for example, a certain kind of planning with a certain form of structuring with a certain style of leading.

This finding stimulated the interest of one of us in the concept of configuration, reflected especially in two books that categorized organizations, one in terms of their structures (Mintzberg, 1979), the other in terms of their power relationships (Mintzberg, 1983). Taking these two together, as in the following box, organizations were described as being entrepreneurial, machine, professional, adhocracy, diversified, political, and missionary.

A subsequent book, that reports various studies that tracked strategies in organizations over decades related the four processes of strategy formation identified in Chapter 1—visioning, venturing, planning, and learning – four of these configurations in particular (Mintzberg, 2007: 345–61). This is noted here and explained near the end of the next chapter.

A major research project began at McGill in 1971 to track the strategies of various organizations over long periods of time, typically thirty to fifty or more years. The approach was therefore historical, designed to identify periods of stable strategy and of transformation, and then to address a number of broad questions—for example, how do different strategies connect to each other, what forces drive strategic change, when are strategies imposed deliberately, and when and how do they emerge? (We have already discussed some of these studies elsewhere, for example that of Air Canada in Chapter 3, the Steinberg retail chain in Chapter 5, and the National Film Board of Canada in Chapter 7, where a note lists all of the published studies.)

box 11.1

Configurations of structure and power
(adapted from Mintzberg, 1989, based on his earlier work)
The entrepreneurial organization

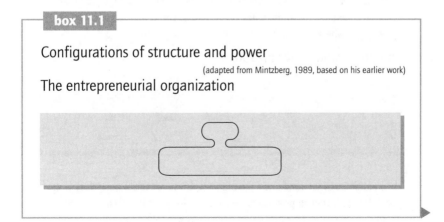

The organization is simple, often small, usually young, not much more than one unit consisting of the boss and everyone else. The structure is informal and flexible, with much of the coordination handled by the chief. This allows it to operate in a dynamic environment where it can outsmart the bureaucracies. The classic case is, of course, the entrepreneurial firm (which can sometimes grow large under the control of its founder). But even rather large organizations, under crisis, often revert to this form of leadership. Here, especially, is where we find strategy formation as visioning (as described in the entrepreneurial school).

The machine organization

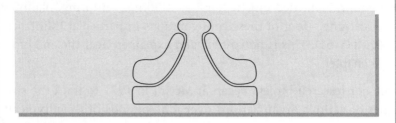

This organization, which operates as a highly programmed, well-oiled machine, is the offspring of the industrial revolution, when jobs became increasingly specialized and work highly standardized. As can be seen in the little figure, in contrast to that for the entrepreneurial organization which shows a leader over the operating base, this one elaborates, to one side, a technocratic staff (planners, time study analysts, etc.) that programs everyone else's work, and to the other side a support staff to provide help (public relations, legal counsel, mailroom, etc.). It also elaborates a line hierarchy down the middle to control the many people who do rather low skilled work. The machine organization tends to be found in stable, mature industries with established mass production or mass service technologies, as in the automobile, airline, and postal sectors. Here, especially, is where we find strategy formation as planning.

The professional organization

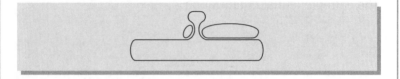

Here professionalism dominates: the organization surrenders a good deal of its power to highly trained professionals who take charge of the operating work— doctors in a hospital, for example, or researchers in a laboratory. Hence the structure emerges as highly decentralized. But because the work is rather standardized (who wants a creative surgeon?), the professionals can work largely independently of each other, coordinating being achieved by what they automatically expect of each other. As shown, the professionals are backed up by much support staff, but little technocracy or line management is necessary (or able) to control what they do. Here, especially, is where we find strategy formation as venturing (namely individual or small group learning).

The diversified organization

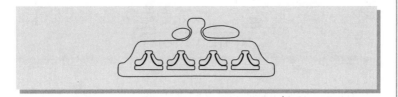

The diversified organization is not so much an integrated organization as a set of rather independent units, coupled together by a loose administrative structure. As in a conglomerate corporation or a multi-campus university, each 'division' has its own structure, to deal with its own situation, subject to performance control systems from a remote, central 'headquarters.' So the various schools of strategy formation can be found within the divisions, depending on their own configurations).

The adhocracy organization

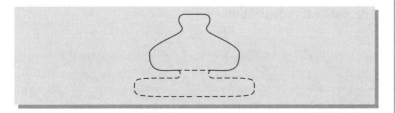

Many contemporary industries, such as aerospace and film making, even guerrilla warfare, have to innovate in complex ways. That requires projects which fuse experts from different specialties into effective teams, so that they can coordinate by 'mutual adjustment,' aided perhaps by standing committees, task forces, matrix structure, and the like. With power based on expertise, as implied in the figure the line-staff distinction diminishes, as does that between top management and everyone else. Some adhocracies carry out projects directly for their clients (as in advertising agencies), while others do so for themselves (as in companies dependent on a great deal of new product development). Here, especially, is where we find strategy formation as collective learning (as well as venturing).

The missionary organization

When an organization is dominated by a strong culture, its members are encouraged to pull together, and so there tends to be a loose division of labor, little job specialization, and a reduction in the distinction between line managers, staff groups, operating employees, and so on. Values and beliefs shared among all the members hold the organization together. So each person can be given considerable freedom to act, which suggests an almost pure form of decentralization. While certain religious orders and clubs are obvious examples, shades of this can be found in many Japanese corporations, as well as in western ones that are organized around strong cultures. Here, therefore can be found especially strategy formation in the cultural school.

The political organization

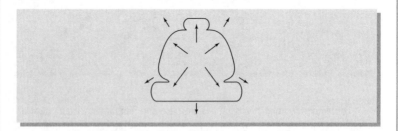

When an organization is able to settle on no stable system of power, with no dominant element (as in those above), conflicts tend to arise and possibly run out of control, leading to a political form, characterized by the pulling apart of the different parts. Some political organizations are temporary, especially during periods of difficult transformation, while others can be more permanent, as in a

> government agency pulled apart by different forces or a moribund business corporation too long protected from market forces. Here, therefore, can be found especially strategy formation in the power school.
>
> It should be emphasized that, as presented, each configuration is idealized—a simplification, really a caricature of reality. No real organization is ever exactly like any one of these, although some do come remarkably close.

In this research, strategies were identified as patterns in action that sustained themselves for identifiable periods of time, for example with regard to aircraft purchase at Air Canada or store openings at Steinberg's. These strategies were then lined up against one another along a common time scale (as shown in Figure 11.1 for Steinberg's) to identify distinct stages in the history of the organization. Among the types of stages identified were:

- stage of *development* (hiring people, establishing systems, firming up strategic positions, etc.)
- stage of *stability* (fine-tuning the strategies and structures, etc., in place)
- stage of *adaptation* (marginal changes in structures and strategic positions)
- stage of *struggle* (groping for a new sense of direction, whether in limbo, in flux, or by experimentation)
- stage of *revolution* (rapid transformation of many characteristics concurrently)

Of interest as well was how such stages tend to sequence themselves over time. Four main patterns were recognized:

- **periodic bumps**, which were common, especially in conventional organizations: long periods of stability interrupted by occasional periods of revolution
- **oscillating shifts**, when stages of adaptive convergence toward stability were followed by ones of divergent struggle for change, sometimes in surprisingly regular cycles
- **life cycles**, where a stage of development was followed by one of stability or maturity, etc.

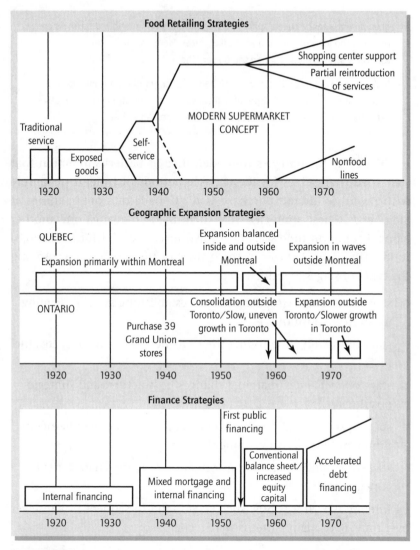

figure 11.1 Some of the strategies identified in the Steinberg Inc. retail chain

■ **regular progress**, in which the organization engaged in more-or-less steady adaptation

Clearly the first three of these are more compatible with the premises of the configuration school than the fourth.

These patterns seem to map rather well onto the forms of organization outlined in the earlier box. Periodic bumps may be especially characteristic of the machine organization, which tends to change by occasional revolutions, known as 'turnaround.' The adhocracy, in contrast, seems to prefer the oscillating shifts, alternately diverging to allow for maximum creativity in its projects and then converging after too much variety to 'get some order around here.' The professional organization seems to favour regular progress, which means almost perpetual adaptation at the operating level with rarely any dramatic transformation overall. Life cycles may be characteristic of all organizations, in some sense, except that some live longer than others (perhaps through repeated mid-life crises). The entrepreneurial organization is obviously favoured in the earliest stage of this cycle, but it also appears during the turnaround of the mature organization, when a strong leader tends to exercise decisive control.

Miller's contribution to configuration

Danny Miller, affiliated initially with McGill University and since with the École des Hautes Études Commerciales of Montreal, has been prolific in this area. His work has been especially ambitious in its integration across different attributes of organizations, and in its combination of breadth (large samples) with depth (probes into specific organizations). He has also, as shown in the box below, explored links with positioning school.

---

box 11.2

What are configurations?

Excerpted from Danny Miller and John O. Whitney (1999)

In the abstract, configurations may be defined as constellations of organizational elements that are pulled together by a unifying theme, such as unequaled service or pioneering invention. The first constellation is called the core, it consists of the mission, the means (the fundamental abilities and resources required to accomplish the mission) and the market. These constitute the raison d'être of the enterprise. The second constellation includes the systems, processes, and structures that support the core. . . . In a well-configured organization, there is harmony within and between the two constellations that creates the synergies required to make a company uniquely effective. In short, building configurations is about two things: (1) making choices about what a company does and how it will do it, and (2) ensuring that the things a company does reinforce each other. . . .

▶ Configurations can be a potent weapon. Indeed, the heart of distinctive competence and competitive advantage may lie not in the possession of specific organizational resources or skills which can often be imitated or purchased by others, but in the power of the orchestrating theme and the degree of complementarity it engenders among [different organizational] elements: mission, means, market, and support systems. In fact, companies may be seen as systems of interdependency among these elements, all of which must be harmonized to compete effectively. . . .

The mission of the firm

All configurations must embody a mission: something to focus attention—to tell people what is and is not critical. 'Encircle Caterpillar' was the mission that effectively focused the new powerful Japanese competitor. . . .

Means: core competencies and activities

Means constitute the very basis of an organization's identity, both to its employees and its customers. Means—technologies, procedures, programs, and unusual talents or resources—shape the tasks and interactions of everyone on the organization. . . . And when they are distinctive, means create unique products and services that set a firm apart and instill client loyalty.

Market: matching capability and customer needs

Means matter only when the market values them, and especially when competitors cannot match them. A firm's central talents or resources must be amply rewarded by outside parties; otherwise a configuration will be useless and sterile. Indeed, most configurations are built with specific niches or customer needs in mind. . . .

Building comprehensive support

The seeds of configuration are unlikely to take root unless they are cultivated and nurtured by an appropriate support structure. Such support includes rituals and ceremonies, the power and reporting structure, plans and information systems, human resources policies, and administrative routines. . . .

Excellent wines have complexity and nuance, blending together different tastes into a harmonious balance. They avoid clashing cacophonies of flavors as well as the strident dominance of a single sharp note. So too must it be for the configured company.

While some of Miller's research reflects traditional contingency theory, as discussed in the last chapter, most fits squarely into the configuration school of strategic management. It deals with what Miller likes to call *archetypes*, that is, states of strategy, structure, situation, and process, also with *transitions* between archetypes, and it views strategic and structural change as *quantum* rather than incremental.[1]

Archetypes

Miller's doctoral dissertation (Miller 1976; see also 1979) used published studies of companies to induce ten archetypes of strategy formation, four of failure and six of success. For example, in the *Stagnant Bureaucracy* 'a previously placid and simple environment has lulled the firm to sleep. The top management is emotionally committed to the old strategies, and the information systems are too feeble to provide it with evidence of the need to change' (from Miller and Friesen, 1984: 94). Other failure archetypes include the *The Headless Giant* (a set of businesses with weak central authority) and *The Aftermath* (where a new team is trying to effect a turnaround with scarce resources and inadequate experience). Among the success archetypes are *The Dominant Firm* (well established, generally immune from serious challenge, with key patents, centralized structure, and traditional strategies), *The Entrepreneurial Conglomerate* (an extension of the rather bold and ingenious person who built and continues to run the organization), and *The Innovator* (generally a smaller firm with niche strategies, a simple structure, and an undiversified product line, with much product innovation).

A quantum view of change

In later work, Miller and Friesen (1980b, 1982a, also Miller and Friesen, 1984) described change in organizations as *quantum*, an idea that goes to the very heart of the configuration school. Quantum change means the changing of many elements concurrently, in contrast to 'piecemeal' change—one element at a time, say strategy first, then structure, then systems. Such change may be rapid—*revolutionary*, to use their word—although it can also unfold gradually.

---

1 See Miller (1982, 1983, 1986), and Miller and Friesen (1977, 1978, 1980a and b, 1982a, b, and c, and especially 1984) for a summary of this work.

This view suggests that organizations resolve the opposing forces for change and continuity by attending first to one and then to the other. While some strategic or other position may always be changing at the margins, it seems equally true that major shifts in strategic perspective occur only rarely. For example, in the Steinberg study cited earlier, only two important reorientations were found in 60 years, while at Air Canada, no major shift was found over the airline's first four decades, following its initial positioning. Otherwise, organizations spend most of their time pursuing given strategic perspectives (perfecting a particular retailing formula, for example). This suggests that success is achieved, not by changing strategies, but by exploiting those already in place.

While this goes on, however, the world changes, sometimes slowly, occasionally in a dramatic shift. Thus, at some point the configuration falls out of synchronization with its environment. Then what Miller and Friesen call a *strategic revolution* has to take place, during which many things change at once. In effect, the organization tries to leap to a new stability, to reestablish as quickly as possible an integrated posture among a new set of strategies, structures, and culture—in other words, a new configuration.

But what about all those emergent strategies discussed in the learning school, growing like weeds all over the organization? What the quantum theory suggests is that the really novel ones are generally held in check in some corner of the organization until a strategic revolution becomes necessary. Then, instead of having to develop new strategies from scratch or having to copy those of competitors, the organization can find its new deliberate direction within its own emerging patterns.

The quantum theory of change seems to apply particularly well to large, established, mass-production organizations—the machines. Because they are so reliant on standardized procedures, they tend to resist serious strategic change fiercely. So these are the organizations that tend to experience the long periods of stability punctured by the short bouts of transformation. Adhocracies, in contrast, seem to follow a more balanced pattern of change and stability, earlier labelled oscillating shifts (see Mintzberg and McHugh, 1985, on the film-making company). Organizations in the business of producing novel outputs apparently need to fly off in all directions for periods of time to sustain their creativity, then settle down for a time to find some order in the resulting chaos.

Change as revolutionary or incremental?

Miller's notion of change as revolutionary, here in the configuration school, is countered by Quinn's notion of change as incremental, as discussed in the learning school. This, in fact, has become one of the debates of strategic management, paralleled by the great debate in biology (mentioned in the last chapter) between Stephen Jay Gould's claims about punctuated equilibrium and Charles Darwin's concept of change as evolutionary. Of course, which it is depends on how closely you look, and from which vantage point. (Gould, for example, has described a million years as barely a moment in his perception of time.) Thus, change that appears incremental to one observer may seem revolutionary to another.

Researchers in strategic management who have come to these different conclusions have, in fact, focused on different types of organizations and different episodes in their development; they have also studied different phenomena (see Wischnevsky and Damanpour, 2006). For example, whereas Quinn interviewed individual executives about their thought processes (namely their intentions and perceptions), Miller tracked the recorded behaviours of organizations (namely their actions and outcomes). So the two might in fact have been describing two sequential stages in the same process: strategists may learn incrementally and then drive strategic change in revolutionary fashion. In other words, organizations may bide their time until they figure out where they have to go, and then, when a strategic window opens, they leap.

This indicates how important it is to appreciate each school of thought about the strategy process as well as to combine them into some kind of comprehensive framework. For example, the cognitive school seeks to tell us how strategists think, the entrepreneurial school how they leap, and the cultural school how they land. The configuration school suggests the sequence.

Excellence and the perils of excellence

In an early paper, Miller together with Mintzberg (1983) argued that the approach of configuration—what they called 'the perspective of synthesis'—offers a rich basis for describing organizations. Many factors can be taken into account in describing various forms. Moreover, configuration might well be a natural state of affairs: Darwinian forces could drive organizations to seek some kind of coherence among their different parts, which can be synergistic and so efficient. Indeed, such coherence could also make these organizations easier to understand and so to manage, for example, by enabling managers to apply only those techniques appropriate for a given configuration (matrix structures in adhocracies, quality circles in machine organizations, etc.).

In a later paper, Miller (1996) went further. He suggested that configuration may be 'the essence of strategy': since strategy is pattern, no coherence or consistency over time implies no overall strategy. Miller also elaborated upon the advantages of configuration, for example that it makes imitation more difficult and allows the organization to react more quickly.

❝ simplicity is dangerous because it can blind managers ❞

But it may have a serious downside as well, making things too simple for the manager: 'simplicity is dangerous because it can blind managers and tether their organizations to a confining set of skills, concerns, and environmental states.' Thus, while writers such as Peters and Waterman (1982) and Porter (1980) have suggested 'that outstanding performance often *demands* dedicated, even passionate, single-mindedness' (130–1), that may become the very problem. The very things that make an organization excellent can breed subsequent failure.

Miller has elaborated upon this point in a book called *The Icarus Paradox* (1990), about the perils of excellence, drawing on the legend of the Greek figure whose ability to fly drew him close to the sun, which melted his wings and sent him tumbling to his death. In a similar vein, Miller described four main 'trajectories' he uncovered in his research that lead from success to failure:

■ The *focusing* trajectory takes punctilious, quality-driven *Craftsmen*, organizations with masterful engineers and airtight operations, and turns them into rigidly controlled, detail-obsessed *Tinkerers*, firms whose insular, technocratic cultures alienate customers with perfect but irrelevant offerings.

■ The *venturing* trajectory converts growth-driven, entrepreneurial *Builders*, companies managed by imaginative leaders and creative planning and financial staffs, into impulsive, greedy *Imperialists*, who severely overtax their resources by expanding helter-skelter into businesses they know nothing about.

■ The *inventing* trajectory takes *Pioneers* with unexcelled R&D departments, flexible think-tank operations, and state-of-the-art products, and transforms them into utopian *Escapists*, run by cults of chaos-loving scientists who squander resources in the pursuit of hopelessly grandiose and futuristic inventions.

■ Finally, the *decoupling* trajectory transforms *Salesmen*, organizations with unparalleled marketing skills, prominent brand names, and broad markets, into aimless, bureaucratic *Drifters*, whose sales fetish obscures design issues, and who produce a stale and disjointed line of 'me-too' offerings. (4–5)

Notice how constructive configurations become destructive ones— yet remain configurations nonetheless. Indeed, configuration becomes the very problem. Lest anyone be inclined to doubt Miller's argument, the firms he names as having been 'trapped' by these trajectories at one time or another include IBM, Procter & Gamble, Texas Instruments, Chrysler, General Motors, Apple Computer, and Walt Disney Productions, among many others. Quite the blue ribbon list! Maybe we simply have to put up with cycles of success and failure, growth and decline (which is, of course, the 'natural' human condition.)

Probes into configuration

Research work on configuration as well as transformation has hardly been absent from the discussions of our other schools, for example on strategic groups in the positioning school, reframing in the cognitive school, turnaround in the entrepreneurial school, and stagnation in the cultural school (as the absence of transformation). In fact, we have infiltrated configurational thinking into our closing discussion of the context of each school (and so tipped our own hand), when we described the types of organizations and the kinds of periods that might be most applicable to it. Here we consider several research probes into configuration, and, in the next section, into transition.

Strategy and structure

In turning to other studies about configuration that have had wide circulation in strategic management, we must begin with Chandler's (1962) pathbreaking work on strategy and structure. As noted earlier, in studying the evolution of 'the large American industrial enterprise,' Chandler identified four 'chapters' in their history, which, in sequence, represent *stages* in their *life cycles*.

- First was the initial acquisition of resources of plant, equipment, and people, or else of the purchase and consolidation of smaller firms that had already done this (as in the origins of General Motors). Marketing and distribution channels were built and control was obtained over supplies (which came to be known as vertical integration).

- Second, the executives turned to the more efficient use of these resources, with the establishment of functional structures (production, sales, etc.) to coordinate the throughput.

- Third, there followed another period of growth, as limits were met in the initial markets: the firms diversified into new markets or new lines of business related to the existing ones.

- Fourth, that required a second shift in structure too. This came to be known as the divisionalized form, pioneered by Dupont, so that each business could be managed by a particular unit, reporting for overall financial control to a central headquarters.

Chandler completed his study long ago. Were he to update it today, he might have been inclined to add a stage of consolidation of the businesses and outsourcing of certain activities, reversing the earlier moves toward diversification and vertical integration. Large firms now typically concentrate on key businesses and core competences, while shedding many of their activities in favour of an extended network of associates. This, together with Chandler's four stages, suggests oscillating cycles of control and release.

Chandler's work was extended particularly by a string of doctoral theses at the Harvard Business School. These were not, however, done as similar deep probes into specific companies, but rather as larger sample surveys of many firms, to understand better the relationships between the strategies of diversification and the structures of divisionalization.

Probably best known is the study by Richard Rumelt (published as a book in 1974), who found that although some 70 percent of the firms in the *Fortune* 500 were in a *single* or a *dominant* business in 1949, by 1969 over half of these firms had diversified, many into categories he called *related* or *unrelated* (namely conglomerate) businesses (or else had been acquired and so had their places usually taken by other, more diversified firms). In parallel with this, much as Chandler had found, these firms matched their new strategies with new structures, of product-based diversification (from 20 percent of the firms in 1949 to 75 percent in 1969).

While there has been some backtracking since, a broader conclusion that Rumelt drew may now hold even more strongly: besides strategy, 'structure also follows fashion' (1974: 149); reinforced more generally by studies of management fashion more generally by Abrahamson and Fairchild (1999), and Carson *et al.* (2000).

Prospectors and defenders

A very different study of configuration, but no less popular among academics as well as some practitioners, has been that of Miles and Snow (1978; also Miles *et al.*, 1978). Based on a study of firms in four industries (textbook publishing, electronics, food processing, and health care), they classified corporate behaviours into four broad categories, which they labelled *defenders*, *prospectors*, *analyzers*, and *reactors*, each with 'its own unique strategy for relating to its chosen market(s),' as well as its related 'particular configuration of technology, structure, and process' (Miles *et al.*, 1978: 550).

- The *defender* is concerned with stability, namely how to 'seal off a portion of the market in order to create a stable domain . . . a limited set of products [is] directed into a narrow segment of the total market' (550). There, to keep out competitors, the defender prices competitively or concentrates on quality. Technological efficiency is important, as is strict control of the organization.

- The *prospector*, in contrast, actively searches out innovative new product and market opportunities (sometimes even at the expense of profitability). Key here is to maintain flexibility, in both technology and administrative arrangements.

- The *analyzer* sits between the defenders and the prospectors, seeking to 'minimize risk while maximizing the opportunity for profit,' so that the approach is best described as 'balanced' (553, 555).

- The *reactor*, unlike the other three, reacts to its environment. This is a failure, 'inconsistent and unstable.' In other words, here we have a '"residual" strategy, arising when one of the other three strategies is inappropriately pursued' (557).

Hence, the Miles and Snow typology reduces to two basic forms (which seem to correspond to the machine and adhocracy organizations), with the third a hybrid, form and the fourth really a collection of inappropriate responses.

Rational, bureaucratic, and political actors

In Chapter 8, we mentioned Graham Allison's (1971) celebrated study of the behaviour of the Soviet and American decision makers during the Cuban missile crisis. This is another excellent example of configurational work, linking dimensions of strategy (or 'policy' in government), structure, and managerial style. Allison claimed that people 'think about problems of foreign and military policy in terms of largely implicit conceptual models that have significant consequences for the content of their thought.' In other words, they have configurations of the mind, whether or not these exist as distinct realities. Allison outlined three in particular.

The *Rational Actor Model* sees government actions 'as the more or less purposive acts of unified national governments.' Goals are clear, choices are made, actions follow. 'Predictions about what a nation will do or would have done are generated by calculating the rational thing to do in a certain situation, given specified objectives.'

Allison called this model 'useful' but in need of being 'supplemented, if not supplanted,' by the two others. *The Organizational Process Model* puts attention on the internal systemic process of government—'the strengths, standard operating procedures, and repertoires' of the various parts of the organization as a bureaucratic system. The key is to understand the patterns of behaviours among the relevant units—as gears and levers in decision making.

The *Governmental Politics Model* concentrates on the politics of government: 'what happens is characterized as a *resultant* of various bargaining games among players in the national government.' The focus is on the 'perceptions, motivations, power, and maneuvers of the players.' The events are explained by understanding 'who did what to whom,' based on the relative power and skills of the different players (3–7).

The behaviour of an organization may therefore be the result not only of a rational design process, but also of social and political processes that permeate the organization. This raises the question of how decision makers think about different configurations. In an intriguing study, Dyck (1997) points out that while decision makers may carry out their day-to-day operations in a given configuration, they are aware and even interested in alternative configurations. Thus, whether configurations persist or are discarded depends on how decision makers evaluate these existing configurations relative to competing ones. Dyck tracks a small religious college across 40 years; tracing debates and discussions on configurations that were established and also others that were considered and rejected, finding 'that members experience an ongoing tension between a rational status quo and rational alternatives (1997: 817).

> ❝ members experience an ongoing tension between a rational status quo and rational alternatives ❞

Probes into periods of transition

Another body of configuration research probes into the periods of major change in organizations. A good example of this is Andrew Pettigrew's (1985, 1987) study of transformation at ICI, the chemical company in the United Kingdom. Pettigrew viewed this change, not as *an* episode, but as a *series* of episodes.

Pettigrew drew the following conclusions about the change process at ICI from 1969 to 1986:

1 Change did not occur as a continuous incremental process.

2 The pattern of change was for radical eras of change to occur at periodic intervals. Of the three periods of high levels of change activity, two, the ones between 1960 and 1964 and 1980 to 1986, could be sensibly labeled as revolutionary in that they featured substantial ideological, structural, and business strategy change. . . . The periods between these packages of changes were occasions for implementing and stabilizing changes, and . . . eras of organizational learning when ideological justification was prepared for the revolutionary break. . . .

3 Each of these periods of high levels of change activity was associated with world economic recessions, with their associated effects on . . . ICI's relative business performance. In other words, ICI made substantial changes only when it was in severe economic difficulties. However, a critical facet of these change periods was . . . also the active strategies by managers to construct a climate for change around the performance difficulties. . . .

4 The revolutionary periods of change were also connected with changes in leadership and power in ICI. . . .

5 Finally, within the eras of revolutionary change there was little evidence to support Chandler's . . . dictum that structure follows strategy. Rather the pattern of change in ICI was a complex mixture of adjustment in core beliefs of the top decision-makers, followed by changes in structure, systems, and rewards, with the business strategy changes emerging and being implemented rather more slowly after [these] changes . . . had been legitimated and implemented. (1987: 664–5)

Notice how Pettigrew's conclusions support Miller's notion of quantum change. Notice too how he has woven the notions of a number of the strategy schools around distinct periods in the life of this organization.

Another probe of a similar nature was carried out by Gerry Johnson (1987) into a British clothing retailer. His conclusions tended to focus on the interpretative view of strategy that we discussed in Chapter 9, but woven together with a rationalistic and adaptive (or incremental) view. Johnson concluded that the managers he studied 'saw themselves as logical incrementalists, and believed that this was a sensible way to manage.' However, they were driven by a set of core beliefs that determined how they interpreted and acted upon the complexity they faced. This set up barriers to change against which challenges had to be seen 'as political and cultural actions rather than a matter of intellectual debate.' But as 'strategic drift' occurred, and performance declined, incremental adjustments had to be replaced by fundamental change: 'there is a need to "unfreeze" the paradigm . . . [to] break up . . . political alliances and [challenge and change] rituals and routines,' with outsiders perhaps playing a key role in introducing new perspectives and ideas.

It is likely that the change process that occurs will be, relatively speaking, ill defined and general. Members of the organization will know that change is occurring but may not be that clear about where it is leading or what it signifies. However, it may be that this process of change is a necessary precursor to the introduction of specific strategies.

This may 'require the sorts of analytical, planning approaches more usually identified with rationalistic, scientific management.' But these 'cannot be effective unless the change processes to break down the [old beliefs] are already in process' (270–4).

Finally, in a fascinating book published recently by David Hurst (1995), based on his own experiences as an executive, organizational change is described through an 'ecocycle' model of crisis and renewal. As shown in Figure 11.2, the model consists of two loops that intersect to form the symbol of infinity. The ecocycle of the forest runs through phases of growth and exploitation: there is 'the rapid colonization of any available space' (98), then conservation, namely stable relationship among established organisms, followed by creative destruction, a role played by natural forest fires, which leads to renewal, and so on.

Hurst argued that human organizations cycle around similar phases, between emergent and constrained actions. Entrepreneurial action leads to conservation, or settling down to established procedure, much as Chandler described, which eventually provokes crisis and confusion, which stimulates creative response, and so a new cycle begins. The 'front' half, or 'performance loop' of the model, shown as a solid line, is the 'conventional life cycle.' This, according to Hurst, is where 'strategic management' is found. The back half, or 'learning loop,' shown dotted, represents 'a less familiar, renewal cycle of 'death' and 'reconception.' This is the realm of 'charismatic leadership' (104).

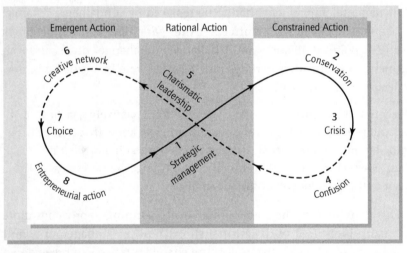

figure 11.2 The organizational ecocycle   from Hurst (1995: 103).

In sharp contrast to the linear life cycle, as that of Chandler, this model describes an unending looping between crisis and renewal, in which the approaches of many of our other schools can be seen in sequence. Sometimes the connections between the stages are smooth and almost linear (in other words, imperceptible or 'seamless,' more in the spirit of splitting), while at other times, they tend to be rapid and nonlinear (namely lumpy).

Transforming organizations

There is an enormous literature and consulting practice aimed at helping managers deal with major change in their organizations—turnaround, revitalization, downsizing, and the like. To do this justice here would be to add a Volume II, a thought we would rather not entertain just now (nor you, we suspect). Instead, we seek to provide some overall structure for this work as well as some illustrations of it.

One word of caution before we begin. All of this is about 'managed change.' But a case can well be made—indeed is done so articulately in Box 11.3—that this term is an oxymoron, that change should not be 'managed,' at least when this word is used to mean forced, made to happen. Managers often claim that people in their organizations resist changing. True enough. But maybe that is because these people have for so long been *over*managed. The cure might actually prove to be just more of the cause. If so, then perhaps the best way to 'manage' change is to allow for it to happen—to set up the conditions whereby people will follow their natural instincts to experiment and transform their behaviors. To quote from this box, 'You deal with change by improving you. And then your time must come.'

❝ you deal with change by improving you. And then your time must come ❞

---

box 11.3

'Change management' is an oxymoron

(adapted by Jim Clemmer from his book, *Pathways to Performance*, 1995)

A dubious consulting industry and 'profession' has developed, claiming to provide 'change management' services. Those two words make about as much sense together as 'holy war' [and] 'nonworking mother.' . . . 'Change management' comes from the same dangerously seductive reasoning as strategic planning. They're both based on the shaky assumption that there's an orderly thinking and implementation process which can objectively plot a course of action, like Jean Luc Picard on the starship *Enterprise*, and then 'make it so.' But if that ever was possible, it certainly isn't in today's world of high velocity change.

> ### ► Successful change flows from learning, growth, and development
>
> Change can't be managed. Change can be ignored, resisted, responded to, capitalized upon, and created. But it can't be managed and made to march to some orderly step-by-step process. . . . Whether we become change victims or victors depends on our readiness for change. . . . [As Abraham Lincoln] once said, 'I will prepare myself and my time must come.' That's how change is managed.
>
> . . . We can't quickly win back customers who've quietly slipped away because of neglect and poor service. We can't suddenly turn our organization into an innovative powerhouse in six months because the market shifted. We can't radically and quickly re-engineer years of sloppy habits and convoluted processes when revolutionary new technology appears. When cost pressures build, we can't dramatically flatten our organizations and suddenly empower everyone who has had years of traditional command and control conditioning. These are long-term culture, system, habit, and skill changes. They need to be improved before they're needed. In the words of an ancient Chinese proverb, 'dig a well before you are thirsty.'
>
> . . . . To effectively deal with change you don't focus on change as some kind of manageable force. You deal with change by improving you. And then your time must come. . . .
>
>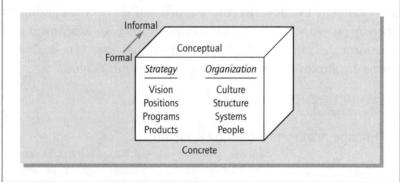

Changing what?

The first question is: *what* can be changed in an organization? One way to think of this is in terms of the change cube, discussed in the accompanying box. It indicates what comprehensive change in an organization really means: about strategy and structure, ranging from the conceptual to the concrete and from highly formal behaviours to rather informal ones.

---

box 11.4

The change cube

by Henry Mintzberg

Change in organizations is greatly spoken about, yet all too often done in bits and pieces. We hear about turnaround, revitalization, cultural change, total quality management, venturing, new product development, and so on. Somehow all of this has to be put into perspective. The change cube is designed to do that.

The face of the cube shows two major dimensions of change. On the left side, change can be about *strategy*, the direction an organization is headed, and on the right, about *organization*, the state it is in. Both have to be considered when changing an organization.

Looking up and down the cube, both strategy and organization can range from the highly *conceptual*, or abstract, to the rather concrete, or tangible. On the strategy dimension, vision (or strategic perspective) is the most conceptual (rethinking, reconceiving), as is culture on the organization dimension (reenergizing, revitalizing). And going down the cube toward the more concrete, you can change, on the two sides, strategic positions (repositioning, reconfiguring) and organization structure (reorganizing, reducing), then programs and systems (reprogramming, reworking, reengineering), finally products and people (redesigning, retraining, replacing), which can also be thought of as changing actions on one side and actors on the other. Put differently, the broadest but most abstract things you can change in an organization are vision and culture, the most specific, actual products and real people (either by replacing the people who are there or by changing their behavior).

An organization can easily change a single product or an individual. But changing, say, a vision or a structure without changing anything else is silly, just an empty gesture. In other words, wherever you intervene on this cube, you have to change everything below. For example, it makes no sense to change structure without changing systems and people, or to change vision without rethinking strategic positions as well as redesigning programs and products.

Finally, all of this can range from the overt and formal, shown on the front face of the cube, to the rather more implicit and informal, shown on the back face. For example, a strategic position can be more deliberate (formal) or more emergent (informal), while people can be changed formally through education or informally through coaching and mentoring.

The point of this description is that serious change in organizations includes the entire cube: strategy and organization, from the most conceptual to the most concrete, informally as well as formally.

© Henry Minzberg, all rights reserved

Mapping processes of change

Now we can consider the methods of change. Needed here is some kind of *map*, to sort out and place into perspective the confusing array of approaches that have been developed over the years to change organizations. Figure 11.3 presents such a map, in which the methods of change are plotted on two dimensions. Along the top is a scale of the breadth of change, which runs from micro to macro. Micro change is focused within the organization: it might involve, for example, job redesign in a factory or the development of a new product. Macro change is aimed at the entire organization, for example, repositioning its place in the market or shifting all of its physical facilities.[2]

David Hurst has expressed this in another way: 'The *helmsman* manages change all the time [micro]. But the *navigator* changes course quite infrequently and then only as circumstances dictate. Changes in destination can be made by the *captain* even less frequently, for they require a total value change in the organization. And *discoverers* may find a new world only once in a lifetime [most macro]' (unpublished material).

We are obviously concerned in this book with the more macro side of this scale. But we map the whole range here for two reasons. One is simply to provide a guide to the different means of change, to put them all into context. The other is that micro changes can have macro consequences. That is the very meaning of emergent strategy: that single actions can lead to significant patterns of action. A new product might cause the organization to reposition its markets.

On the horizontal scale of Figure 11.3, we suggest that there are three basic approaches to the process of change: planned change, driven change, and evolved change. *Planned* change is programmatic: there exists a system or set of procedures to be followed.

---

2 Micro change tends to focus on the concrete level of the change cube, but it need not. One can change the vision of work design in a factory. Likewise macro change, while it often starts at the conceptual level, need not. The organisation can shift all its physical facilities without any overarching vision, although that would hardly seem to be logical (which does not mean it never happens!).

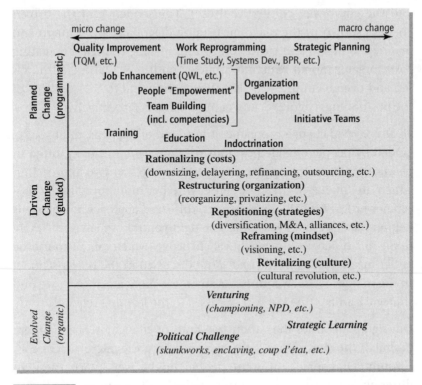

figure 11.3 **Map of change methods** © Henry Mintzberg August 1997.

These range from programmes of quality improvement and training (micro) to ones of organizational development and strategic planning (more macro). Consider, for example, this classic statement of organization development:

Organizational development is an effort (1) *planned*, (2) *organization-wide*, and (3) *managed* from the *top*, to (4) increase organization *effectiveness* and *health* through (5) *planned interventions* in the organization's 'processes' using *behavioral science* knowledge. (Beckhard, 1969: 9; italics in original)

Driven change is guided: a single individual or small group, usually in an influential position of authority, oversees the change and ensures that it happens. Here we find all the currently popular (mostly) 're' words, ranging from rationalization through restructuring to revitalizing.[3] Doz and Thanheiser (1996) have referred to various among these as changing the strategic context, the organizational context, and the emotional context (culture). The sequence of the driven changes shown in the diagram, reading diagonally from micro and planned to macro and closer to evolved, include changing operating costs, organizational structure, strategic positions, managerial mindset, and overall culture. (The last three correspond to the concerns of the positioning, cognitive, and cultural schools respectively.)

Finally, *evolved* change is organic: it just kind of happens, or at least is guided by people outside positions of significant authority, often in obscure places in the organization. Unlike the first two approaches, which are 'managed' in some sense, whether more formally by procedures or less formally by managers, this third approach to change is neither managed nor even under the tight control of managers.[4] More to the micro side, we show political challenge (which can, of course, be rather macro too, as in the *coup d'état* discussed in the power school). In the middle, we see venturing. And on the more macro side, we find strategic learning (the last two discussed in the learning school).

Our figure identifies the various methods of change by placing them in one of the above three categories and along the micro–macro continuum. Of course, different people might well place these in different positions (for example, proponents of planned change might claim that the real intention is to evoke organic response). We are prepared to engage in no great debate over this—the figure represents only our opinion. Like any map, which necessarily simplifies, it is intended to offer the viewer some kind of comprehensive overview of an otherwise confusing terrain.

---

3 To the 're' words in this figure could be added, as synonymous or variations, renewing, rethinking, revisioning, reconfiguring, retrenching, reforming, rearranging and reducing.

4 Hence, planned through driven to evolved change corresponds to the scale of formal to informal on the change cube. It should be noted, however, that all can range from the conceptual to the concrete. Strategic planning (as we pointed out in Chapter 3) can be rather conceptual, although it is meant for concrete results, while strategic learning or political challenge can range from one to the other.

Programmes of comprehensive change

A manager can simply pick something and try to change it: enhance the training of the sales force, for example, or reorganize the research laboratory. Most change is of this *piecemeal* type; it goes on all the time, here and there. Indeed Tom Peters has long been a fan of such change, which he has called 'chunking.' Don't get bogged down, just grab something and change it.

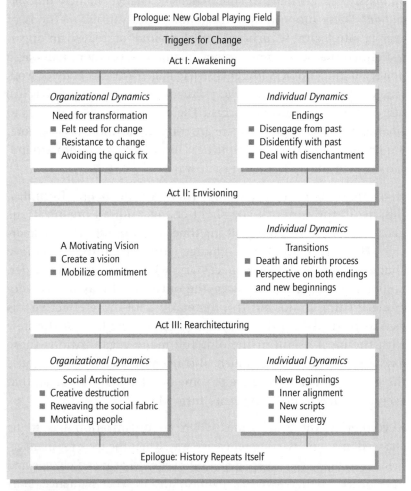

figure 11.4 Transformational leadership: a three-act drama

Source: From *CONTROL YOUR DESTINY OR SOMEONE ELSE WILL* by Noel M. Tichy, Stratford Sherman, copyright © 1993 by Noel M. Tichy and Stratford Sherman. Used by permission of Doubleday, a division of Random House, Inc.

The change cube suggests, however, that this probably works better at the more concrete (and micro) level than the conceptual (and macro) end. You can retrain a group of workers or reorganize one department, perhaps, but you cannot reposition strategy or change culture without making a lot of other associated changes. Indeed, 'changing culture' alone is just a lot of empty words: as noted earlier, culture is not changed at all when nothing else changes.

So there has arisen a great deal of literature and consulting practice on massive programmes of comprehensive change, namely *transformation*. These propose how to combine the various methods of change into logical sequences to 'turn around' or 'renew' an organization. (Turnaround implies quick, dramatic revolution; renewal, a slower building up of comprehensive change.) But this body of work can be confusing: just about every writer and consulting firm has his, her, or its own formula for success. There is no consensus at all as to what works best, although there are certainly periodic fads—galore. But because of fads, for example bear in mind that to 'turn around' can mean to end up facing the same way!)

Here, then, as everywhere else, there are no magic formulas. Despite all the current hype about change, not all organizations need to change everything all the time. The word for that is 'anarchy.' The trick is to balance change with continuity: to achieve change when and where necessary while maintaining order. Embracing the new while sweeping out the old may be the very modern thing to do, but it is generally a lot more effective—as well as difficult—to find ways to integrate the best of the new with the most useful of the old. Too many organizations these days are subjected to too much ill-conceived change. Just because there is a new chief executive or some new fad does not mean that everything has to be thrown into turmoil.

Nevertheless, there are times when an organization has to be changed in a serious, comprehensive way. Then the trick for management is to figure out where it can intervene, what it can change and have others change—when, how fast, and in what sequence. Start small and build up, or do something dramatic? Begin by replacing people, reconceiving vision, or redoing the chart? After that, concentrate on strategy, structure, culture, or shareholder value? Change everything at once, or 'chunk' along?

On the other hand, maybe management should just create the conditions for change and then let it happen, in the belief that the best change begins on the ground, in the corner of some factory or a visit to some customers, and then flows from there, even up to the 'top.'

> " it is the state you are no longer in that seems impossible "

If all this may seem confusing, then consider this comment of the French philosopher Alain: 'All change seems impossible. But once accomplished, it is the state you are no longer in that seems impossible.' With this in mind, let us sample some of the frameworks for comprehensive change.

In 1995, three McKinsey consultants, Dickhout, Denham, and Blackwell, published an interesting article on change, outlining six different 'strategies' used by the 25 companies studied:

- **Evolutionary/institution building**: this involved a gradual reshaping of the 'company's values, top-level structures and performance measures so that line managers could drive the change.'
- **Jolt and refocus**: to 'shake up a gridlocked power structure,' leaders 'in one fell swoop . . . delayered top management, defined new business units, and redesigned management processes.'
- **Follow the leader**: for immediate results, leaders 'initiated major changes from the top,' for example, by selling off weak businesses, 'while removing only the most critical organizational bottlenecks.'
- **Multifront focus**: in this case, 'change is driven by task teams whose targets are more wide ranging'—cost reduction, sales stimulation, etc.
- **Systematic redesign**: again task teams drive the process to boost performance, but 'core process redesign and other organizational changes tend to be planned in parallel.'
- **Unit-level mobilizing**: here the 'change leaders empower task teams to tap into the pent-up ideas of middle managers and front-line employees.' (102–4)

These describe various initial or focal activities. But a key question is how different activities should be sequenced over time to effect a major transformation. Let us consider first top-down change and then bottom-up.

Top-down change?

Well known has been the approach at General Electric under the leadership of Jack Welch between 1981 and 2001, which David Ulrich, who worked with Welch, in an article with Richard Beatty (1991) have described as a five-step process (which may occur simultaneously as well as in sequence), including both the 'hardware' of the organization (strategy, structure, systems) and its 'software' (employee behaviour and mindset). The description begins with *restructuring*, which is meant downsizing and delayering, followed by *bureaucracy bashing*, to 'get rid of unnecessary reports, approvals, meetings, measures,' and the like. Then there is a stage of *employee empowerment*, which gives rise to one of *continuous improvement*, before, as 'an outgrowth of the other four,' the culture is fundamentally changed (1991: 22, 24–9). This is illustrated in Figure 11.5.

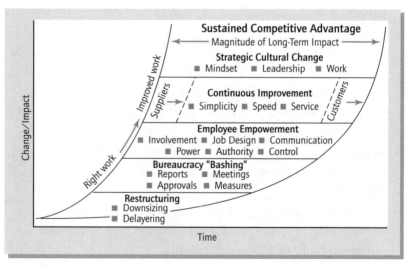

figure 11.5 A process for reengineering mature organizations

Source: Beatty and Ulrich (1991: 25).

Baden-Fuller and Stopford's 'crescendo model of rejuvenation' is similar:

1 Galvanize: create a top team dedicated to renewal.

2 Simplify: cut unnecessary and confusing complexity.

3 Build: develop new capabilities.

4 Leverage: maintain momentum and stretch the advantages. (1992)

Doz and Thanheiser (1996) noted in a survey of forty companies that almost all included in their transformational efforts portfolio restructuring, downsizing and outsourcing, benchmarking, and some sort of process improvement and quality management efforts. They found 'periods of intense activity where high energy . . . [was] typically triggered by various "turning points" [or "crucible"] events such as retreats, workshops, or other employee-manager gatherings' (7). In the 'more effective, longer term' transformations, they describe the following pattern:

■ 'from internal to external focus': first improve efficiency, then create new opportunities.

■ 'from top-down to delegated action': 'the inertia breaking process was usually strongly driven from the top' even though 'the transformation was sometimes piloted in a subunit . . . before being implemented in the whole company'; subsequent activities were often 'at the initiative of subunits.'

■ 'from emotion and intellect to organization': 'in nearly all the cases . . . the initial transformation cycle was driven by a new strategic understanding that was brought into focus through an emotional process (part and parcel of "crucible" events), then later reflected in more extensive, subtle, and multifaced changes in organizational context.' (10–11)

In effect, the chief executive took some quick initial strategic actions, such as divesting some business or replacing key executives, but 'winning the hearts' of others was key to the next step. These 'changes in the emotional context permitted further, more subtle changes in strategic context,' as well as in the organizational context, so that the chief executive could 'let go' to allow for more 'decentralized emergent initiatives.'

In summary, over time the nature of the transformation process kept alternating from cycle to cycle between *bursts* of energy concentration and *periods* of energy diffusion, to smaller, less visible pulsations. Successful transformation processes shifted from corporate upheavals to ongoing learning and renewal. (11)

Bottom-up change?

The above has been the dominant view from strategic management: top-down (at least initially), leader-driven, and strategic. But, stemming from earlier work in 'organizational development,' others have described transformation as far more of a bottom-up process, in which small changes taken within pockets of the organization drive the overall change process (see Nutt *et al.* 2000). Change is an exploratory journey rather than a predetermined trajectory, more of a learning process than a planned or driven one. Yet if it works, it can end up being significantly strategic.

This is the spirit of a 1990 article by Beer *et al.* in the *Harvard Business Review*, entitled 'Why Change Programs Don't Produce Change.' After discussing 'the fallacy of programmatic change,' they discuss the 'more successful transformations' they studied that 'usually started at the periphery of the corporation in a few plants and divisions far from corporate headquarters' and were 'led by the general managers of those units, not by the CEO or corporate staff people' (159). The best chief executives created 'a market for change,' but let others decide how to initiate changes and then used the most successfully revitalized units as models for the rest of the company. The accompanying box presents their 'Six Steps to Effective Change' for the managers of such units.

Opposite this box we juxtapose another, from an article that appeared a few years later, also in the *Harvard Business Review*, with a remarkably similar title, 'Leading Change: Why Transformation Efforts Fail.' This was written by John Kotter, a colleague of Beer, in the same department at the Harvard Business School. But Kotter's 'Eight Steps to Transforming Your Corporation' are more top-down. 'Change, by definition,' Kotter wrote, 'requires creating a new system, which in turn always demands leadership. [The start of] a renewal process typically goes nowhere until enough real leaders are promoted or hired into senior-level jobs' (1995: 60).

So should the change process be top-down or bottom-up? If you are to believe the experts, then you will have to flip a coin. Or else try to understand what is broken in your own organization before you decide how to fix it. There is no formula for transforming any organization, and that includes the very notion that the organization needs transforming in the first place.

In fact, the McKinsey consultants, Dickhout and colleagues, whose set of change strategies were presented at the outset of this discussion, are among the few in this literature who have made the welcome claim that which approach your use depends on your organization's goals, needs, and capabilities. In their study, 'each transformation was a unique response to a specific set of problems and opportunities. . . . The leader appeared to have "cracked a code" embedded within the organization . . . [so that] energy was released and channeled to improve performance' (20). Wise words to end discussion of a literature and a practice that has not always been terribly wise.

The popular literature on transformation is really about planned and driven change—in other words, about change that is 'managed,' whether more formally through procedures or less formally by a leader (even if that leader acts well within the organization, as in the Beer *et al.* approach). This may provoke organic change in the organization—that is the object of a number of these approaches—but the approaches themselves are hardly organic. Their proponents may counter that change has to be managed in organizations; we, in turn, wonder if much of this is not about managers' egos and consultants' earnings.

Imagine a meeting in which the chief executive has called everyone together: 'Hey gang, I've been thinking about all this change stuff. I'm not the hero you think I am. If this is going to happen, *you* are going to do it. I am here to help, to facilitate, even to inspire. But making this place great is *your* responsibility.' Would that earn this person a place on the cover of *Fortune* magazine? Or how about this from your favourite consulting boutique: 'It's really very rough out there. But you actually have a bunch of mature intelligent people in your organization. They would just love to seize the initiative, if only you gave them half a chance. Try it. You may be surprised. That will be $55 please.'

And then, what about the corporation that is beyond hope, or at least would cost a lot more to fix than to let die a natural death? Do we need all these geriatric consulting practices, all those people manning the corporate life-support systems?

---

box 11.5

More bottom-up change

'Six Steps to Effective Change' for managers at the business unit or plant level

(from Beer, Eisenstat, and Spector, 1990: 161–164)

1 **Mobilize commitment to change through joint diagnosis of business problems**. . . . By helping people develop a shared diagnosis of what is wrong in an organization and what can and must be improved, a general manager [of a unit] mobilizes the initial commitment that is necessary to begin the change process. . . .

2 **Develop a shared vision of how to organize and manage for competitiveness**. Once a core group of people is committed to a particular analysis of the problem, the general manager can lead employees toward a task-aligned vision of the organization that defines new roles and responsibilities. . . .

3 **Foster consensus for the new vision, competence to enact it, and cohesion to move it along**. . . .

4 **Spread revitalization to all departments without pushing it from the top**. . . . The temptation to force newfound insights on the rest of the organization can be great, particularly when rapid change is needed, but it would be the same mistake that senior managers make when they try to push programmatic change throughout a company. It short-circuits the change process. It's better to let each department 'reinvent the wheel'—that is, to find its own way to the new organization. . . .

5 **Institutionalize revitalization through formal policies, systems, and structures**. . . . The new approach has to become entrenched. . . .

6 **Monitor and adjust strategies in response to problems in the revitalization process**. The purpose of change is to create . . . a learning organization capable of adapting to a changing competitive environment. . . . Some might say that this is the general manager's responsibility. But monitoring the change process needs to be shared. . . .

---

box 11.6

More top-down transformation

'Eight Steps to Transforming Your Corporation' for its overall managers

(from Kotter, 1995: 61)

1 **Establishing a sense of urgency**: examining market and competitive realities; identifying and discussing crises, potential crises, or major opportunities.
2 **Forming a powerful guiding coalition**: assembling a group with enough power to lead the change effort; encouraging the group to work together as a team.
3 **Creating a vision**: creating a vision to help direct the change effort; developing strategies for achieving that vision.
4 **Communicating the vision**: using every vehicle possible to communicate the new vision and strategies; teaching new behaviors by the example of the guiding coalition.
5 **Empowering others to act on the vision**: getting rid of obstacles to change; changing systems or structures that seriously undermine the vision; encouraging risk taking and nontraditional ideas, activities, and actions.
6 **Planning for and creating short-term wins**: planning for visible performance improvements; creating those improvements; recognizing and rewarding employees involved in the improvements.
7 **Consolidating improvements and producing still more changes**: using increased credibility to change systems, structures, and policies that don't fit the vision; hiring, promoting, and developing employees who can implement the vision; reinvigorating the process with new projects, themes, and change agents.
8 **Institutionalizing new approaches**: articulating the connections between the new behaviors and corporation success; developing the means to ensure leadership development and succession.

Critique, context, and contribution of the configuration school

McGillomania

The most pointed criticism of the configuration school has been mounted by Lex Donaldson (1996), who once described it as 'McGillomania.' Donaldson argues that configurations represent a flawed approach to theorizing, precisely because they are so easy to understand and teach:

Few real organizations are simple structures or machine bureaucracies: almost all organizations lie somewhere in the middle. Students, be they MBA or executives, mostly come from organizations which have intermediary levels of size, standardization, organicness and so on. Managers are involved in managing change, usually of degree: some growth in size, a little more innovation, maturing of this product line but not that product line and so on. They need a framework on to which they can map their experience and which yields highly differentiated and gradated prescriptive advice. In configurations they find stark, but simplistic caricature: simple structures, machine bureaucracy, innovating adhocracies. These models provide scant help. (127)

> " organizations come in many shades of gray and not just black and white "

Organizations come in 'many shades of gray and not just black and white' (114), he added. These 'ideal types' therefore provide a vocabulary, but this vocabulary is relatively crude when it comes to describing the diversity of the organizational world. 'Each configuration has problems' (117). For example, multidivisional firms may have units with different structures which pursue different strategies.

Donaldson reserved the brunt of his criticism for the other major plank of the configuration school: quantum change. It is empirically and conceptually erroneous, he argued, to maintain that firms are either static or changing rapidly. 'Most organizations, most of the time, are changing incrementally' (122). Furthermore, to say that organizations at intermediate points between different configurations are in disequilibrium—With strategies that are nonviable until they reach a configuration which is more stable—begs the question of how they manage to make this transition at all.

Donaldson's criticism is based on the question of accuracy, as if theories are true or not. But all theories are false: they are just words or pictures on pieces of paper. Reality is always more complex. (The world may not be flat, for example, but neither is it round. It bulges at the equator, and has all kinds of bumps, called mountains.) So usefulness becomes a key criterion, especially for practising managers. (The flat earth theory is particularly useful for building airport runways in Holland.)

This does not negate Donaldson's criticisms—the world seen as configurations is flawed too—but it does raise at least equally important questions about his preferred alternative, which is in the spirit of contingency theory discussed in Chapter 10. In other words, managers have to choose from among flawed theories.

And as we tried to show in this chapter, configuration can often be very helpful, even as a vocabulary by which to understand how different forms of organizations combine. Moreover, theories, as tools, evolve. It took a long time for biological taxonomists to evolve today's highly complex and powerful classification. They would have gotten nowhere if they had thrown the entire enterprise overboard because it was not sufficient to encompass all the variety of species they could observe.

In the mid-1990s, a group of doctoral students led by Professor Craig Russell embarked on a class project: evaluating all empirical studies of the relationship between organizational configurations and performance (Ketchen *et al*, 1997). The group identified 40 studies that attempted to test this relationship. They then estimated the strength of the configuration-performance relationship found in these studies. Their findings suggests that the strength of the relationship increased when researchers adopted broad definitions of configurations, focused on single industries, and looked at the evolution of configurations over time.

As to whether the pace of change should be slow or fast, the jury is out on this one, as it likely always will be, since there is plenty of evidence (cited in various of our chapters) for both incremental and quantum—and plenty of usefulness for both as well. Of course, one is more compatible with contingency theory, the other with configuration theory, so we had better be careful whom we believe in this debate.

Lumping

Because pattern is in the eye of the beholder, all lumping must be considered somewhat arbitrary. To describe by configuration is to distort in order to explain. But that is true of every concept, every theory, indeed every word (which is just a category). All simplify in one way or another. So the issue really amounts to how serious is this form of distortion compared with some other. Like it or not, we need categories to help us understand our complex world. (Imagine a world without words.) And so, we need lumping, even though we must be aware of its limitations.

To take one visible example, we all find useful the categorization of the continents. Australia is one such continent: it sits geographically distinct, even the character of its people can be distinguished (with regard to language and accent, for example). But Greenland fits these criteria too, maybe even more so, although this 'island' is not quite so large. So why is it excluded? Africa is included: it is huge, although rather more diverse in language, etc. But why is Europe considered a continent? It has a huge diversity of languages and no evident boundary to the east. Is Europe a continent simply because it was Europeans who designated the continents?

We conclude that categories, including configurations, are figments of our imagination (or lack of it) at least as much as they are identifiable things.

The edges

The configurational approach should not, therefore, allow us to ignore the nuances of our messy world. We need fine-grained work that exposes the complex interrelationships among things. As Raphael (1976) has pointed out, the richest forms of life exist on the edges, between sea and land, forest and field, and so on. That is where much of the exciting innovation takes place in the world of organizations too, outside the pat categories, beyond the neat configurations. In one sense, then, while we cannot specify a context for this school—it is, after all, the school of contexts—we can draw attention to the contexts it misses: nuanced ones, not (or not yet) categorized, perhaps not even categorizable.

> **selecting the right degree of configuration is a complex balancing act**

Likewise, at the same time that organizations benefit from configuration, they can also suffer from it. This came out clearly in Miller's work on the Icarus Paradox: the very consistency that promotes success can lead to failure. 'Selecting the right degree of configuration is a complex balancing act. Managers must avoid the blandness or chaos of too little configuration while skirting the obsessionality of too much. Excellent wines have complexity and nuance, blending together different tastes into a harmonious balance' (Miller, 1996: 511).

Overall, the contribution of the configuration school has been evident in strategic management. It brings order to the messy world of strategy formation, particularly to its huge, diverse literature and practice. Bear in mind what you have just been through in this book: not a safari across the edges—in between swamps and fields, forests and rivers—but through ten distinct eco (or mind) systems, ten configurations imagined out of a single world that is not nearly so lumpy as suggested. But if you are still aboard, this far, then you must have some appreciation for all these lumps. Just bear in mind that admonition of Whitehead: 'Seek simplicity and distrust it.'

'Hang on, ladies and gentlemen, you have yet to meet the whole beast'

This is not a cow

This is an organizational chart that shows the different parts of a cow. In a real cow the parts are not aware that they are parts. They do not have trouble sharing information. They smoothly and naturally work together, as one unit. As a cow. And you have only one question to answer. Do you want your organization to work like a chart? Or a cow?

(Adapted from Anderson & Lembke, NY, advertisement for SAP Canada)

Like many other safaris, we cannot deliver quite as much as we may seem to promise. So this chapter is not an elephant.

We warned in Chapter 1 that only you, the reader, can see the whole elephant. It can exist, not on these pieces of paper, but only in your mind's eye. As Robert Ornstein wrote in *The Psychology of Consciousness*:

Each person standing at one part of the elephant can make his own limited, analytic assessment of the situation, but we do not obtain an elephant by adding 'scaly,' 'long and soft,' 'massive and cylindrical' together in any conceivable proportion. Without the development of an over-all perspective, we remain lost in our individual investigations. Such a perspective is a province of another mode of knowledge, and cannot be achieved in the same way that individual parts are explored. It does not arise out of a linear sum of independent observations. (1972: 10)

These pieces of paper have been about the conventional mode of knowledge—words in linear order. That other mode takes place beyond words, perhaps, as some kind of image in the mysterious reaches of the human mind. So we cannot even show you the elephant. But maybe we can help you to find it. That is the purpose of this final chapter.

❝ we cannot show you the elephant, but maybe we can help you to find it ❞

We begin with a review of various attributes of the ten schools, to provide a summary of the material of the preceding chapters. Then, in a vain effort to tame the wilds of strategic management, we address various issues that cut across the whole field. Finally, we discuss some ways in which glimpses of the whole beast might be caught.

Of tails and tusks, plans and patterns

An elephant *is* body and legs, trunk and tusks, ears and tail. It may be more than the sum of these parts, but as we noted at the outset, you have to understand the parts to appreciate the whole. Accordingly, we draw together here various attributes of our beast of strategy formation.

Actually, we begin by describing other wholes—different beasts we have encountered on our safari, each a metaphor for one of the schools. Then we plot the development of these schools over time, to show their comings and goings—the attention each received and how some replaced others as prominent. And third, we offer a massive table that summarizes a whole host of attributes of the ten schools.

A metaphorical beast for each school

Why just elephants? Who goes on a safari to see a single animal? In fact, we have been coming across all sorts of other beasts along the way. Now it is time to name them.

First thing we saw on our safari was a spider, that solitary figure so carefully designing its web, strong enough to exploit its distinctive competences. Nearby was a squirrel, gathering and planning its resources in preparation for the coming months. A water buffalo ignored all this, sitting contentedly in its carefully selected position. What could possibly disrupt that?

A lone wolf thought he could. Why compete with the lions for the gazelles, thought this entrepreneur, when he could have that water buffalo all to himself. Risky? The owl sitting up in the tree thought so. She took everything in—very cognitive. But did she get it right? Maybe she was creating some kind of fantasy world of her own.

As we moved on, we saw a whole troop of monkeys, leaping in and out of the trees, playful and adaptive learners, responding to what each other picked up. Meanwhile, the powerful lions were eyeing the gazelles, picking out the one they would try to run down. Some of the younger lions seemed to be eyeing each other too, wondering who would get to eat first.

The peacock was oblivious to all this. All he cared about was looking beautiful. Much like a culture, he doesn't change. So too the ostrich, except that this bird did not want to look at all—at anyone else in the environment, let alone himself. Very dangerous behaviour in the wilds of strategic management.

Finally, did you catch sight of the chameleons darting around? They seem to change a lot, from one configuration to another, but you have to wonder if they really end up being so different.

Come to think of it, we never did see an elephant.

The evolution of the schools

An elephant is a complex system that grows and develops. That is true of each elephant as well as the species called elephant. The beast that the blind men stumbled upon was the product of a long process of evolution. Imagine, then, the problem biologists have in trying to build a coherent picture of the evolution of all species, from the rather simple to the remarkably complex.

Likewise, although somewhat more quickly, the field of strategic management has come a long way since the early 1960s. A literature and practice that grew slowly at first, then faster but in a one-sided way in the 1970s, and another-sided way in the 1980s, took off on a variety of fronts in the 1990s, and shows no sign of slowing down in the new millennium. Today it constitutes a dynamic if disparate field. Early schools that were easy to identify have given rise to later ones that are more complex, and more nuanced, one with the other.

Figure 12.1 seeks to capture this development by plotting activity in the ten schools. These graphs are impressionistic, our own subjective estimates of the amount of attention each school has received from writers and practitioners.

The graphs show the successive dominance of the three prescriptive schools—design in the early years, then planning in the 1970s, followed by positioning in the 1980s, which has since lost some of its popularity but remains influential. From the 1990s on, the field has became far more eclectic, with all the other schools gaining in importance.

There has been growing attention of late, especially in practice but also in scholarship, to the micro side of the power school, namely the role of boards of directors, the dynamics of top management teams, the use of rhetoric to assert control, and the like, and in research associated with the entrepreneurial school. But two other schools have really taken off in recent years—configuration and learning. Of course, no one runs around talking about the configuration approach to strategy making—as they did earlier about planning and then positioning. But academics talk a lot about types of strategy processes and stages in strategic development, while practitioners in many quarters have become almost

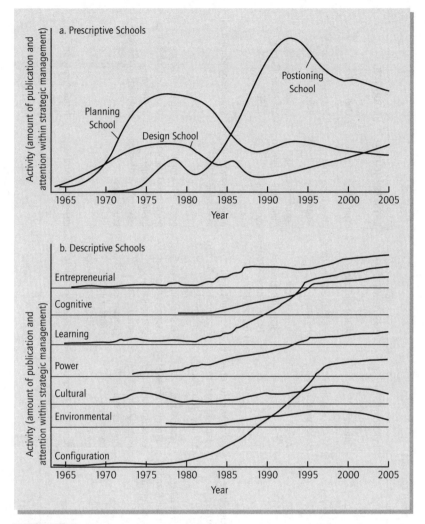

figure 12.1 Evolution of the ten schools

obsessed with strategic transformation. On a rather different front, learning approaches have come into great prominence too, especially under the guise of 'strategic learning' and 'dynamic capabilities.'

Dimensions of the schools

Table 12.1 lists all sorts of dimensions of the different schools. The table is offered as a summary as well as a reference source; do not feel obligated to read it all!

table 12.1 Dimensions of the ten schools

	DESIGN	PLANNING	POSITIONING	ENTREPRENEURIAL	COGNITIVE
A Metaphorical Beast for Each School	Spider	Squirrel	Water Buffalo	Wolf	Owl
A homily for each school	"Look before you leap."	"A stitch in time saves nine."	"Nothin' but the facts, ma'am."	"Take us to your leader."	"I'll see it when I believe it."
Foundation Writers	Selznick 1957, Andrews 1971	Ansoff 1965	Purdue work (Schendel, Hatten) 1970s, Porter 1980 and 1985	Schumpeter 1950, Cole 1959, others in economics	Simon 1947, 1957, March and Simon 1958
Underlying Discipline(s)	none (architecture as metaphor)	(some links to urban planning, systems theory, cybernetics)	Economics (industrial organization), Military History	none (early writings in economics)	Psychology (cognitive)
Champions	case study teachers, leadership aficionados; especially in America	"professional" managers, MBAs, staff experts, consultants, especially in France, America and communist governments	as in planning school, especially analytical staff people, consultants "boutiques," and military writers; notably in America	popular business press, novelists, small business people, especially in developing economies	the psychology-orientated; pessimists in one wing, optimists in the other
Intended Message/Realized Message	fit/think	formalize/program	analyze/calculate	envision/centralize	frame/worry or imagine

A Metaphorical Beast for Each School	LEARNING	POWER	CULTURAL	ENVIRONMENTAL	CONFIGURATION
A homily for each school	"If at first you don't succeed, try, try again."	"Look out for number one."	"An apple never falls far from the tree."	"It all depends."	"To everything there is a season. . . ."
	Monkeys	Lion	Peacock	Ostrich	Chameleon
Sources	Lindblom 1959, 1968; Cyert and March 1963; Weick 1969; Quinn 1980	Allison 1971 (micro); Pfeffer and Salancik 1978; Astley, 1984 (macro)	Rhenman and Normann 1960s; no obvious source elsewhere	Hannan and Freeman 1977; contingency theorists (e.g., Pugh et al., 1960s)	Chandler 1962, McGill group (Mintzberg, Miller, etc.) 1970s
Base Discipline	none (links to learning theory in psychology, chaos theory in mathematics)	Political Science	Anthropology	Biology, Political Sociology	History
Champions	experimentors, adaptors, especially in Japan and Scandinavia	the power and conspiracy-orientated people, especially in France	the social, spiritual and community-orientated people, especially in Scandinavia and Japan	population ecologists, positivists, especially in the Anglo-Saxon countries	synthesizers
Intended Message/ Realized Message	learn/play	grab/hoard	coalesce/perpetuate	cope/capitulate	integrate or transform/ lump or revolutionize

	DESIGN	PLANNING	POSITIONING	ENTREPRENEURIAL	COGNITIVE
Key Words	congruence/fit, distinctive competence, SWOT, formulation/ implementation	programming, budgeting, scheduling, scenarios	generic strategy, strategic groups, competitive analysis	bold stroke, vision, insight	map, frame, schema, interpretation, cognitive style
Strategy as	planned perspective	decomposed plans (or positions)	planned generic positions, also ploys	unique perspective (vision)	mental perspective
Basic Process	personal, judgmental, deliberate	formal, deliberate	analytical, deliberate	visionary, intuitive, deliberate umbrella, (positions can emerge)	mental, emergent
Pattern of change	occasional, quantum	periodic, incremental	piecemeal, frequent	occasional, opportunistic and revolutionary	infrequent
Central Actor(s)	the chief executive	planners and procedures	analysts and analysis	the leader	the brain

	LEARNING	POWER	CULTURAL	ENVIRONMENTAL	CONFIGURATION
Key Words	incrementalism, emergent strategy, sense making, venturing, champion, core competence	bargaining, conflict, coalition, stakeholders, collective strategy, alliance	values, beliefs, myths, symbolism	adaptation, evolution, contingency, selection, complexity, niche	configuration, archetype, stage, life cycle, transformation, revolution, turnaround, revitalization
Strategy as	learned patterns	political and cooperative patterns and positions, also ploys	collective perspective	specific generic positions (niches)	any of those to the left, in context
Basic Process	emergent, informal	conflictive, emergent (micro), deliberate (macro)	ideological, collective, deliberate	passive, imposed, emergent	integrative, episodic, plus all of those to the left, in context (deliberate for transformations)
Patterns of Change	continual, incremental or piecemeal, occasionally quantum	frequent, piecemeal	infrequent	rare and quantum (piecemeal in contingency theory)	occasional, revolutionary
Central Actor(s)	any learners	anyone with power (micro), whole organization (macro)	collectivity	"environment"	any of those to the left, in context

	DESIGN	PLANNING	POSITIONING	ENTREPRENEURIAL	COGNITIVE
Environment, Leadership, or Organization	Leadership dominant, Organization acquiescent	Organization dominant, Environment acquiescent	Organization, dominant, Environment to be analyzed	Leadership dominant, Organization malleable, Environmental niche	Leadership source of cognition, Environment overwhelming or constrained
Favoured Context	stable and comprehensible	simple, stable, ideally controllable	simple, stable, mature (i.e. quantifiable)	dynamic but simple (i.e. comprehensible)	complex
Favoured form of Organization	machine	large machine	large machine	entrepreneurial	any
Most likely during stage of	reconception	development and programming	assessment	startup, turnaround, small size	original conception, reconception, inertia

	LEARNING	POWER	CULTURAL	ENVIRONMENTAL	CONFIGURATION
Environment, Leadership or Organization	Leadership (any learners) dominant	Power in or of the organization dominant	Organization (as established) dominant	Environment dominant	Any of those to the left
Favoured Content	complex, dynamic (i.e. unpredictable)	divisive, malevolent (micro), controllable or cooperative (macro)	passive	competitive, delineated	any of those to the left
Favoured Formal (implicitly favored)	adhocracy or professional	adhocracy or professional (micro), closed machine (macro)	missionary, also stagnant machine	machine	any of those to the left, preferably adhocracy and missionary for transformation
Most likely during stage	evolution, unprecedented change	flux (micro), domination, cooptation (macro)	stability (reinforcement, inertia)	maturity, death	revolution (turnaround revitalization), otherwise any to the left

Some of this material is for the record—early writers,[1] base disciplines, key words, and the like for each school. Other material describes the strategy process as seen by each school: the basic process, the central actor(s), the view of organization and of environment, the favoured situation and stage, and so on.

Some other columns worth a special look are those that list a homily for each school, and two that compare the intended message of each school with what we take to be its realized message—what it really seems to be saying.

Taming the wilds of strategic management

Moving ever closer to the whole beast, if never quite there, we now consider a set of issues that cut across our schools—for example, how generic should a strategy be and how controlled should be the process to create it. All are fundamental to our understanding of the strategy process.

Each issue is introduced under a label, by a question, and as a dilemma. But in each case we reject the extreme answers—in favour of conditional ones. In other words, we believe the answers usually lie not at the extremities, but in how the contradictions are reconciled in practice, whether by lumping or by splitting. We discuss eight issues in all, the first three related to strategy content, the other five to the strategy process. Each begins and ends with a question. To quote the sage words of Sam Goldwyn, the movie mogul: 'For your information, let me ask you a few questions.'

Complexity issue

How complex should a good strategy be? On one hand, we are directed by Ashby's 'Law of Requisite Variety' (1970) to ensure that a system contains sufficient variety to meet the challenges it faces. Complex and unstable environments, for example, call for considerable variety in responses, meaning strategies that are complex, and nuanced. On the other hand is the equally plausible KISS imperative

---

1 For a time line of some of the main writers, see Gaddis (1997: 41).

('Keep It Simple, Stupid,' as in Peters and Waterman, 1982). Thus Andrews argued in the design school for strategies as simple informing ideas, while Pascale (1982), in the spirit of the learning school, criticized Americans for 'getting off' on simplistic notions of strategy the way the Japanese get off on sumo wrestling.

Kenneth Boulding has addressed the dilemma well: 'Somewhere . . . between the specific that has no meaning and the general that has no content, there must be . . . for each purpose and each level of abstraction, an optimal degree of generality' (1956: 197–8). The complexity issue has hardly been addressed in strategic management: how elaborate, how nuanced, how comprehensible, how general do we want our strategies to be, when and where?

Integration issue

How tightly integrated should a good strategy be? In the positioning school, especially in the growth-share matrix, the impression given is that strategy is a portfolio, a loosely coupled collection of components. The planning school, despite its use of the word 'synergy,' takes a similar view—especially seen in capital budgeting. And then there are those in the entrepreneurial and cultural schools who see no components at all, only strategy as one fully integrated perspective—'seamless,' to use the popular expression.

A variety of mechanisms to integrate strategies have been proposed: plans to integrate formally, cognition or vision to integrate mentally, culture to integrate normatively, communication to integrate collectively, and so on. How much integration is desirable, of what kind, when and where?

Generic issue

How unique or novel should a good strategy be? Is the number of available strategies infinite, or is there a 'generic' set from which organizations must choose? Correspondingly, do organizations succeed by respecting the rules or by breaking them?

The positioning school tells us that strategies are generic, that they exist a priori, clearly defined. Strategic positions are like pears, to be plucked off the tree of environmental opportunity. (In the environmental school, the pears fall on your head and knock you senseless.)

No doubt there are many industry recipes out there, and no shortage of 'mainline' and 'me-too' strategies. But the entrepreneurial and cultural schools, in particular, tell us that strategies can be unique—perspectives particular to the vision of one person or the culture of one organization, no two alike. The learning school adds that all strategies are the products of idiosyncratic adaptive processes. And the design school claims that strategies are unique because they are *created* in a personalized process of design (even though this school refers repeatedly to the 'choice' of strategy).

So the question becomes not just which is it—novel or generic—when and where, but how do the two interrelate? When and how do novel strategies become generic, how do strategic groups (as clusters of generic strategies) form, and so on?

Note how our three content issues themselves combine. Generic strategies would seem to be simpler, less integrated (as portfolios of components), but perhaps more flexible. They are also easier to articulate. Novel strategies are likely to be more complex, presumably more integrated, and therefore less flexible (because if you change any part of an integrated strategy, you risk *dis*integrating it). They may also be more difficult to articulate, yet once done, more easily remembered. Moreover, if strategies are generic, then their content becomes the natural focus, while if they are unique, then the focus must turn to the process of creating them. So let us now turn to the issues of process.

Control issue

How deliberate or emergent should an effective strategy formation process be: how predetermined, how cerebral, how centralized? In other words, to what extent is there a need for a priori control as opposed to a posteriori learning? We discuss this first among the issues of process because it is also one of content—concerning strategies as intended plans as opposed to realized patterns. (Indeed the more emergent the strategy, the more a central management must treat content as process—in other words manage people and structures deliberately in the hope that they will come up with the desirable strategies.)

The first three (prescriptive) schools aggressively promote deliberate-ness, as does the entrepreneurial school (although less formally). One side of the cognitive school raises doubts about the power of the strategist's mind over strategic matter, while the learning school dis-misses the deliberate in favour of the emergent. But, as we noted in Chapter 1, no real world strategy can be purely deliberate or purely emergent, since one precludes learning while the other precludes control. So the question becomes: what degree of each is appropriate, where and when?

Collective issue

Who is the strategist? How do we read the'organization's mind'? In Table 12.1, we listed the candidates for the job of strategist—each school has its own. At one extreme, it is the *him* or *her* of the design and entrepreneurial schools; at the other extreme, the *them* of the learning, political, and cultural schools. Or perhaps the strategist is the *it* of the environmental, planning, positioning, and cognitive schools—respectively, the world out there, procedure, analysis, and the biological brain. To put all this in another way, is strategy forma-tion fundamentally a personal process, a technical process, a physiological process, a collective process, even a non-process? Maybe it is all of the above. If so, which, or how much of each, when and where?

Change issue

Here we really wish to discuss three different issues related to strat-egic change—its presence, its pattern, and its source.

First, how do strategists reconcile the conflicting forces for change and for stability? How do they maintain alignment and promote order, efficiency, pattern, and control, while having to reconfigure and adapt, respond, innovate, and learn? To repeat an earlier point, despite the impression conveyed in most of the literature, strategy is a concept rooted in stability, not change. Organizations pursue strat-egies for purposes of consistency. But they sometimes need strategic change too—they have to discard their established directions in response to a changed environment.

The planning school claims that organizations can have stability and change concurrently: they can set course by explicit plans, yet change every year, on schedule. Very convenient. But very questionable. Other schools come down clearly on one side or the other: organizations are either changing all the time or else they hardly ever change. Under politics, strategies are in a constant state of flux, as new challenges arise. Likewise, strategic learning is a never-ending process: patterns may form, but since initiatives are always forthcoming, strategies can never quite settle down. But to the environmental and cultural schools as well as a part of the cognitive school, strategies rarely if ever change: the organization, or its strategist, slots into a niche, settles on a culture, slips into a mental frame, and then holds on for dear life. (In the environmental school, they would rather die than switch.) But surely real-world behaviour must fall largely between these extremes.

Next, we consider the pattern or pace of change. The configuration school makes a strong case for occasional but quantum and revolutionary change. A similar pattern of change is implied in the design and entrepreneurial schools, where strategy appears as some kind of immaculate conception. Even the cognitive and cultural schools support this pattern, but on the other side: to them, strategies hardly ever change. In contrast, the learning school permits change that is incremental, as strategists come to know a complex situation through experimentation (although they can sometimes leap to a new perspective when struck by a sudden insight). The planning school also tends to promote incremental change, in fact if not by intention, while the political school (micro) describes the disjointed, piecemeal change that arises from conflict.

All of these views seem plausible. Indeed, we have discussed empirical evidence in support of various ones. For example, the quantum theory shows that most of the time organizations change incrementally, in the direction of their established strategies, but occasionally they shift direction in revolutionary fashion. This may be especially true for entrepreneurial and mass production organizations, while the more innovative adhocracies may tend to swing back and forth between balanced periods of change and continuity. A variety of patterns of change is thus possible; questions remain as to which, when, where, and why.

A last issue of change concerns its source. Where do new strategies come from? Extending the concept of learning beyond just one school, do organizations learn by doing (as in the learning school), by thinking (as in the design school), by programming (as in the planning school), by analyzing (as in the positioning school), or by arguing (as in the power school)? While the learning school suggests that organizations learn with ease, the cognitive and cultural schools imply that they learn only with great difficulty. And the environmental school suggests that organizations don't learn at all. How much, then, do organizations learn, how easily, and how, when, and where?

Choice issue

We have discussed this issue at some length already: the question is not whether there exists strategic choice, but how much. Hence, we rejected the pure determinism of the environmental school as well as the closely related views of the cognitive and cultural schools, that the circumstances overwhelm the strategists. Likewise, we rejected the easy voluntarism of the design and entrepreneurial schools, in which the 'great leader' can do almost anything. As for the assumed voluntarism of the planning and positioning schools—a world ripe for plucking by those clever planners and analysts—on closer examination we found other things: a planning school upset by unexpected changes, and a positioning school wary of real choice, in both cases with determinism parading under the guise of free will.

Perhaps it is the macro side of the power school that achieves a good balance here, with its notion that the power of an organization reflects its dependency on the environment for resources. Some organizations must largely acquiesce, at least some of the time, while others can sometimes dominate. (Some, of course, acquiesce while believing they dominate, like the king in Saint-Exupery's *The Little Prince* who could order the sun to set, but only at a certain time of the day!) A balance is also struck in the learning school, which suggests that strategists cope with a difficult world by learning over time, occasionally even achieving leaps of insight that belie their supposed cognitive limitations.

The question then becomes: what, when, and where is the power of proactive leadership, personalized intuition, and collective learning against the forces of environmental demand, organizational inertia, and cognitive limitation?

Thinking issue

Finally, we come to perhaps the most intriguing issue of all, related also to deliberate control. Pascale (1982, 1984) poses it as how much strategic thinking do we want anyway, implying that organizations obsessed with the strategy formation process lose control of it. Approaching this from the perspective of the learning school, Pascale believes organizations should get on with acting.

But again, the issue need not be dichotomized. Certainly, we need to think—we are cerebral animals—and even sometimes to formalize. Yet, as we critiqued the prescriptive schools, we can become too conscious at the expense of our ability to act ('paralysis by analysis'). Indeed, conscious thought did not fare so well in the cognitive school, although ironically, it did get redeemed somewhat in the learning school (through the acknowledgment of insight and inspiration). Perhaps Karl Weick (1979) strikes the right balance here with his point that we need to act but then we need to make sense of our actions. That is why we reviewed his work in both the learning and cognitive schools.

Given that this book has, we hope, encouraged a good deal of thinking about strategy formation, perhaps we should convert Pascale's point into the following question, which remains largely unaddressed in the literature of strategic management: What is 'strategic thinking' anyway? And what forms of it—what 'strategic styles'—are most effective? How is thought best coupled with action in strategy making: in other words, how is the specific made to inform the general and the general brought to bear on the specific? When and where?

Toward seeing the whole beast

Our safari is now heading back to base, which means you will soon be back home with only your images of the trip. So let us try to draw together some of its loose ends.

There has been at least one consistent ambiguity throughout this book: whether these schools describe different processes, used in different organizations, or different parts of the same process, used at different stages of the same organization. In other words, is this, various species (spider, wolf, etc.), or one species—the elephant in its many parts should strategists pick and choose from among all these ideas, like diners at a buffet table, or should they try to combine them into one or another palatable dish, as chefs do back in the kitchen? We have gone both ways on this question for one good reason: the answer has to be 'yes' both times.

We have gone both ways on this question for one good reason: the answer has to be 'yes' both times.

Every strategy process has to combine various aspects of the different schools. Can anyone possibly imagine strategy making in any serious organization without mental and social aspects, or that ignore the demands of the environment, the energy of leadership, and the forces of organization? And can any strategy process be realistically pursued as purely deliberate or purely emergent? To deny learning is as silly as to deny control.

Yet practice tilts too. Sometimes it becomes more individually cognitive than socially interactive (in much of small business, for example). Some strategies seem to be more rationally deliberate (especially in mature mass-production industries), while others tend to be more adaptively emergent (as in high technology industries). The environment can sometimes be highly demanding (during social upheavals), yet other times (even the same times) entrepreneurial leaders are able to manoeuvre through it with ease. There are, after all, identifiable stages and periods in strategy making.

Of course, the very format of this book has favoured the latter interpretation—of different processes. Ours has been a book mostly about lumping, not splitting—about the various species of the strategy process. This made it easier to write, and, we hope, easier to read. Bear in mind too that this has been a review of a field, and the field of strategic management has been a rather lumpy one these past forty years—from planning to positioning to learning, and so on. This has most likely reflected the influence of the academic writers and the consultants: it is they who have been driving the thinking in this field. Like butchers, we all chop up reality for our convenience, in some cases using one part of the beast while throwing out the rest, like poachers who grab the tusks of the elephant and leave the carcass to rot. Of course, the further back we look, the lumpier it all appears in retrospect. The nuances get lost.

> " like butchers, we all chop up reality for our convenience "

But those who have ultimate responsibility for strategy—the managers of our organizations—can allow themselves no such luxuries. They have to deal with the entire beast of strategy formation, as a living thing. True, they can make use of the process in various ways: an elephant, after all, can be a beast of burden or a symbol of ceremony—but only if it remains intact and alive.

Why then write this book (other than for the historical record)? Why not leave the field to the splitters, who weave together all the nuances? Because they do not seem to have the necessary impact, at least on practice. It is not that managers do not appreciate nuance—they live nuance every day. Rather, like the rest of us, they seem to understand the world more easily in terms of categories, at least initially. Categories strike us sharply. The nuances can follow.

The trick, of course, is to make use of this simplicity while distrusting it, as we earlier cited Whitehead. We all have to appreciate the categories and we all have to get beyond them.

As we tried to point out in our critiques of the different schools, at times rather harsh, the greatest failings of strategic management have occurred when managers took one point of view too seriously. We had our obsession with planning. Then everything had to be generic positions based on careful calculations. Later the learning organization became all the rage, somehow to be reconciled with perpetual transformation. 'Learn, all of you,' the pundits seemed to be saying, 'but do it quickly and dramatically.' No wonder there is so much confusion.

By having juxtaposed the messages of all ten schools, we hope we have revealed the fallaciousness of all this. In other words, it is the whole book that matters, not any single chapter. There are categories out there, but they should be used as building blocks, or, better still, as ingredients of a stew.

Three figures follow. The first maps the schools as distinct approaches to strategy formation under different conditions. The second sequences the schools as organizations progress in the development of their strategies. And the third depicts the schools as different aspects of one integrated process of strategy formation. Together all three help us to understand the whole beast.

Mapping the schools

Figure 12.2 identifies the various approaches to strategy formation along two dimensions—how controllable the external environment is thought to be (ranging from comprehensible to confusing), and how open-ended is the proposed internal strategy process (ranging from rational to natural). Our ten lumps are mapped on this space of strategy formation. (We could have selected other dimensions; our purpose here is simply to show how the different approaches spread out.)

All four corners are filled. Planning and positioning are seen at one corner—rational processes in an environment considered to be controllable. Facing this at the opposite corner are the cognitive and, nearby, learning and power (micro) schools—more natural or organic processes in environments considered to be unpredictable. In the other two corners are the entrepreneurial school, seen as an open-ended process in some niche of the environment that can ostensibly be controlled, and the environmental school, which expects the organization to respond rationally to an environment it cannot control. All the other schools fit somewhere in between. So do some of the hybrid views we have discussed, shown by the lines joining pairs of the schools.

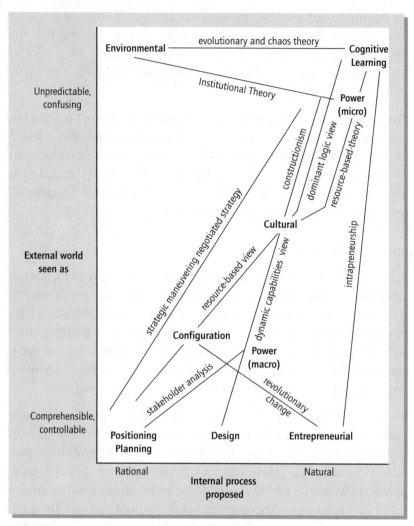

figure 12.2 Mapping the schools of strategy formation

Sequencing the schools

Figure 12.2 has lumped the schools according to external condition and internal process. In a similar way, in Chapter 11 we lumped some of the schools according to the form of organization that seem to favour them: in particular, the entrepreneurial organization favouring a visionary approach, the machine organization favouring planning and positioning, the professional organization favouring venturing (individual learning), and the adhocracy organization favouring collective learning and visioning.

But organizations do not usually stay with one approach to the strategy process all their lives. They typically use different ones in early development, under conditions of maturity, and later perhaps in renewal. So here we consider how our ten schools most commonly (but not exclusively) seem to sequence themselves along the development trajectory of different kinds of organization, as shown in Figure 12.3.[2]

Early development

Organizations, business and often non-business too, generally begin their lives with the strong leadership of the founder: an entrepreneur, or champion, who takes the lead to get them started and on the road to development. He or she usually begins with some kind of vision—a new form of retailing, the provision of some specialized hospital service—derived from earlier personal learning. Or else the initial vision is copied from some other organization. In some cases, however, the founder develops that vision as the organization itself develops. (The founder of the IKEA furniture chain began by trying to sell pens!) Both the entrepreneurial and the design schools, as well as the construction side of the cognitive school, describe the strategy process in this stage.

This vision, in turn, is designed to stimulate more learning, in the form of venturing, especially to clarify and elaborate the vision (for example, how that new form of retailing will work in the marketplace). So here the learning school becomes especially significant.

Small organizations often remain in this state (as in the small town newspaper described in Mintzberg *et al.*, 1984), as sometimes do even ones that have grown large still under the control of their founders (as in the retail chain and women's undergarment manufacturer described in Mintzberg and Waters, 1982, 1984), cycling between visioning and venturing (the entrepreneurial and learning schools).

---

2 This discussion is adopted from material in Chapter 12 of Mintzberg's 2007 book *Tracking Strategies: toward a general theory*, with evidence from the studies reported in the rest of that book.

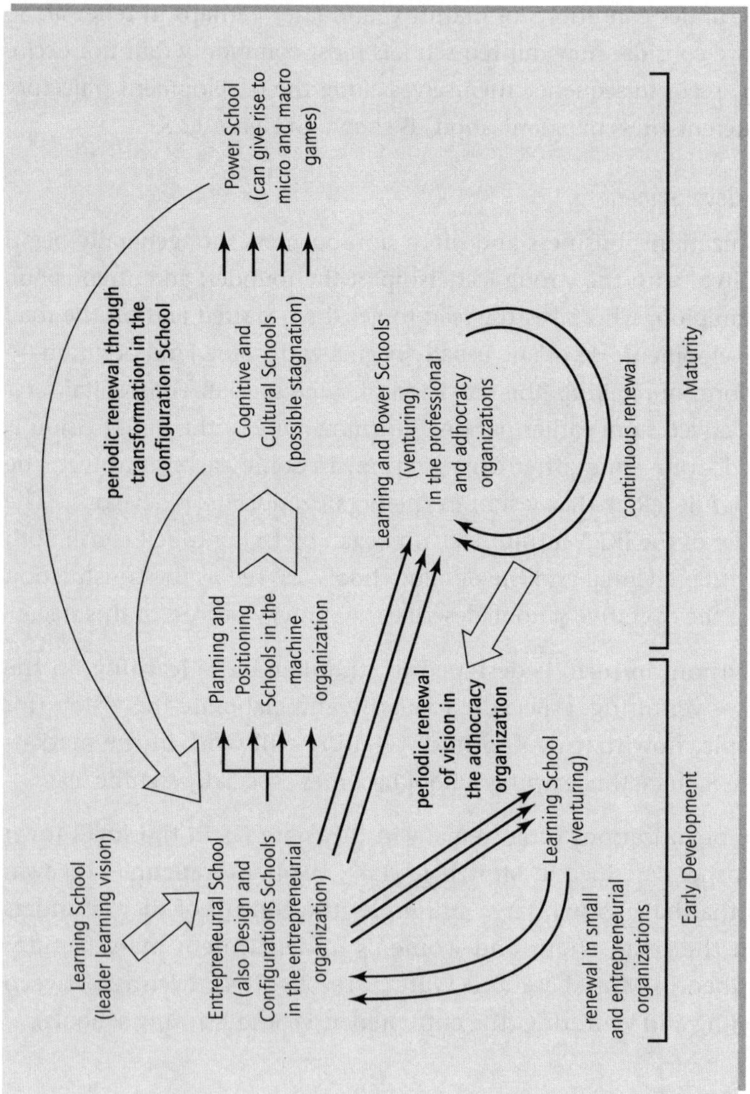

Learning School
(leader learning vision)

Entrepreneurial School
(also Design and
Configurations Schools
in the entrepreneurial
organization)

Learning School
(venturing)

renewal in small
and entrepreneurial
organizations

Planning and
Positioning
Schools in the
machine
organization

**periodic renewal
of vision in
the adhocracy
organization**

**periodic renewal through
transformation in the
Configuration School**

Cognitive and
Cultural Schools
(possible stagnation)

Power School
(can give rise to
micro and macro
games)

Learning and Power Schools
(venturing)
in the professional
and adhocracy
organizations

continuous renewal

Early Development

Maturity

figure 12.3   **Sequencing the schools of strategy formation**

Many organizations, however, grow beyond their entrepreneurial origins, into another form, such as machine, professional, or adhocracy. As their visions stabilize, and they learn their way into tangible strategic positions (Wal-Mart, for example, in various countries), they move toward maturity. But as described in Chapter 11, this can happen in quite different ways.

Maturity in the professional organization

Professional organizations continue with a good deal of individual or small group venturing, for example, by the doctors in a hospital coming up with new procedures. So these organizations tend not so much to renew themselves collectively as to stimulate all kinds of learning all over the place. So don't look for great turnarounds in hospitals, universities, and other professional organizations (Mintzberg and Rose, 2003; Hardy *et al.*, 1983). And so don't look for the configuration school so much as steady evolution and renewal, more consistent with the learning school.

But by the same token, the extensive form of decentralization of the professional organization leads to a good deal of conflict, as the professionals challenge each other for the limited resources. So do look for the power school (micro), and to some extent the positioning school, as the professionals use all sorts of strategic analyses to justify their own ventures and challenge those of their colleagues.

Maturity as renewal in the adhocracy organization

Adhocracies engage in much venturing too, but usually in teams of experts more than by individuals (as in an Olympic Organizing Committee preparing a new games, or an advertising agency developing a new campaign). Indeed, as a project organization, the adhocracy is above all a venturer (whereas ventures, in the professional organization result in new services that become regular operations, as in the introduction of a new surgical procedure in a hospital). So the adhocracy settles down to maturity by never settling down: it remains in a state of constant renewal, which means that the learning school tends always to be predominant.

But that learning extends beyond the project themselves. Evidence from two studies, of a film company and an architectural firm (Mintzberg and McHugh, 1985; Mintzberg *et al.*, 1988; also in Mintzberg 2007: Chapters 4 and 9), suggest that this learning extends beyond the projects themselves, to the organization at large. For example, in the film company, isolated initiatives—as in the first effort to produce films for television in the 1950s—led other teams to follow suit, and so carried the organization to a new overall emergent strategy.

We found that in the film company, this happened in a remarkably regular pattern. In cycles of about six years each, there was convergence around some strategic theme, or new perspective (for example, making films for television), followed by another six years or so of divergence into many themes. We called this 'cycling into and out of focus.' With some supporting evidence in the architectural firm, this may be how adhocracy organizations tend to renew themselves.

With these organizations so decentralized too, there tends to be a good deal of conflict. So once again, while the learning school seems to be dominant, the power school (micro) is close behind.

Maturity in the machine organization

Mass production and mass service organizations exhibit a very different pattern (see Mintzberg, 2007: Chapter 2, 6, 8, on a European automobile company, a state airline, and a large textile firm).

These organizations really do settle down, typically in the machine form, to pursue their given strategic perspective and strategic positions. There may still be some venturing—there is always some of that same learning, except in the most decrepit of organizations. But mostly there is planning, not to create new overall strategies so much as to programme the consequences of the strategies already created, through procedures of budgeting, operational planning, and the like. (As noted in Chapter 2, mostly 'Strategic Planning' is an oxymoron.)

There also tends to be some strategic positioning to find new positions and rearrange existing ones under the umbrella of the overall strategic perspective (for example, establishing new routes in an airline, or new overseas markets for existing products in an automobile company). The mature stage of the industry usually means that there is a great deal of industry and competitive data available, and the organization, tending to be large and established, can make good use of it. So we tend to find here a considerable amount of strategic analyzing too (also part of the positioning school).

Stagnation and renewal through transformation in the machine organization

When they are large and well-established, machine organizations can sustain themselves for long periods of time, even without much strategic renewal. In fact, many turn to the power school (macro) to do so; they use their overall power to bully competitors and governments, etc., or else they enter into cooperative, cartel-like arrangements with would-be competitors.

But eventually there tends to come stagnation, especially as the environment changes (in the form of new technologies and changed competition, etc.). So the cultural and environmental schools come to the fore, also the side of the cognitive school that explains resistance to change. At the same time, political games tend to become more pervasive (the power school—micro), as people battle each other over turf and for the diminishing resources. (Here, too, strategic analyses are used in these battles.)

When things get bad enough, or if the organization is lucky enough before that happens, new entrepreneurial leadership may arise or be brought in to effect a 'turnaround.' (As noted in Chapter 8, the political battles can also help to unfreeze the organization, setting the stage for the turnaround.) In effect, under strong leadership, the organization reverts to the entrepreneurial school (reinforced by the design school, and the construction side of the cognitive school, with renewed strategic learning), in the form of a transformation, as described in the configuration school.

Such turnaround tends to take one of three forms: operating (to cut costs), strategic (to shift strategic positions), and visionary (to bring in a new strategic perspective). But no matter which it is, this period of renewal is usually temporary, because such organizations generally remain in mass production or the mass provision of service, and so soon revert to their machine form, with its heavy reliance on planning and less tolerance for entrepreneurial leadership. We saw this especially in the studies of the automobile and textile companies mentioned earlier.

The design and planning schools give the impression that such change can be rather regular in machine organizations. But the evidence from our studies (reported in Mintzberg, 2007) provide strong support instead for the quantum nature of change described in the configuration school: irregular, infrequent, and often dramatically revolutionary. In fact, the airline exhibited no such transformation at all across the forty years of its history.

Splitting the schools

Figure 12.4 shows the schools taking their place around and within one integrated process of strategy formation.

At the centre is the actual creation of strategy, shown as a black box, to indicate how it is seen by most of the schools: as mysterious, or ignored. Only the cognitive school really tries to get inside it, but, as we noted in Chapter 6, without much success. Some other schools claim to do so, especially the design and planning schools, but as Gary Hamel was quoted in Chapter 4, the 'dirty little secret of the strategy industry is that it doesn't have a theory of strategy creation' (1997: 80). Indeed, try to find a box amidst the great many on the 'strategic planning' charts that gives the remotest hint of this. The learning and power schools do make some tentative efforts in this regard, at least to understand how organizations learn and how political games drive strategic change. All the other schools, in our view, take their place around this black box, whether above, below, before, after, or beyond it (which brings this diagram close to the one about 'strategic thinking as seeing' presented in Chapter 5).

The positioning school looks *behind*, at established (historical) data, which it analyzes and feeds into the black box of strategy making. On the other side, coming out of the black box, in succession, are the planning, design, and entrepreneurial schools. The planning school looks *ahead*, but just ahead, to programme the strategies created inside the box. The design school looks farther *ahead*, to a strategic

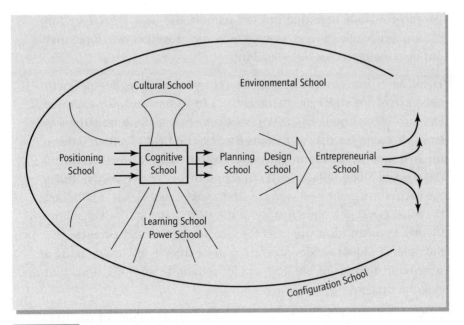

figure 12.4 Splitting the schools*

(*Our thanks to Patricia Pitcher, who suggested a similar diagram)

perspective, while the entrepreneurial school looks *beyond* as well as *beside*, past the immediate situation to a unique vision of the future—but with an intuitive process even less articulated than that of the design school.

The learning and power schools, in our opinion, look mainly below, to what underlies strategy formation, concentrating on trees more than forests. The learning school looks on the ground, sometimes into the grass roots for evidence of learning. The power school, in a sense, looks lower (but not deeper): under the rocks, sometimes even underground, to places that organizations do not always like to expose—their political games.

Looking down from *above* is the cultural school, enshrouded in clouds of beliefs, while well above that is the environmental school, looking *on*, so to speak. And in contrast to the cognitive school, which tries to look *inside* the process (through the microscope, as opposed to the reversed telescope of the environmental school), the configurational school looks *at* it, or, we might say, *all around it*.

We can conclude here that our ten schools also look at strategy formation as a single process, every which way. Together, we hope, they can help managers see *through* all this.

There have been several efforts in recent years to integrate different perspectives of strategic management. In some cases, for example Farjoun (2002) and Frery (2006), scholars analyze the foundations of strategic management for threads that tie the field together. Others, for instance Alvarez and Busenitz (2001), Gavetti and Levinthal (2004), and Sloan (1996), argue that one theory or perspective holds the key for integrating all views of strategy. Hoskisson *et al.*, (1999), on the other hand, trace the history of the field, looking for overarching themes that can form the basis for integration. Hutzschenreuter and Kleindienst (2006) tackle integration more directly by undertaking a systematic analysis of publications for a handful of dimensions that describe strategy.

In Box 12.1, we present one such effort by Pamela Sloan of the HEC Montreal business school, based on her doctoral dissertation and summarized for this edition. It synthesizes by seeing the schools as complementary instead of competing.

---

box 12.1

Strategy as synthesis: the schools as complementary

Strategy, at its essence, is integrative. It's a bringing together—a synthesis—of actions and intentions that shape a company and influence its performance.

Integration and coherence were at the core of the design school. Andrews—who provided the clearest statement of this school—conceived of strategy as having four identifiable components: what a company *might do* in terms of market opportunity; what it *could do* in terms of corporate capability; what the leaders of the company want to do; and what the company *should do* in acknowledging its obligations to society. The challenge in formulating strategy was to balance these components and reconcile them into a coherent whole.

But, as the different schools of strategy have emerged, the field has become more and more fragmented. More colourfully stated, we have created the strategy beast. One of the consequences is that we have lost sight of the essential integrative character of strategy formation, a holistic view of strategy itself, and coherence as its key test. This doesn't make much sense. Every company has a position in the market, a set of resources and capabilities, leaders who have desires and, in a scandal-ridden world, a growing need to incorporate—as done in the design school—ethical values into the formation of strategy.

Getting back to an integrated view strategy shouldn't mean abandoning the different schools. Each makes a valuable contribution toward understanding how and why strategies form, as well as helping to explain performance. But, we do need to re-orient our strategic thinking to see the different schools as parts of a whole that come together and interact with one another.

My research took a holistic view of strategy formation as its starting point and explored how different strategic influences interacted with one another. I studied 15 years of strategy formation in one company and found evidence of many of the schools. The premises of the positioning school explained aspects of competitive strategy, while the learning school offered insight into the evolution of the company's resources and capabilities. The vision of top management, a key dimension of the entrepreneurial school, combined with the cognitive framing of strategy, also played a role. Ethical values enabled and constrained strategy formation in ways consistent with the cultural school. Each different influence provided the means to attain different goals.

But the study also showed that none of the different influences alone could explain either strategy formation or the coherence of strategies. Rather it was the schools' collective influence that accounted for how strategies formed and how effective they were. The different influences did not work on simple parallel tracks – nor were they always mutually reinforcing. They were deeply connected and tied together by an identifiable process of synthesis.

Synthesis takes place through a complex process of change and transformation. Like the configuration school, the basic process is integrative, centring on the relationship and interaction of the market, firm, leadership and ethical influences. But, drawing on the power school, the process of synthesis pays particular attention to contradictions, inconsistencies and conflicts among them.

The relationships among the components are susceptible to change and can be disturbed in a variety of ways. A rupture or major discontinuity in one of the components can have a profound effect on the relationship among them. Some discontinuities may be under the control of the company, such as the appointment of a new CEO. Others, such as unanticipated market shocks, are not. Here is where the environmental school comes in.

The first stage of synthesis. When the relationship is disturbed, contradictions and conflicts emerge. A firm's market position, and its resources and capabilities may

▶ no longer be coherent after a major market shock. Similarly, executive succession that brings a different vision may generate inconsistencies with the firm's resources and capabilities or its position in the market. Conflicts may emerge when the interests of different shareholders become opposed—as when a restructuring needed to protect the interests of shareholders harms the interests of employees or communities.

The second stage of synthesis. Reconciling these contradictions is part of the process of synthesis. This is not always easy, for it involves making changes to one or more of components of strategy in a way that both reconciles the contradictions and ensures the ongoing attainment of different strategic goals. This process of reconciliation continues until a new—and more stable—synthesis emerges. Syntheses with higher coherence survive; those with lower coherence are eventually dissolved.

The process of synthesis is intended to move the components into a coherent, mutually reinforcing relationship and to generate positive, sustainable performance. But recurrent, unreconciled contradictions or strategic blind spots caused by neglecting one of the strategic influences can make synthesis a chaotic effort that results in little coherence, negative performance and ultimately the disintegration of strategy.

This research brings out two long forgotten aspects of strategy formation. First, it points to the importance of the set of strategic influences and understanding their concurrent effects. Second, it stresses the critical role of *integrative* thinking and recasts how we see the different schools, moving them from competing to complementary ways to explain the formation of strategy. This integrative approach brings their complex connections and interactions to light, surfaces the contradictions, conflicts and inconsistencies that can arise in the formation of strategy, and reconciles them in ways that yield coherent, sustainable strategies.

Beyond the parts

It is convenient that strategic management has, for the most part, slotted neatly into these ten categories. That has made our jobs as writers, readers, researchers, and consultants that much easier. But not as managers: unfortunately this may not have been the best thing for practice.

That is why we are pleased—now that we have completed this book, at least—that the field is becoming more eclectic, more nuanced. We celebrate its newfound messiness—so much better than its old order.

Some bemoan this. The field is out of control, they say. Bring on some sort of dominating 'paradigm.'[3] But we have already had that, thank you, in the strategic planning of the 1970s (was having everyone filling out all those silly forms some sort of strategic utopia?), followed by all that obsessive positioning, and then that passionate learning, or else constant transforming.

But is this what is needed in practice? Can anyone really believe that it has to be one to exclusion of the others? We need good practice, not neat theory. The appearance of various hybrids of the schools is thus a welcome sign.[4] It means not only that the field is coming of age, but also that the practice is becoming more sophisticated.

The blind men never saw the corpus callosum of the elephant, the tissue that joins the two hemispheres of its brain. Nor did they see the ligaments that connect its different bones. But we are beginning to get a bit of that perspective in strategic management. It is a good thing, that these parts exist too, because without them all elephants would be dead elephants. And without an understanding of equivalent connections in organizations, all strategies risk becoming dead strategies.

Not that understanding of these connections will come easily. Strategy formation is a complex space. And ten is a big number for brains accustomed to seven plus or minus two. But the fault, dear Brutus, lies neither in the stars nor in ourselves, but in the process itself. Strategy formation is judgmental designing, intuitive visioning, and emergent learning; it has to be about transformation as well as perpetuation; it depends on individual cognition and social interaction, cooperation as well as conflict; it requires analyzing before and programming after as well as negotiating during; and all of this must be in response to what can be a demanding environment. Just try to leave any of this out and see what happens!

---

3 For a related debate, concerning organization theory in general rather than strategic management in particular, see the proposal by Pfeffer (1993, 1995) and the counterargument by Van Maanen (1995a and b).

4 Of course, they are hybrids only in our terms. Reverse the perspective, like that famous image of a wine goblet that becomes the profile of a woman's face, and the schools become the hybrids.

The hunt for strategic management

It is now time to end our safari, to leave our libraries, classrooms, offices, retreats, and easy chairs, and really plunge into the tangled wilds—where we shall need clear vision to see the real beasts. We should certainly encourage scholars and consultants to continue probing the important parts of each school: we need to know more about tusks and trunks and tails. But, more importantly, we have to get beyond the narrowness of each school: we need to know how this beast called strategy formation, which combines all of these schools and more, really lives its life.

We need to ask better questions and generate fewer hypotheses—to allow ourselves to be pulled by the concerns out there rather than being pushed by the concepts in here. And we need to be more comprehensive: to concern ourselves with process and content, statics and dynamics, constraint and inspiration, the cognitive and the collective, the planned and the learned, the economic and the political. In other words, in addition to probing its parts, we must give more attention to the whole beast of strategy formation. We shall never find it, never really see it all. But we can certainly see it better. And so (forgive us):

> It was the gang from strategy
> To action much inclined,
> Who went to find their cagy beast
> As they left the schools behind.
> Cried they, 'Having rode on that safari
> Can we be no longer be so blind?'

References

Abrahamson, E., and Fombrun, C. J. "Macrocultures: Determinants and Consequences." *Academy of Management Review* (19, 4, 1994:728–755).

Abrahamson, E., and Fairchild, G. "Management Fashion: Lifecycles, Triggers, and Collective Learning Processes." *Administrative Science Quarterly* (44, 1999:708–740).

Ackoff, R. L. "Beyond Prediction and Preparation." *Journal of Management Studies* (XX, 1[January], 1983:59–69).

Afuah, A. "Redefining Firm Boundaries in the Face of the Internet: Are Firms Really Shrinking?" *Academy of Management Review* (28, 1, 2003:1231–1246).

Alberts, W. "The Experience Curve Doctrine Reconsidered." *Journal of Marketing* (53, 3, 1989:36–49).

Allaire, Y., and Firsirotu, M. "How to Implement Radical Strategies in Large Organizations." *Sloan Management Review* (26, Spring 1985:19–33).

Allison, G. T. *Essence of Decision: Explaining the Cuban Missile Crisis* (Boston: Little, Brown, 1971).

Alvarez, S. A., and Busenitz, L. W. "The Entrepreneurship of Resource-Based Theory." *Journal of Management* (27, 2001:755–775).

Amram, M., and Kulatilaka, N. *Real Options: Managing Strategic Investment in an Uncertain World* (Boston, MA: Harvard Business School Press, 1999).

Anand, N., and Peterson, R. A. "When Market Information Constitutes Fields: Sensemaking of Markets in the Commercial Music Industry." *Organization Science* (11, 3 [May/June], 2000:270–284).

Andrews, K. R. *The Concept of Corporate Strategy* (Homewood, IL: Irwin, editions 1971, 1980, 1987).

Andrews, K. R. "Directors' Responsibility for Corporate Strategy." *Harvard Business Review* (58, 6, November-December 1980:28–43).

Andrews, K. R. "Replaying the Board's Role in Formulating Strategy." *Harvard Business Review* (59, 3, May-June 1981a:18–27).

Andrews, K. R. "Corporate Strategy as a Vital Function of the Board," *Harvard Business Review* (59, 6, November-December 1981b:174–184).

Ansoff, H. I. *Corporate Strategy* (New York: McGraw-Hill, 1965).

Ansoff, H. I. "The State of Practice in Planning Systems." *Sloan Management Review* (Winter 1977:1–24).

Argyris, C. *Increasing Leadership Effectiveness* (New York: Wiley, 1976).

Argyris, C. "Teaching Smart People How to Learn." *Harvard Business Review* (69, 3, May-June 1991:99–109).

Argyris, C., and Schön, D. A. *Organizational Learning: A Theory of Action Perspective* (Reading, MA: Addison-Wesley, 1978).

Ashby, W. R. *An Introduction to Cybernetics* (London: Chapman and Hall, 1970).

Astley, W. G. "Toward an Appreciation of Collective Strategy." *Academy of Management Review* (9, 3, 1984:526–533)

Astley, W. G. "The Two Ecologies: Population and Community Perspectives on Organizational Evolution." *Administrative Science Quarterly* (30, 2, 1985:224–241).

Astley, W. G., and Fombrun, C. J. "Collective Strategy: Social Ecology of Organizational Environments." *Academy of Management Review* (8, 4, 1983:576–587).

Baden-Fuller, C., and Stopford, J. M. *Rejuvenating the Mature Business: the Competitive Challenge*, Chapter 6 (Boston: Harvard Business School Press, 1992)

Balogun, J., and Johnson, G. "Organizational Restructuring and Middle Manager Sensemaking." *Academy of Management Journal* (47, 4, 2004:523–549).

Barkema, H., and Shvyrkov, O. "Does Top Management Team Diversity Promote or Hamper Foreign Expansion?" *Strategic Management Journal*, (28, 7, 2007:663–680).

Barney, J. B. "Organizational Culture: Can It Be a Source of Sustained Competitive Advantage?" *Academy of Management Review* (11, 3, 1986:656–665).

Barney, J. B. "Firm Resources and Sustained Competitive Advantage." *Journal of Management* (17, 1, 1991:99–120).

Barney, J .B. "Resource-Based Theories of Competitive Advantage: A Ten Year Retrospective on the Resource-Based View." *Journal of Management* (27, 2001:643–650).

Barr, P. S., Stimpert, J. L., and Huff, A. S. "Cognitive Change, Strategic Action, and Organizational Renewal." *Strategic Management Journal* (13, 1992:15–36).

Bateson, G. "A Theory of Play and Fantasy." Reprinted in *Steps to an Ecology of Mind* (New York: Ballantine Books, 1972:117–193).

Bateson, G. *Steps to an Ecology of Mind* (New York: Ballantine Books, 1972).

Baughman, J. P. "Problems and Performance of the Role of Chief Executive in the General Electric Company, 1882–1974" (working paper, Graduate School of Business Administration, Harvard University, 1974).

Baumol, W. J. "Entrepreneurship in Economic Theory." *American Economic Review* (58, May 1968:64–71).

Bazerman, M. *Judgment in Managerial Decision Making*, 6th edition. (New York: John Wiley and Sons, Inc., 2005).

Beatty, R. W., and Ulrich, D. O. "Re-Energizing the Mature Organization." *Organizational Dynamics* (Summer 1991:16–30).

Beckhard, R. *Organizational Development: Strategies and Models* (Reading, MA: Addison-Wesley, 1969).

Beer, M., Eisenstat, R. A., and Spector, B. "Why Change Programs Don't Produce Change." *Harvard Business Review* (November-December, 1990:158–166).

Bello, F. "The Magic that Made Polaroid." *Fortune* (April 1959:124–164)

Bennis, W., and Namus, B. *Leaders: The Strategies for taking Charge* (New York: Harper & Row, 1985).

Bettis, R. A., and Prahalad, C. K. "The Dominant Logic: Retrospective and Extension." *Strategic Management Journal* (16, 1995:3–14).

Bhide, A. "How Entrepreneurs Craft Strategies That Work." *Harvard Business Review* (March-April 1994:150–161).

Bigley, G. A., and Wiersema, M. F. "New CEOs and Corporate Strategic Refocusing: How Experience as Heir Apparent Influences the Use of Power." *Administrative Science Quarterly* (47, 2002: 707–727).

Bjorkman, I. "Factors Influencing Processes of Radical Change in Organizational Belief Systems." *Scandinavian Journal of Management* (5, 4, 1989:251–271).

Bogner, W. C., and Barr, P. S. "Making Sense in Hypercompetitive Environments: A Cognitive Explanation for Persistence of High Velocity Competition." *Organization Science* (11, 2, 2000:337–370).

Bogner, W. C., and Thomas, H. "The Role of Competitive Groups in Strategy Formulation: A Dynamic Integration of Two Competing Models." *Journal of Management Studies* (30, 1, 1993:51–67).

Boisot, M. H., ed. *Information Space: A Framework for Learning in Organizations, Institutions and Culture* (London: Routledge, 1995).

Bolman, L. G., and Deal, T. *Reframing Organizations: Artistry, Choice, and Leadership,* 2nd edition (San Francisco: Jossey-Bass Publishers, 1997).

Boston Consulting Group Inc., The. *Strategy Alternatives for the British Motorcycle Industry* (London: Her Majesty's Stationery Office, 1975).

Boulding, K. E. "General Systems Theory: The Skeleton of Science." *Management Science* (2, 3, 1956:197–208).

Bower, J. L. *Managing the Resource Allocation Process: A Study of Planning and Investment* (Boston: Graduate School of Business Administration, Harvard University, 1970).

Bower, J. L., and Doz, Y. "Strategy Formulation: A Social and Political Process." In D. E. Schendel and C. W. Hofer, eds., *Strategic Management* (Boston: Little, Brown, 1979:152–166).

Bowman, E. H. "Strategic History: Through Different Mirrors." *Advances in Strategic Management* (11A, JAI Press, 1995:25–45).

Boyd, B. K. "Strategic Planning and Financial Performance: A Meta-Analytical Review." *Journal of Management Studies* (28, 4 [July] 1991:353–374).

Brandenburger, A. M., and Nalebuff, B. J. "The Right Game: Use Game Theory to Shape Strategy." *Harvard Business Review* (July-August 1995:57–81).

Brandenburger, A. M., and Nalebuff, B. J. *Co-opetition* (New York: Doubleday, 1996)

Branson, R. "Reflections of a Risk-Taker." *The McKinsey Quarterly* (Summer 1986:13–18).

Braudel, F. *The Wheels of Commerce: Civilisation and Capitalism* (Weidenfeld & Nicolson History, 2002).

Braybrooke, D., and Lindblom, C. E. *A Strategy of Decision* (New York: Free Press, 1963).

Bresser, R. K., and Bishop, R. C. "Dysfunctional Effects of Formal Planning: Two Theoretical Explanations." *Academy of Management Review* (8, 4, 1983:588–599).

Brinton, C. *The Anatomy of Revolution* (New York: Vintage Books, 1938).

Broms, H., and Gahmberg, H. *Semiotics of Management* (Helsinki School of Economics, 1987).

Brook, P. *The Empty Spare* (Markham, Ont.: Penguin Books, 1968).

Brown, J. S., and Duguid, P. "Organizational Learning and Communities-of-Practice: Toward A Unified View of Working, Learning and Innovation." *Organization Science* (2, 1991:40–57).

Brown, S. L., and Eisenhardt, K. M. *Competing on the Edge: Strategy as Structured Chaos* (Harvard Business School Press, 1998).

Bruner, J. S., Goodnow, J. J., and Austin, G. A. *A Study of Thinking* (New York: John Wiley, 1956).

Brunsson, N. *Propensity to Change: An Empirical Study of Decisions on Reorientations* (Göteborg: BAS, 1976).

Brunsson, N. "The Irrationality of Action and the Action Rationality: Decisions, Ideologies, and Organizational Actions." *Journal of Management Studies* (1, 1982:29–44).

Burgelman, R. A. "Managing Innovating Systems: A Study of the Process of Internal Corporate Venturing" (Ph.D. dissertation, Graduate School of Business, Columbia University, 1980).

Burgelman, R. A. "A Process Model of Internal Corporate Venturing in the Diversified Major Firm." *Administrative Science Quarterly* (28, 1983a:223–244).

Burgelman, R. A. "A Model of the Interaction of Strategic Behavior, Corporate Context, and the Concept of Strategy." *Academy of Management Review* (8, 1, 1983b:61–70).

Burgelman, R. A. "Strategy Making as a Social Learning Process: The Case of Internal Corporate Venturing." *Interfaces* (18, 3, May–June 1988:74–85).

Burgelman, R. A. "A Process Model of Strategic Business Exit: Implications for an Evolutionary Perspective on Strategy." *Strategic Management Journal* (17, 1996:193–214).

Burgelman, R. A., and Sayles, L. R. *Inside Corporate Innovation: Strategy, Structure, and Managerial Skills* (New York: Free Press, 1986).

Busenitz, L. W., and Barney, J. B. "Differences Between Entrepreneurs and Managers in Large Organizations: Biases and Heuristics in Strategic Decision-Making." *Journal of Business Venturing* (12, 1997:9–30).

Business Week, "The New Breed of Strategic Planner" (September 17, 1984:62–66, 68).

Buzzell, R. D., Bradley, T. G., and Sultan, R. G. M. "Market Share: A Key to Profitability." *Harvard Business Review* (January-February 1975:97–111).

Carson, P., Lanier, P., Carson, K., and Guidry, B. "Clearing a Path through the Management Fashion Jungle: Some Preliminary Trailblazing" *Academy of Management Journal* (43, 6, 2000:1143–1158).

Casson, M. "Entrepreneurship and the Theory of the Firm." *Journal of Economic Behavior and Organization* (58, 2, 2005:327–348).

Chaffee, E. E. "Three Models of Strategy." *Academy of Management Review* (10, 1, 1985:89–98)

Chandler, A. D. Jr. *Strategy and Structure: Chapters in the History of the Industrial Enterprise* (Cambridge, MA: MIT Press, 1962).

Chandler, A. D. "The Functions of the HQ Unit in the Multi-business Firm." *Strategic Management Journal* (12, 8, 1991:31–50).

Christensen, C. R., Andrews, K. R., Bower, J. L., Hamermesh, G., and Porter, M. E. *Business Policy: Text and Cases,* 5th edition (Homewood, IL: Irwin, 1982).

Clark, E. "Power, Action and Constraint in Strategic Management: Explaining Enterprise Restructuring in the Czech Republic." *Organization Studies* (25, 4, 2004: 607–627).

Clausewitz, C. von. *On War* (Penguin Books, 1968).

Clausewitz, C. von. *On War* (Princeton, NJ: Princeton University Press, 1989).

Clemmer, J. *Pathways to Performance: A Guide to Transforming Yourself, Your Team, and Your Organization* (Toronto: Macmillan Canada, 1995).

Coffey, W. *303 of the World's Worst Predictions* (New York: Tribeca Communications, 1983).

Cohen, M. D., March, J. G., and Olsen, J. P. "A Garbage Can Model of Organizational Choice." *Administrative Science Quarterly* (17, 1, March 1972:1–25).

Cole, A. H. *Business Enterprise in Its Social Setting* (Cambridge, MA: Harvard University Press, 1959).

Collins, O., and Moore D. G. *The Organization Makers* (New York: Appleton-Century-Crofts, 1970).

Collins, J. C., and Porras, J. I. "Organizational Vision and Visionary Organizations." *California Management Review* (Fall 1991:30–52).

Collins, J. C. and Porras, J. I. *Built to Last: Successful Habits of Visionary Companies* (New York: Harper Business, 1997).

Collis, D., and Rukstad, M. G. "Can You Say What Your Strategy Is?" *Harvard Business Review* (86, 4, 2008:82–90).

Conner, K. R., and Prahalad, C. K. "A Resource-Based Theory of the Firm: Knowledge Versus Opportunism." *Organization Science* (7, 5 [September-October] 1996:477–501).

Connolly, T. "On Taking Action Seriously: Cognitive Fixation in Behavioral Decision Theory." In G. R. Ungdon and D. N. Braunstein, eds., *Decision-Making: An Interdisciplinary Inquiry* (Boston: Kent, 1982:42–47).

Cornelius, P., Van de Putte, A., and Romani, M. "Three Decades of Scenario Planning in Shell." *California Management Review* (48, 1, 2005:92–109).

Corner, P. D., Kinicki, A. J., and Keats, B. W. "Integrating Organizational and Individual Information Processing Perspectives on Choice." *Organization Science* (3, 1994:294–308).

Cornford, F. M. Microcosmo-graphia Academica (Cambridge, UK: Mainsail Press, 1993:39).

Cressey, P., Eldridge, J., and MacInnes, J. *"Just Managing": Authority and Democracy in Industry* (Milton Keynes, England: Open University Press, 1985).

Crossan, M., Lane, H., and White, R. "An Organizational Learning Framework: From Intuition to Institution." *Academy of Management Review* (24, 3, 1999:522–537).

Cyert, R. M., and March, J. G. *A Behavioral Theory of the Firm* (Englewood Cliffs, NJ: Prentice Hall, 1963).

Dacin, M. T., Goodstein, J., and Scott, W. R. "Institutional Theory and Institutional Change: Introduction to the Special Research Forum." *Academy of Management Journal* (45, 1, 2002:45–57).

Dane, E., and Pratt, M. "Exploring Intuition and its Role in Managerial Decision Making." *Academy of Management Review* (32, 1, 2007:33–54).

Darwin, F., ed. *The Life and Letters of Charles Darwin, Including an Autobiographical Chapter*, 3 vols. (London: John Murray, 1887).

Das, T. K., and Teng, B. "Cognitive Biases and Strategic Decision Processes: An Integrative Perspective." *Journal of Management Studies* (36, 1999:757–778).

Davenport, S., and Leitch, S. "Circuits of Power in Practice: Strategic Ambiguity as Delegation of Authority." *Organization Studies* (26, 11, 2005:1603–1623).

D'Aveni, R. A. *Hypercompetiton: Managing the Dynamics of Strategic Maneuvering* (New York: The Free Press, 1994).

De Geus, A. P. "Planning as Learning." *Harvard Business Review* (March-April 1988:70–74).

Denrell, J. "Selection Bias and the Perils of Benchmarking." *Harvard Business Review* (83, 4, 2005:114–119).

Devons, E. *Planning in Practice, Essays in Aircraft Planning in War-Time* (Cambridge, England: The University Press, 1950).

Dickhout, R., Denham, M., and Blackwell, N. "Designing Change Programs That Won't Cost You Your Job." *The McKinsey Quarterly* (4, 1995:101–116).

Dixit, A. K., and Pindyck, R. S. "The Options Approach to Capital Investment." *Harvard Business Review* (73, 3, 1995:105–115).

Dobbin, F., and Sutton, J. R. "The Strength of a Weak State: The Rights Revolution and the Rise of Human Resources Management Divisions." *American Journal of Sociology* (104, 1998:441–476).

Dollinger, M. J. "The Evolution of Collective Strategies in Fragmented Industries." *Academy of Management Review* (15, 2, 1990:266–285).

Donaldson, L. "For Cartesianism: Against Organizational Types and Quantum Jumps." In *For Positivist Organization Theory: Proving the Hard Core* (London: Sage, 1996:108–129).

Donaldson, L. *The Contingency Theory of Organizations* (Thousand Oaks, CA: Sage, 2001).

Downing, S. "The Social Construction of Entrepreneurship: Narrative and Dramatic Processes in the Coproduction of Organizations and Identities." *Entrepreneurship: Theory and Practice* (29, 2, 2005:185–204).

Doz, Y. L., and Thanheiser, H. "Embedding Transformational Capability." ICEDR, October 1996 Forum Embedding Transformation Capabilities (INSEAD, Fontainebleau, France, 1996).

Drucker, P. F. "Entrepreneurship in Business Enterprise." *Journal of Business Policy* (I, 1, 1970:3–12).

Drucker, P. F. "The Theory of the Business." *Harvard Business Review* (September-October, 1994:95–104).

Duhaime, I. M., and Schwenk, C. R. "Conjectures on Cognitive Simplification in Acquisition and Divestment Decision Making." *Academy of Management Review* (10, 2, 1985:257–295).

Durand, R. "Firm Selection: An Integrative Perspective." *Organization Studies* (22, 3, 2001:393–417)

Dutton, J. E., Ashford, S. J., O'Neil, R. M., and Hayes, E. "Reading the Wind: How Middle Managers Assess the Context for Selling Issues to Top Managers." *Strategic Management Journal* (18, 5, 1997:407–425).

Dyck, B. "Understanding Configuration and Transformation through a Multiple Rationalities Approach, *Journal of Management Studies*" (34, 5, 1997:793–823).

Economist, "The Return of von Clausewitz—The Fine Art of Being Prepared." (March 9, 2002).

Edwards, J. "Strategy Formulation as a Stylistic Process." *International Studies of Management and Organizations* (7, 2, Summer 1977:13–27).

Eisenhardt, K. M., and Martin, J. A. "Dynamic Capabilities: What are They?" In C. E. Helfat, ed., *The SMS Blackwell Handbook of Organizational Capabilities: Emergence, Development, and Change* (Blackwell: Oxford, 2003:341–363).

Eisenhardt, K. M., and Sull, D. N. "Strategy as Simple Rules." *Harvard Business Review* (79, 1, 2001:107–116).

El Sawy, O. A., and Pauchant, T. C. "Triggers, Templates, and Twitches in the Tracking of Emerging Strategic Issues." *Strategic Management Journal* (9, September-October 1988:455–474).

Eliot, O. *Felix Holt, The Radical* (Oxford: Clarendon Press, 1980).

Engwall, L. "The Viking Versus the World: An Examination of Nordic Business Research." *Scandinavian Journal of Management* (12, 4, 1996:425–436).

Fadiman, C., ed. *The Little Brown Book of Anecdotes* (Boston: Little, Brown, 1985).

Farjoun, M. "Towards an Organic Perspective on Strategy." *Strategic Management Journal* (23, 2002:561–594).

Feld, M. D. "Information and Authority: The Structure of Military Organization." *American Sociological Review* (24, 1, 1959:15–22).

Feldman, S. P. "Management in Context: An Essay on the Relevance of Culture to the Understanding of Organizational Change." *Journal of Management Studies* (23, 6, 1986:587–607).

Feldman, M. S., and Rafaeli, A. "Organizational Routines as Sources of Connections and Understandings." *Journal of Management Studies* (39, 3, 2002:3019–331).

Finkelstein S. "Power in Top Management Teams: Dimensions, Measurement, and Validation." *Academy of Management Journal* (35, 1992:505–538).

Firsirotu, M. "Strategic Turnaround as Cultural Revolution" (doctoral dissertation, McGill University, Faculty of Management, Montreal, 1985).

Floyd, S. W., and Wooldridge, B. "Dinosaurs or dynamos? Recognizing Middle Management's Strategic Role." *Academy of Management Executive* (8, 4, 1994:47–57).

Fombrun, C., and Astley, W. G. "Strategies of Collection Action: The Case of the Financial Services Industry," R. Lamb (ed.) *Advances in Strategic Management, Volume 2* (Greenwich, CT.: JAI Press, 1983:125–139).

Fortune, "GM's $11 Billion Turnaround" (130, 8, October 17, 1994:54–69).

Fortune, "The Entrepreneurial Ego" (65, 2, August 1956:143).

Fortune, "14 INNOVATORS Staying Creative, Jazzing Employees, Keeping That Startup Vibe, and Other Tales From the Front "(November, 15, 2004).

Freeman, R. E. *Strategic Management: A Stakeholder Approach* (London: Pitman, 1984).

Frery, F. "The Fundamental Dimensions of Strategy." *MIT Sloan Management Review* (48, 1, Fall 2006:71–75).

Gaddis, P. O. "Strategy Under Attack," *Long Range Planning* (30, 1, 1997:38–45).

Gagliardi, P., ed., *Symbols and Artifacts: View from the Corporate Landscape* (New York: Aldine de Gruyter, 1992).

Garud, R. G., Kumaraswamy, A., and Nayyar, P. "Real Options Or Fool's Gold? Perspective Makes the Difference." *Academy of Management Review* (23, 2, 1998:212–214).

Gartner, J. "America's Manic Entrepreneurs." *American Enterprise* (16, 5, 2005:18).

Garvin, D. A., and Levesque, L. C. "Meeting the Challenge of Corporate Entrepreneurship." *Harvard Business Review* (84, 10, 2006:102–112).

Gavetti, G., and Levinthal, D. A. "The Strategy Field from the Perspective Management Science: Divergent Strands and Possible Integration." *Management Science* (50, 10, 2004:1309–1318).

Gerhard, D. "Periodization in European History." *American Historical Review* (61, 1956:900–913).

Gilbert, X., and Strebel, P. "Developing Competitive Advantage." In J. B. Quinn, Mintzberg, H., and James, R., eds., *The Strategy Process* (Englewood Cliffs, NJ: Prentice Hall, 1988:82–93).

Gimpl, M. L., and Dakin, S. R. "Management and Magic." *California Management Review* (Fall 1984:125–136).

Glaister, K., and Falshaw, J. R. "Strategic Planning: Still Going Strong?" *Long Range Planning* (32, 1, 1999:107–116).

Goffee, R., and Jones, G. "What Holds the Modern Company Together." *Harvard Business Review* (74, 6, 1996:133–148).

Goold, M. "Design, Learning and Planning: A Further Observation on The Design School Debate." *Strategic Management Journal* (13, 1992:169–170).

Goold, M. "Learning, Planning, and Strategy: Extra Time." *California Management Review* (38, 4, Summer 1996:100–102).

Goold, M., and Campbell, A. *Strategies and Styles: The Role of the Center in Managing Diversified Corporations* (Oxford: Basil Blackwell, 1987).

Goold, M., and Quinn, J. J. "The Paradox of Strategic Controls." *Strategic Management Journal* (11, 1990:43–57).

Goold, M., Campbell, A., and Alexander, M. *Corporate-Level Strategy: Creating Value in the Multi-Business Company* (New York: John Wiley & Sons, 1994).

Gould, S. J. *The Panda's Thumb* (New York: W. W. Norton, 1980).

Gould, S. J. "Free to Be Extinct." *Natural History* (August 1982:12–16).

Greene, R., and Elffers, J. *The 48 Laws of Power* (New York: Viking Penguin, a division of Penguin Group (USA) Inc, 1998).

Greve, H., and Mitsuhashi, H. "Powerful and Free: Intra-Organizational Power and the Dynamics of Corporate Strategy." *Strategic Organization* (2, 2, May 2004:107–132).

Greve, H., and Mitsuhashi, H. "Power and Glory: Concentrated Power in Top Management Teams." *Organization Studies* (28, 8, 2007:1197–1221).

Grinyer, P. H., and Spender, J. C. *Turnaround—Managerial Recipes for Strategic Success* (London: Associated Business Press, 1979).

Gulati, R. "Alliances and networks." *Strategic Management Journal* (19, 4, 1998:293–313).

Hadamard, J. *An Essay on the Psychology of Invention in the Mathematical Field* (Princeton, NJ: University Press, 1949).

Hage, J. "Choosing Constraints and Constraining Choice" (paper presented at the Anglo-French Conference at the Tavistock Institute, London, 1976).

Hakansson, H., and Snehota, I. "No Business is an Island: The Network Concept of Business Strategy." *Scandinavian Journal of Management* (5, 3, 1989:187–200).

Halberstam, D. *The Reckoning* (New York: Avon Books, 1986).

Hambrick, D. C. "Upper Echelons Theory: An Update." *Academy of Management Review* (32, 2, 2007:334–343).

Hambrick, D. C., and Fredrickson, J. W. "Are You Sure You Have a Strategy?" *Academy of Management Executive* (19, 4, 2005:51–62).

Hambrick, D. C., and Mason, P. "Upper Echelons: The Organization as a Reflection of its Top Managers." *Academy of Management Review* (9, 2, 1984:193–206).

Hamel, G. "Strategy as Revolution." *Harvard Business Review* (July-August, 1996:69–82).

Hamel, G. "Strategy Innovation and the Quest for Value." *Sloan Management Review* (39, 4, Winter 1998:7–14).

Hamel, G., and Prahalad, C. K. "Strategic Intent." *Harvard Business Review* (May-June 1989:63–76).

Hamel, G., and Prahalad, C. K. "Strategy as Stretch and Leverage." *Harvard ard Business Review* (71, 2, March-April 1993:75–84).

Hamel, G., and Prahalad, C. K. "Competing for the Future." *Harvard Business Review* (72, 4, 1994:122–128).

Hamel, G., and Prahalad, C. K. *Competing for the Future* (Boston: Harvard Business School Press, 1994).

Hamel, G., and Prahalad, C. K. "Competing in the New Economy: Managing Out of Bounds." *Strategic Management Journal* (17, 1996:237–242).

Hamel, G., Doz, Y. L., and Prahalad, C. K. "Collaborate with Your Competitors and Win." *Harvard Business Review* (January-February 1989:133–139).

Hamermesh, R. G. *Making Strategy Wok: How Senior Managers Produce Results* (New York: Wiley, 1986).

Hannan, M. T. "Ecologies of Organizations: Diversity and Identity." *The Journal of Economic Perspectives* (19, 1:2005:51–70).

Hannan, M. T., and Freeman, J. "The Population Ecology of Organizations." *American Journal of Sociology* (82, 5, 1977:929–964).

Hannan, M. T., and Freeman, J. "Structural Inertia and Organizational Change." *American Sociological Review* (49, April 1984:149–164).

Harbison, F., and Myers, C. A. *Management in the Industrial World* (New York: McGraw-Hill, 1959).

Hardy, C., Langley, A., Mintzberg, H., and Rose, J. "Strategy Formation in the University Setting." *The Review of Higher Education* (6, 1983:407–433).

Hart, S. "Intentionality and Autonomy in Strategy-Making Process: Modes, Archetypes, and Firm Performance." *Advances in Strategic Management* (7, 1991:97–127).

Hatten, K. J., and Schendel, D. E. "Heterogeneity within an Industry: Firm Conduct in the U.S. Brewing Industry, 1952–1971." *Journal of Industrial Economics* (26, 1977:97–113).

Hayes, R. H. "Strategic Planning—Forward in Reverse?" *Harvard Business Review* (November-December 1985:111–119).

Hayes, R. H., and Jaikumar, R. "Manufacturing's Crisis: New Technologies, Obsolete Organizations." *Harvard Business Review* (September-October 1988:77–85).

Hedberg, B. "Organizational Stagnation and Choice of Strategy: Observations from Case Studies" (working paper, International Institute of Management, Berlin, 1973).

Hedberg, B. "Reframing as a Way to Cope with Organizational Stagnation: A Case Study" (working paper, International Institute of Management, Berlin, 1974).

Hedberg, B. "How Organizations Learn and Unlearn." In P. C. Nystrom and W. H. Starbuck, eds., *Handbook of Organizational Design*, Vol. 1: *Adapting Organizations to Their Environments* (New York: Oxford University Press, 1981:3–27).

Hedberg, B., and Jonsson, S. A. "Strategy Formulation as a Discontinuous Process." *International Studies of Management and Organization* (7, 2, Summer 1977:88–109).

Hedberg, B., and Targama, A. "Organizational Stagnation, a Behavioral Approach." *Proceedings of the Conference, TIMS XX* (1973:635–641).

Helfat, C. E., Finkelstein, S., Mitchell, W., Peteraf, M. A., Singh, H., Teece, D. J., and Winter, S. G. *Dynamic Capabilities: Understanding Strategic Change in Organizations* (Oxford, Blackwell Publishing, 2007).

Hellagren, B., and Melin, L. "The Role of Strategists' Ways-of-Thinking in Strategic Change Processes." In J. Hendry, G. Johnson, and J. Newton, eds., *Strategic Thinking: Leadership and the Management of Change* (Chichester: John Wiley, 1993:47–68).

Henderson, A. D. "Firm Strategy and Age Dependence: A Contingent View of the Liabilities of Newness, Adolescence, and Obsolescence." *Administrative Science Quarterly* (44, 2, 1999:281–314).

Henderson, B. D. "The Experience Curve-Reviewed. IV. The Growth Share Matrix, or The Product Portfolio." *Boston Consulting Group Reprint 135*. (1973).

Henderson, B. D. *Henderson on Corporate Strategy* (Cambridge, MA: Abt Books, 1979).

Herrman, P. "Evolution of Strategic Management: The Need for New Dominant Designs." *International Journal of Management Review* (7, 2, 2005:111–130).

Hill, T., and Westbrook, R. "SWOT Analysis: It's Time for a Product Recall." *Long Range Planning* (30, 1, 1997:46–52).

Hirsch, P. M. "Organizational Effectiveness and the Institutional Environment." *Administration Science Quarterly* (20, September 1975:327–344).

Hogarth, R. M., and Makridakis, S. "Forecasting and Planning: An Evaluation." *Management Science* (27, 2 [February] 1981:115–138).

Hopwood, B. *Whatever Happened to the British Motorcycle Industry?* (San Leandro, CA: Haynes Publishing, 1981).

Hoskisson, R. E., Hitt, M. A., Wan, W. P., and Yiu, D. "Theory and Research In Strategic Management: Swings of A Pendulum." *Journal of Management* (25, 3, 1999:417–456).

Huff, A. S., ed. *Mapping Strategic Thought* (Somerset, NJ: Wiley, 1990).

Hunt, M. S. "Competition in the Major Home Appliance Industry, 1960–1970" (doctoral dissertation, Harvard University, 1972).

Hurst, D. "Changing Management Metaphors—To Hell with the Helmsman" (unpublished manuscript).

Hurst, D. K. *Crisis & Renewal: Meeting the Challenge of Organizational Change* (Boston: Harvard Business School Press, 1995).

Hutzschenreuter, T., and Kleindienst, I. "Strategy-Process Research: What Have We Learned and What Is Still to Be Explored." *Journal of Management* (32, 5, 2006:673–720).

Huy, Q. "In Praise of Middle Managers." *Harvard Business Review* (79, September, 2001: 72–79).

Iansiti, M., and Levien, R. "Strategy as Ecology." *Harvard Business Review* (82, 3, 2004:68–78).

Inkpen, A., and Chouldhury, N. "The Seeking of Strategy Where It Is Not: Toward a Theory of Strategy Absence." *Strategic Management Journal* (16, 1995:313–323).

Itami, H., with T. W. Roehl. *Mobilzing Invisible Assets* (Cambridge, MA: Harvard University Press, 1987).

James, B. G. "Reality and the Fight for Market Position." *Journal of General Management.*" (Spring, 1985:45–57).

Janis, I. L. *Victims of Groupthink* (Boston: Houghton Mifflin, 1972).

Jarzabkowski, P., Balogun, J., and Seidl, D. "Strategizing: The Challenges of a Practice Perspective." *Human Relations* (60, 1, 2007:5–27).

Jelinek, M. *Institutionalizing Innovation: A Study of Organizational Learning Systems* (New York: Praeger, 1979).

Jelinek, M., and Amar, D. "Implementing Corporate Strategy: Theory and Reality" (paper presented at the Third Annual Conference of the Strategic Management Society, Paris, 1983).

Jelinek, M., and Schoonhoven, C. B. *The Innovation Marathon: Lessons from High-Technology Firms* (Oxford: Basil Blackwell, 1990).

John K., and Pomerantz, G. "USFL Is Awarded $1 In Suit Against NFL Young League Had Sought $1.69 Billion." *Washington Post* (July 30, 1986).

Johnson, G. *Strategic Change and the Management Process* (New York: Basil Blackwell, 1987).

Johnson, G. "Managing Strategic Change—Strategy, Culture and Action." *Long Range Planning* (25, 1, 1992:28–36).

Johnson, G., and Huff, A. S. "Everyday Innovation/Everyday Strategy." In G. Hamel, C. K. Prahalad, H. Thomas and D. O'Neal., eds., *Strategic Flexibility: Managing in a Turbulent Environment* (New York: John Wiley & Sons Inc., 1998:13–27).

Johnson, G., Melin, L., and Whittington, R. "Micro Strategy and Strategizing: Towards an Activity-Based View?" *Journal of Management Studies* (40, 1, 2003:1–22).

Jonsson, S. A. "City Administration Facing Stagnation: Political Organizational and Action in Gothenburg" (Swedish Council for Building Research, no date).

Jonsson, S. A., and Lundin, R. A. "Myths and Wishful Thinking as Management Tools." In P. C. Nystrom and W. H. Starbuck, eds., *Prescriptive Models of Organizations* (Amsterdam: North-Holland, 1977:157–170).

Jonsson, S. A., Lundin, R. A., and Sjoberg, L. "Frustration in Decision Processes: A Tentative Frame of Reference." *International Studies of Management and Organization* (Fall-Winter 1977–1978:6–19).

Kaplan, R., and Norton D. *The Balanced Scorecard: Translating Strategy Into Action* (Harvard Business School Publishing, 1996).

Kaplan, R. and Norton, D. *The Strategy-Focused Organization: How Balanced Scorecard Companies Thrive in the New Business Environment* (Harvard Business School Publishing, 2000).

Katz, R. L. *Cases and Concepts in Corporate Strategy* (Englewood Cliffs, NJ: Prentice Hall, 1970).

Keller, M., *Rude Awakening: The Rise, Fall and Struggle for Recovery of General Motors* (New York: Morrow, 1989).

Kennedy, J., and Pomerantz, G. "USFL Is Awarded $1 In Suit Against NFL Young League Had Sought $1.69 Billion." *Washington Post.* (30 July 1986).

Ketchen, D. J., Combs, J. G., Russell, C. J., Shook, C., Dean, M. A., Runge, J., Lohrke, F. T., Naumann, S. E., Haptonstahl, D. E., Baker, R., Beckstein, B. A., Handler, C., Honig, H., and Lamoureux, S. "Organizational Configurations and Performance: A Meta-Analysis." *Academy of Management Journal* (40, 1:223–240).

Ketokivi, M., and Castañer, X. "Strategic Planning as an Integrative Device." *Administrative Science Quarterly* (49, 3, 2004:337–365).

Kets de Vries, M. F. R. "The Entrepreneurial Personality: A Person at the Crossroads." *Journal of Management Studies* (February 1977:34–57).

Kets de Vries, M. F. R. "The Dark Side Entrepreneurship." *Harvard Business Review* (November-December 1985:160–167).

Keys, J. B., and Miller, T. R. "The Japanese Management Theory Jungle." *Academy of Management Review* (9, 2, 1984:342–353).

Khandwalla, P. N. "The Effect of the Environment on the Organizational Structure of Firm" (doctoral dissertation, Cambridge-Mellon University, 1970).

Kiechel, W. III. "Sniping at Strategic Planning." *Planning Review* (May 1984:8–11).

Kiesler, C. A. *The Psychology of Commitment: Experiments Linking Behavior to Belief* (New York: Academic Press, 1971).

Kirzner, I. "Entrepreneurial Discovery and the Competitive Market Process: An Austrian Approach." *Journal of Economic Literature* (35, 1997:60–85).

Knight, K. E. "A Descriptive Model of the Intra-Firm Innovation Process." *Journal of Business of the University of Chicago* (40, 1967:478–496).

Knuf, J. "Benchmarking the lean enterprise: Organizational learning at work." *Journal of Management in Engineering* (16, 4, 2000:58–72).

Kogut, B., and Zander, U. "What Firms Do? Coordination, Identity, and Learning." *Organization Science* (7, 5 [September-October] 1996:502–518).

Kohler, W. *The Mentality of Apes* (New York: Humanitarian Press, 1925).

Kotler, P., and Singh, R. "Marketing Warfare in the 1980's." *Journal of Business Strategy* (Winter 1981:30–41).

Kotter, J. P. "Leading Change: Why Transformation Efforts Fail." *Harvard Business Review* (March-April, 1995:59–67).

Kress, G., Koehler, G., and Springer, J. F. "Policy Drift: An Evaluation of the California Business Program." *Police Sciences Journal* (3, Special Issue, 1980:1101–1108).

Lampel, J. "Rules in the Shadow of the Future: Prudential Rule Making Under Ambiguity in the Aviation Industry." *International Relations* (20, 3, 2006:343–349).

Lampel, J., and Bhalla, A. "Let's Get Natural: Communities of Practice and the Discourse of Spontaneous Sharing in Knowledge Management." *Management Decision* (45, 7, 2007:1069–1082).

Lampel, J., and Bhalla, A. "Embracing Realism and Recognizing Choice In Its Offshoring Initiatives." *Business Horizons* (51, 5, 2008).

Lampel, J., and Shamsie, J. "Probing the Unobtrusive Link: Dominant Logic and the Design of Joint Ventures by General Electric." *Strategic Management Journal* (21, 2000:593–602).

Lampel, J., and Shamsie, J. "Capabilities in Motion: New Organizational Forms and the Reshaping of the Hollywood Movie Industry." *Journal of Management Studies* (40, 8, 2003: 2189–2210).

Lampel, J., and Shapira, Z. "Judgmental Errors, Interactive Norms and the Difficulty of Detecting Strategic Surprises." *Organization Science* (12, 5, 2001:599–611).

Land, E. "The Most Basis Form of Creativity." *Time* (June 26, 1972:84).

Langley, A. "Between 'Paralysis by Analysis' and 'Extinction by Instinct'." *Sloan Management Review* (36, 3, 1995:63–76).

Langley, A. "Patterns in the Use of Formal Analysis in Strategic Decisions." *Organization Studies* (11, 1, 1990:17–45).

Langley, A., Mintzberg, H., Pitcher, P., Posada, E., and Saint-Macary, J. "Opening Up Decision Making: The View from the Black Stool." *Organization Science* (May-June 1995).

Lapierre, R. *Le Changement Stratégique: Un Rêve en Quête de Réel* (Ph.D. Management Policy course paper, McGill University, 1980).

Lauriol, J. "Une analyse des représentations de la stratégie et de son management dans la production d'ouvreges de la langue française (prepared for La Journeé Recherche of AIMS, for FNEGE, in France, 11 October 1996).

Lawrence, T. B., Mauws, M. K., Dyck, B., and Kleysen, R. F. "The Politics of Organizational Learning: Integrating Power Into the 4I Framework." *Academy of Management Review* (30, 1, 2005:180–191).

Learned, E. P., Christensen, C. R., Andrews, K. R., and Guth, W. D. *Business Policy: Text and Cases* (Homewood, IL: Irwin, 1965).

Levitt, T. "Marketing Myopia." *Harvard Business Review* (July-August 1960:45–56).

Levy, D. "Chaos Theory and Strategy: Theory, Application, and Managerial Implications." *Strategic Management Journal* (15, 1994:167–178).

Lewin, K. *Field Theory in Social Science* (New York: Harper & Row, 1951).

Liedtka, J. "Strategy as a 'Little Black Dress'." In H. Mintzberg, B. Ahlstrand, and J. Lampel eds., *Strategy Bites Back: It is Far More and Less, Than you Ever Imagined...*" (Edinburgh Gate, Harlow: Prentice Hall, Financial Times, 2005:41–43).

Lindblom, C. E. "The Science of Muddling Through." *Public Administration Review* (19, 2, 1959:79–88).

Lindblom, C. E. *The Policy-Making Process* (Englewood Cliffs, NJ: Prentice Hall, 1968).

Lipsky, M. "Standing the Study of Public Policy Implementation on Its Head." In W. D. Burnham and M. W. Weinberg, eds., *American Politics and Public Policy* (Cambridge, MA: MIT Press, 1978:391–402).

Livingston, J. S. "The Myth of the Well-Educated Manager." *Harvard Business Review* (49, 1, January-February 1971:79–89).

Lorange, P. "Formal Planning Systems: Their Role in Strategy Formulation and Implementation." In D. E. Schendel and C. W. Hofer, eds., *Strategic Management: A New View of Business Policy and Planning* (Boston: Little, Brown, 1979).

Lorange, P. *Corporate Planning: An Executive Viewpoint* (Englewood Cliffs, NJ: Prentice Hall, 1980).

Lorange, P., and Vancil, R. F. *Strategic Planning Systems* (Englewood Cliffs, NJ: Prentice Hall, 1977).

Lorenz, B. N. *The Essence of Chaos* (Seattle: University of Washington Press, 1993).

Lorsch, J. W. "Managing Culture: The Invisible Barrier to Strategic Change." *California Management Journal* (28, 2, Winter 1986:95–109).

Lovallo, D. P., and Mendonca, L. T. "Strategy's Strategist: An Interview with Richard Rumelt". *Harvard Business Review* (4, 2007:56–67).

Lyles, M. A. "A Research Agenda for Strategic Management in the 1990s." *Journal of Management Studies* (27, 4, 1990:363–375).

Macmillan, I. C. *Strategy Formulation: Political Concepts* (St. Paul: West, 1978).

Macmillan, I. C., and Guth, W. D. "Strategy Implementation and Middle Management Coalitions." In R. Lamb and P. Shrivastava, eds., *Advances in Strategic Management*, Vol. 3 (Greenwich, CT: JAI Press, 1985:233–254).

Majone, G., and Wildavsky, A. "Implementation as Evolution." *Policy Studies Review Annual* (2, 1978:103–117).

Makridakis, S. *Forecasting, Planning, and Strategy for the 21st Century* (New York: Free Press, 1990); also extracts from 1979 draft.

Malmlow, E. G. "Corporate Strategic Planning in Practice." *Long Range Planning* (5, 3, 1972:2–9).

March, J. G., and Olsen, J. P., eds. Ambiguity and Choice in Organizations (Bergen, Norway: Universitetsforlaget, 1976).

March, J. G., and Simon, H. A. *Organizations* (New York: John Wiley, 1958).

Marsh, P., Barwise, P., Thomas, K., and Wensley, R. "Managing Strategic Investment Decisions in Large Diversified Companies" (Centre for Business Strategy Report Series, London Business School, 1988).

Martinet, A. C. "Pensée strategique et rationalitiés: Un examen épistémologique" (papier de recherche numéro 23, Institut d'Administration des Enterprise, Lyon, France, 1996).

McClelland, D. C. *The Achieving Society* (Princeton, NJ: D. Van Nostrand, 1961).

McConnell, J. D. "Strategic Planning: One Workable Approach." *Long Range Planning* (4, 2, 1971:2–6).

McGahan, A., and Porter, M. E. "How Much Does Industry Matter, Really?" *Strategic Management Journal* (18, 1997:15–30).

McGee, J., and Thomas, H. "Strategic Groups: A Useful Linkage Between Industry Structure and Strategic Management." *Strategic Management Journal* (7, 1986:141–160).

McGrath, R. G., and Macmillan, I. "Assessing Technology Projects Using Real Options Reasoning." *Research Technology Management.* (43, 4, 2000:35–50).

Mechanic, D. "Sources of Power of Lower Participants in Complex Organizations." *Administrative Science Quarterly* (1962:349–364).

Melin, L. "Structure, Strategy and Organization: A Case of Decline" (paper for an EIASM-workshop, Strategic Management under Limited Growth and Decline, Brussels, 1982).

Melin, L. "Implementation of New Strategies and Structures" (paper for the Third Annual Strategic Management Society Conference, Paris, 1983).

Melin, L. "Strategies in Managing Turnaround." *Long Range Planning* (18, 1, 1985:80–86).

Meyer, J. W., and Rowan, B. "Institutionalized Organizations: Formal Structure as Myth and Ceremony." *American Journal of Sociology* (83, 1977:340–363).

Miles, R. E., and Snow, C. C. *Organization Strategy, Structure, and Process* (New York: McGraw-Hill, 1978).

Miles, R. E., and Snow, C. C. *Fit, Failure and the Hall of Fame* (New York: Macmillan, 1994).

Miles, R. E., Snow, C. C., Meyer, A. D., and Coleman, H. J., Jr. "Organizational Strategy, Structure, and Process." *American Management Review* (July 1978:546–562).

Miles, R. H. *Coffin Nails and Corporate Strategies* (Englewood Cliffs, NJ: Prentice Hall, 1982).

Miller, D. "Strategy Making in Context: Ten Empirical Archetypes" (Ph.D. thesis, Faculty of Management, McGill University, Montreal, 1976).

Miller, D. "Strategy, Structure, and Environment: Context Influences upon Some Bivariate Associations." *Journal of Management Studies* (16 [October] 1979:294–316).

Miller, D. "Evolution and Resolution: A Quantum View of Structural Change in Organizations." *Journal of Management Studies* (19, 1982:131–151).

Miller, D. "The Correlates of Entrepreneurship in Three Types of Firms." *Management Science* (29, 1983:770–791).

Miller, D. "Configurations of Strategy and Structure: Towards a Synthesis." *Strategic Management Journal* (7, 1986:233–249).

Miller, D. *The Icarus Paradox* (New York: Harper Business, 1990).

Miller, D. "The Generic Strategy Trap." *Journal of Business Strategy* (13, 1 [January-February] 1992:37–41).

Miller, D. "Configurations Revisited." *Strategic Management Journal* (17, 1996:505–512).

Miller, D., and Friesen, P. H. "Strategy-Making in Context: Ten Empirical Archetypes." *Journal of Management Studies* (14, 1977:253–279).

Miller, D., and Friesen, P. H. "Archetypes of Strategy Formulation." *Management Science* (24, 9, 1978:921–933).

Miller, D., and Friesen, P. H. "Momentum and Revolution in Organizational Adaptation." *Academy of Management Journal* (23, 1980a:591–614).

Miller, D., and Friesen, P. H. "Archetypes of Organizational Transition." *Administrative Science Quarterly* (25, 1980b:268–299).

Miller, D., and Friesen, P. H. "Structural Change and Performance: Quantum Versus Piecemeal-Incremental Approaches." *Academy of Management Journal* (25, 4, 1982a:867–892).

Miller, D., and Friesen, P. H. "Strategy-Making and Environment: The Third Link." *Strategic Management Journal* (4, 1982b:221–235).

Miller, D., and Friesen, P. H. "Successful and Unsuccessful Phases of the Corporate Life Cycle." *Organization Studies* (4, 4, 1982c:339–356).

Miller, D., and Friesen, P. H. *Organizations: A Quantum View* (Englewood Cliffs, NJ: Prentice Hall, 1984).

Miller, D., and Mintzberg, H. "The Case for Configuration." In G. Morgan, ed., *Beyond Method* (Beverly Hills: Sage, 1983).

Miller, D., and Shamsie, J. "The Resource-Based View of the Firm in Two Environments: The Hollywood Film Studios from 1936 to 1965." *Academy of Management Journal* (39, 3, 1996:519–543).

Miller, D., and Whitney, J. O. "Beyond Strategy: Configuration as a Pillar of Competitive Advantage." *Business Horizons* (May-June 1999:5–17).

Miller, G. A. "The Magic Number Seven Plus or Minus Two: Some Limits on Our Capacity for Processing Information." *Psychology Review* (March 1956:81–97).

Mink, M. "Military Strategist Clausewitz—Be Bold." *Investor's Business Daily* (February 19, 2004).

Mintzberg, H. "Research on Strategy-Making," *Proceedings of the 32nd Annual Meeting of the Academy of Management* (Minneapolis, 1972).

Mintzberg, H. "Strategy-Making in Three Modes." *California Management Review* (16, 2, Winter 1973:44–53).

Mintzberg, H. "Patterns in Strategy Formation." *Management Science* (24, 9, 1978:934–948).

Mintzberg, H. *The Structuring of Organizations: A Synthesis of the Research* (Englewood Cliffs, NJ: Prentice Hall, 1979).

Mintzberg, H. "A Note on that Dirty Word 'Efficiency'" *Interface* (October 1982:101–105).

Mintzberg, H. *Power In and Around Organizations* (Englewood Cliffs, NJ: Prentice Hall, 1983).

Mintzberg, H. "The Strategy Concept 1: Five Ps for Strategy." *California Management Review* (30, 1, June 1987:11–24).

Mintzberg, H. *Mintzberg on Management: Inside Our Strange World of Organizations* (New York: Free Press, 1989).

Mintzberg, H. "The Design School: Reconsidering the Basic Premises of Strategic Management." *Strategic Management Journal* (11, 1990:171–195).

Mintzberg, H. "Strategic Thinking as 'Seeing.'" In J. Nasi, ed., *Arenas of Strategic Thinking* (Foundation for Economic Education, Helsinki, Finland, 1991).

Mintzberg, H. *The Rise and Fall of Strategic Planning* (New York: Free Press, 1994).

Mintzberg, H. "Reply to Michael Goold." *California Management Review* (38, 4, Summer 1996a:96–99).

Mintzberg, H. "Musings on Management." *Harvard Business Review* (July-August, 1996b:5–11).

Mintzberg, H. *Tracking Strategies: Toward a General Theory* (Oxford University Press, 2007).

Mintzberg, H., and Austin, B. "Mirroring Canadian Industrial Policy: Strategy Formation at Dominion Textile from 1873 to 1990." *Canadian Journal of Administrative Sciences* (13, 1, 1996:46–64).

Mintzberg, H., and McHugh, A. "Strategy Formation in an Adhocracy." *Administrative Science Quarterly* (30, 1985:160–197).

Mintzberg, H., and Rose, J. "Strategic Management Upside Down: Tracking Strategies at McGill University from 1829 to 1980." *Canadian Journal of Administrative Sciences* (20, 4, 2003:270–290).

Mintzberg, H., and Waters, J. A. "Tracking Strategy in an Entrepreneurial Firm." *Academy of Management Journal* (25, 3, 1982:465–499).

Mintzberg, H., and Waters, J. A. "Researching the Formation of Strategies: The History of Canadian Lady 1939–1976." In R. B. Lamb, ed., *Competitive Strategic Management* (Englewood Cliffs, NJ: Prentice Hall, 1984:62–93).

Mintzberg, H., and Waters, J. A. "Of Strategies, Deliberate and Emergent." *Strategic Management Journal* (6, 1985:257–272).

Mintzberg, H., and Waters, J. A. "Studying Deciding: An Exchange of Views Between Mintzberg and Waters, Pettigrew and Butler." *Organization Studies* (11, 1, 1990:1–16).

Mintzberg, H., Brunet, J. P., and Waters, J. A. "Does Planning Impede Strategic Thinking? Tracking the Strategies of Air Canada from 1976." *Advances in Strategic Management* (4, 1986:3–41).

Mintzberg, H., Otis, S., Shamsie, J., and Waters, J. A. "Strategy of Design: A study of 'Architects in Co-Partnership.'" In J. Grant, ed., *Strategic Management Frontiers* (Greenwich, CT: JAI Press, 1988:311–359).

Mintzberg, H., Taylor, W. D., and Waters, J. A. "Tracking Strategies in the Birthplace of Canadian Tycoons: The Sherbrooke Record 1946–1976." *ASAC Journal* (1, 1, 1984:11–28).

Mitchell, R. K., Busenitz, L., Lant, T., McDougall, P. P., Morse, E. A., and Smith, J. B. "Entrepreneurial Cognition Theory: Rethinking the People Side of Entrepreneurial Research." *Entrepreneurship Theory and Practice* (27, 2, 2002:93–104).

Montgomery, C. "Putting Leadership Back into Strategy." *Harvard Business Review* (86, 1, 2008:54–60).

Morgan, G. *Images of Organzations* (Beverley Hills, CA: Sage, 1986).

Morgan, G. *Imaginization: The Art of Creative Management* (Newbury Park: Sage, 1993).

Moulton, W. N., and Thomas, H. "Bankruptcy as a Deliberate Strategy by Troubled Firms" (paper presented at the Annual Conference of the Strategic Management Society, Boston, 1987).

Myers, I. B. *Introduction to Type: A Description of the Theory and Applications of the Myers-Briggs Type Indicator* (Palo Alto, CA: Consulting Psychologists Press, 1962).

Nasi, J., ed. *Arenas of Strategic Thinking* (Foundation for Economic Education, Helsinki, Finland, 1991).

Nelson, R. R., and Winter, S. G. *An Evolutionary Theory of Economic Change* (Boston: Harvard University Press, 1982).

Neustadt, R. E. *Presidential Power: The Politics of Leadership* (New York: Wiley, 1960).

Newbert, S. "Empirical research on the resource-based view of the firm: An assessment and suggestions for future research." *Strategic Management Journal* (28, 2, 2007:561–594).

Newman, W. H. *Administrative Action: The Technique of Organization and Management* (Englewood Cliffs, NJ: Prentice Hall, 1951).

Noda, T., and Bower, J. L. "Strategy Making as Iterated Processes of Resource Allocation." *Strategic Management Journal* (17, 1996:159–192).

Nonaka, I. "Toward Middle-Up-Down Management." *Sloan Management Review* (29, 3, Spring 1988:9–18).

Nonaka, I. "Toward Middle-Up-Down Management: Accelerating Information Creation." *Sloan Management Review* (29, 3, 1998:9–18).

Nonaka, I., and Takeuchi, H. *The Knowledge-Creating Company: How Japanese Companies Create the Dynamics of Innovation* (New York: Oxford University Press, 1995).

Normann, R. *Management for Growth* (New York: Wiley, 1977).

Nutt P., Backoff, R., and Hogan, M. "Managing the Paradoxes of Strategic Change." *Journal of Applied Management Studies* (9, 1, 2000:5–31).

Oliver, C. "Strategic Responses to Institutional Processes." *Academy of Management Review* (16, 1991:145–179).

Ornstein, R. F. *The Psychology of Consciousness* (New York: Viking, 1972).

Palich, L. E., and Bagby, R. D. "Using Cognitive Theory to Explain Entrepreneurial Risk-Taking: Challenging Conventional Wisdom." *Journal of Business Venturing* (10, 1995:425–438).

Pascale, R. T. "Our Curious Addiction to Corporate Grand Strategy." *Fortune* (105, 2 [January 25] 1982:115–116).

Pascale, R. T. "Perspectives on Strategy: The Real Story Behind Honda's Success." *Califoinia Management Review* (Spring 1984:47–72).

Pascale, R. T., and Athos, A. G. *The Art of Japanese Management: Applications for American Executives* (New York: Simon & Schuster, 1981).

Pekar, P., Jr., and Allio, R. "Making Alliances Work: Guidelines for Success." *Long Range Planning* (27, 4, 1994:54–65).

Pennington, M. W. "Why Has Planning Failed?" *Long Range Planning* (5, 1, 1972:2–9).

Penrose, E. T. *The Theory of the Growth of the Firm* (New York: Wiley, 1959).

Peteraf, M. A. "The Cornerstones of Competitive Advantage: A Resource-Based View." *Strategic Management Journal* (14, 3, 1993:179–191).

Peters, T. H., and Waterman, R. H., Jr. *In Search of Excellence* (New York: Harper & Row, 1982).

Peters, T. J. "A Style for All Seasons." *Executive Magazine* (Summer, Graduate School of Business and Public Administration, Cornell University, 1980:12–16).

Perrigrew, A. M. "Strategy Formulation as a Political Process." *International Studies of Management and Organization* (Summer 1977:78–87).

Pettigrew, A. M. *The Awakening Giant: Continuity and Change in Imperial Chemical Industries* (Oxford: Basil Blackwell, 1985).

Pettigrew, A. M. "Context and Action in Transformation of the Firm." *Journal of Management Studies* (24, 6, November 1987:649–670).

Pfeffer, J. "Barriers to the Advance of Organizational Science: Paradigm Development as a Dependent Variable." *Academy of Management Review* (18, 1993:599–620).

Pfeffer, J. "Mortality, Reproducibility, and the Persistence of Styles of Theory." *Organization Science* (6, 6, November-December 1995:681–686).

Pfeffer, J., and Salancik, G. R. *The External Control of Organizations: A Resource Dependence Perspective* (New York: Harper & Row, 1978).

Pinchot, G., III. *Intrapreneuring* (New York: Harper & Row, 1985).

Pokora, T. "A Theory of the Periodization of World History." *Archiv Orientali* (34, 1966:602–605).

Polanyi, M. *The Tacit Dimension* (London: Routledge & Kegan Paul, 1966).

Popescu, O. "Periodization in the History of Economic Thought." *International Social Science Journal* (17,4, 1965:607–634).

Porter, M. E. *Competitive Strategy: Techniques for Analyzing Industries and Competitors* (New York: Free Press, 1980).

Porter, M. E. "The Contributions of Industrial Organizations to Strategic Management." *Academy of Management Review* (6, 4, 1981:609–620).

Porter, M. E. *Competitive Advantage: Creating and Sustaining Superior Performance* (New York: Free Press, 1985).

Porter, M. E. "Corporate Strategy: The State of Strategic Thinking." *The Economist* (303, 7499 [May 23, 1987]:21–28).

Porter, M. E. "What Is Strategy?" *Harvard Business Review* (November-December 1996:61–78).

Porter, M. E. Response to Letters to the Editor, *Harvard Business Review* (March-April, 1997:162–163).

Porter, M. E. "The CEO as Strategist." In H. Mintzberg, B. Ahlstrand, and J. Lampel, eds., *Strategy Bites Back: It is Far More and Less, Than you Ever Imagined..."* (Edinburgh Gate, Harlow: Prentice Hall, Financial Times, 2005: 44–45). First published in *Fast Company* magazine with the title "Great Strategies are a Cause".

Potts, M. "New Planning System Aims to Boost Speed, Flexibility." *Washington Post* (September 30, 1984).

Power, D. J., Gannon, M. J., McGinnis, M. A., and Schweiger, D. M. *Strategic Management Skills* (Reading, MA: Addison-Wesley, 1986).

Prahalad, C. K., and Bettis, R. A. "The Dominant Logic: A New Linkage Between Diversity and Performance." *Strategic Management Journal* (7, 1986:485–501).

Prahalad, C. K., and Hamel, G. "The Core Competence of the Corporation." *Harvard Business Review* (68, 3, May-June 1990:79–91).

Priem, R. L., and Butler, J. E. "Is the Resource-Based Theory a Useful Perspective for Strategic Management Research?" *Academy of Management Review* (26, 1, 2001:22–40).

Prown, J. D. "The Truth of Material Culture: History or Fiction." In S. Lubar and W. D. K. Kingery, eds., *History from Things: Essays on Material Culture* (Washington, DC: Smithsonian Institution Press, 1993:1–19).

Pugh, D. S., Hickson, D. J., and Hinings, C. R. "An Empirical Taxonomy of Structures of Work Organizations." *Administrative Science Quarterly* (1969:115–126).

Pugh, D. S., Hickson, D. J., and Hinings, C. R., MacDonald, K. M., Turner, C., and Lupton, T. "A Conceptual Scheme for Organizational Analysis." *Administrative Science Quarterly* (8, 1963–64:289–315).

Pugh, D. S., Hickson, D. J., and Hinings, C. R., and Turner, C. "Dimensions of Organizational Structure." *Administrative Science Quarterly* (13, June 1968:65–105).

Quinn, J. B. "Strategic Change: 'Logical Incrementalism.'" *Sloan Management Review* (Fall 1978:7–21).

Quinn, J. B. *Strategies for Change: Logical Incrementalism* (Homewood, IL: Irwin, 1980a).

Quinn, J. B. "Managing Strategic Change." *Sloan Management Review* (Summer 1980b:3–20).

Quinn, J. B. "Managing Strategies Incrementally." *Omega, The International Journal of Management Science* (10, 6, 1982:613–627).

Raghu, G., Kumaraswamy, A., and Nayyar, P. "Real options or fool's gold? Perspective makes the difference." *Academy of Management Review* (23, 2, 1998:212–214).

Rafaeli, A., and Vilnai-Yavetz, I. "Emotion as a Connection of Physical Artifacts and Organizations." *Organization Science* (15, 6, 2004:671–686).

Raphael, R. *Edges: Backcountry Lives in America Today on the Borderlands Between the Old Ways and the New* (New York: Knopf, 1976).

Reger, R. K., and Huff, A. S. "Strategic Groups: A Cognitive Perspective." *Strategic Management Journal* (14, 1993:103–124).

Reger, R. K., Gustafson, L. T., De Marie, S. M., and Mullane, J. V. "Reframing the Organization: Why Implementing Total Quality Is Easier Said Than Done." *Academy of Management Review* (19, 1994:565–584).

Rhenman, E. *Organization Theory for Long-Range Planning* (London: John Wiley, 1973).

Rieger, F. "The Influence of National Culture on Organizational Structure, Process, and Strategic Decision Making: A Study of International Airlines" (doctoral dissertation, McGill University, Faculty of Management, Montreal, 1987).

Rigby, D. K. "How to Manage the Management Tools." *Planning Review* (November/December 1993:8–15).

Rostow, W. W. *The Stages of Economic Growth*, 2nd edition (Cambridge, MA: Harvard University Press, 1971).

Roth, K. and Ricks, D. A. "Goal Configuration in a Global Industry Context." *Strategic Management Journal* (15, 1994:103–120).

Rothschild, W. E. "How to Ensure the Continued Growth of Strategic Planning." *Journal of Business Strategy* (1, Summer, 1980:11–18).

Ruef, M. "The emergence of organizational forms: A community ecology approach." *American Journal of Sociology* (106, 2000:658–714).

Rugman A. M., and Verbeke, A. "Edith Penrose's Contribution to the Resource-Based Views of Strategic Management." *Strategic Management Journal* (23, 2002:769–780).

Rumelt, R. P. *Strategy, Structure, and Economic Performance* (Boston: Harvard Business School Press, 1974).

Rumelt, R. P. "How Much Does Industry Matter?" *Strategic Management Journal* (12, 3, 1991:167–185).

Rumelt, R. P. "Inertia and Transformation." In C. A. Montgomery, ed., *Resources in an Evolutionary Perspective: A Synthesis of Evolutionary and Resource-based Appioaches to Strategy* (Norwell, MA: Kluwer Academic and Dordrecht, 1995:101–132).

Rumelt, R. P. "The Evaluation of Business Strategy." In H. Mintzberg and J. B. Quinn, *The Strategy Process*, 3rd edition. (Englewood Cliffs, NJ: Prentice Hall, 1997).

Saint-Exupéry, A. *Le Petit Prince* (New York: Harcourt Brace Jovanovich, 1943).

Sarrazin, J. "Le Role des Processus de Planification dans les Grandes Entreprises Françaises: Un Essai d'Interpretation" (thèse 3ième cycle, Universite de Droit, d'Economic et des Sciences d'Aix-Marseille, 1975).

Sarrazin, J. "Decentralized Planning in a Large French Company: An Interpretive Study." *International Studies of Management and Organization* (Fall/Winter 1977/1978:37–59).

Schendel, D. E., and Hofer, C. H., eds., *Strategic Management: A New View of Business Policy and Planning* (Boston: Little, Brown, 1979).

Schoeffler, S. "Nine Basic Findings on Business Strategy." *The Strategic Planning Institute* (Cambridge, MA: 1980).

Schoeffler, S., Buzzell, R. D., and Heany, D. F. "Impact of Strategic Planning on Profit Performance." *Harvard Business Review* (March-April 1974:137–145).

Schön, D. A. "Organizational Learning." In G. Morgan, ed., *Beyond Method: Strategies for Social Research* (Beverly Hills, CA: Sage, 1983).

Schulz, M. "Organizational Learning." In J. A. C. Baum, (ed.) *Companion to Organizations* (Blackwell Publishers, Oxford, 2001:415–441).

Schumpeter, J. A. *The Theory of Economic Development* (London: Oxford University Press, 1934).

Schumpeter, J. A. "The Creative Response in Economic History." *Journal of Economic History* (November 1947:149–159).

Schumpeter, J. A. *Capitalism, Socialism, and Democracy*, 3rd edition. (New York: Harper & Row, 1950).

Schwartz. H., and Davis, S. M. "Matching Corporate Culture and Business Strategy." *Organizational Dynamics* (Summer 1981:30–48).

Schwenk, C. "The Cognitive Perspective in Strategic Decision-Making." *Journal of Management Studies* (25, 1988:41–56).

Seeger, J. A. "Reversing the Images of BCG's Growth Share Matrix." *Strategic Management Journal* (5, 1, 1984: 93–97).

Selznick, P. *Leadership in Administration: A Sociologial Interpretation* (Evanson, Il: Row, Peterson, 1957).

Senge, P. M. *The Fifth Disicipline: The Art and Practice of the Learning Organization* (New York: Doubleday, 1990).

Shimizu, R. *The Growth of Firms in Japan* (Tokyo: Keio Tsushin, 1980).

Shrader, C. B., Taylor, L., and Dalton, D. R. "Strategic Planning and Organization Performance: A Critical Appraisal." *Journal of Management* (10:2, 1984:149–171).

Shrivastava, P. "A Typology of Organizational Learning Systems." *Journal of Management Studies* (21, 1, 1983:7–28).

Simon, H. A. *Administrative Behavior* (New York: Macmillan, editions 1947 and 1957).

Simon, H. A. *The New Science of Management Decision* (Englewood Cliffs, NJ: Prentice Hall, 1960, also revised edition, 1977).

Simon, H. A. "Making Management Decisions: The Role of Intuition and Emotion." *Academy of Management Executives* (1, February 1987:57–64).

Simons, R. "Rethinking the Role of Systems in Controlling Strategy" (presented at the 1988 Annual Meeting of the Strategic Management Society, Amsterdam, October 1988: published 1991 by Publishing division, Harvard Business School, #9-191-091).

Simons, R. *Levers of Control: How Managers Use Innovative Control Systems to Drive Strategic Renewal* (Boston: Harvard Business School Press, 1995).

Sirmon, D. G., Hitt, M. A., and Ireland, R. D. "Managing Firm Resources In Dynamic Environments to Create Value: Looking Inside the Black Box." *Academy of Management Review* (32, 1, 2007:273–292).

Sloan, P. "Strategy as Synthesis." Ph.D dissertation (*HEC Montreal*. 1996).

Smalter, D. J., and Ruggles, R. L., Jr. "Six Business Lessons from the Pentagon." *Harvard Business Review* (March-April 1966:64–75).

Smith, W. "3 Years After Apple Went Sour, Steve Jobs Has Returned." *The Orange County Register* (November 13, 1988:3).

Smircich, L., and Stubbart, C. "Strategic Management in an Enacted World." *Academy of Management Review* (10, 4, 1985:724–736).

Snodgrass, C. R. "Cultural Influences on Strategic Control System Requirements." (Ph.D. dissertation, University of Pittsburgh, Graduate School of Business, 1984).

Spender, J. C. *Industry Recipes* (Oxford: Basil Blackwell, 1989).

Spender, J. C. "Strategic Theorizing: Expanding the Agenda." *Advances in Strategic Management* (8, 1992:3–32).

Sperry, R. "Messages from the Laboratory." *Engineering and Science* (1974:29–32).

Stacey, R. *Managing Chaos: Dynamic Business Strategies in an Unpredicatable World* (London: Kogan Page, 1992).

Starbuck, W. H. "Organizational Growth and Development." In J. G. March, ed., *Handbook of Organizations* (Chicago: Rand-McNally, 1965).

Starbuck, W. H. "Unlearning Ineffective or Obsolete Technologies." *International Journal of Technology Management* (11, 1996:725–737).

Starbuck, W. H., and Hedberg, B. L. T. "Saving an Organization from a Stagnating Environment." In H. B. Thorelli, ed., *Strategy + Structure = Performance: The Strategic Planning Imperative* (Bloomington: Indiana University Press, 1977:249–258).

Starbuck, W. H., Greve, A., and Hedberg, B. L. T. "Responding to Crises." *Journal of Business Administration* (9, 2, 1978:107–137).

Staw, B. M. "Knee Deep in the Big Muddy: A Study of Escalating Commitment to a Chosen Course of Action." *Organizational Behaviour and Human Performance* (16, 1976:27–44).

Steinbruner, J. D. *The Cybernetic Theory of Decision: New Dimensions of Political Analysis* (Princeton, NJ: Princeton University Press, 1974).

Steiner, G. A. *Top Management Planning* (New York: Macmillan, 1969).

Steiner, G. A. *Strategic Planning: What Every Manager Must Know* (New York: Free Press, 1979).

Steiner, G. A., and Kunin, H. E. "Formal Strategic Planning in the United States Today." *Long Range Planning* (16, 3, 1983:12–17).

Stevenson, H. H., and Gumpert, D. E. "The Heart of Entrepreneurship." *Harvard Business Review* (March-April 1985:85–94).

Stewart, R. F. *A Framework for Business Planning* (Stanford, CA: Stanford Research Institute, 1963).

Summers, H. G., Jr. *On Strategy: The Vietnam War in Context* (Washington, DC: GPO, Strategic Studies Institute, U.S. Army War College, Carlisle Barracks, PA, 1981).

Sun Tzu, *The Art of War* (New York: Oxford University Press, 1971).

Taylor, S. S. "Overcoming Aesthetic Muteness: Research In Organizational Members' Aesthetic Experience." *Human Relations* (55, 7, 2002:755–766).

Taylor, W. D. "Strategic Adaptation in Low-Growth Environments" (Ph.D. thesis, Ecole des Hautes Etudes Commerciales, Montreal, 1982).

Tichy, N. M., and Sherman, S. *Control Your Destiny or Someone Else Will: How Jack Welch Is Making General Electric the World's Most Competitive Corporation* (New York: Doubleday, 1993).

Toynbee, A. J. *Study of History. Abridgement of Vol. I–X* (New York: Oxford University Press, 1946–57).

Tregoe, B. B., and Tobia, P. M. "An Action-Oriented Approach to Strategy." *Journal of Business Strategy* (January-February, 1990:16–21).

Tregoe, B. B., and Zimmerman, J. W. *Top Management Survey* (New York: Simon &. Schuster, 1980).

Trigeorgis, L. "A Real Options Application in Natural Resource Investments." *Advances in Futures and Options Research* (4, 1990: 153–164).

Trigeorgis, L. "Real Options and Interactions with Financial Flexibility." *Financial Management* (22, 3, 1993:202–224).

Tripsas, M., and Gavetti, G. "Capabilities, Cognition and Inertia: Evidence from Digital Imaging." *Strategic Management Journal* (21, 2000:1147–1161).

Tung, R. L. "Strategic Management Thought in East Asia." *Organizational Dynamics* (22, 4 [Spring] 1994:55–65).

Tverskv, A., and Kahneman, D. "Judgment Under Uncertainty: Heuristics and Biases." *Science* (185, 1974:1124–1131).

Van de Ven, A. H. "Review of Howard E. Aldrich's Organizations and Fnvironments." *Administration Science Quarterly* (24, 2, June 1979:320–326).

Van Maanen, J. "Style as Theory." *Organization Science* (6, 1, 1995a: 132–143).

Van Maanen, J. "Fear and Loathing in Organization Studies." *Organization Science* (6, 6, November-December 1995b:687–692).

Van Putten, A. B., and MacMillan, I. C. "Making Real Options Really Work." *Harvard Business Review* (82/12 December 2004:134–141).

Venkatesan, R. "Strategic Sourcing: To Make or Not to Make." *Harvard Business Review* (November-December 1992:98–107).

Venkatraman, N., and Camillus, J. "Exploring the Concept of 'Fit' in Strategic Management." *Academy of Management Review* (9, 3, 1984:513–526).

Venkatraman, N., and Prescott, J. "Environment-Strategy Coalignment: An Empirical Test of its Performance Implications." *Strategic Management Journal* (11, 1, 1990:1–23).

Volberda, H. W., and Elfring, T., eds., *Rethinking Strategy* (Sage Publications, 2001).

von Neumann, J., and Morgenstern, O. *Theory of Games and Economic Behavior,* 2nd edition (Princeton, NJ: Princeton University Press, 1947).

Vorhies, D. W., and Morgan, N. "Benchmarking Marketing Capabilities for Sustainable Competitive Advantage." *Journal of Marketing* (69, 1, 2005:80–94).

Wack, P. "Scenarios: Uncharted Waters Ahead." *Harvard Business Review* (September-October 1985:73–89).

Waterman, R. H., Jr., Peters, T. J., and Phillips, J. R. 'Structure Is Not Organization." *Business Horizons* (23, 3 [June] 1980:14–26).

Weber, M. *Economy and Society* (Berkeley, CA: University of California Press, 1978).

Webster's New World Collegiate Dictionary, 2nd College Edition. 1984. Simon and Schuster, New York.

Weick, K. E. *The Social Psychology of Organizing* (Reading, MA: Addison-Wesley, first edition 1969, second edition 1979).

Weick, K. E. 'Cartographic Myths in Organizations," In A. S. Huff, ed., *Mapping Strategic Thought* (New York: Wiley, 1990: 1–10).

Weick, K. E. *Sensemaking in Organizations* (Thousand Oaks, CA: Sage Publications, 1995:54).

Wernerfelt, B. "A Resource-based View of the Firm." *Strategic Management Journal* (5, 1984:171–180).

Wernerfelt, B. "The Resource-based View of the Firm: Ten Years After." *Strategic Management Journal* (16, 1995:171–174).

Westley, F. "Middle Managers and Strategy: Microdynamics of Inclusion." *Strategic Management Journal* (11, 1990:337–351).

Westley, F., and Mintzberg, H. "Visionary Leadership and Strategic Management." *Strategic Management Journal* (10, 1989:17–32).

Whittington, R. "Strategy as Practice." *Long Range Planning* (29, 1996:731–735).

Whittington, R. "Completing the Practice Turn in Strategy." *Organization Studies* (27 (5): 2006:613–634).

Wilkinson, L. "How to Build Scenarios: Planning for 'Long Fuse, Big Bang' Problems In an Era of Uncertainty." *Scenarios: The Future of the Future* special issue of *Wired,* 1995.

Wilson, I. "Strategic Planning Isn't Dead—It Changed." *Long Range Planning* (27, 4 [August] 1994:12–24).

Wischnevsky, J. D., and Damanpour, F. "Organizational Transformation and Performance: An Examination of Three Perspectives." *Journal of Managerial Issues* (28, 1, 2006:104–128).

Wrapp, H. E. "Good Managers Don't Make Policy Decisions." *Harvard Business Review* (September-October 1967:91–99).

Wright, J. P. *On a Clear Day You Can See General Motors: John Z. de Lorean's Look Inside the Automotive Giant* (Grosse Pointe, MI: Wright Enterprises, 1979).

Wright, P., Pringle, C., and Kroll, M. *Strategic Management Text and Cases* (Needham Heights, MA: Allyn and Bacon, 1992).

Yelle, L. E. "The Learning Curve: Historical Review and Comprehensive Survey." *Decision Sciences* (10, 1979:302–328).

Yukl, G. A. *Leadership in Organizations* (Englewood Cliffs, NJ: Prentice Hall, 1989).

Zajac, E. J., Kraatz, M. S., and Bresser, R. K. F. "Modelling the Dynamics of Strategic Fit: A Normative Approach to Strategic Change." *Strategic Management Journal* (21, 2000:429–453).

Zald, M. N., and Berger, M. A. "Social Movements in Organizations: Coup d'Etat, Insurgency, and Mass Movements." *American Journal of Sociology* (83, 4, January 1978:823–861).

Zan, L. "What's Left for Formal Planning?" *Economia Aziendale* (6, 2 [March] 1987:187–204).

Index